INSIGHT
GUIDES

GreatBarrierReef

Edited and Produced by John Borthwick
and David McGonigal
Editorial Director: Geoffrey Eu

A P A
PUBLICATIONS

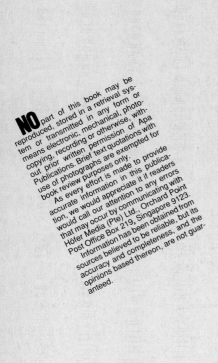
GREAT BARRIER REEF

First Edition
© 1991 APA PUBLICATIONS (HK) LTD
All Rights Reserved
Printed in Singapore by Höfer Press Pte. Ltd

ABOUT THIS BOOK

Three *Insight Guides* to Australia, it seems not enough. In 1983, APA Publications published its first coverage of the island continent, *Insight Guide: Australia*. With the vivid text, photographics and up-to-the-minute information which are APA's signature, it was soon one of most popular *Insight Guides*. Later, *Australia* was joined by two new Insight Guides to this Great South Land, *Cityguide: Sydney* and *Cityguide: Melbourne*, and soon after, was itself completely updated. Meanwhile, stretching along the northeast rim of the continent was one of the natural wonders of the world, the Great Barrier Reef. Located just off the Queensland coast, this Pacific treasure trove lacked only one thing – an APA *Insight Guide*.

APA Publications was established in 1970 by German-born designer and photographer **Hans Höfer**. Höfer, Bauhaus-trained and footloose when he arrived in Asia, sweated to produce the first of APA's titles *Insight Guide: Bali*. Instantly acclaimed, it presented information for travellers in a way that no publisher had done before; the pictures and text, capturing the essence of that island, combined to produce a book that inspired as it informed.

The same combination of aesthetics and accessible information became the driving force behind the subsequent titles in the series of Insight Guides which went on to focus on a score of Asian, Pacific, African, American and European destinations over the next two decades. Always, Höfer went to great pains to see that his team of writers, photographers and editors kept close touch with their subject. To that end he invited the best writers and photographers on each of the

Insight Guide's destinations to work on the series.

In order done before; the pictures and text, capturing the essence of that island, combined to produce a book that inspired in travel and in producing Insight Guides. **John Borthwick** and **David McGonigal**, both from Sydney, had already edited three APA books, *Cityguide: Sydney* and *Cityguide: Melbourne* and the completely revised *Insight Guide: Australia*. To them fell the enviable task of exploring and reporting on the Barrier Reef and the developments among its pellucid waters and islands – ranging from the first coral polyps of 10 million years ago to today's booming tourist resorts.

As ever, their brief was clear: for all the travellers who would venture to 'the Reef' (as the Aussies call it) and its lush doorstep, the Queensland coast, the facts had to be instantly at hand, and the writing on all aspects of the Reef full of colour and clarity.

An "old APA hand" since the original *Insight Guide: Australia*, **John Borthwick** has combined for years the multiple roles of travel writer-photographer for many Australian and international magazines, plus adventure tour leader in far corners of the world, as well as working in a Sydney art college. With this book he renews a long relationship with Queensland which started when he hitchhiked to Cairns in the early 1970's and which has more recently found him surfing the Gold Coast, diving off Cairns and sailing the Whitsunday Islands. He took a long look at the history of Queensland's coast, and an on-the-spot one at various aspects of the coast, then filed his first-hand impressions on a personal archipelago of his favourite islands. Tough job!

Full-time writer and photographer **David**

Borthwick

McGonigal

Matthews

Eu

McGonigal took to the project with his characteristic enthusiasm for hard work. A perpetual traveller, over the years he has explored and written about most of the untouched regions of Australia. His book *Wilderness Australia* and *The Kimberley* display the same excellence in photography and writing which he now brings to *The Great Barrier Reef*. A qualified lawyer, in the late 1970s David radically changed his notion of "conveyancing" when he set off on a four-year motorcycle odyssey which took him across Nepal, Afghanistan, Turkey, Europe and North America. Now he combines Australian and overseas travel with writing for many leading publications. For this book, David examined the marine life and natural history of the Reef - and the threats to it - before plunging into 'resort mode' and visiting a chain of his favourite islands.

In editing *The Great Barrier Reef*, McGonigal and Borthwick turned to their trusty Apple Macintosh SEs, as did APA Editorial Director **Geoffrey Eu** in Singapore, with whom they worked closely throughout the project. Geoffrey is no stranger to this form of publishing adventure, having worked with the editors on three previous APA books.

Anne Matthews, who produced the extensive Travel Tips, is a freelance Sydney book editor, researcher and writer, as well as a long-time associate of the editors from the days when all three worked in adventure travel. Having spent several years as a trek leader in Nepal, Kashmir and China, English-born Anne has adapted to living in inner-city Sydney – although with intermittent bursts of wanderlust. She has produced *The Australian Adventure*, an encyclopedic, Australia-wide guide to excursions and tours and, more recently, *Jack Thompson's Australia* and a book with gardening personality Don Burke.

Alex McRobbie, a Scottish-born journalist is, more than most people, a 'native' of Queensland's Gold Coast. Having spent more than half his life in Surfers Paradise, he has seen the area develop from 'sand tracks to skyscrapers.' Alex (who once walked across Australia's vast Nullarbor Plain) has literally written the book of the Gold Coast – *The Real Surfers Paradise*. Obviously he was the ideal writer to do an 'inside job' on the area for this guide.

Ron and Viv Moon who penned the essays on Cape York and Cooktown have been travelling Australia extensively for the past 20 years. Both freelance travel writers, they have also produced two comprehensive guide books of their own, one to the Kimberley region in the far north-west of Western Australia, and the other on Cape York. Their expertise is evident in their contributions on these, the remotest areas of coastal Queensland.

Margery Smith writes with authority on cruising and bareboat charter in Queensland waters. A freelance travel writer living in Melbourne, Margery (who has Danish seafaring ancestry) has spent a great deal of time at sea, writing professionally about vessels of all shapes and sizes.

Brisbane-based **Warren Steptoe** has gone fishin' – and then come back with a story that didn't get away. One of Australia's few full time professional fishing writers and photographers, and a columnist in *Modern Fishing*, Australia's largest selling fishing magazine, Warren is also a top fishing and boating photographer. He is the holder of several Australian fishing records, and father of two fishing-enthused sons.

Phil Tressider who penned our chapter on golf, is perhaps Australia's leading golf writer. Managing editor of *Australian Golf Digest*, and a sports writer for over 30 years, he is author of a number of books on golfing and cricket - and not surprisingly, as a member of the prestigious Australian Golf Club in Sydney, is a keen golfer.

Apart from the editors, a group of Aussie-based photograhers lent their expert lenses to the book. Long-time APA hands **Paul Steel** and **Manfred Gottschalk** were primary contributors, together with the talented team from **Stockshots** and wildlife specialist **Kathie Atkinson**.

– APA PUBLICATIONS

CONTENTS

MAPS

TRAVEL TIPS

WELCOME TO 'THE REEF'

In a familiarity bred of respect not contempt, Australians often call the Great Barrier Reef simply 'the Reef.' *The* Reef: the title is apt, for the Great Barrier Reef, the most extensive structure ever built by living creatures and the only life form on Earth visible from the moon, is our planet's ultimate reef.

'My inner eye is flooded with those marvellous greens and blues of unpolluted water...' wrote Australian poet Judith Wright of the Reef. She noted that the myriad fish, anenomes, sponges, corals and shellfish all seemed to be 'trying to outdo each other in elegance and beauty of pattern, form and colour.'

One of the natural wonders of the world, the Great Barrier Reef holds a fascination for overseas visitors and Australians alike. It is the largest coral reef in the world - hence the claim that it is the world's largest living thing. Made up of 2500 separate reefs, it stretches over 2000 km (1240 miles) from the northern tip of the continental shelf near Papua New Guinea to Bundaberg in the south.

The islands of the Great Barrier Reef are of two distinct types - continental and coral cay. The former make up the vast majority - some 540 in all - and were formed by separation from mainland Australia at the end of the Ice Age, as isolated mountaintops clad in greenery. The cays, on the other hand, are sandy knolls of coral, dotted with palm trees and a variety of other tropical vegetation.

The Barrier Reef fringes Australia's north-eastern coast, just offshore of the state of Queensland, which oversees the Reef's many National Parks. With a land mass which can contain nearly five Japans, seven Britains or 1,672 Hong Kongs, Queensland - like its Reef - is one of those larger than life places. More than any other region of Australia, Queensland might be described as a state of mind - though not necessarily of *minds*. Here, actions speak loudest: doing, building, growing, getting, and of course, travelling.

Preceding pages, mixed grille with a contented message; rainbow 'Teewah' sands of the Sunshine Coast; taking off into the blue yonder; dense coastal greenery; a Queensland beauty. **Left,** cruising with a tender behind.

To 'do' this 'Sunshine State,' one needs to remember that Queensland is far more than one spectacular reef. The expansive Outback, Cape York Peninsula, the hinterland rain forests, the Sunshine and Gold coasts, and the stretches of un-labelled coast: each one offers more action than even most 'locals' could fit into a lifetime. To the traveller then falls the challenge of seeing the most, and the best, in the time available. And that is the aim of *Insight Guide: The Great Barrier Reef and Queensland Coast*, to find the places, both on and off the map, in which the visitor can meet the people, plumb the depths, dangle a line and 'go troppo' in the nicest possible way.

Sixty percent of foreign tourists to Australia have Queensland as their primary destination. Eighty percent of Queensland's visitors are Australians. And both groups combine to invade the Gold Coast alone in an annual force of three million visitors. The sheer *popularity* of it all could sound overwhelming, until you realise that there are plenty of beaches in Queensland where you can stride out the miles and never see more than the occasional Person Friday footprint. Stretches of sea and reef still almost as empty as on the morning of the earth - despite the Reef being the most popular tourist diving destination in the world.

In order to come to grips with Queensland, the Reef and all that bloom within them, the reader will find this book and its sections arranged in a north to south sequence. As the 'Islands' section starts with the southernmost resort of Lady Elliott Island and tacks north to Lizard Island, so too the 'Mainland' section crosses the border at Coolangatta and lopes and lingers ever northwards until Cape York. Some activities defy all directions, bar gravity and luck - think of golfing, sailing, fishing, surfing, and eating - these are covered in a compass-free zone.

Visitors, particularly environmentally-mindful ones, are welcome in Queensland and on the Reef. However, tourism, like any industry, has the capacity to damage the fragile equilibrium of the coral, the beaches and the coastal rain forests - and Australians today have a growing awareness of their stewardship of these gifts. The editors hope that this book will enhance your pleasure in visiting this great region. Mindful of the old adage, the best travellers here, as anywhere, will be those who leave only their footprints. And on the Reef itself, not even footprints!

<u>Right</u>, Aboriginal dancer in far north Queensland.

A line-up of the history-makers of Queensland's coast would present as odd an array of mugs, thugs and opportunists as ever assembled in a single document. Dreamers, heroes and victims are there too. Such a cast cannot be constrained to parade neatly upon the page of history; facts and anecdotes jostle each other, and a single-strand chronology gives way to multiple themes.

Aboriginals: It is likely that an ancient land bridge connected Australia's Cape York Peninsula to New Guinea for more than 40,000 years, before disappearing about 10,000 years ago. Over this would have come the ancestors of the Australian Aborigines, who ever since have intermarried and traded with Melanesians of the Torres Strait Islands.

There is evidence in the central Queensland highlands of Aboriginal occupation from at least 19,000 years ago, and of exploration of the Great Barrier Reef by Aborigines, who set out in canoes for the offshore islands and reefs. Their craft eventually evolved up to 20 metre (65 feet) long and, as late as 1873, Cairns Aborigines had 12 metres (40 feet) outriggers capable of carrying up to 20 people. North Queensland's Aborigines hunted shark, dugong, mullet, shellfish and turtle with spears, nets and harpoons; and on land, wallabies, kangaroos and cassowaries.

With the arrival of Europeans, a familiar history was played out. Colonial authorities proclaimed tribal domains to be 'waste lands' ripe for their appropriation, and, for example, within 40 years of contact the Rockhampton clan was reduced to ten people. Defeated tribes were forced to work for new masters on cattle stations and pearling luggers, sometimes to be paid in opium, and then banished to distant reserves. European diseases further contributed to the collapse of tribal structures.

With the Palmer River gold rush of the 1873, Cape York Aborigines were squeezed from their lands by miners and cattlemen, as were their coastal relatives by *trepang* and pearl fishers. Christian missions opened in the 1890s, and having no appreciation of traditional cultures, contributed to further fragmentation of kin groups. There was black resistance: between 1840 and 1890 it is estimated that 500 whites were killed by Aborigines; meanwhile, 5,000 to 15,000 Aborigines were killed by whites.

Today, almost 100,000 Aborigines and Torres Strait Islanders live in Queensland, both as urban dwellers and on reserves, such as the coastal settlements at Palm Island, Wujal Wujal, Cooktown, Hopevale and Lockhart River. Paternalism for 150 years has left them disadvantaged (to say the very least), but increasingly determined to assert themselves in both cultures.

The next wave: Two thousand generations of Aborigines roamed the continent since those first epic migrations, but only during the last millennium did white sails and skins appear along their coasts. There is reliable cartographic evidence of Japanese and Chinese awareness of Australia, and Chinese merchants of the 13th and 14th centuries seeking sandalwood and spices may have landed here. The Bugis seamen of Macassar certainly did. For at least at least 400, and possibly 1000 years, Macassan *praus* made annual excursions to Cape York in order to gather the sea delicacy, *trepang (bêche-de-mer* or sea cucumber). Processing plants, pottery, tamarind trees, and offspring, remained from these visits, which ceased around 1906 when the Navy enforced the 'White Australia Policy.'

The first Europeans: Documents show that Portuguese navigators were familiar with the whole eastern half of Australia at least 250 years before James Cook's arrival. Their great rivals, the Spanish, also sought the Great South Land, and in 1595 Alvaro Mendana made an unsuccessful excursion from Lima. In 1605, Pedro Fernando de Quiros also tried, and failed, to reach the coast of the Great South Land, arriving instead on a New Hebrides (now Vanuatu) island which he named 'Austrialia del Espiritu Santo.'

Preceding pages: the striking Aboriginal rock art of Cape York. Left, gold at last!

In 1606-7 Luis Vaez de Torres sailed west towards the Moluccas, but instead of navigating the north coast of New Guinea, was forced to the south, becoming the first European to pass through the strait between Australia and New Guinea which now bears his name. Also in 1606, Dutchman William Jansz sailed east from Java and reached the western shore of Cape York Peninsula. He failed to find spices, silver or gold, but became the first recorded European to set foot on the continent.

James Cook: In 1762 the British captured Manila and found secret Spanish reports indicating the existence of a strait between New Guinea and a south land, the legendary

ing on the continent took place near the town of 'Seventeen Seventy' at Bustard Bay between Bundaberg and Gladstone.

On June 3 and 4 *Endeavour* cautiously wended its way through the 70 km (44 miles) long Whitsunday Passage, named so by Cook '... as it was discovered on the day the Church commemorates that Festival.' By June 11, he had sailed more than 1600 km (1000 miles) hemmed in by the Great Barrier Reef, the coral bulwark preventing his exit seaward to safer, deeper waters. His progress was halted abruptly that night, off Cape Tribulation above Cairns, when *Endeavour* 'stuck and stuck fast' on a small coral reef. Ballast and cannons were jettisoned. The

'Terra Australis Incognita.' Six years later Frenchman Chevalier de Bougainville almost beat the British to it. Bougainville's Reef, 200 km (125 miles) off Cooktown marks the point of his closest approach to land. Finally, it fell to a small converted English collier named *Endeavour* and to James Cook, the humbly-born genius who commanded her to become, in April 1770, the first European expedition to sight the east coast of Australia. After landing at the future first site of Sydney, Botany Bay, he continued north along the coast and on May 17 entered Moreton Bay, near today's Brisbane. In late May, Cook's second land-

ship was dragged for four days by longboat crews, during which time Cook epithetically named nearby Mt Sorrow and Weary Bay. On June 18 *Endeavour* was beached near the mouth of the Endeavour River, where Cooktown now stands, and spent seven weeks under repair.

Under way again, Cook reconnoitred the maze of the Reef from the peak of Lizard Island, and on August 22 risked a gap to the open sea now known, predictably, as Cook's Passage. Reaching Cape York, the northernmost tip of the continent, on small rocky Possession Island, Cook '... once more hoisted English Coulers and in the name of

His Majesty King George the Third took possession of the whole Eastern Coast ... by name of New South Wales.'

Bligh and co.: During an epic 43 day voyage in 1789 (following the famous mutiny on the *Bounty*) from Tonga to Timor, William Bligh and his 18 men found a way through the Barrier Reef, at Bligh Reef Island near Cape Direction. They put ashore at several places for water, and passing through Endeavour Strait above the Cape, headed for Dutch Timor. In March 1791, transported convicts Mary and William Bryant, their two young children and seven other escapees stole a small cutter in Port Jackson (Sydney Harbour). Ten weeks and 5200 km (3254

Guinea. The first recorded merchant ship through more southerly Torres Strait was the brig *Shah Hormuzeer*, which crossed the outer Barrier Reef in 1793 and threaded its way east through the treacherous reefs. Thereafter an increasing number of vessels attempted this perilous passage.

When Matthew Flinders circumnavigated Australia in 1802-1803, he charted the Queensland coast and became the first to use the term 'The Great Barrier Reef,' and also to press for the continent to officially be called 'Australia.' In 1803 whaling captain Eber Bunker charted the southernmost islands and reefs of the Barrier Reef, today known as the Capricorn-Bunker group, including

miles) later they had become the first Europeans to sail the entire eastern seaboard of Australia (Cook had sailed part of the distance outside the Barrier Reef.) Rounding Cape York, they reached Coupang in Dutch Timor, only to be arrested.

Opening up the coast: From 1788, with the establishment of the British penal colony at Port Jackson, there was strong pressure on ships to the Indies to shave time off the lengthy journey around the north of New

Above, after striking the Barrier Reef, Captain Cook's *Endeavour* was careened for repairs near the site of today's Cooktown.

Lady Elliott and Lady Musgrave Islands; and in 1804 Capt. James Aitken established the first beche-de-mer curing station on Lady Elliott. This was one of Australia's very first export industries. He was followed by others (usually escaped convicts and similar motley crew) who worked their way up the sheltered waters inside the Reef, thus establishing the first real industry of Great Barrier Reef. From 1818 to 1822 the passage between the Barrier Reef and the coast was charted by Phillip Parker King - and the population of the Australian colonies reached 33,500.

'Queensland' at last: In 1823 N.S.W Surveyor-General John Oxley, looking for a new prison site, explored Moreton Bay by cutter. Anchored off Bribie island, he was approached by a group of friendly Aborigines, one of whom hailed him in English. It was Thomas Pamphlett a wood cutter who with three companions had sailed from Sydney eight months earlier, been blown out to sea, and after drifting north, was wrecked on Moreton Island. The men fell in with friendly local Aborigines, and became Queensland's first European dwellers.

September 1824 saw Redcoats and convicts establish a penal settlement at Redcliffe Peninsula in Moreton Bay. This was soon moved to the current site of Brisbane on the

tribe. Then in 1848 explorer Edmund Kennedy's party of 12, plus black guide Jackey-Jackey, set out to cross the interior of Cape York peninsula, from Rockingham Bay, near Hinchinbrook Island. Difficulties with supply, hostile natives and rugged terrain forced him to despatch his companions to the coast at Weymouth Bay, while he pushed on with Jackey-Jackey. Kennedy was speared several times by local Yaraikana natives, and died in Jackey's arms. The latter was also wounded, but struggled gamely through the jungle to the Cape in order to hasten a waiting schooner to the successful rescue of the two remaining survivors who were stranded at Weymouth

Brisbane River, until its penal role was abandoned in 1839 as the pressure for free settlers (and anti-convict agitation) grew. In 1843 the first land sale was held in Brisbane, and soon dairying began in Moreton District, followed later by the sugar and timber industries. Thereafter, pastoral industries dominated southern Queensland until well into the 20th Century.

In 1846 Englishman James Morrill and his companions were wrecked on the Reef, then drifted for 42 days until washed ashore south of Townsville. They were eventually rescued, but Morrill returned to live at least another 13 years with a local Aboriginal

Bay, encircled by hostile Aborigines.

The transportation of convicts to Australia was phased out between 1840 and 1868; and in 1858 the country's white population reached one million. On December 10, 1859 the colony of 'Queensland' - the name was Queen Victoria's own modest suggestion - separated from NSW, and adopted a coat of arms which featured a bull, ram and deer - significantly, none was a native species. (In 1977 this was revised to feature an Australian brolga and an English red deer.) At this time, the Canoona gold rush established Rockhampton as the major sea port of central Queensland. Thereafter, migration induced by the impetus of gold rushes raised the state population from 30,000 to 100,000 in only seven years.

In the 1860s the extractive industries commenced: guano mining on Lady Elliott Island, Bird Islet and Raine Island; pearl diving in Torres Strait, plus a large industry in Trochus, Turban and pearl-shells (for mother-of-pearl buttons); sandalwood was cut and whales hunted. Starting in 1863, the logging of hoop pine, kauri and white beech proceeded on Fraser Island until these soft-woods were exhausted; the hardwoods were then taken, the logging of which still continues today. Sugar farming commenced near the capital, Brisbane, then spread quickly up

efficient labour acclimatised to humid conditions and the sugar and cattle economy soon depended on them. Farmers, traders, their financiers and conservative politicians believed the coast could not be successfully developed without this cheap labour; but trenchant criticism came from missionaries, anti-slavers and philanthropic bodies, especially against the unnecessary brutality of the recruiting practices. Mendacious white agents known as 'blackbirders' would lure (or simply kidnap) Islanders aboard their rotten luggers, cramming as many as possible into tiny holds. (The natives soon retaliated with ambushes, massacres and cannibalism.) In some cases greedy local chiefs

the coast to Maryborough, Bundaberg, Mackay and, by the 1880s, as far as Cairns. By 1885 areas like Mackay were economically dependent upon the sugar industry.

'Blackbirding': In 1863 one Robert Towns imported 67 Melanesians from the New Hebrides to work in his cotton fields. Thereafter many 'Kanakas' (from the Hawaiian word for man) from the Solomons and New Hebrides were brought to Queensland on three year 'contracts.' They provided cheap,

Left, Chinese miners coming ashore in Queensland during the gold rush of the mid 1870s. Above, on 7 August 1875, the gold rush boom town of Cooktown suffered a devastating fire.

would sell their people: for a man the price was a gun; for a woman, bullets and powder.

Some Queenslanders opposed the importation of any non-whites, Indian, Chinese or Kanakas, on the grounds of erosion of a 'white' nation and that standards for white labourers would be lowered by the competition with plentiful, cheap coloured workers. By 1900 half the sugar crop was grown by Kanakas, but with Federation, further importation was forbidden by the new Commonwealth Government, and in 1906 and 1907 the Kanakas were returned to their islands. During 40 years of indentured labour, 50,000 Kanakas were imported. Ten thousand remained here in graves.

Gold fever: The discovery in 1867 of gold in Gympie, and the subsequent production of 3.5 million ounces (100 tonnes) of refined gold saved the colony from bankruptcy. In 1870 gold became the stimulus for the development of Rockhampton, Gympie, Charters Towers and Ravenswood. In 1873, a 36 year old Irishman, James Venture Mulligan heard of gold in the Palmer River region of the Cape and went in pursuit. With six companions he won 3,000 gms (6.6 lb) of gold from the river in a few days. He then blazed an overland trail to Cooktown, enabling thousands more European and Chinese prospectors to join the rush. Between 1873 and 1876,

left the coast at Bowen with 250 cattle for a 1400 km (870 miles) overland trek to the Cape on what was to became one of Queensland's epic pioneering journeys. Fire destroyed half their provisions, they fought Aborigines, lived off shark meat, crossed innumerable bogs and rivers, battled through 'the wet,' discovered rich new pastures, had many of their horses die from poisonous plants, and even lost their boots and trousers. Nine months later, after rafting across a large river (which was eventually named the Jardine) flowing into the Gulf of Carpentaria, they were guided by a friendly tribe to their father's settlement.

In 1864 a small colony of rabbits was

30 tons (30.5 tonnes) of Palmer River gold were shipped out of Cooktown; and at least twice that official amount is estimated to have been smuggled to China. Cooktown's population had errupted to 30,000 by the 1880s, and 18,000 Chinese laboured on the Palmer River diggings.

Extraordinary stories: In 1863 the Queensland government sent magistrate John Jardine by sea from Rockhampton to the tip of Cape York where he established Somerset, a shipwreck rescue point and coaling station for vessels passing through Torres Strait. Soon after, Jardine's sons, Frank and Alexander, plus drovers and black trackers,

introduced to Hervey Bay district. In one year they had multiplied to 12,000. And in 1881 on Lizard Island (north of Cooktown) Capt. Robert Watson, his young wife, Mary and their infant and two Chinese servants lived in a small stone house (the ruins of which still partially remain). During Capt. Watson's absence from the island a group of mainland Aborigines attacked, fatally spearing one of the Chinese men. In an extraordinary escape attempt, Mary, the baby and the other Chinese, Ah Sam (wounded by spears) paddled away from their island in a one-square-metre iron boiler tank (which is now in the Queensland Museum, Brisbane). They reached several other islands but could find no water. Two weeks after the attack, Mary recorded in her diary that Ah Sam died of his wounds. The baby, too, perished from dehydration. 'Nearly dead with thirst.' was Mary's last diary entry before she too died.

The Queensland Government learned in 1883 that Germany intended to 'annex' most of New Guinea, so it attempted a pre-emptively claim upon the south-eastern part of the island, Papua. A colony was not able to colonise another land, protested the British, who in turn proclaimed *their* 'protectorate' over the area. Germany responded by claiming the whole north coast of New Guinea. In 1887, Port Douglas, which was established during the Palmer gold rush, was intended to be North Queensland's major port, but instead Cairns became the coastal rail terminus. Between 1857 and 1891, the Cairns-Kuranda rail line was built by 1500 Irish and Italian navvies, who braved landslides, washouts, waterfalls, fever and hostile natives to construct 15 tunnels over a 24 km (15 miles) section of track which is still in daily use.

Over the 1880s and 1890s there was persistent agitation to divide Queensland into three states. The movement for the northern state was dominated by sugar interests, but in the south there was a real fear of that this would be a 'black' state based on quasi-slavery. In 1897 writer E. J. Banfield ('The Beachcomber') and his wife settled on Dunk (Coonanglebah) Island. Aged 45 and a physical wreck who, according to his doctors, had six months to live, Banfield hired the island from the government for 2 shillings 6 pence (about 25 cents) per acre per annum. Twenty five years later a visitor described him as 'the youngest man who had ever foiled time ... a small wiry man burned nut-brown by the sun ... and a chest like a gym instructor.'

In 1935 the cane toad *(buffo marinus)* was introduced from Hawaii in order to exterminate the sugar-cane beetle. The beetles are long gone, but, like the star of a horror film, the cane toad is still eating anything in its way and inexorably heading south.

Shipwrecks: The small wooden schooners

Far left, Aborigine of the Coolangatta region. **Left**, explorer Edmund Kennedy was fatally speared in December 1848 at Cape York. **Above**, panning for gold.

and brigs of the 1850s, which competed for coastal cargo and passengers were replaced in the mid-19th century by steam vessels which could manoeuvre through Torres Strait. Yet even they ran afoul of the Reef and Strait's shoals and cyclones. In all there are nearly 1500 known historic shipwrecks in the Barrier Reef region. The earliest known one inside the Reef was the 135-ton Batavia-bound brig *Morning Star* which went down in 1814; many others followed, until in 1844 a stone marker was erected on the Reef at Raine Island (incidentally, the largest mass breeding ground in the world for turtles), marking the safest passage through the Reef. So many ships were wrecked in the far north-

ern waters and survivors perished on subsequent open boat journeys that a cave on Booby Island in Torres Strait was stocked with provisions for shipwreck victims.

In 1836 the *Stirling Castle* was wrecked on Swain Reefs north of Rockhampton. Having drifted in the ship's longboat to Great Sandy Island (now known as Fraser Island), some 300 km (180 miles) to the south, the survivors were found by Aborigines of the Dulingbara tribe. Within a fortnight the seriously injured Capt. James Fraser and his first mate died. Fraser's wife, Eliza, who had given birth to a child during the longboat voyage, only to have it drown in the bottom of the boat, lived with the island Aboriginals for some time, until rescued by an escaped convict who had 'gone native.' Eliza Fraser returned to civilisation, to tour English fairgrounds with exaggerated tales about her captivity to anyone who would pay to listen.

SS *Gothenburg*, a three-masted iron schooner, carrying cargo and gold bullion, struck Old Reef off Ayr in 1875, drowning 106, including miners laden with gold in their money belts. A tropical cyclone in 1899 swept across Bathurst and Princess Charlotte Bays on Cape York, causing the loss of 300 crew on the 59 pearling boats sheltering there. In 1911 the *SS Yongala* disappeared in another cyclone, with 120 lives lost. During World War II the intact hull was discovered by a minesweeper, off Cape Bowling Green, near Townsville, and is now one of the most popular wreck diving sites in the world, albeit a difficult and dangerous one.

The 20th century: The Commonwealth of Australia was born in 1901 (the year Queen Victoria died) and the young country's population reached 3,773,801. In 1903 the railroad from Rockhampton to Brisbane was opened. South Keppel Island (now known as Great Keppel) was first settled by white graziers in 1906. After several of their sheep were killed by Aborigines, the new settlers gave the natives strychnine-laced flour. This grotesque method of eliminating competition was common in Australia during the early years of settlement. First elected to government in 1915, the Labor Party thereafter ruled Queensland almost continuously until 1957.

Throughout the 1920s Queensland was Australia's most decentralised, least urban state. The majority of settlers had come from the British Isles and northern Europe, and exhibited strong antagonism to Italian immigrants, more than 3000 of whom arrived during the sugar boom of the '20s. Most Italians were male cane cutters who quickly united to buy their own farms so that by 1924, in the Innisfail district alone, 'foreign' growers were almost as numerous as 'British' farmers, and Anglo cutters were outnumbered four to one. Southern Italians were characterised as 'knife wielding, inferior, racially-minded (!!) Sicilians,' while Northerners were preferred by the comparably 'racially-minded' local Anglo settlers.

In 1922 the Great Barrier Reef Committee was established for marine research and capital punishment was abolished in Queensland, the first Australian state to do so. A turtle soup factory was opened on Heron Island in 1923 and thousands of green turtles were slaughtered until a mere seven years later there were too few to continue profitable operation of the factory.

With World War II and the fear of a Japanese invasion, there were mass evacuations from North Queensland; Townsville's civilian population declined by 25 percent. Several of the hundreds of navigable passages through the Reef were mined in order to prevent a possible inva-

sion; rumours circulated of enemy submarines inside the Reef, and of a US battle fleet sheltering among the Whitsunday Islands - neither of which was ever confirmed. General Douglas MacArthur, Allied Commander in the Pacific had his HQ in Brisbane. A line drawn across the continent, known as 'the Brisbane Line,' indicated the portion of Australia which would be abandoned should the Japanese invade the north; but the only hostilities on Queensland soil were the savage street battles in Brisbane between Australian and US servicemen.

In 1949 the Labor government introduced the 'gerrymander' (electoral boundaries drawn to the advantage one party), which was further refined from 1957 onwards by the Country (later National) Party to be the art form by which Queensland's political integrity was corrupted until 1989. Entrenched conservative government clotted into a bloody-minded alliance with an equally conservative public service, judiciary and police force.

Coastal development: 'Free enterprise', 'stability' and 'development' were post-War Queensland's pillars of unquestioned wisdom. The 'El Dorado Syndrome' held sway, a chauvinistic belief that the natural wealth and prosperity of this 'state bigger than Texas' must one day lead it to becoming

California of Australia, minus the accompanying veneer of intellectual or cultural sophistication.

Until the early '60s the state economy was principally pastoral and agricultural. The emphasis then changed to extractive and manufacturing industries, and tourism. The sugar industry remained the backbone of the coastal agricultural economy, and, despite price drops, is proud of its reputation as the most efficient in the world, in terms of both growing and milling cane. The '70s and '80s decades of prosperity, especially in the mining of coal, copper and bauxite, and later in tourism, coincided with the domination of state politics by one man.

the most important in the Commonwealth. The 50's brought a large influx of settlers to the Gold Coast, many of them retirees from NSW and Victoria, including one Bruce Small - who drained a mangrove swamp and subdivided it, then went on to become Mayor and a member of state parliament. As historian Ross Fitzgerald notes, with Small's 1967 entry into politics, 'local government and land development became inseparable on the Gold Coast.' Queensland became the

Left, A diver recovers 3,500 oz. of gold from the *S.S. Gothenburg*. **Above**, Qantas was based in the outback town of Longreach in 1922.

In August 1968, Johannes Bjelke-Petersen, fundamentalist Christian, passionate anti-socialist and one-eyed advocate of unfettered development became state Premier. He believed religiously that hard work equalled money, success and salvation. Instead of salvation this creed begat greed, corruption, nepotism, more greed and environmental rape. During late '60s exploratory drilling for oil on the Barrier Reef, which was supported by Bjelke-Petersen, was stoppped by industrial action: there was near-unanimity among Queenslanders and other Australians in rejecting the prospect of oil wells on the Reef. A Royal Commission which considered the likely effects of oil drilling came up with an inconclusive result, but the Federal Government ruled that there should be no further exploration. In 1975 the Federal Government established the Great Barrier Reef Marine Park Authority, which has been proclaimed in stages until it now includes 98 percent of the Reef. It is on the World Heritage Listing of our planet's unique and precious places. According to historian Fitzgerald, the Barrier Reef is '... the only area in the world where trans-national oil companies have been opposed successfully despite their continuing pressure and the exhortations of a number of state government politicians ...'

percent of its local forest area. Only half the original North Queensland rainforest remains. Despite this, as recently as 1985, in the Daintree-Cape Tribulation region, where the rainforest reaches its optimum in size, beauty and diversity, the National Party state government had constructed through the region a controversial road, causing incalculable ecological damage.

Tourism: In 1899 an entrepreneur called Robert Hayles established the first tourist resort at Magnetic Island, but later moved to Cairns in 1926 to open the Green Island resort. In 1917 a holiday resort opened on the south coast at Elston, which was once known as Umbigumbi ('place of the ant') and would

The 1970s saw a prolonged battle over sand mining on Fraser Island, the largest sand island in the world. Rainforest, lakes, beaches and coloured sands were all threatened by a multinational mining company that had mined 160 hectares until the Federal government refused an export licence for the extracted minerals. Leader of the opposition to mining was a local public servant John Sinclair, who although named Australian of the Year for his inspirational efforts, was victimised for them by his employer, the Queensland Government.

Since white settlement, every region of Queensland coast has lost between 50 and 90

later be known as Surfers Paradise. Nothing remained by then of Umbigumbi's bora rings and ceremonial grounds where the Aboriginal Bundjalung nation, which extended as far south as the Clarence River, had once gathered. In 1925 James Cavill erected the 'Surfers Paradise Hotel' at Elston, and in 1933, by popular demand, the name of 'Surfers Paradise' replaced Elston. When in 1950 a Brisbane journalist sarcastically called the Surfers Paradise area 'the Gold Coast,' he was referring to its avariciously escalating land prices. The irony was lost, but the name, and the land game, remain.

Lindeman Island was the first Queensland

island to welcome tourists in 1927 although it did not have any resort facilities until 1929. Neighbouring Whitsunday islanders began to switch from grazing leases to tourism, such as the Baeur family building the beachfront cabins for visitors on their farm on South Molle Island. In 1932, Captain Christian Poulson converted the mercifully defunct Heron Island turtle soup factory into a tourist resort, which remained with his family until 1977 when it was sold to P&O, the shipping line. After World War II, Capt. Tom McLean converted a Navy gunboat for tourist work out of Mackay Harbour, and so began Roylen Cruises, one of the oldest and most famous of the Reef cruise companies.

By 1960 the Reef was already drawing around 250,000 visitors annually. A decade later, the Gold Coast's summer population was trebling to 165,000 - although rampant and unchecked development had lead to serious foreshore erosion. By the '80s the tourist boom was also bringing large numbers of Japanese and American tourists, and Japanese investment. By 1989 most of Queensland's five-star hotels were at least partly Japanese owned, a development which has not been without controversy.

In 1971 Yohachiro Iwasaki, the third richest man in Japan quietly purchased 6,840 ha (1,700 acres) of coastal land at Yeppoon north of Rockhampton, intending to establish a $100 million resort for Japanese tourists. He expanded this with other leased, freehold and 'option to purchase' lands to a total of 9,100 ha (22,483 acres) including 15.3 km (9.5 miles) of beachfront. There was strong local opposition, and equally strong support from the state government, which in 1978 introduced special legislation blocking any public accountability for the project. Protests against the alienation of coastline, the proposed woodchipping of native forests and the destruction of sensitive wetlands culminated in the bombing of the project in 1980. It proceeded, although not yet to its grandiose ultimate conclusion, and now operates as a successful resort.

A new spirit: During the '80s, Queensland came of age with four major events, two touristic, two political. The 1982 Brisbane Commonwealth Games saw that sunny city emerge from its reputation as 'just a big country town.' The capital's gains were more than consolidated with its 1988 World Expo, which drew three million interstate and overseas visitors. On a darker note, 1987 saw the commencement of the Fitzgerald Royal Commission into corruption within the Queensland police force. What started as a damage-control exercise (into the usual policemen's secret ball of prostitution kick-backs and the sort of money that only drugs can buy), went awfully wrong for Queensland's entrenched National Party. In the end, many members of the government, excluding the wiley old Bjelke-Petersen, were found with their hands in the till, and the separation of powers between executive, police, public service and judiciary was found to be almost non-existent. Bjelke-Petersen lost his leadership; and in November 1989, after 22 years, the National Party lost power.

The newly-elected Labour Government froze the freeholding of land on Cape York (where the previous administration had sold vast tracts to a handful of owners for negligible sums), banned logging in virgin rainforests and considered closing the disastrous Cape Tribulation road. 'The days of the rape of the Cape are finished,' said the new Minister for Environment and Heritage. However, renewed plans for a futuristic space station on Cape York look set to revive the controversy.

Looking towards the future it is predicted that by the turn of the century, when there will be a state population of around three million, another one million visitors per year are expected to visit the Reef. A rocket station, to launch commercial satellites, is proposed near Temple Bay on Cape York, but, slated to occupy up to 200,000 ha (5000,000 acres) of national estate land, it is already facing strong opposition.

The days have passed when one could say that in Queensland a national park is a piece of land that nobody can find a reason to exploit. And there is plenty of hope. Says Queensland journalist Quentin Dempster, 'I have great optimism for this, our rorted old colonial outpost of the British Empire. A new Queensland will be forged from the sins, lies and skullduggery of the past.'

<u>Left</u>, 'British' and Italian sugar-cane cutters in the Ingham region, circa 1931.

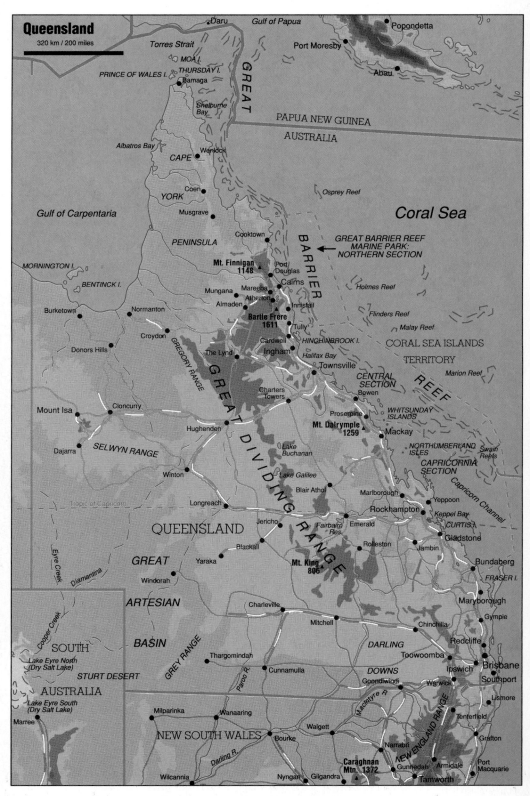

Queensland

320 km / 200 miles

Torres Strait
Daru
Gulf of Papua
Popondetta
Port Moresby
Abau

MOA I.
PRINCE OF WALES I.
THURSDAY I.
Bamaga
Shelburne Bay

GREAT

PAPUA NEW GUINEA
AUSTRALIA

Albatros Bay
Wenlock
CAPE
YORK
Coen
Musgrave
Gulf of Carpentaria

Osprey Reef
Coral Sea

PENINSULA
Cooktown

GREAT BARRIER REEF
MARINE PARK:
NORTHERN SECTION

MORNINGTON I.
BENTINCK I.
Mt. Finnigan
1148
Port Douglas
Mungana
Mareeba
Cairns
Atherton
Almaden
Innisfail
Bartle Frere
1611
Tully
Burketown
Normanton
Croydon
Donors Hills
The Lynd
Cardwell
Ingham

BARRIER

Holmes Reef
Flinders Reef
Malay Reef
HINCHINBROOK I.
Halifax Bay
Townsville

CORAL SEA ISLANDS
TERRITORY

GREGORY RANGE

Charters Towers
CENTRAL SECTION
Bowen
Marion Reef

Mount Isa
Cloncurry
Hughenden
GREAT DIVIDING RANGE
Lake Buchanan
Proserpine
Mt. Dalrymple
1259
Mackay

WHITSUNDAY ISLANDS

REEF

Dajarra
SELWYN RANGE
Lake Galilee

NORTHUMBERLAND ISLES
Swain Reefs

Winton
Blair Athol
CAPRICORNIA SECTION

Tropic of Capricorn
Longreach
Marlborough
Yeppoon
Keppel Bay

QUEENSLAND
Jericho
Fairbairn Res.
Emerald
Rockhampton
CURTIS I.
Capricorn Channel

GREAT
Yaraka
Blackall
Rolleston
Jambin
Gladstone

Mt. King
806
Bundaberg

ARTESIAN
Windorah
FRASER I.

Eyre Creek
Diamantina
Charleville
Maryborough

BASIN
Mitchell
Chinchilla
Gympie

GREY RANGE
DARLING
Redcliffe

SOUTH
Lake Eyre North
(Dry Salt Lake)
Thargomindah
Toowoomba
Ipswich
Brisbane

STURT DESERT
Cooper Creek
Cunnamulla
DOWNS
Warwick
Southport

AUSTRALIA
Lake Eyre South
(Dry Salt Lake)
Goondiwindi
Macintyre R.
Lismore

Marree
Milparinka
Wanaaring
Walgett
NEW ENGLAND RANGE
Tenterfield

NEW SOUTH WALES
Bourke
Narrabri
Grafton

Pardo R.
Darling R.
Caraghnan
Mtn. 1372
Gunnedah
Armidale
Port Macquarie

Wilcannia
Nyngan
Gilgandra
Tamworth

46

OF CITIES AND COASTS

With over 2800 km (1740 miles) of Pacific Coast, Queensland's coastline might represent a lifetime of exploration. Mangroves, marinas, bomboras, bars, bays, casinos and whale playgrounds crowd the visitor's possible itinerary. Predictably, it's not all Man Friday beaches. 'Progress' has also thrown up cities, suburbs and status-conscious resorts. The visitor must target his or her desire.

It all starts with a rush at the Gold Coast, a giant theme park of sand, shopping and 300,000 visitors each summer. North and inland of its glitz is Brisbane, the state capital, an even-paced city which administers 'The Sunshine State's' prosperity and growing population - 2.8 percent increase per annum, almost twice the national average. (Appropriately, the state emblem bird is the jabiru stork.)

North of the capital, the density of development decreases significantly. One also notices an insistence on tagging almost every inch of coastline with a promotional title. These 'promogenous zones' sometimes have smaller, unofficial zones such as the 'Pineapple Coast' and the 'Coral Coast' embedded within them, or larger ones like the 'Sugar Coast' overarching them. The whole mega-realm could be called the 'Cane Toad Coast.' The list runs something like:

Gold Coast - Coolangatta to the Southport Spit
Sunshine Coast - Caloundra to Rainbow Beach
Fraser Coast- Fraser Island to Bundaberg
Capricorn Coast - Bundaberg to Yeppoon
Whitsunday Coast- Mackay to Bowen
Tropic Island Coast - Ingham to Innisfail
Marlin Coast - Cairns to Port Douglas
Far North Queensland - Cardwell to Cape York.

Halfway up this littoral ladder, the Tropic of Capricorn bisects the state at Rockhampton. The area of Queensland is so large, at 1.7 million sq km (667,000 sq miles) or 22.4% of the continent, that flying is often the best (though not the cheapest) way to get around. There are international airports at Brisbane, Townsville and Cairns, as well as domestic airfields almost everywhere. Once there (wherever that may be), a vast array of activities awaits the mainland traveller: bushwalking, gem fossicking, coastal kayaking, rodeos, golfing, and of course fishing.

Queensland is not a monoculture. Strong regional variations exist, ranging from the urbanity of the south-east and the pockets of intense tourist culture located along the coast, to the rural ways of the 'deep north' and Outback; an important part of Queensland's culture lies with its Aborigines and Torres Strait Islanders whose ancestors have been here for more than 40,000 years.

Preceding pages: massive grain harvesters on the Darling Downs; road trains require lots of passing room; the Gold Coast is Queensland's most developed seaside resort area.

Seasons 'Down Under' reverse those of the Northern Hemisphere: September to November is spring, December to February summer, March to May autumn, and June to August winter. Queensland is semi-tropical to tropical, with year-round sunshine. Above the Tropic of Capricorn (Rockhampton), the coastal summer is hot and humid, while winter day temperatures rarely fall below 27 C (80 F). In summer high coastal humidity (up to 98 percent) makes things uncomfortable - if you're flying to Cairns or Townsville then, allow a day to acclimatise.

The southern regions have hot summers (up to 28 C [82 F] is common), while the winters are mild with cool nights. Seasonal variations are less as you head north, until there are only two seasons: hot and dry, or hot and wet. As a rule, from November to March, it's warm to boiling everywhere. North Queensland during the December-March monsoon ('the wet') cops a lot of rain.

The coast between Tully and Babinda has an annnual average rainfall of four metres (157"). The 'Golden Gumboot Award' for Australia's highest rainfall is closely contested by neighbouring Babinda, Tully and Innisfail. Babinda's pub owner says: 'When you can see the mountains, it's going to rain. When you can't see them, it's bloody well raining again.'

Hurricanes are known here as tropical cyclones; they occur mainly in summer on the coast between Cooktown and Mackay. Good warning systems and building codes mean that damage is kept to a minimum.

Fortunately, the Reef weather is predictable, and at its best from May through October. The clear skies and moderate breezes offer perfect conditions for coral viewing, diving and fishing.One seasonal hazard from October to May is the sea wasp or box jellyfish *(chironex fleckeri)*. The venom from these marine stingers can be fatal, and mainland beaches all carry signs warning against ocean swimming during that period.

Some have netted enclosures. Island beaches do not attract these stingers.

Seasonal clothing:Queenslanders are informal dressers. However, for special occasions at better hotels or restaurants, a tie and jacket are recommended. Sunglasses, a hat and blockout sun lotion are essential. (With the highest skin cancer rate in the world, this could be known as the 'Melanoma Coast.') Good walking shoes are necessary for bushwalking; and for reef-walking, a pair of sneakers is indispensible.

School Holidays: Book all accommodation and travel arrangements well in advance if visiting Queensland during the following school holiday 'high seasons': mid to late April; Easter week; final two weeks of June; first three weeks of September; and mid December to end of January.

Special seasonal events: Mid November: turtle invasion of Heron and Wilson Islands to lay eggs. Mid August to mid October: humpback whale migrations - Fraser Island, Hervey Bay and Capricorn and Bunker Groups. August to December: black marlin season, with the action centering on Lizard Island.

Left, a few clouds dissipating at sunset is a better sign than (**above**) solid cumulus clouds rolling in during 'the Wet'.

Staying: Perhaps it's a combination of the warm climate and easy going lifestyle, but Queensland offers a wider range of accommodation options than just about anywhere else on the planet. At one extreme there are some of the world's best resorts - both on the coast and sprinkled around the islands. At the other end of the spectrum are more backpacker lodges and camping grounds than you can poke a Volkswagen Kombi van at. And in the middle is a cornucopia of family lodges, holiday apartments, and motels.

A special treat is reserved for those who move out of reach of the sea breezes. Queensland country pubs are an experience - some are classics, others should be condemned, but all will provide an unequalled insight into the Australian psyche.

Island resorts: Most of this book is aimed at providing you with the information you need to make a sensible decision on what islands would suit you best. Contrary to what tourist literature would have you believe, it is possible to have a bad holiday in Queensland - the easiest way to ensure this is to select an island holiday at random.

For example, if you want to dive every day you'll be a lot happier at the cay resorts of Heron Island or Lady Elliot Island than you would be at a mainland resort or islands with only fringing reefs. On the other hand, neither of the above cays has a raging night life. If you want to get away from it all, you wouldn't go to Daydream, Hamilton or Green Island. Similarly, if you want an up-market island resort, you should aim for Bedarra, Hayman or Lizard islands rather than Hook Island's simple facilities. In some cases, the choice is made for you - for instance, young children are not welcome at Orpheus Island or Bedarra Island.

Bear in mind that the islands of the Queensland coast are not so developed that the choice is to pay resort prices or miss out altogether. Several islands have camping grounds or other simple lodges as well as up market resorts. On many camping is the only

option - a real desert island fantasy. However, camping permits are required for national park islands and these should be obtained in advance. (See Travel Tips)

By definition, islands are limited and many people are put off by the prospect that they may be trapped somewhere they don't like. In the course of researching this book, the authors island-hopped more in a year than most will in a lifetime. From marlin-chasing millionaires down to impoverished backpackers counting every dollar the al-

most universal plaint was "I don't want to leave the island ... ever."

Indeed, our advice would be to pick one island and stay for at least a week rather than flit, with one night here and another there. It takes time to drop into each island's mood, and to fully appreciate the special charm of being surrounded by water.

Mainland accommodation: The greatest density of mainland resorts is along the Gold Coast, the Sunshine Coast and in the Cairns region. Best known are the Sheraton Mirage resorts of the Gold Coast and Port Douglas: these grand palaces of marble and designer furniture measure their swimming pools in hectares and list every imaginable facility.

Left, Hamilton Island offers every facility imaginable. Above, hotel provides a new backdrop to Brisbane's railway station.

But there are many other resorts catering to every taste and budget. The Hyatt Regency Coolum, for example, specialises as a health resort while the exquisite Reef House outside Cairns is a Bogart-induced vision in white cane and indoor plants.

Some resorts are aimed at giving guests a chance to appreciate nature, rather than the facilities to dominate it. This is the case of Binna Burra Lodge in the hinterlands behind the Gold Coast, Cape York Wilderness Lodge, and Oasis Lodge at Carnarvon National Park via Roma.

Not all resorts are for the rich. Along the coast, there are clusters of two and three star resorts catering for families of young travel-

discovered that these apparently impecunious travellers were the core of their business. Today, the expensive expansive resorts are again doing well and the simple backpacker lodges continue to thrive.

Queensland has a well developed network of youth hostels. A few are inland (Mt Isa, Longreach and Warwick) but most are along the coast from Coolangatta to Cairns and Cooktown. The hostels are open to overseas members of associations under the International Youth Hostels Federation and, of course, to members of YHA Australia. If you are an Australian resident, you can join YHA at most hostels: membership also provides discounts on a range of tours and at equip-

lers. Perhaps the highest single concentration of these establishments is in the Airlie Beach/Whitsunday region.

The follow-the-sun youth culture ensures that there is a never-ending stream of backpackers flowing up the coast and into Cairns in vans, cars and buses or by thumb, bicycle or even by air. As Cairns went wildly upmarket in the 1980's, backpackers came to be regarded as second-class visitors. However, the 1989 airline dispute proved to be a watershed: the rich stopped arriving but the backpackers hardly faltered. Those providing tours - to islands and dive sites, rafting, into the Atherton Tablelands, and the like -

ment suppliers across Australia. Lots of the Queensland hostels are very busy so booking in advance is advisable. A list of YHA hostels can be obtained from the Youth Hostels Association of Queensland, 462 Queen St, Brisbane, Qld 4000 (tel: 07/831 2022).

The middle range of Queensland accommodation extends from new motels to old colonial hotels. Although the motels frequently lack character, they are usually very clean and comfortable, and economical. An Australian innovation to hospitality on the road is that most motels provide tea and coffee-making facilities - cups, jug, spoons, teabags, coffee sachets, and packets of sugar and whitener at the most basic. This can extend up to everything you'd need for breakfast, including cooktop, sink, microwave and toaster.

The height of "Australianess" in hospitality is the country pub. Extreme examples of this are wedding-cake creations with wide upstairs verandahs decorated in ornate wrought iron lace. Although there are exceptions, in many cases the rooms appear to have fallen through a time warp from the 1950s. Simple wooden furniture, comfortable beds with chintz bedspreads and curtains and bedside lights with floral shades predominate. Food in the dining room is often ordinary, but bonhomie in the bars is

and the tales spun can make the bar scene in *Crocodile Dundee* look like *High Society*.

For the more adventurous traveller who ventures off the beaten trail - in Queensland that means anywhere away from the coast - accommodation can't be taken for granted. There are long stretches of road without towns and some of the communities along the way are very small. It's worthwhile having a complete listing of Queensland accommodation on hand when planning any driving holiday.

Fortunately, the automobile associations in each state and territory of Australia publish lists of accommodation and camping grounds (which also provide cheap accom-

always extraordinary.

In large expanses of the outback regions, the pub may well be the only accommodation available. Some of these establishments look as if they were hand carved out of slabs of wood and slate. The facilities can be primitive: one of the authors remembers trying to chew a barbecued steak with the texture of an old boot (the pub's only menu offering) when a local said "Jeez, the food here is wonderful since Jim bought the freezer". On the other hand, the characters you'll meet

Left, Queensland pubs range from the laced-ornate to (**above**) simple 'watering holes'.

modation in the form of on-site vans), ranked by the associations' inspectors from five stars to none at all. These are available to members of affiliated motoring organisations around the world, upon proof of membership. The controlling body in Queensland is the Royal Automobile Club of Queensland, 190 Edward St, Brisbane, Queensland 4000 (tel. 07/253 2444). Like the publications of other state motoring bodies, the RACQ books have listings for accommodation right around Australia. These same organisations have travel counters where you can book accommodation in advance - essential if you're travelling in peak periods.

If this book were written a decade or so ago, it's unlikely that this chapter would have been included. A simple warning along the lines of "Queensland food can be a health hazard" would have sufficed. Fortunately, there has been such a dramatic improvement in Queensland dining opportunities in recent years that a visit can now be culinary delight rather than a dining desert.

Australia in general, and the Queensland tropics in particular, have always had a head start in the quality of ingredients in terms of freshness and variety. Queensland beef, an endless array of fresh fish and shellfish, and a climate that sees mangos, coconuts, pawpaw, and bananas growing wild all ensured that there would be some memorable meals. However, it was content rather than cooking that made the difference.

Then the tourist boom struck and the major international hotel chains of Sheraton, Hyatt and Hilton arrived. They knew the standards expected by their guests around the world and in a giant leapfrog the quality of the top Queensland hotel restaurants came into world league. Independent restaurants rose to the challenge and matched them.

The best cuisine along the Queensland coast is simple enough to let the quality of ingredients shine through. Many dishes are innovative combinations of tropical fruit and seafood. And you'll often find local game such as crocodile on the menu - it tastes rather like chicken that's been cooked in a lightly-flavoured fish sauce. Despite that, it's a pleasant dish and reverses the natural order of "croc bites visitor".

In Far North Queensland are a couple of special Australian table ventures. Near Innisfail is the Nerada Tea Plantation, the country's only commercial tea growers. In the highlands of the Atherton Tablelands behind Cairns is an orchard that specialises in bringing new species of tropical fruits into the country. As part of Gondwanaland, Australia separated from Asia before many fruits now found there had evolved. The Queensland climate is perfect for the rambutans,

lychees and jackfruit of Asia.

On the other hand, few American realise that macadamia nuts are native Australia - the first plants were taken to Hawaii this century and thrived so well that many visitors think these islands are their natural home.

There are a few other tricks awaiting the visitor to Australia - especially those from North America. Like much of the civilised world, Australian regard an entree as a small dish before the main course: in other words, an Australian entree is an American

"starter". Then, there's a peculiarly Australian trait (among some of the population) of calling the evening meal "tea". If you are invited over for tea, especially in rural areas, clarify whether this is for an afternoon tea, normally of copious tea or coffee served with scones, jam and cream, or whether it's the evening meal.

An essential anagram in the Australian lexicon is "BYOG", often abbreviated to "BYO". This represents Bring Your Own Grog. Many moderately priced restaurants are BYO - you bring a bottle of wine or some cans of beer bought at a bottle shop (liquor store) at a price much less than the usual

Left, an array of seafood. **Above**, buffet pub meals are filling and relatively inexpensive.

restaurant mark up. If you are invited to someone's home for dinner, the normal practice is to bring a bottle or two of wine.

A considerable part of conversation in Queensland relates to beer. For decades, the local brew called "XXXX" - and pronounced "Fourex" - dominated Queensland's beer consumption. Then in the 1980s, the Western Australian based Bond Brewing took over XXXX. After years of enduring jokes from southern states that the main Queensland drink was only called XXXX because Queenslanders couldn't spell "beer", local drinkers didn't take kindly to their own beer being made south of the border. When a local company bought the

Downs on the state's southern border, is over 100 years old but has yet to make significant inroads into an industry dominated by southern producers.

There is one town in Queensland that completely dominates its sector of the Australian drinking scene, however. Just as the French town of Champagne is synonymous with its bubbly product, Scotland with whisky, and Kentucky with bourbon, rum has made Bundaberg famous. Inevitably, Australians have abbreviated Bundaberg Rum to simply "bundy" - ask for a bundy anywhere in Australia and the barman will immediately understand.

It's claimed that Canadian border guards

now-redundant XXXX brewing plant and started producing Powers beer few could have predicted the success it has proven to be. Powers is now seen in the parochial Queensland market as "our beer".

Australia's wine industry is rapidly gaining acceptance in the world market. The vineyards of the Hunter region of NSW, northern Victoria, South Australia's Barossa and Clare valleys and the Margaret River region of Western Australia produce most of the country's wine. Unlike beer, wine transcends state boundaries so most wines can be found throughout Australia. Queensland's wine industry, based around the Darling

used to detect American draft dodgers by asking them to recite the alphabet. If the last letter was pronounced "zee" rather than "zed", they were turned back. In Australia, the test would be just as simple - offer suspects a Vegemite sandwich and if they wolf it down, they are surely Australian. Vegemite is a black yeast extract that looks rather like road tar - many claim it tastes like it, too! Spread thinly on bread it is guaranteed to bring on homesickness in even the staunchest Australian expatriate. Visitors to Australia should try it - like one's first root beer, it's a cultural rite of passage.

More universally attractive is Queensland's range of seafood. Foodists will argue endlessly about the relative merits of barramundi (a giant perch that many regard as Australia's finest eating fish) versus coral trout but, cooked fresh, both are excellent. A good seafood sampler is the ubiquitous seafood platter on the menu at most Queensland restaurants. Typically, this would cost about $50 for two people and would include prawns (despite Paul Hogan's advertisements Australians don't call them "shrimp"), Moreton Bay bugs (looking rather like a mutant crayfish but with a distinctive flavour), oysters (Sydney rock oysters are world renowned), mussels, calamari, lobster (the traditional Australian name -

fish. The toxin is often present on the reef, it accumulates in the tissue of small fish which are in turn eaten by larger fish. Thus concentrations of ciguatera are likely to be higher in large fish (say, those weighing over four kilograms/nine pounds). A few reef fish such as red bass and red snapper are notorious for their ciguatera potential. If you are planning on fishing around the reef, the best advice is to check with local fishermen to see what fish, if any, pose a threat at the time. Cooking doesn't destroy the toxin.

The symptoms of ciguatera poisoning normally appear a few hours after the meal and medical aid is essential as ciguatera can be fatal.

although "crayfish" is becoming more common on menus), crab (either freshwater crabs in which most of the meat is in the pincers or the better known ocean crabs), and some pieces of fish (either battered and fried, or grilled). Basically, you can expect half the ocean to turn up on your plate, barring the odd dolphin or whale.

If you are sailing and fishing and putting together your own seafood platter, you should be aware of the dangers of ciguatera, a form of food poisoning from some reef

Left, travellers' hostels have good cooking facilities. **Above**, a desert island entree.

This hazard is only applicable to amateur fishing: professional knowledge and health regulations protect the restaurant patron. Australia has some of the most stringent health regulations in the world so anything on the menu can be eaten with impunity (except perhaps Vegemite) and tap water from municipal water supplies is always safe to drink.

For a simple gourmet repast, buy a few avocados, a lemon and a kilo of fresh cooked prawns and make your own lunch on a river bank or by the beach. It will give a good insight into one reason Australia is known as "the lucky country".

CRUISING AND BAREBOAT CHARTER

It should go without saying that there is no better way to explore Queensland's reefs, beaches and bays than by boat. However, not all areas are suitable for boat charters; local experience is often needed to cope with capricious seas, tides and winds.

Bareboat charters can be arranged for yachts with power and motor cruisers. 'Bare' here doesn't mean no sails, empty cupboards and a naked crew - although, for a price, no doubt the latter can be arranged. It means without crew supplied. You are the skipper, your family or friends are the crew - or vice versa. There is freedom to do what you like, where you fancy. Unlike in the Mediterranean, there are no flotillas of boats sailing in company, but skippers and sail guides are available to assist for hours, days or weeks, depending on your wishes. A crewed charter allows you to have a full crew and to go where you please.

There are also 'share' boats where a berth or cabin on a yacht or motor cruiser can be taken. A skipper and hostess/chef is in charge, and on some vessels you may be required to pull the occasional rope and lend a hand in the galley. Other boats may have a full crew and offer total luxury.

Marine regulations allow no more than eight people on bareboat charters. No licence is. needed, but at least one member should have had some boating experience. A questionnaire to be completed when booking will assess your degree of experience. Basic needs are common sense: an ability to read a chart and keep track of where you are going. There is no necessity to have a knowledge of navigation as sailing is by sight - an island or land will always be nearby. You will need to know enough to set the sails or turn on the engine.

Sail guides are available at a cost of $130 per day for any period of time. If the charterer thinks you need someone to assist you, there is no way you will be turned loose with his boat. You will be given a briefing session (around three hours) when information will be imparted on the implications of your

Preceding pages: yachts moored on the outer reef; a boat gives you freedom to explore. <u>Left</u>, Heron Island's commuter craft.

charter, the layout and operation of the boat, tides, coral bays, anchorage and radio calls. Tips will be given on the best fishing and snorkelling spots, island resort facilities and general help to plan your itinerary. Some briefing sessions include viewing a video.

You will sign a contract which outlines your responsibilities and the company's. You agree to return the boat on time and in good condition. A bond of $500 is held to cover any damage - a waiver is offered if your past competency can be proven - and the bond is returned 10 to 14 days after your charter. Final payment is at least one month prior to your charter date. Cancellation fees apply and insurance to cover this contin-

of the sun's rays. At 8.15 a.m. the weather forecast is given and each boat notifies its proposed course for the day. At 4.15 p.m. there is an updated weather report and anchorage details are received by the base. When base goes off air, there is a 24 hour emergency number to contact.

Types of yachts vary from company to company (nine in the Whitsunday area) but a typical selection includes a Holland 25 (7.8 metres in length, beam 2.45 metres, with an 8 hp diesel) maximum suggested - 2 people; Farr 10.20 (10.4 m, beam 3.2 m, 18 hp diesel) for 4 people; Beneteau 40 (length 12.3 m, beam 3.9 m, 36 hp diesel) for 6 people (this French-built boat is a popular choice); and

gency would be wise. Major credit cards can be used for extras with the larger charterers. Charters are usually on a noon to noon basis.

Extra crew that can be hired include a skipper, sail guide, dive instructor/master, deckhand, cook and galley help. Food for the helpers is supplied by you. Children aged one to four are not ideal on small boats. If you bring a child too small for an adult lifejacket, make sure you acquire one to fit the kid.

A two-way radio is mandatory and morning and afternoon calls are made daily. All bare boats must be moored by 4.00 p.m.; after that time it is difficult to see coral or obstacles beneath the surface, due to the angle

Woodward 47 (length 14.2 m, beam 4.37 m, 80 hp diesel) recommended for 8 people.

These boats have one or two extra berths, but to guarantee comfort, it is better to have less people than the total berths, especially for extended cruising. Also take into account that it is easier to handle a larger and more stable boat that can be more forgiving of any mistakes you might make.

Most charterers insist on a five day minimum (sometimes seven at peak times) but fewer days can be negotiated. Sample charter costs, per vessel, per night are: Holland 25, $230; Farr 10.20, $350; Beneteau 40, $490; Woodward 47, $720. For 10 or more nights, rates reduce. Fuel is sometimes included in the charter cost of yachts and motor cruisers. If not, a deposit may be requested - $70 for yachts and $200 for motor cruisers. A guide to possible consumption is $12-$14 per engine hour for motor cruisers and $3 daily for yacht fuel. Marina fees are extra: typically $20-$40 per day at resorts.

What equipment to expect on board your charter yacht? Types of boats differ and the charterer supplies a specific list. General equipment usually includes stereo radio/cassette, boarding/swimming ladder, aluminium dinghy with outboard motor, snorkelling and fishing gear, spray jackets, anchors, mooring lines, tool kit, blankets, pillows

and cleaning equipment. Navigation and safety equipment will be SSB radio transceiver, depth sounder, hand bearing/fixed compass. Sailboard hire (if not supplied) is $25 per day.

What *you* need to take: water-resistant suntan lotion, a wide hat that doesn't blow off, rubber soled shoes (for the boat and also for reef walking), polarised sunglasses, camera (also with a polarising lens) and film, your favourite music tapes, snorkelling mask, a wet suit if you plan to remain in the water for more than 30 minutes. (Even though the water is comparatively warm, at 20 - 24 C in winter, you begin to chill after that time.) A shirt and trousers can be useful

(some supply towels, sheets, pillow slips - if not, they can be hired locally), life raft and jackets, flares, fog horn, extinguisher, flashlights, binoculars, parallel rule and dividers, charts and tide tables, first aid kit, barometer/clock, safety harnesses, toilet paper, clothes pegs, coathangers, bilge pumps, sun awning, deck barbecue. Phew!

Galley equipment includes a gas stove (full oven on larger vessels), refrigerator and freezer, crockery, cutlery, cooking utensils,

Left, boom netting is like sailing without a boat. Above, sailing in the Whitsundays ranges from the most luxurious (left) to the most basic (right) modes.

for wearing while snorkelling if you are prone to sunburn. Disinfectant - essential to be applied immediately with a coral cut. Soft stowable travel bag. There is no room to store hard suitcases (charterer may be able to arrange storage for excess baggage). Spray jacket (if not supplied), sweaters, jeans, track suit for cooler periods, May to August. Smart casual wear for resort evenings. Beach towel. A light raincoat.

Charterers will stock up on food for you if given advance notice. Package prices vary; a standard one is around $25 per person per day, and includes food for three meals, morning and afternoon tea. Special menus, such as vegetarian or diabetic can be met.

Queensland's most popular sailing area is the **Whitsunday region**, with the bases of Airlie Beach, Shute Harbour and Hamilton Island catering to holidaymakers who are looking for an exceptional boating experience. The sea is clear (although not as clear as further north), beaches white and the islands lush, green gems. The Whitsunday Passage is often likened to the Caribbean as a boating paradise and is protected from the South Pacific ocean swells by the Great Barrier Reef, 40 km (25 miles) to the east. On the same latitude as Tahiti, the Whitsundays offer unrivalled sailing opportunities among 74 continental islands. (More than three-

also the time for cyclones; however, a leading charter operator claims they have never had to cancel a charter for this reason. With warning from the weather bureau, boats would be called into port before there was a serious danger. It's an ill wind that doesn't blow some good - discounted rates for boats occur around this time.

The **Great Barrier Reef** itself is too complex and dangerous for novices to navigate and only a handful of crewed boats are licenced to sail there. An alternative and memorable way to visit the Reef is by floatplane which can be arranged over the radio from your boat. (Visits are always 'weather permitting.') The plane lands

quarters of which are National Parks: you need a permit if you wish to camp on any of these.) Resort islands which welcome sailing visitors include Hamilton, South Molle, Whitsunday, Lindeman and Daydream. The most luxurious, Hayman Island, doesn't. The Whitsunday Village Fun Race in October starts from Airlie Beach; with up to 300 yachts competing it's the biggest yacht race in the southern Hemisphere.

South-easterly trade winds keep the temperature down in the main season, April to October. November to March is hotter and wet, with balmy - but rainy - nights when the local breezes are mostly from the north. It is

nearby to collect passengers. Once landed on the Reef, you can reef-walk or snorkel, dive or view the marine life from a glass bottom boat or moored pontoon. However, even without such an excursion, some of the best snorkelling and diving can be experienced from your boat, around the fringing reefs within the charter area. In fact, fringing reefs normally have better coral than the outer Reef though it, on the other hand, has incomparable fish life. The clearest water is usually at the northern end of islands.

Swimming at the islands and on the Reef is safe all year from the dangerous jelly fish which make an appearance in coastal waters from October to April/May. Washed out from the tidal rivers, the poisonous marine life are rarely found beyond 30 metres from shore. Whatever your choice of boat, the main activities to fill the days will be swimming, snorkelling, sailboarding, fishing, beachcombing and lazing in the sun. In the evenings (which can be magic), it might be a barbecue on board or on a secluded beach, or a visit to an island resort.

Airlie Beach: Proserpine airport is 26 km (16 miles) from the tourist town of Airlie Beach which has shops, restaurants and motels. Four charter companies operate from the protected marina, Queensland Yacht Charters being the largest. Mandalay

Association, PO Box 83, Airlie Beach. 4802, tel. 079/46 6673.

Coral Trekker, a beautiful Danish-built 22 metre square-rigger and *Golden Plover,* a 30 metre brigantine built in Melbourne in 1910 are among a small number of genuine old-time sailing ships which ply the Whitsunday waters, capturing hearts and minds. Such vessels offer true sailing safaris - great for the young at heart, and even the young. There are weekly departures for seven days of sailing and camping on islands at night. Two person tents, sleeping bags, air mattresses, sailboards and snorkelling gear are provided. Scuba diving is available for those with certificates. The cost of passage starts at

Boat Charters have their own boat jetty a few kilometres towards **Shute Harbor**. Shute, 10 km from Airlie is also accessible by water taxi 18 km from the airport at Hamilton Island. A natural harbour, Shute Harbor doesn't have the tourist support facilities of Airlie Beach. Three companies charter from here. Whitsunday Rent-a-Yacht, with 12 years' experience, have 18 yachts and three motor cruisers to charter. For additional information, contact the Whitsunday Tourism

Left, the *Coral Trekker* is a popular Whitsunday square rigger. **Above**, from watching the pattern of sails and sky to being up amongst them, sailing is a special experience.

around $700 per person per week. Somewhat newer is *Romance,* a 26 metre square rigged brigantine, which sails the Whitsundays and the Great Barrier Reef for five nights. The twin rate is $740 per person, multi-share rate is $685 and a single berth cabin costs $1200. All meals are included.

Fully crewed boats with share berths offer regular departures sail from Airlie and Shute. Twenty-one metre luxury ketches and motor cruisers, holding up to ten, take you for varying durations. Costs are around $696 per person for seven nights with a food kitty of $175 paid direct to the boat. Private charters are available for approximately $1000 per day. Share berths on crewed boats allow passengers to take some turns with boat duties on sailings of six, eight or 15 days with no set itineraries. Rates from $575 per person include meals; marina and mooring fees are extra. These informal sailings are particularly enjoyable for young singles. Share berths are also available for seven day itineraries on some of the most famous racing yachts in Australia's history. They are captained by a racing skipper. Regular departures are every Sunday. As a sample cost - $519 for seven days on *Apollo III*.

Serviced by a jet airport, **Hamilton Island** Marina has space for 200 boats. Developed in recent years for tourism, there are many restaurants and night life venues from which to choose. Hamilton Island Charters have 15 boats - yachts and motor cruisers for bareboat charter. The island hosts a week of races in April each year. If you don't qualify - it's open to monohull and multihull yachts entered by a member of a yacht club recognised by a national yachting authority - you might enjoy the excitement and social activities surrounding the event. More information from the Hamilton Island Yacht Club, PO Box 10, Hamilton Island, Qld, 4803.

Hamilton Island Tall Ship Cruises sails the 27 metre sailing schooner *Mentor* with twin share cabin accommodation for seven nights departing Saturdays. Carrying 12 passengers, the cost is $751 per person with a food kitty of $140 extra. At the upper end of the market is a berth on the luxurious *Southern Spirit* a ketch rigged auxiliary catamaran worth $4.5 million. All possible comforts are provided. Food is gourmet prepared by international chefs. In the Wildean spirit of 'no success like excess,' there's Georg Jensen cutlery, gold plated fittings and hand printed fabrics to contribute to the ambience. For these pleasures, ten passengers (maximum) with each part from $3550 to $6150. No children under 16 or people without diamond dusted credit cards are accepted. If you prefer to dine alone, *Southern Spirit* is available for private charter at $55,000 per week.

At the southern end of the Whitsundays, **Mackay** is home to two well-run cruise operations. Family operated Elizabeth E Coral Cruises have regular Monday departures of *Elizabeth E II* on a four day cruise visiting Lindeman Island, South Molle, Whitsunday Island and the Barrier Reef. The

ship is 33 metres in length and carries 28 passengers in ensuite cabins and old style charm, with excellent food. The chef's freshly baked cakes and biscuits for morning and afternoon tea are a hazard for anyone watching the figure. Weather permitting, an overnight stay is scheduled on the Reef. Twin share is $731 per person, sole occupancy $1097. Children under 15, $366.

The other option is with Roylen Cruises and their two 35 metre catamarans, *Roylen Endeavor* and *Roylen Endeavor II*. They operate five day trips to the reef, Brampton, Hamilton, South Molle, Lindeman, Daydream and Hook Islands. With 45 passengers and a crew of 10, ensuite cabins are

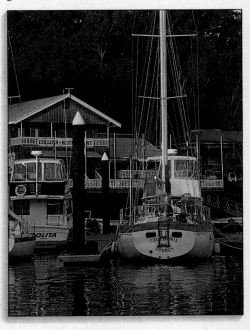

double, twin or triple. Designed for stability and comfort, the beam of the cats is 13.25 metres. There are two grades of accommodation costing $741 or $879 per person.

In the far north, **Cairns** has opportunities for crewed sailing. (A quick visit to Ben Cropp's Shipwreck Museum at Port Douglas will explain the reason for the lack of bareboating in these waters.) Day trips are popular on catamarans and launches to visit Green Island, Fitzroy Island, Michaelmas Cay, Cooktown and the Great Barrier Reef. Coach pickups are available from hotels.

There are some interesting extended cruises to be taken. A regular departure of

Coral Princess takes passengers on a four day itinerary to Townsville. The 35 metre catamaran carrying 54 passengers in luxury visits Palm, Dunk and Frankland islands and the Great Barrier Reef. Three to four hours are spent cruising each day, anchoring at night. The rate of $692 per person ($939 in a deluxe suite) includes all meals, fishing, snorkelling equipment.

Scuba diving equipment is available at an extra cost and an introductory dive course can be taken. There are special rates for children up to 14 years.

Kangaroo Explorer sails seven days to Cape York and return. The itinerary is flexible but visits are usually made to Cooktown,

heads north to Cape York visiting Lizard, Thursday Islands and Cooktown. The ambience is described as 'refined yet informal.' The 36 passengers are accommodated in modern cabins with two, three or six berths. Costs range from $850 to $1250 for sole use of a cabin.

The unprotected waters around **Townsville** make this an unsuitable area for bareboat charters. *Coral Princess* (see under preceding heading of Cairns) begins a four day return cruise to Cairns on a regular basis.

Goldcoast Bareboat Charters offer yachts to sail in the **Gold Coast's** hundreds of kilometres of secluded waterways.

Departures can be arranged from the Sanc-

Lizard Island, Flinders Islands, Torres Strait Island and Claremont Island. The 25 metre catamaran is specially designed to sail the Barrier Reef coast and carries 15 passengers. Cabins are all ensuite, air-conditioned and can sleep two, three or four passengers. Per person rates begin at $1235.

With a little more character, but still with complete comfort, Sailaway Cruises operate the brigantine *Atlantic Clipper*, a 38 metre sailing ship, built in 1987. Each Saturday she

Left, **Hamilton Island marina. Above**, sunset over the Whitsunday Passage.

tuary Cove Marina or the Southport Yacht Club. The boats will sleep six, but four persons would be more comfortable. The cost is $158 per night. At the Marina Mirage, Surfers Paradise, it is also possible to charter a luxurious motor cruiser, complete with crew.

Bookings and more information can be obtained through the Queensland Government Travel Centre, 196 Adelaide Street, Brisbane. 4000, tel. (07)833 5255. Fax: 07/ 221 5320. Or Charter World Pty Ltd., 579 Hampton Street, Hampton, Victoria. 3188, tel. (03)521 0033. Fax: (03) 521 0081. Happy Sailing!

Among fishermen, the annual gathering of big black marlin near Cairns is a world famous event. However, these 'mega marlin' aren't all there is to Queensland fishing. From ultra light line sportfishing for queenfish, to some of the world's largest sharks, to the tasty reef dwellers and the acrobatic barramundi of the northern estuaries, there's enough superlative fishing in Queensland to fill a lifetime, let alone a holiday.

Thirty years ago Brisbane's **Moreton Bay** was renowned as *the* place to fish for big sharks. Whaling operations based at Tangalooma on **Moreton Island** attracted so many great white and tiger sharks that Brisbane was (and still is) the only place in the world ever to simultaneously hold the all tackle world records for both species. Whaling ceased in the late 60's and although a couple of days' judicious berleying may still attract the big sharks, the main focus of attention around Brisbane has changed to billfish.

To the north of Moreton Island's **Cape Moreton** an eddy, fed by nutrient outfall from Moreton Bay's mangrove wetlands, attracts large numbers of juvenile black marlin (up to 50 or 60 kg [110-130 lbs]) and sailfish. The small marlin arrive shortly after Christmas and frequent the area until March when sailfish begin to predominate. Cape Moreton's sailfish are notable for their habit of feeding in co-operation near the surface where they are clearly visible. They average around 35 kg (77 lbs) and are usually taken by casting live baits to feeding fish off special 6-10 kg (13-22 lbs) line class spinning outfits, or (when not feeding on the surface) by deep drifting live baits on similar line class conventional game fishing gear.

Winter's approach in late May heralds the end of Brisbane's light tackle billfish season. It's then that the boats head wide to fish heavy tackle on much larger marlin which have recently been discovered along the edge of the continental shelf, off the **Gold and Sunshine Coasts** and Brisbane. 'The

big three: black, blue and striped marlin are all present and already record fish have been brought in. Strike and capture rates are proving to be at least twice as good as the much vaunted Hawaiian grounds.

Charter skippers to contact for heavy and light tackle billfishing off southern Queensland are: Gold Coast - Ross McCubbin (018)729 393; Brisbane - Ken Brown (07)396 0080 and Geoff Ferguson (07)393 3573; Sunshine Coast - Bob Jones (07)283 3568. Alternatively, Judy Gay runs a booking agency on (07)398 7910.

Fraser Island (see chapter), some 190 km (120 miles) north of Brisbane, is the world's largest sand island. The island itself is over 120 km (75 miles) long and as might be expected on an island where one beach is called 'Seventy Five Mile Beach,' fishing interest centres around beach fishing. Each winter and spring the Australia's east coast tailor ('bluefish' in the US) migrates to Fraser Island to spawn. Many of Australia's fishing enthusiasts follows them.

Not far north of Fraser Island begins the **Great Barrier Reef.** Here at its very beginnings, the Reef is widely separated scatterings of coral with deep channels between them. The adjacent **Capricorn and Bunker Island Groups** and the **Swains Reefs** are popular Australian fishing holiday destinations. Both are a good distance offshore (the Capricorn/Bunkers, 60-70 km [37-43 miles]; the Swains, 160 km [100 miles]), and are best fished as a party hiring a charter boat from Bundaberg, Gladstone or Yeppoon and living aboard the boat for the duration of the trip. At least one week is the normal trip to the Swains, bearing in mind its distance offshore. Shorter trips of only a few days fish the Capricorn/Bunker reefs. Most fishing on charter trips to the Swains and Capricorn Bunker reefs is heavy handline bottom fishing for a host of species, of which coral trout and red emperor are the most popular table fare. The pelagic Spanish mackerel is also keenly sought.

Many charter boats in this region never advertise, relying instead on a regular clientele who make their trip an annual event. Boats to either grounds tend to be booked

Left, early morning is a popular time for beach fishing all along the Gold Coast from Coolangatta to Broadbeach.

well in advance, making it important to plan up to 12 months ahead. Try booking agent Os Blacker in Gladstone, on (079)72 4033.

From the Swains to Cape York, angling target species are consistent: members of the sweetlip and emperor family follow coral trout and red emperor, as do members of the wrasse, *lutjanid* and parrot fish families. Pelagic sport and game fish include cobia, quite a few of the trevally family (notably the giant trevally *(catanx ignubilis)*, job fish and longtail, kawa kawa, yellowfin and dogtooth tuna. Reef fish are generally fished with either rail winches or heavy handlines. Heavy spinning and light game fishing tackle is used for sport and game fishing.

the Reef. In Mackay, Shute Harbour, Townsville, Cairns and Port Douglas boats are always available. Smaller ports such as Bowen and Hamilton Island may also have boats for charter. Most resorts offer some type of fishing option, but these are sometimes fairly casual arrangements which may not suit really dedicated anglers. It is advisable to check out exactly what is entailed in fishing from a resort before booking. Resorts at Tangalooma, Hamilton Island, Dunk Island and Lizard Island have either resident game fishing boats or professionally crewed game boats on call.

The **Whitsunday Group** of islands, accessed through Airlie Beach, Shute Harbour

Visitors to the Barrier Reef should be aware of ciguatera, a toxin always present in a number of species common along the Barrier Reef (eg. red bass and Chinaman fish) and a potential problem (due to its cumulative properties) if present in other reef species. Poisonous species will be quickly identified by crew on any boat fishing the Reef. The best way to avoid poisoning from other species is not to eat large specimens of any fish which (due to their longer life span) are likely to have accumulated dangerous levels of ciguatoxin.

North of Bundaberg, all large ports along the coast have charter boats available to fish

and Hamilton Island are justifiably famous cruising grounds. Fishing is of course part of any bareboat charter and anybody with any expertise will have no trouble finding a meal of fresh fish around the Whitsundays. Those folk interested in tossing small metal lures and jigs from a light spinning rig will also find enjoyable small fish sport fishing in the Whitsundays. As an ideal boating and fishing holiday the Whitsundays have few peers.

The largest city in North Queensland, **Townsville**, has light tackle billfishing comparable to Brisbane. At **Cape Bowling Green** 60 km (37 miles) south of Townsville, is a nutrient cell fed by the wetlands of nearby Bowling Green Bay. Here, small black marlin and sailfish can be present in such numbers that the capture of a dozen in a day just might arouse comment on the waterfront. Cape Bowling Green is one of the few places in the world where billfish are regularly taken on fly tackle. Charter skippers Calvin Tiley (077)724 205 and Dave Pemberton (077)72 3180 are supported by several other part time boats working the Cape Bowling Green grounds.

To change tack(le) for a moment: in Townsville can be found the first of the professional fishing guides who work the coastal rivers and inshore waters for several sportfishing species - including a red eyed bucket-mouthed tail-walking member of the perch family called barramundi. 'Barra' (as they are known) are joined by queenfish, mangrove jacks and a very tasty *lutjanid* (known to Americans as 'snappers') which locals call 'fingermark.' Guides take their clients into mangrove creek mazes in the massive wetland systems behind Hinchinbrook Island, in Trinity Inlet near Cairns, and in Kennedy Inlet near the tip of Cape York.

Mangrove inlet and inshore sportfishing is almost exclusively carried out with light spinning or pistol grip 'baitcasting' outfits. Much of the fishing is lure casting around snagpiles of fallen timber where king barra lurks. Contacts for guides are: Townsville - Steve Jetson (077)79 6370; Cairns - John Cross (070)53 6404; Cooktown - Carl Grist (070)69 5280 and Cape York - Gary Wright (070)69 1444.

Guide-cum-charter skipper Barry Cross who operates out of **Cairns** specialises in casting big cup-faced 'blooper' lures for giant trevally up to and over 20 kg (45 lbs). This spectacular and adrenalin charged form of sportfishing has established Barry a regular flow of clients from Australia and overseas. Some people who come out each year to fish the giant black marlin off Cairns now set aside extra days to fish with Barry. He may be contacted on (070)54 5497.

What can be said about the huge black marlin that, from September to November, congregate to breed along the outside of the Barrier Reef off Cairns? A 'grander' (a fish

Left, captured marlin are usually rewarded with a tag, and freedom, for its resistance, unless it's a record-breaking catch like the one above.

of over 1000 lbs [450 kg]) can weigh as much as a small motor car and moves with similar speed and power. Attaching oneself to one of these is not for the faint of heart. Also not for the faint of wallet.

The best way to tangle with a 'grander' is to spend several days fishing as far north as **Lizard Island**. From here it's too far to return to Cairns each day, making the additional cost of accommodation aboard a mother ship anchored behind a convenient reef or at the resort on Lizard Island an almost essential part of Cairns marlin fishing. Day charters are available along the Cairns waterfront during the marlin season; however, bookings for trips of several days

duration including use of a mother ship or the resort are best organised well ahead because of heavy demand in peak season. Jack Erskine's Tackle Shop on Mulgrave Road in Cairns will be able to help in booking a marlin charter boat. 'Jack's shop' (phone (070) 51 6099) is Australia's most famous tackle supply house and the home of Jack's custom built tackle.

Spearfishing is a sport which is rarely specifically catered for by charter boat operators along the Queensland coast, although most will accept spearfishing charters by special arrangement. However, spearfishing with scuba is illegal in Queensland.

There can hardly be a stronger imperative for learning to dive than a planned trip to the Great Barrier Reef. Although diving isn't essential to appreciate the Reef, it certainly adds an extra dimension to a Reef holiday. And learning to dive is likely to change the character of your holidays forever: a dive certificate is a passport to the watery two thirds of the earth's surface.

However, there are a few inhibitions to be overcome on the way to becoming a diver. For a start, diving is a completely unnatural act and there are a few times along the way when you'll come face to face with situations that will test your will power. A good diving instructor will be able to take you past those without trauma.

Snorkelling: While diving may be an added feature of a Reef holiday, snorkelling is a near-essential. Without this very basic skill, you are restricted to viewing the corals and fish of the Reef through a glass bottomed boat. And that's only marginally more immediate than seeing it on television.

There are three parts to a snorkelling kit: mask, snorkel and flippers (or fins). Although most resorts supply these free of charge it's a good idea to bring your own, as that way you'll be sure of a perfect fit every time. To that should be added a T-shirt and waterproof sun block - there is nothing more certain than chronic sun burn after hours of floating face down, completely absorbed in the wonders below, while your unprotected back and legs cook while being kept deceptively cool by the salt water.

The better flippers these days are at least partially made of silicon, which is much more endurable than rubber. Divers generally prefer flippers that end in a single strap rather than ones that have a fitting like a shoe because the former can be more easily used with wet suit booties. However, if you're not going to wear booties, the shoe-style flippers afford better protection against coral cuts.

Snorkels come in an almost infinite vari-ety of colours and designs. They all work as well as each other - except for the old dangerous ones that terminated at the top with a ping pong ball in a cage. The most vital point in selecting a snorkel is to get one with a soft, comfortable mouthpiece. Again, silicon is the favoured mouthpiece material. It is not chance that all snorkels are roughly the same length - there is a limit to the length of tubing that a human lung can clear of water with a single exhalation. When a snorkeller dives below the surface the snorkel fills with water and upon returning to the surface the snorkeller expels that water before taking the next breath.

Purchasing a mask should be done with great deliberation. After all, this will be used for both snorkelling and diving, and nothing is worse than an ill-fitting mask. A good mask should seal so completely against your face that you can hold it there, unsupported, while standing upright, merely by breathing in through your nose. Inevitably, the best masks are made of silicon.

For very obvious reasons, one needs a mask with good strong glass, so it is essential to buy a diver's mask of a reputable brand. All diver's goggles allow you to pinch your nose between thumb and forefinger to equalise pressure in your ears when descending. If you wear glasses your options are limited - it's impossible to wear glasses and goggles together. Goggles can be made up of prescription glass but these are expensive and are normally only considered by regular divers.

The only two tricks to snorkelling are making it into the water without sand in your flippers (virtually impossible) and getting used to breathing with your head underwater. The first few breaths taken this way seem very strange indeed but it soon becomes perfectly natural.

Diving: There are several schools of diving tuition with acronyms that sound like Santa's gnomes: FAUI, NAUI and PADI. Disciples of each will extol the virtues of their system but, in practice, the teaching skills of the instructor are more important than the system taught. A good instructor will be both patient in the water and thorough

Left, snorkelling is best done in pairs (so there is a companion on hand if you encounter difficulties), but holding hands is optional.

in the classroom. After all, diving at recreational level isn't difficult, but safety should be so ingrained that it become pyschologically impossible for you to take risks.

The Queensland coast and islands are littered with diving schools. Almost every resort has a diving instructor and courses start weekly or, in some cases, daily. On the coast, the main concentration of diving schools is in the Cairns/Port Douglas area but there are also many around Airlie Beach/Shute Harbour. Prices vary greatly, and so do the services offered. You should check particularly how much of the course is conducted in a pool and how much in the open water - some initial time in the pool is useful

but you'll enjoy diving a lot more if you can see the reef while you learn. Also, some apparently cheap dive courses may pad the bill by charging you for every extra beyond the most basic core of the course.

Anyone considering learning to dive while in Queensland should obtain a diver's medical certificate from a doctor, stating that you are fit to dive. You won't be permitted to start a course without it. Of course, certified divers wishing to dive must bring their certificates with them, as the rule on checking certification is closely policed. Many certified divers decide to dive while visiting the Reef even if they haven't been underwater

for years. So you can expect to be asked to give details of your most recent diving experience. If you haven't dived for a while, it's a good idea to bring a current diver's medical certificate and your first few dives are likely to be under the close supervision of an instructor or dive master.

A "resort dive" is the best compromise for someone who is interested in learning to dive but doesn't want to make the commitment in advance, or for one who just wishes to experience the Great Barrier Reef from a diver's perspective. In a resort dive, people who have never been diving before are given very basic instructions on the use of dive equipment then taken for a dive under the close personal supervision of instructors and dive masters. However, anyone contemplating doing a resort dive would be well advised to bring a diver's medical certificate in any case - diving is addictive and many go straight from the water after a resort dive and sign up to do a full certificate course.

If you are keen on diving or learning to dive, the best places to go are the southern resorts right on the Reef - Heron and Lady Elliot islands. However, if you are going with your family and not everyone is so enthusiastic about getting to know the Reef, other islands or mainland resorts will give them more to do.

Divers must remember that, with the exception of Lady Elliot, they will have to take a boat from their accommodation to the dive site. The trip may vary from a few minutes in a small runabout to a lengthy excursion from the coast to the outer Reef. There are several dedicated dive cruise boats operating - these are obviously for the enthusiast whose only interest in the area is as a series of dive sites. Other excursions such as those out of Port Douglas are geared equally to the diver, snorkeller and glass bottomed boat passenger. Quicksilver is a good example of such a mixed operation that manages to cater for all groups very well - some others are less successful in this. Another option is to join a "diving safari" that takes an air compressor to a coral cay such as Lady Musgrave Island, sets up camp and dives, dives, dives.

Experienced divers with their own diving equipment must balance up the inconvenience of lugging gear around the world against the advantage of using familiar equipment. Unlike some countries, most

Australian dive operations use good new BCs and regulators: if suitcase space is limited, using hired gear will be little hardship.

A never-ending source of conversation among divers is the argument about the relative merits of the north and south, outer reefs and inner reefs, cays versus fringing reefs, and so on. As always, these are battles that will never be settled. As a general principle, the outer Reef has more large fish, but fringing reefs have better displays of coral.

Running from north to south, a brief rundown of diving possibilities would be:

North of Cairns, there are several diving operations out of **Port Douglas** operating sites such as **Agincourt Reef** and the **Low**

from 50 km (30 miles) to 250 km (150 miles) off-shore. South of Cairns around **Mission Beach** there is too much river run off to make diving very attractive around the rainforest islands but dive vessels do run out to **Beaver Reef**.

Around **Townsville** some of the reefs have been badly affected by the Crown Of Thorns starfish that decimated the coral over the past decade and more. However, there are still some excellent fringing reefs to be found. Even so, the inner reefs off Townsville are further out than the outer reefs along other parts of the coast so longer boat voyages are required. **The Whitsundays** don't have great visibility - sometimes down to three

Isles. The Reef is at its closest point to the mainland in this northern region but there are few close centres of civilisation as stepping off points. When the trade winds abate around October it's possible to dive on the ocean side of the Reef. This is a fascinating and vertiginous world where the Reef and all its associated life suddenly end at the deep Pacific. **Cairns** is the heartland of the Queensland diving industry and there are several vessels operating to the Reef which is

Left, Merlin, the giant moray eel of the Cod Hole near Lizard Island, and friend. **Above**, divers setting out from Heron Island.

metres or less, but they do have some very good fringing reefs and a wide variety of corals in relatively small areas. The main Reef is some 60 km (40 miles) offshore here and some dive boats operate out here to take advantage of the great visibility - around 25 to 30 metres (80-100 feet). Further south around **Great Keppel** the diving is all on fringing reefs but the visibility in summer isn't very good. In the southern part of the Reef there are a lot of platform reefs to chose from and some coral cays to stay on. The visibility is very good (especially in winter) but at that time of the year a wetsuit is essential.

An Englishman once speculated- as only an Englishman could- that surfing might be 'like having a cup of tea with God'. Which just goes to prove that when you're screaming through the liquid hoop of a tubing wave, words are no help at all. However, in blessing Queensland with the Great Barrier Reef, that tea-drinking God shortchanged it on surf, for only the southernmost 250 km (155 miles) of the coast catches the full Pacific swell, with the Reef blocking it from that point northwards.

Queensland's warm waters ensure that at any time of year you will find surfers flinging their boards, wave skis, boogey boards, surfboats and windsurfers onto anything which resembles a swell. At the heart of all this is the simple pleasure of being thrust shorewards by the great free-ride pulse of the ocean. Having begged, borrowed or rented a surfcraft of any kind, get someone to instruct you on a few pointers. Observe the 'No surfcraft between the flags' signs; surf in the company (but not in the way) of others and stay out of the water if it looks too rough. Beginners in surfing are pathologically resented when they 'drop in' on a wave which

another surfer is already riding, so stay clear of other riders when they're up. If the verbal abuse doesn't bother you, consider your body being impaled with a very sharp surfboard. Seriously consider starting on a soft boogey board instead of a hard board.

Sharks too enjoy Queensland's tepid summer waters, so unless you'd enjoy a cup of tea with Jaws, don't swim or surf in rivermouths, or at dawn or dusk, feeding time. If you hear the shark alarm ... you've got about 30 seconds to do the hundred metres back to shore. On the other hand, tropical stingers like the box jelly fish are not found in the southern, surfable waters - they begin where the surf ends, above Bundaberg.

Surf Lifesaving Clubs hold summer carnivals, with events like the belt race, rescue and resuscitation drills, and spectacular, hazardous surf boat races. Collisions and capsizes are frequent, and a boat 'cracking' a two metre wave all the way to shore is a fine and, when things go wrong, dramatic sight.

The Surfari: The Gold Coast has almost 40 km (25 miles) of surf, from **Duranbah** (in NSW) at Tweed Heads to the Southport Spit. Not all of it is good - but some is brilliant, notably the right-hand point breaks. Queensland's surf begins at pretty **Coolangatta**: Point Danger, Snapper Rocks, Rainbow Bay and Greenmount. They are usually crowded, but work in a variety of wind and swell conditions. A few minutes drive up the coast brings you to the legendary point surf of **Kirra**, which, like much Queensland surf, is best during cyclone season (December through March). Kirra's 'filthy' tubes need a heavy cyclonic north swell to be perfect. When they are, heros surf here.

Currumbin, another few kilometres north is more gentle, good for skis, malibus, beginners. Eight kilometres (five miles) up the road is **Burleigh Heads**, whose 'Burleigh Barrels' are the most famous waves on the Coast. It's best in a south swell, and with a ringside vista from the headland, great for spectators too. Further on, the name **'Surfers Paradise'** is a misnomer because the best waves are actually elsewhere (as is Paradise itself), and Surfers has mostly beach breaks, rather than the classic point surfs further south. The Cavill Avenue break here is fairly consistent.

In Moreton Bay, on **North Stradbroke Island** there can be excellent waves at Cylinders, Fishermans, Main Beach and Point Lookout, but it's definitely sharky. **Moreton Island** is a real surfari. Bring a sturdy vehicle and all supplies, catch the ferry from Scarborough near Redcliffe on the mainland - and be prepared for sharks.

Back on the mainland at **Caloundra** there are beach breaks on Kings Beach, working best in a north-easterly wind, and at Ann Street. Also at nearby Moffat Heads is a very good right hander. Moving up the **Sunshine Coast**, there is plenty of surf: Kawana Beach

Granite, Ti-Tree, National Park, Johnson's and Main Beach, all of which can provide liquid ecstacy, except for the 200 other grommets and wax-heads out there too. Noosa is best during summer.

You'll need a four-wheel drive to get to the remote breaks on **Double Island Point**, 80 km (50 miles] north from Noosa. Keep going to the magnificent **Fraser Island**, where the breaks aren't necessarily consistent but they're all yours. Half way along the island's Seventy Five Mile Beach is a surf spot at the wreck of the *Maheno,* then another 50 km (31 miles) north is Indian Head and Waddy Point, probably the island's best waves.

Coastal Queensland's northernmost break

just south of Point Cartwright, Alexandra Headland below Maroochydore, Mudjimba Island, Yaroomba, Coolum, Perigian Beach and Sunshine Beach just south of Noosa.

Noosa Heads: When surfers discovered Noosa in the '60s it was a sleepy little settlement, but the perfect waves of its National Park points soon changed that. Noosa's waves rank among the world's finest. The coastline is scalloped with five linking bays,

is at **Agnes Waters** near the town of Seventeen Seventy, between Bundaberg and Gladstone. It's a right point break which works only in heavy cyclone swell, so don't expect it to be pumping just because you've dropped in. Beyond here the Barrier Reef and its islands block the swell.

Out there, on the Reef proper, 100 kilometres or so offshore, surfers have ridden perfect breaks so remote and unpredictable that unless you live on an island and have a boat, and you don't mind perfect waves, friendly whales and bodysurfing dolphins combined with sharp coral and large sharks, it's just too bad.

Left, 'Nipper' lifesavers plant a swimming zone flag on a surf beach. **Above,** cutting-back on a Queensland wave.

A fairway philosopher once asserted that a round of golf is a round of life. If sinking little white eggs into far green cups is life as you'd like to know it, then Queensland's coast spawns some of the world's most colourful versions of this golfing life.

Gold Coast: From Coolangatta to Hope Island, the Gold Coast (a.k.a. 'the Golf Coast') is richly endowed for the enthusiast. It wasn't always so. Gold Coast courses were once few and far between. Then the early 1980s resort boom arrived, which seemed to

options while clubs like **Gold Coast Burleigh, Surfers Paradise** and **Southport** also drew hefty fields. In the Gold Coast hinterland, **Kooralbyn Valley** resort created, with a few millions dollars, a challenging layout through natural bush country.

Palm Meadows, designed by prominent Australian pro golfer Graham Marsh and lavishly funded by Japan's Daikyo corporation, set new standards in course and clubhouse facilities. The Palm Meadows Cup, climbing steadily towards $1 million prize-

coincide with the enormous local impetus which Greg Norman (golf's 'Great White Shark') gave the game. Courses sprang up, on bland sugar cane fields (or, sadly for wildlife, on so-called 'useless' swamp lands), and the golf enthusiast found himself in a sporting heaven.

The NSW-Queensland border was the springboard for this golf onslaught, with the prosperous **Coolangatta-Tweed Head** fairways fingering out in a dozen different directions from a massive clubhouse with its symbolically revolving golf ball on the rooftop. **Twin Towns** and the hilly **Terranora Lakes** courses provided attractive

money, is established as a highlight in the Australian tournament calendar. The world's finest, including Norman (a Queenslander), Strange, Ozaki and Floyd, have played here. **Parkwood**, a 10-minute drive from Southport, has been sculpted in a lovely valley and with a lacework of ponds to test the player's nerve and arm.

Sanctuary Cove heralded its arrival with a ritzy tournament presentation, combining golfers and high ticket entertainers. Curtis Strange maintained concentration on his winning final round despite the background crooning of 'Ol' Blue Eyes,' Frank Sinatra. **The Palms** course was Sanctuary Cove's first venue but recently it has been overshadowed by **The Pines** course, a tough pond and pine-flanked layout that can bring the finest player to his knees. Arnold Palmer designed the new course which reflects the bold approach of this power-house golfer .

Golf in Australia is a democratic sort of game, catering to all ages and classes of players. Most Gold Coast courses encourage visitors, and green fees are as low as $5 at Terranora Lakes and $8 at Twin Towns (Japanese visitors keep thinking that several zeros have fallen off the fee notice). They rise to around $55 at the resort courses - still an absolute 'steal' for overseas visitors.

Brisbane is well catered for in golf venues

with **Royal Queensland** undisputed as the premier layout. **Gailes** is another former Australian Open venue, while **Indooroopilly, Brisbane (Yeerongpilly), Keperra** and **Pacific** are some of the other clubs offering Brisbane golfers first class facilities.

The **Sunshine Coast** has been recently enriched by the establishment of the **Hyatt Regency Coolum** resort and golf course. The hotel itself is like the ultimate clubhouse, or golf church: Nature here has been

Left, Lindeman Island has the perfect terrain for a golf course. **Above**, using every minute of the day.

completely, tastefully re-fashioned in the image of a new god, Golf Culture. Master American designer, Robert Trent Jones Jr. sculpted this stunning layout, taking an 'unattractive' parcel of bush and sandy mangrove country and transforming it into a lush championship quality course. Noosa, Caloundra and Headlands are all within easy proximity of Coolum, offering splendid golf for the Sunshine Coast devotees. Kangaroos share the fairways with golfers at both **Buderim** and **Tewantin-Noosa,** the latter well known for its staging each year of the Jack Newton Classic, in which Prime Minister Bob Hawke is a regular participant.

Toowoomba, Townsville, Rockhampton, Mackay, Gympie and Maryborough are some of the big coastal towns proud of their golfing facilities. Visitors are welcome, and fees are modest. True to the 'no holds barred' spirit of the huge development at Yeppoon known as the **Capricorn Iwasaki Resort**, its golf course layout, carved through natural bushland on the outskirts of Yepoon township, is a real challenge.

The Great Barrier Reef islands have a fair smattering of golf opportunities. **Lindeman, South Molle, Dunk, Brampton** and **Magnetic** islands all have courses where cool sea breezes and perhaps a turtle bobbing languidly in the bay make island golf a fun thing. Hamilton Island's developers have even taken a large chunk of nearby Dent Island and manicured it into an 18 hole course, complete with all facilities including a new name, **Hamilton West Island**.

An hour's run north of Cairns is the **Sheraton Mirage** resort, pride of **Port Douglas**. Most Australians will recognise it through the massive exposure it has received. In its 'Super Skins' tournaments, Norman and Nicklaus, Ozaki, Strange and Faldo have played for huge 'skin' stakes along fairways that border the Coral Sea or reach towards low mountains to the west.

You'll find **Paradise Palms** 28 km (17.5 miles) north of Cairns; it is a remarkable venue. The site was once cane fields but has been transformed into a rich, rolling golfing oasis. Another Daikyo construction, its grandiose clubhouse of Queensland-cum-Bali design is memorable. Royal palms, mango trees, palms, and vivid bougainvillea make the usually unwelcome trek through the rough a trip through a paradise garden.

The Outback: The claim has been made that Australians are intimidated by the immensity of their country, and so cling to their shores living in cities and looking ever outwards rather than towards the 'red heart' of the continent. If this is so (and population patterns support the thesis) it is also an accusation that can be levelled against visitors to Australia, too. Most may venture inland to see Ayers Rock but they arrive by jet, stay in air conditioned hotels and retreat to the coast as soon as they can.

In Queensland, the ambit of visitor activities is even more circumspect. Few venture further from the coast than the day trip from Cairns to Kuranda - still almost within sight of the coast. The rest of inland Queensland is largely ignored. That's an oversight: Queensland's outback is just as special as the Reef but in a very different way. Out here, adversity has become a lifestyle. Of course, talking about non-coastal Queensland as a single entity is a nonsense. As the crow flies, from the NSW border to the Jardine River on Cape York Peninsula is 2300 kilometres (1400 miles) - more than the length of the US west coast from Canada to Mexico or the distance from Athens to Stockholm.

Inland Queensland spans five tourist regions from the evocatively-named Golden West to the pedestrianly-titled North West Queensland, with Gulf Savannah, Outback Queensland and the Darling Downs/Southern Border region in between.

The part of Queensland least likely to be found on the tourist itinerary is the **Gulf Savannah** that extends from the Northern Territory border to the Cape York Peninsula, following the edge of the Gulf of Carpentaria. **Normanton** is the largest population centre in the region - with a massive 1100 souls. The prawn fishing fleet of **Karumba** (a very different place to Kuranda) boosts its population to 550 but the other towns: Burketown, Croydon and Georgetown have less than 300 each.

During the wet season from December to March this 'channel country' is in flood and

moving around on the ground is difficult. However, after the rains, the rivers and waterholes of the region are home to teeming wildlife - from kangaroos and wallabies, to crocodiles and barramundi and myriad waterfowl. It's a nature lover's delight. Anyone seeking an experience light years away from the tourist trail will love the Gulf Savannah region. You can get there by bus, 4WD or air from Cairns or Mount Isa. Railway enthusiasts probably already know that the "Gulflander" rail service from Normanton to Croydon, which was completed in 1891 still uses the 1922 rail motor to pull two cars on the four hour journey. It departs Croydon on Wednesdays and Normanton on Thursdays.

Mount Isa is very much the centre of **North West Queensland**. This town of some 24,000 people is more than 10 times to size of any other in the region. It is the home of one of the world's largest copper, silver, lead and zinc mines - its spoils are carried by rail to the port at Townsville. This is one of the most cosmopolitan cities in Australia - people of some 60 nationalities work in the mine and ancillary industries. Mount Isa is also the world's largest city - its city limits encompass an area of 41,000 square kilometres (15,830 square miles), almost exactly the same area as Switzerland. There are daily underground mine inspections and a Royal Flying Doctor service base.

The Royal Flying Doctor Service is a uniquely Australian solution to the paucity of roads and the lack of population in Central Australia. The service was the brain child of the Reverend John Flynn of the Australian Inland Mission. Its first flight was from Cloncurry in North West Queensland in 1928. But transportation was only half the solution - the other necessity was an improvement in communications. That became possible in the early 1930s when Alfred Traeger of Adelaide invented the pedal radio. At last, people on remote homesteads could have direct communications with a doctor. By linking this assistance to a comprehensive medical chest kept by the radio receiver, cattle station owners could treat illnesses and injuries far beyond the level of first aid. Visitors to Mount Isa can come to the RFDS base and see John Flynn's "mantle of safety" still in operation today, near where it began more than sixty years ago.

While in North West Queensland, film afficionados may like to head out to **McKinlay** for a beer. The Federal Hotel in McKinlay was used as "Walkabout Creek Hotel" in the first *Crocodile Dundee* film. And just outside Mount Isa is the Riversleigh fossil deposits that is providing a wealth of insight into long extinct life forms.

Anyone touring the channel country or the land around Mount Isa would be pardoned for thinking that they were in the outback. This is a part of the world where meeting another person outside town is an event

Australia's unofficial national song "Waltzing Matilda" - the events in the song are alleged to have taken place at nearby Dagworth Station. Indeed, Winton with a present population of 1200 has had an influence out of all proportion to its size: Australia's national airline Qantas was founded here in 1920. Qantas is an anagram for Queensland And Northern Territory Aerial Service Ltd.

Between 1922 and 1924, Qantas had its home in **Longreach** - the original hangar still stands at the airport. Only a few years ago, the Stockman's Hall of Fame and Outback Heritage Centre opened in Longreach - this multimillion dollar project is proving a strong lure in drawing hundreds of thou-

worthy of note and where warm hospitality is genuine, and a matter of survival. However, the Queensland government defines the state's **Outback** zone much more closely - it's the region around the corner of the state bounded by NSW, South Australia and the Northern Territory. Still, that takes in more than a third of this giant state.

The outback is part of the national psyche and is ingrained into every Australian - even those who have never set foot west of the Great Dividing Range. The Queensland outback has played more than its share in that part of the national character. It was in Winton that A. B. ("Banjo") Patterson wrote

sands of visitors to the outback town of 3000. As the name implies, this complex honours the people who opened up Australia and those living in the outback. It has also proven to be a focal point for historic events such as a dinner for all surviving drovers who moved the herds of cattle and sheep around the country before the advent of road trains.

On a similarly rural note, Blackall, south east of Longreach, was the site of shearer Jackie Howe's legendary feat in shearing 321 sheep with hand shears in a single day in 1892. Mechanical shears had been in use for many years before his record was finally broken in 1950. Barcaldine to the north also had a seminal part to play in Australian history. It was the centre for the shearer's strike of 1891 and under the "tree of knowledge" in front of the Barcaldine railway station, the Australian Labor Party was formed.

In the far south western corner of the state is the tiny community of **Birdsville** (population 30). The main structure in town, the hotel, stands on Main street - patrons frequently arrive by light plane, and park directly opposite the pub. Birdsville started life as the customs check point for stock coming to Queensland up the infamous desert crossing, the Birdsville Track. Each year in September, the population of Birdsville swells dramatically for the running of the

Much closer to Brisbane and the coast, Roma is the entrance point for spectacular **Carnarvon Gorge** and its surrounding national park. Unlike the dry surrounding countryside, the 30 km (16 mile) sandstone gorge has a permanent water supply and is of international significance because of the diversity of orchids, ferns, palms and mosses it supports. It has been inhabited for thousands of years and there are some fine Aboriginal rock paintings within the park.

Despite its proximity to the coast, Roma is within the **Golden West** region. The fertile soils of this region supports a much greater population than those further west - **Toowoomba**, its major city, has 80,000

Birdsville horse races.

For adventurers coming off the Birdsville Track, **Windorah** is most notable as the place where the sealed road commences. However, it also has a bizarre geographical feature - it's the only place in the world where two rivers (the Barcoo and the Thomson) join to form a creek - Cooper Creek. Such is the high rate of evaporation in the desert air that Cooper Creek flows southwestwards into the desert and just disappears into the dry salt lakes of South Australia.

Left, A meeting of commonly used off-road vehicles. **Above**, outback motoring can be on rudimentary tracks.

inhabitants. This unusual, hilly city is known for its cool climate (a rarity in Queensland), interesting colonial architecture, and the proliferation of flowers and plants that flourish in its mountain air.

The **Darling Downs** is one of the most beautiful rural areas in Australia. Its rich black volcanic soil produces much of Queensland's crops including the majority of its wheat and half the maize. Visitors coming into Queensland from NSW along the New England Highway enter the region as they cross the border - with wide grain fields, formal stands of trees and green pastures, it's a spectacular introduction.

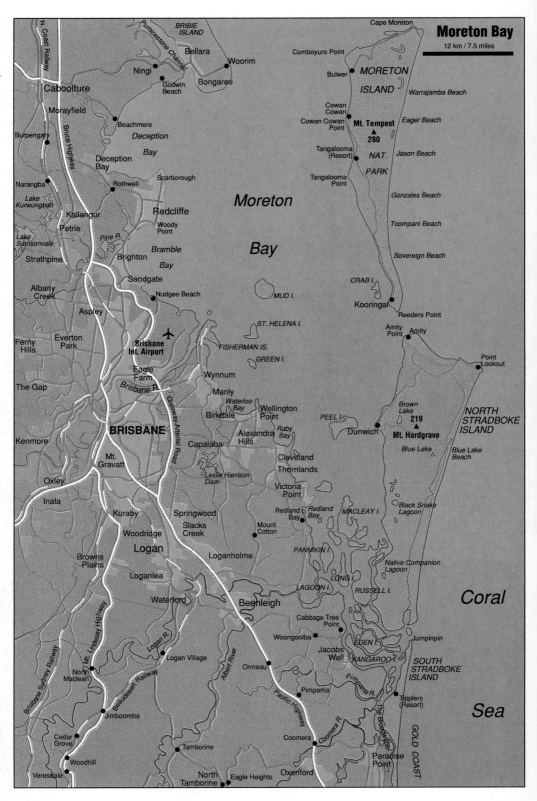

Moreton Bay

12 km / 7.5 miles

Cape Moreton

Comboyuro Point

MORETON

Bulwer

ISLAND

Warrajamba Beach

Cowan Cowan

Cowan Cowan Point

Mt. Tempest
280

Eager Beach

Tangalooma (Resort)

Jason Beach

NAT.

Tangalooma Point

PARK

Gonzales Beach

Toompani Beach

Sovereign Beach

CRAB I.

Kooringal

Reeders Point

Amity Point

Amity

Point Lookout

Brown Lake
219

PEEL I.

NORTH
STRADBROKE
ISLAND

Dunwich

Mt. Hardgrave

Blue Lake

Blue Lake Beach

Black Snake Lagoon

MACLEAY I.

Redland Bay

Redland Bay

PANMIKIN I.

Native Companion Lagoon

Coral

LONG I.

LAGOON I.

RUSSELL I.

Cabbage Tree Point

Jumpinpin

Woongoolba

EDEN I.

KANGAROO I.

SOUTH
STRADBROKE
ISLAND

Jacobs Well

Sea

Pimpama

Tipplers (Resort)

Coomera

The Broadwater

GOLD
COAST

Paradise Point

BRIBIE ISLAND

Bellara

Woorim

Ningi

Godwin Beach

Bongaree

Caboolture

Morayfield

Beachmere

Deception

Burpengary

Bay

Narangba

Deception Bay

Rothwell

Scarborough

Lake Kurwungbah

Kallangur

Redcliffe

Moreton

Petrie

Woody Point

Pine R.

Lake Samsonvale

Strathpine

Brighton

Bramble

Bay

Albany Creek

Sandgate

Bay

Aspley

Nudgee Beach

MUD I.

Ferny Hills

Everton Park

ST. HELENA I.

Brisbane Int. Airport

FISHERMAN IS.

The Gap

Eagle Farm

GREEN I.

Brisbane R.

Wynnum

Kenmore

BRISBANE

Manly

Waterloo Bay

Wellington Point

Birkdale

Gateway Arterial Road

Alexandra Hills

Raby Bay

Mt. Gravatt

Capalaba

Oxley

Leslie Harrison Dam

Cleveland

Thornlands

Inala

Victoria Point

Kuraby

Springwood

Woodridge

Slacks Creek

Mount Cotton

Browns Plains

Logan

Loganholme

Loganlea

Waterford

Logan R.

Beenleigh

North Maclean

Logan Village

Ormeau

Albert River

Mt. Lindesay Highway

Jimboomba

Beaudesert Railway

Pacific Highway

Pimpama

Brisbane Sydney Railway

Cedar Grove

Coomera R.

Woodhill

Tamborine

Oxenford

Veresdale

North Tamborine

Eagle Heights

N. Coast Railway

Pumicestone Channel

Bruce Highway

BRISBANE AND MORETON BAY

A harsh start: **Brisbane** did not begin with a boom. The governor of the new colony of Queensland, Sir George Bowen noted in his report in 1859: 'As to money wherewith to carry on Government, I started with just seven pence halfpenny in the Treasury. A thief broke in a few nights after my arrival and carried off the seven pence halfpenny mentioned.' Things have improved.

It is ironic that such an easy-going city as today's 'Brissie' should have emerged from nightmarish beginnings as a penal settlement for 'the worst class of offenders.' Named after Scottish soldier Sir Thomas Brisbane, a convict outpost was established at Moreton Bay in September 1824 by a party of Redcoats and convicts from Sydney. Three Aboriginal nations, the Undangi, Jagaro and Jukambe had long occupied this fertile river and bay region prior to the arrival of Europeans. From 1845 to 1854, the Aborigines put up strong resistance to white occupation, and to one of their warriors fell the honour of slaying Captain Patrick Logan, a particularly brutal commandant of the concentration camp on Stradbroke Island.

Once the economic Cinderella of Australian capital cities, Brisbane and its satellite coastal resorts are now booming with revenues from tourism and the state's mining and manufacturing industries. During the last decade 50,000 new settlers per year have arrived in the state, and Brisbane has seen billions of dollars worth of resulting development, and has celebrated it all with two big events, the 1982 Commonwealth Games and the 1988 World Expo. Australia's third largest city scatters its 1,140,000 inhabitants so effectively over its low hills that it's easy to forget that Brisbane is situated on a meandering river. It is Australia's largest capital city (1,220 sq km; 471 sq miles), but, until recently, in spirit Brisbane remained (according to some) 'the world's biggest country town.'

Brisbane's character is still part-urban, part-rural, and certainly not as class-conscious as Sydney, Melbourne or the Gold Coast. Clothes are casual; men wear shorts and shirt-sleeves even in winter. Accents are as Australian and broad as the hat brims; and no-one calls the place 'Bris-bane' - it's 'Brisb'n.'

Yin-yang map: The city's main commercial streets follow a grid, with those running north-east having feminine names, and those running north-west masculine. Maps, leaflets and helpful information are available from the Queensland Government Tourist Bureau, on the corner of Adelaide and Edward streets (tel. 312-211) and open from 8.30 - 5 weekdays and 8.30 - 11.15 a.m. Saturdays. The best place to begin exploring Brisbane is with the soles of your shoes. The usual, but nevertheless delightful, civic landmarks dominate the historical architecture: the 1879 freestone **Post Office**; **King George Square** with its neo-classical 1930 City Hall; the Gothic revival red-and-white gingerbread of an 1889 **Methodist Church**; an Edwardian **Lands Build-**

Preceding pages: moonrise over the Brisbane business district. Right, the new Heritage Hotel on the Brisbane River.

ing; the 1868 French Renaissance **Parliament House** (spoilt by a towering, newer annex); and an Italianate **Treasury**. The **Botanic Gardens**, 20 ha (50 acres) of flowers, shrubs and trees, border the Brisbane River next to Parliament House and are open from sunrise to sunset.

Many of these buildings can be seen from the **City Hall Tower** observation platform (open 9 - 4). The City Hall, in Queen Street, is one of the largest in Australia, and also houses a museum and art gallery on the ground floor. While you're there, pick up a map to the city's **Heritage Trail** (available in the foyer). One of Brisbane's earliest buildings dating from 1829 is the **Old Observatory and Windmill** which stands on Wickham Terrace, overlooking the city. Built by convict labour, it was originally designed to be driven by wind, but the sails never worked, so it was converted to a barbarous, convict-powered treadmill. For a tour of Brisbane's other historic city buildings pick up a copy of the National Trust's

Historic Walks brochure from the Trust's headquarters in **Old Government House** (tel. 229 1788) at the end of George Street. The **Riverside Plaza** Brasserie is purpose-built for eating fine food *al fresco* in the subtropical climate, while the city's main street, **Queen Street**, is now a pedestrian mall with trees and sidewalk cafes.

The **Queensland Cultural Centre** (opposite South Brisbane railway station) is the new cultural heart of the city. It incorporates a Performing Arts Complex, Art Gallery, Museum, Library and restaurant. Guided tours are available. (Telephone 11631 for recorded information.) From an earlier era, the **Queensland Museum**, at the corner of Gregory Terrace and Bowen Bridge Road, has many interesting exhibits on the marine life of the Great Barrier Reef and also displays of Aboriginal artefacts, history and customs. The hours are 10 - 5 Mondays to Saturdays and 2 - 5 Sundays and holidays.

Overshadowed by the grandiose colonial edifices and official institutions

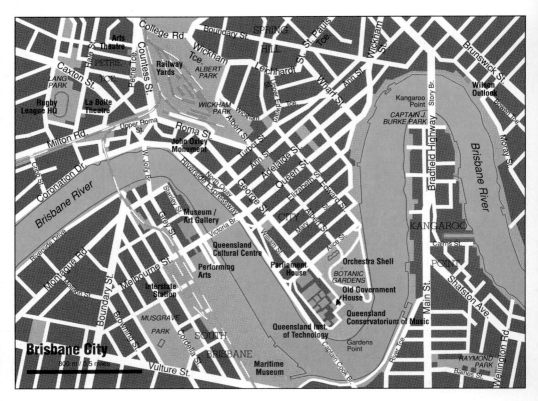

are some wonderful older haunts, Brisbane's elegant 19th century pubs. These old kings and queens are usually found enthroned upon a corner from which they gaze imperiously through their triple balconies and mantillas of wrought iron lace upon our modern madness. You can drink downstairs in these, and then fall upstairs for bed and breakfast. The Carlton in Queen Street, the Regatta on Coronation Drive, and The Prince Consort in Fortitude Valley are all suitably regal, in a dethroned sort of way.

One Brisbane 'watering hole,' as famous for its old ways as for its venerable architecture, is the 1889 **Breakfast Creek Hotel**. This fusty gem with turrets, widow's walk and a blazing neon, squats a few miles north of town on the way to the airport. In the Paddy Fitzgerald Bar, workers in steel-capped boots (or rubber thongs), shorts and navy singlets swig 'pots' of XXXX-rated beer served straight from the kegs. Conversation is loud and raucous; women are in the minority; and quiche

Brisbane is a relaxed city.

definitely isn't served. It's a rare sight of the unreformed Australian male in his natural habitat, the public bar. Just behind the 'Brekky Creek' pub is a Chinese Joss House, Brisbane's only Buddhist Temple, a reminder of the thousands of Chinese who came to the Queensland gold fields last century.

Excursions: The Brisbane River is more Conrad than Cunard, its old wharves and warheouses reminders of its days as a hub of South Pacific trading, and as port for the state's wheat, sugar and wool exports. It meanders through a city of lovely terrain and statistics (200 parks, 37 hills), under seven bridges, and then wanders off 34 kilometres to Moreton Bay and the Pacific.

The **William Jolly Bridge**, named after the first mayor of Brisbane, and opened in 1930, was the first bridge. The **Story Bridge** is probably the most famous and often photographed, while the Victoria and Captain Cook bridges were completed later, in 1970 and 1972 respectively. The city has many excursions for the day-tripper, probably the most popular being the one to the riverside **Lone Pine Koala Sanctuary** at Fig Tree Pocket. The Sanctuary also has dingoes, wombats, cockatoos, galahs, emus, Tasmanian devils and platypuses. Hours: 9:30 - 5 daily.

Mt. Coot-tha (Aboriginal for 'place of wild honey') Reserve is only eight kilometres (five miles) from the city centre, but its 57 ha (141 acres) are a complex of parks, ponds and gardens where thousands of plant species thrive. There are Botanic Gardens, a cactus garden, a Tropical Display Dome and a planetarium. From the hill top (about 300 metres [900'] above sea) you can see to the coastal channel and its islands.

Transport: Public transport within the urban area consists of a metro system, buses and river ferries. For information on city buses visit the information centre in the City Plaza behind the City Hall, or call 225-444. The ferries are fast, cheap and clean. They run from Eagle Street to East Brisbane and Hawthorne every half hour, and across the river from Alice Street, by the Botanic Gardens. The popular cruise to the

Lone Pine Koala Sanctuary departs from the Hayles Wharf every afternoon at 1.30, returning at 5.30 and costs $8. Taxis are best booked by phone, call 320-151 or 391-1091. Camping facilities in Brisbane are virtually non-existent. For an excellent guide to Queensland camping grounds ask for the brochure issued by the Government Tourist Bureau.

Dining Out: Brisbane has hundreds of restaurants, many of which are are concentrated in **Fortitude Valley** and near the University at St. Lucia. Local specialities are Queensland Mud Crabs and Moreton Bay "Bugs." Brisbane also has a wide range of ethnic restaurants and a good selection of the traditional steak and salad places. Queenslanders generally dine earlier than other Australians.

Nightlife: Brisbane's city motto is certainly not 'Disco, ergo sum.' Located as it is, only 110 km (68 miles) from the perpetual pizzaz of the Gold Coast, and having once been a bit of a Cinderella, some of the bright lights of investment passed Brisbane by. However, there is ample pub rock, jazz (Crest Hotel or Bonaparte's), nightclubs (Whispers), discos and good movies. A more sophisticated style of distraction can be achieved at Rosie's Tavern, The Brisbane Underground, The Caxton Hotel, Reflections or The Red Parrot Club. You'll find the full rundown on what's on, and where, in the weekend papers or in the free entertainment paper, *Time Off*. In late September, Brisbane takes on a carnival air during 'Warana' — Aboriginal for blue skies - a week-long spring festival with parades, arts shows, beauty contests and other events. Other important annual rituals include the August Royal National Agricultural Show, and during September, two football Grand Finals, in Rugby League and Australian Rules.

If you're a punter, horseracing at **Eagle Farm** and **Doomben** tracks takes place weekly and gives a good chance for a bet and a good day out. Big races on the calendar include the Queensland Derby, the Brisbane Cup and the Castlemaine Stakes, all run in June.

The best months to visit Brisbane are from April through November when day temperatures range from 20 to 27 degrees Celsius (68 to 80°F). There is a year-round average of 7.5 hours of sunlight per day. Most of the rain comes during the very hot, very damp summer months of December to February. Brisbane is also a great launching pad for day-trips to nearby attractions such as the Gold and Sunshine Coasts and **Lamington National Park**.

The two best sources of information on just about everything are: The Queensland Government Tourist Bureau, at 196 Adelaide St., Brisbane, QLD 4000, tel. (07) 833 5255; and, Tourism Brisbane, Ground Floor, City Hall, King George Square, Brisbane, QLD 4000, tel. (07) 221 8411.

Moreton Bay: This huge sheltered body of water at the mouth of the Brisbane River was named by Captain Cook after the Earl of Morton - the spelling has changed since then, and so has the bay. The main islands of North Stradbroke and Moreton form a bulwark against the Pacific, and between

Like the layers of a cake, the new city overshadows the old.

them and the mainland, 365 smaller islands and 1000 sq km (386 sq miles) of water provide a haven for boats, and even for breeding whales. Moreton Bay is regarded as one of the world's best light tackle gamefishing grounds.

Brisbane is the jumping-off point for the following Moreton Bay islands: **Bribie** (by road), **Coochiemudlo** (by ferry), **St Helena** (by ferry), **Moreton** (by air or sea), and **North Stradbroke** (by sea). Coochiemudlo, Lamb, Karragarra, Russell and St. Helena islands have day visiting facilities only. Peel Island permits camping, but there is little water.

South Stradbroke Island can be reached by launch from Runaway Bay Marina north of Southport on the Gold Coast, or by seaplane from Paradise Waters, also on the Gold Coast. There is one resort called **Tipplers**, no cars and a council camp ground. South and North Stradbroke islands are separated by a channel at Jumpinpin (which, considering the unfriendly sharks and rips, you certainly should notnot.)

On St Helena Island, no camping is permitted, nor at Blue Lake National Park on North Stradbroke Island, while on Moreton Island it is permitted. Information about camping varies from island to island: get the facts straight from the National Parks and Wildlife Service, Department of Environment and Conservation, PO Box 155, North Quay, QLD 4002, tel. (07) 227 8185, or (07) 202 0200

North Stradbroke Island: At 37 km by 11km (23 x 6.8 miles) and 27,530 ha (68,000 acres), North Stradbroke is the largest of the Moreton Bay islands. 'Straddie' (population 3000) is reached by launch or vehicle barge from Cleveland (south of Brisbane) or the Gold Coast, with vehicular ferry access also possible from Cleveland. Most tourist facilities are based around **Anchorage Village Beach Resort** at **Point Lookout**, which also features the Quarterdeck Restaurant. Ringed by swamps and mangrove forests, this is the island's only hotel. Points of interest include the old quarantine station at

Dunwich; **Twenty-Two Mile Beach** on eastern side where extensive shell middens are evidence that Aborigines dined for hundreds of years on shellfish; **Blue Lake** and **Brown Lake**; the Golden Stradbroke wallaby (if you can spot one); and in the South Passage which separates 'Straddie' from Moreton Island, plenty of shipwrecks. Whale watching happens from **Point Lookout** during the cetacean migrations of May-July and August-October.

At **Amity Point** on the north of the island, traditional Aborigines are said to have enlisted the aid of dolphins for fishing mullet, an example of interspecies cooperation unknown elsewhere. The island's Noonuccal Aboriginal name is Minjerriba - 'giant in the sun.' Since European contact, North Stradbroke has known many changes. It was the port for Brisbane until the Brisbane River was dredged in the late 1880s. Originally, North and South Stradbroke islands were connected; there are now two versions of how they came to be separated. One says that late last century a white trader with too much dynamite on his hands blew Stradbroke Island in two. The more credible story is that the heavy seas from a cyclone in 1896 washed away the narrow sand spit. The island was heavily sand-mined until the early 1980s for rutile, zircon and titanium.

The distinguished Aboriginal poet, Oodgeroo Noonuccal (previously known as Kath Walker) lives here on her tribal ground and teaches bush lore and conservation to the hundreds of black and white children who visit each year. **Moongalba Sitting Down Place** is the five hectare (12.5 acres) site on which she is determined to preserve both the Aboriginal and European history of her island, with the emphasis on nature as seen through Aboriginal eyes. Some 25,000 children and adults have visited her island base so far.

Moreton Island: This sand mass (the second largest in the world, after Fraser Island) of almost 19,260 ha (47,500 acres) is mostly National Park and has four small settlements, the villages of

The War Memorial is a circle of tranquility in the city centre.

Bulwer, Kooringal and Cowan Cowan, and Tangalooma Island Resort, a former whaling station which ceased operations in 1962. There is daily access (except Monday) from Holt Street wharf, Pinkenba, Brisbane, on the *Tangalooma Flyer*, departing at 9 a.m. The *Moreton Venture* car ferry runs from White Island to Kooringal and Tangalooma.

Moreton Island was known as Moorgumpin by the Nooghie clan who occupied the island for about 3000 years. Its dimensions are 34 km by 16 km (21 x 10 miles), and it is 35 km (21 miles) miles from the mainland. **Mt Tempest**, 282 metres (922'), is the highest dune in world; its crest is made of lightning-fused particles. Unlike Stradbroke Island, it has no kangaroos, wallaby or adders; and also unlike Stradbroke, sand mining here has been resisted - so far. Camping facilities are provided at four grounds, plus bush camping. Get your permit in Brisbane (from the Division of Conservation, Parks and Wildlife) or, failing that,

from the Ranger at Tangalooma Resort.

Points of interest: the 1857 sandstone light house still in use at Cape Moreton; Blue Lagoon, Honeyeater Lake, Jabiru Lake, Eager's Swamp and the coloured sand desert behind Tangalooma; the diverse plant communities, such as Banksia, flowering gums, hibiscus and oleander, which represent fairly intact ecosystems and are thus of great scientific importance; and of course, the great dunes which are slowly moved to the north-west by the predominant southerly winds.

Bribie Island: Mostly undeveloped, this 31 km (19.2 miles) long island is reached via a long bridge across **Pumice-Stone Passage**. It tucks in under Caloundra on the mainland, and was home in the 1950s to famous Australian painter Ian Fairweather, who lived in a shack on the beach. Bribie has two townships, **Bongaree** and **Woorim**, with limited accommodation in hotel, motels and van parks. It is a wildlife sanctuary, and provides good fishing and boating.

Some of Brisbane's ornate colonial architecture, such as 'The Mansions', remains.

THE GOLD COAST

All that glitters: With golden sands, gold in its pockets and gold in those land prices, the aptly-named **Gold Coast** is a 35 km (22 miles) strip of canal developments, town houses and hotels which seems to multiply incrementally each year. It all glitters north from Coolangatta on the Queensland-NSW border (the 'Banana Curtain') to Southport, which is about an hour's drive from Brisbane, the State capital. The Pacific Ocean breaks upon its eastern hem while to the west there are major residential districts on canal estates off the Nerang and other rivers.

One of the prime reasons for the area's development into Australia's leading resort for both local and international tourists is its climate, which is pleasantly warm during winter (average 21°C [70°F]) and not unbearably hot during summer. The balmy weather attracts settlers as well as tourists and within a few years the Gold Coast region will be, in population terms, the sixth largest city in Australia. The resident population is about 250,000. When James Cavill opened his 'Surfers Paradise Hotel' in 1925 at a spot on the dune coast known as Elston (and before that, Umbigumbi), the population of the Gold Coast-to-be was 6,602.

The most up-tempo zone of 'the Coast,' the nation's densest concentration of holiday facilities, is the 10km coastal strip which runs north from Broadbeach to Sea World (sited on an unglamorously named tongue of coast called The Spit). Between them is **Surfers Paradise** - the tourist industry's trend-setter and hyperactive heartland.

'Surfers' (as it is universally known) has no patina of age - if few buildings look more than ten years old, that's because they're not. It is a sundrenched boom town of concrete, glass and crass. The soaring skyscrapers, modish shopping plazas and millionaires' mansions occupy an area of centuries-old Aboriginal fishing grounds which first saw white settlers in 1842; since then suc-

cessive waves of development have erased almost all traces of those pioneers. In 1933, the name 'Surfers Paradise' was officially adopted.

The northernmost town on the Gold Coast, **Southport** is predominantly oriented towards local business and commerce. The southernmost, **Coolangatta**, on the NSW border, is primarily a resort for domestic visitors; somewhat down-at-heel, it has changed less with the times than ritzy-glitzy Surfers. **Tweed Heads**, which is in NSW, adjoins Coolangatta (they are known as the Twin Cities). Tweed Heads has been compared with a Tex-Mex border town, and the description is partly merited. Although it's very much the 'poor cousin,' because of different State laws, Tweed Heads has many clubs with hundreds of poker machines ('one-armed bandits') which are illegal in Queensland. These provide the revenue that permits the occasional staging of shows featuring international artists. Another major attraction of Tweed Heads is its 'adult' book shops (also

Preceding pages: hundreds come down to the Surfers Paradise beach at dawn. **Left,** surfing at Surfers. **Right,** tourist information is readily available.

illegal in Queensland).

'Miami, Fla., without the paranoia': There is nothing puritanical about the Gold Coast. The briefest bikinis in Australia, often worn without tops, are a feature of the resort and the beaches and swimming pools are a voyeur's paradise. On less frequented beaches, total nudity is becoming fairly common and accepted, although it is still technically illegal.

The catalyst for the most recent quantum leap in the Gold Coast's tourist development was the opening in late 1985 of the Hotel Conrad and Jupiters Casino. Operated by the US Hilton group, the hotel/casino set a new standard for the Gold Coast. A number of other five-star hotels opened after the Conrad and many tourist facilities were forced to upgrade to appeal to sophisticated overseas visitors, particularly the Japanese. The Gold Coast is now extremely popular with Japanese visitors and their presence has done more than anything else to give the Coast its cosmopolitan international atmosphere.

December-January is the peak period for ubiquitous Japanese golfers and honeymooners.

Man-made attractions: For a holiday area to achieve international status, it needs unique tourist attractions. The Gold Coast has a wide range of these, including innovative theme parks which appeal to visitors of all ages. One of the Coast's greatest assets is that all of its best attractions are located within less than an hour's drive of each other. This concentration within a few kilometres of Surfers Paradise makes the Gold Coast unique among international resort areas.

The major man-made attractions are **Sea World** on the Spit, **Dreamworld** at Coomera and **Jupiters Casino** at Broadbeach. Sea World is similar to its namesake in San Diego, California while Dreamworld is reminiscent of an Australian-oriented Disneyland. Sea World and Dreamworld offer excellent value for money and a visit to both is virtually a must for visitors. It takes a full day to get round all the attractions in

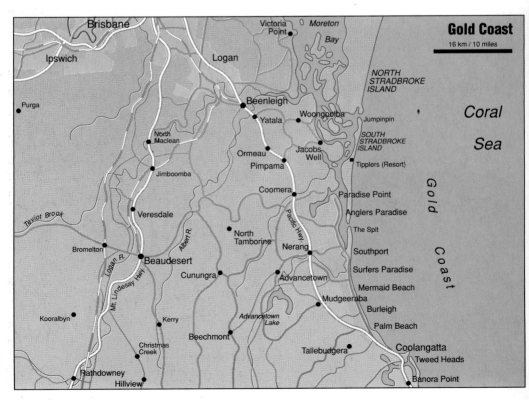

these parks (and with children, it can take two days).

A third major theme park is Warner Brothers' **Movie World** at Oxenford. This $120 million project will be similar to the Universal Studios tours in Hollywood but based upon Warner characters. Australia's largest purpose-built movie studio, the Warner-Roadshow complex, is already established next to the theme park. The area could well become Australia's Hollywood because a new and even larger sound stage is being added to the studio complex. **Jupiters Casino** in the Hotel Conrad at Broadbeach is Australia's only casino which opens 24 hours a day, and is as large as the biggest casinos in Las Vegas. It includes an 'authentic' English pub, the Prince Albert.

Two other major attractions - natural, but man-developed - are the **Currumbin Sanctuary** (operated by the National Trust of Queensland) and **Fleay's Fauna Centre** (operated by the National Parks and Wildlife Service) at West Burleigh. These two pioneer Gold Coast attractions feature Australian birdlife and fauna. They are *the* places on the Gold Coast to see parrots, koalas, kangaroos and even the rare platypus: the lillies, you might say, which even the Gold Coast can't gild.

The Spit and Broadwater: Ten minutes' drive north from Surfers Paradise, the Spit peninsula is the home of Sea World. Enveloped on three sides by water, from the intense Pacific surge on one side to the sheltered **Broadwater** (which is very 'pacific' in the true sense), on the other, the Spit has been extensively developed to include three large restaurant and retail complexes: Fish**ermans Wharf, Mariners Cove** and **Marina Mirage**, and an excellent 5-star hotel, the **Sheraton Mirage** and a nearby 4-star hotel, the **Sea World Nara**. On the Spit there are numerous aquatic attractions and boats of every kind can be hired or chartered. Parasailing operates on the Broadwater, and Sea World Aviation's helicopter tours from the Spit are an excellent (albeit expensive) way to gain an aerial pano-

Several theme parks provide an alternative to the beach.

ramic of the Gold Coast.

Many boat cruises operate from the Tiki Village jetty on the Nerang River in the heart of Surfers Paradise. These cruises cover the Broadwater and the protected waters that run north from the Gold Coast towards Brisbane.

The Hinterland: The Gold Coast is doubly fortunate in that only half an hour by car from Surfers Paradise's turbo-drive tourism is a built-in escape route, the area known as the Hinterland. Much of this rugged mountainous region is protected National Parks and, already a gem of evolution, it will never be further 'developed.' The Hinterland includes some of Australia's finest tropical rain forest areas. At Canungra, the Australian Army maintains its jungle warfare training facility, which gives an idea of the ruggedness of the terrain.

Binna Burra, Natural Arch, Springbrook, Tamborine Mountain and **Advancetown** are all places in the Hinterland which appeal to visitors who want to see the 'real' Australia.

There are many interesting and scenic restaurants in the Hinterland and the Pioneer House at Advancetown is worth a visit. Four wheel drive tours are an excellent way to cover the more remote parts of the region.

Accommodation: On the Gold Coast, it is possible to stay in a five-star hotel penthouse suite costing $1,300 per night, which includes the services of a butler. It is also possible to rent a high rise luxury apartment for $1,300 per week - but the apartment can sleep eight people and includes all facilities for cooking etc. Then again, if you'd like to have some spare change left over, excellently appointed apartments can be rented from as low as $300 per week, and will sleep four people. Sites at caravan parks and camping grounds virtually on the beachfront can be rented for around $100 per week. Backpackers are also well catered for by a number of establishments which charge about $10 per night. The Gold Coast's supply of accommodation has always stayed ahead of demand, except for the annual

A few lucky ones win this lifestyle at Jupiters Casino (right).

102

peak periods, which are mostly during school holidays. This has meant low average occupancy rates for many establishments, so intense competition has kept prices well below those of Sydney and the other capital cities.

High rise and up market: The greatest supply of tourist accommodation is in high rise apartments, or condominiums. (Queensland's tallest buildings are in Surfers Paradise). Apartments with ocean views are usually the most expensive. All 'units' are usually well-equipped, with modern kitchens and amenities such as dishwashers. Swimming pools, saunas, spa baths, etc are widely available. Rates are often negotiable: in essence, the longer your stay, the cheaper the rate you can command.

The Gold Coast's five-star hotels offer all the facilities of their counterparts in the capital cities, but their rates are usually about half those in, for example, Sydney. The Coast's pioneer International class hotel is the 622 room Hotel Conrad, which is Australia's largest hotel (by two rooms over the Sydney Regent with 620 rooms) and also the country's largest hotel convention centre. The second international chain to be represented on the Gold Coast is Ramada, with the 406-room Ramada Surfers Paradise standing on the site of pioneer Jim Cavill's Surfers Paradise Hotel.

All Nippon Airways' Gold Coast Hotel at Surfers Paradise was formerly the Holiday Inn. The Coast's fourth five-star hotel, the Gold Coast International, opened in March 1987, is also Japanese-owned (by Daikyo), as are several other hotels and local golf courses, all indicating how (a) popular and (b) profitable the Gold Coast is for Japan. The 'Honoluluing' of the Gold Coast by Japanese investors has not proceded without public controversy. Strong feelings have been expressed about the issue of foreign investment, with the debate occasionally, and unfortunately, lapsing into knee-jerk racism.

The luxurious Sheraton Mirage, on the Spit at Main Beach is the Gold Coast's only resort hotel with an abso-

lute ocean frontage. The Hyatt Regency at Sanctuary Cove (opened in June 1988) is an excellent hotel and probably the major reason for visiting Sanctuary Cove, a residential and marine development which includes a pseudo-old style 'village'. The 400-room Sea World Nara Resort Hotel, billed as a five-star hotel at four-star prices, is very popular with families, being the only major hotel which fronts the Broadwater's protected beaches.

Shop til you name-drop: At international resorts, shopping is a tourist event in its own right and the existence of a wide range of 'name' retail outlets is a major drawcard for visitors. On the Gold Coast, especially Surfers Paradise, there has been a massive upgrading of the retail sector and today the area's shops offer the variety and sophistication expected, including 24 hours a day trading. 'Glitzy' is often used to describe the new generation of shops in Surfers. Almost every up-market retailer in Australia is now represented there, as well as the usual inter-national name-drop labels such as Lacoste, Ermenigildo Zegna and Louis Vuitton. There is no point in mentioning particular retail complexes in Surfers Paradise, because the entire town centre is a vast, tourist-tagetted shopping hive, a veritable Tower of Label. Bring your credit line.

Good news for visitors is that intense competition keeps most prices low. As with accommodation, the Gold Coast is over-supplied with retailers, so there are always sales taking place, with genuine reductions. Even Duty Free shops (of which there are as many in Surfers Paradise as in Sydney) engage in intense competition, so visitors holding onward overseas airline tickets - and with the time to comparison-shop - can consume at very competitive prices.

Eats and beats: The first licensed premises in Surfers Paradise, Meyer's Ferry Hotel, opened in 1887. Today, the Gold Coast has over 400 cafes, restaurants and nightclubs and it would be possible to eat out at a different place every night for a year. The Coast offers

Whatever you want in Surfers Paradise will be within a block of Cavill Avenue, including pedestrian malls with sidewalk cafes (right).

as much variety in restaurants and night spots as does Melbourne or Sydney and, again, the rivalry to attract tourists is intense. Operators with international experience claim that competition on the Gold Coast is as ferocious as anywhere in the world. While this causes problems to restaurateurs, it ensures their customers usually receive good value for money.

Japanese restaurants have proliferated and most are very good. Enormous amounts (by Australian standards) have been spent on decor and if the test of a good Japanese restaurant is to check how many Japanese eat at them, then many are excellent. Many Gold Coast restaurants have a short life, but those which have stood the test of time include **Danny's Italian Restaurant** and **The River Inn** seafood restaurant, both in the Tiki Village complex on the riverside in Cavill Avenue. **Oskars**, Surfers Paradise and **Oskars on the Beach** at Coolangatta are both deservedly award winning restaurants. **Grumpy's Wharf** on the Spit is an-

other restaurant popular with local residents, as is the **Holy Mackerel**, on Marine Parade, Southport. A small unpretentious French restaurant, **Fanny's**, in the Sands building, Surfers Paradise, provides the best French cuisine on the Gold Coast. Fanny's doesn't advertise and is not well-known, except to a few discerning local residents who are its main patrons.

Good hotel restaurants which provide consistent service and an international ambience include **Nicholsons** at the Hotel Conrad and **Margots** at the Gold Coast International. These are up-market establishments and Nicholsons in particular is a fine example of the best type of American hotel restaurant. A fairly recent newcomer to the restaurant scene is the **Crooked House**, Surfers Paradise. This has an early Australia theme and features a vast collection of Australiana. Apart from eating, you can take an hour or so just browsing around the various displays of items that recall Australia's unusual history. It's well worth a visit.

There are many takeaway services which also specialise in delivering food (pizzas, Chinese, seafood, Italian, etc.) to homes or apartments. Menus are placed in the apartments of most tourist accommodation blocks.

There are between 20 and 30 nightclubs on the Gold Coast, but few have the atmosphere or ambience of the better Sydney or Melbourne clubs. Most nightspots are concentrated in the Orchid Avenue-Cavill Avenue central area of Surfers Paradise. **Fortunes** at the Hotel Conrad is a well-appointed upmarket nightspot, while **Traders** at the Gold Coast International Hotel is also worth a visit. The most spectacular night time entertainment of the Las Vegas revue type is staged at the **Showroom** in the Hotel Conrad.

Getting around: A local bus service runs between Southport and Coolangatta and is well patronised by residents, but less so by visitors because it is not particularly tourist-oriented. However, there are numerous bus services to most major tourist attractions. These buses pick up visitors at their hotels or at central points along the Coast. There is a good Shuttle Bus service between the major hotels and apartment blocks.

As in other fields, competition in the car rental business on the Gold Coast is cut-throat, so very low rates are available, especially standby rates, which are a gift. All the majors - Thrifty, Budget, Hertz, Avis, etc are represented - but there are dozens of independents. These include economic renters such as Rent-A-Moke, Rent-A-Bomb and Topless Car Rentals. *(You* needn't be topless: the cars are VW convertibles). There are also many places which hire a variety of motor scooters (a car driver's license is sufficient to drive one). Pedal cabs, which seat two, are also available in Surfers Paradise. They are similar to the trishaws common in parts of Asia, except for the person pedalling.

The Gold Coast's taxi service is woefully inadequate. Just trying to phone the taxi company requires great patience; the lines appear to be continually engaged. At a recent count, there were only 129 licensed cabs on the Coast; at the same time, there were 148 licensed limousines. Many of these luxury cars are Rolls Royces, Cadillacs and Bentleys, plus 'stretch' Mercedes, including several painted a startling pink. Limousine services began to expand only a few years ago, following the upsurge in overseas visitors. The Gold Coast must now be one of the few places in the world where limos outnumber taxis. The limos cost very little more than taxis and usually arrive on time - probably because the limo companies answer the phone.

This Week on the Gold Coast is a free pocket-size guide to current events and things to do. The obvious ones are spending, surfing, sailing, bushwalking, windsurfing, playing Aussie 'two-up' at the Casino, fishing, and more spending . . . or just reading a book. In a strip once dubbed 'Surfeit's Paradise,' it's a true radical who can turn his or her back on the glitz, soak up some of the 'Godzone' sunshine and curl up with *War and Peace* or an Australian work such as *Oscar and Lucinda*.

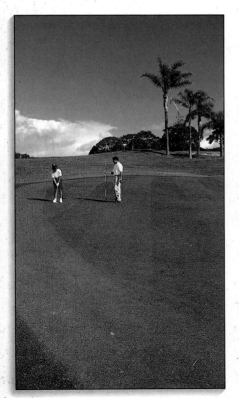

Left, golf courses are plentiful and green fees cheap throughout Queensland. **Right**, taking in the sights.

SUNSHINE COAST AND NOOSA HEADS

Like Clark Kent into a phone booth, slip into the sea at **Noosa**, shed your suit of city worries, and emerge as a tropical Superperson. That's what this 64 km (40 miles) string of beaches known as the **Sunshine Coast** is best for. It's a short flight from most places and a 90 minute drive north of Brisbane.

First settled in the 1870s, the region has grown out of a rural adolescence in timber, sugar and pineapple and into a booming residential and tourism maturity. With almost guaranteed sub-tropical weather (seven hours per day of sunshine), the Caloundra to Rainbow Beach coastal stretch and its hinterlands, from the Glasshouse Mountains to Cooloola, are bursting with possibilities for the visitor.

Caloundra, at the southern end of this coast is a jumble of apartments, 'prehistoric' (that is, from the 1940s) fibro guest houses and good beaches. The streets are full of the video, real estate and fast food shops which characterise the Sunshine Coast of the late '80s-'90s, accommodated in the cheapjack, low rise retail architecture which characterised it in the '60-'70s.

From Caloundra, the coast shimmers up through the beach resorts of Mooloolaba, Alexandra Headland, Maroochydore, Mudjimba, Perigian, and Sunshine Beach to Noosa Heads, all of which have accommodation, camping nearby, shops, beaches and pubs. **'The Wharf'** at Mooloolaba is a new development, featuring the walk-through aquarium, Underwater World, a Barrier Reef-like marine environment. The Sydney-Mooloolaba yacht race in April finishes in this harbour.

At **Coolum Beach**, there is a new Hyatt Regency golf resort, with every fitness facility imaginable. It lolls among manicured greens and pedicured

Preceding pages: the wreck of the *Cherry Venture* is a landmark on the beach drive from Noosa to Rainbow Beach. **Left**, catching a perfect wave at Noosa's National Park breaks.

fairways while Mount Coolum looks on. But not all accommodation on the Sunshine Coast is in this price bracket. At Perigian and elsewhere in offseason it is easy to find a $30 night motel for two. **Buderim** is the site of another golf course (which rolls away from the backdoor of the comfortable, moderately-priced Headland Crest Hotel); kangaroos on the course are one of the attractions, or hazards. You can look down from here to the glittering coast, where the rowboats and dangled lines of an earlier time have given way to powerboats and tower blocks, and the swampy nooks and mangrove crannies once filled by mud crabs and spawning fish are now canalled and estated.

Noosa Heads (off the Bruce Highway via Eumundi or Cooroy) is an intense zone of beauty, sophistication and opportunism. Nestling beside Laguna Bay, Noosa has distilled several versions of the Australian Dream. In the late '60s and '70s, vague hippies charged vague prices for banana smoothies from fibro snack shops along Hastings Street, and nomadic surfers slept in their cars wherever they happened to break down. Today, yuppies and timeshare sharks cruise past the huge, new pink Noosa Sheraton. But, despite the oversupply of accommodation, food and fashion, what lies at the heart of Noosa's original attraction still remains intact, though somewhat more crowded. The perfect waves which wrap around the points of Noosa National Park rank among the world's finest. The breaks at Ti-Tree Bay, Granite Beach, Fairy Pools and Devils Kitchen first drew surfers; later followed the wealthy retirees from the southern capitals, and then came the rest of the world. Noosa has the remains of a remarkable beauty. One day it will have the remains of a remarkable ugliness.

Sheltering the boutique cruisers of Hastings Street from the prevailing southeasterly winds is the 432 ha (1067 acre) national park of quiet forest crisscrossed by walking tracks. This park goes back to 1879 when early settlers had vision to declare it a reserve. A 2.7

Noosa Heads is tucked between river and surf.

112

km (1.7 miles) walk to Hells Gate meanders past beautiful coves of soft white sand which fringe the headland; here fashion inhibitions don't exist and all-over tans are commonplace. After real estate, the biggest industry is sunburn prevention and cure.

Eating: On the hill, the Noosa Heads Hotel is no longer the old bloodbath it used to be. Along with the town and the times, it too has gone pastel; the feral locals have been penned into a side bar, while the tourists bistro nattily among themselves, devouring good $10 seafood plates and big steaks. In the food court next to the Sheraton on Hasting Street, a fair range of quick sustenance from satays to sundaes is at hand. For a little more style, Cafe le Monde opposite the Surf Club allows you to nibble al fresco with good salads and slow service. Upstairs, Palmers Restaurant is said to be best in town: eat fresh lobster (for as little as $30 for the full creature), sluiced with local Eumundi Lager.

Excursion: Unwinding behind Noosa like a metaphor of development is the Noosa Sound and River. The further one moves west from the buildings and boulders of the eroded Main Beach, past the depilated, designer shores of canal estates, and back to the untrammelled reaches and ponds of the river, the healthier the shoreline gets. Houseboats, catamarans, dinghies and barbecue cruises allow access to these delightful 56 km (miles) of waterways. Cruise the Upper Noosa River, starting from Lake Cootharaba - or the lower river, from Booreen Point down to Tewantin - by canoe, kayak, surfski or shallow draught power boat. Or cruise the Noosa Everglades at the northern end of Lake Cootharaba; get your maps and camping permit from Kinaba Island Information Centre. Plenty of day tours are available on these waters.

There are two equally impressive ways of driving north to Rainbow Beach. The **'Cooloola Way'** is a rough (4-WD recommended) inland route via Noosaville, Tewantin, Cooroy, Pomona (and the 1921 Majestic Theatre), Kin Kin (and the Country Life Pub - the

Noosa's main street is quiet at dawn – but not for long.

counter lunch is so big that you need a nap to, well, counter lunch), Wolvi Road and Cooloola National Park (41,000 ha [1000,000 acres]) of dry sclerophyll forest, swamps and wild brumbies). This can be done in two hours - or much more. The area is a vast breathing space of red roads and white trees with silken skin and twisted limbs. Through here also runs the **Cooloola Wilderness Trail**, a beautiful 46 km (28 miles) bushwalk.

The other route is straight up along the beach for approximately 45 km (28 miles), past the **Teewah Coloured Sands**, which are at least 40,000 years old. Beach driving can only be done safely in a 4WD vehicle, and not within two hours either side of high tide. Check conditions with locals before proceeding, and especially before heading up to the wreck of the *Cherry Venture* . Do not cross any beach barricades. When returning to Noosa, there is a car spa on the northern side of the river.

Rainbow Beach is slow and spacious, with a pub, a few motels and restaurants, a hostel, camping ground, National Parks office (for Fraser Island permits) and a few shops. There's a long beach, which arcs around Wide Bay, from Double Island Point in the east to Inskip Point (departure point for Fraser Island) to the north.

The Hinterland: Despite the title 'Sunshine *Coast,*' many of the area's attractions are situated well inland. In the south, the ten **Glasshouse Mountains** (named so by James Cook who spotted them from out at sea in 1770) jut from the plain like volcanic expectorations, which is what they are. Tibrogarn (282 m), the father, Beerwah (552 m), the mother, the child Coonowrin ('Crookneck') (375 m) and so on, are all woven into an elaborate Aboriginal narrative. For those so orientated, this area is great for rockclimbing.

The Blackall Range is about 40 km (25 miles) or 45 mins drive west of Maroochydore. Timber getters arrived here in the 1860s, seeking the prized red cedar, then later came citrus and pineapples plantations, which have more

The tranquil beauty of the Noosa River is legendary.

recently been replaced by macadamia and avocado farms. Now billed as 'the Creative Heart' of the Sunshine Coast, the Blackall Range's galleries, antique shops and craftworkers are a temperate counterpoint to some of the overheated developments of the coast.

This 30 km (18.5 miles) diversion from the Bruce Highway starts in the south at Landsborough and ends at Nambour. By taking this ridge route, known as **The Range Drive**, you can reach Mary Cairncross Park, Maleny, Montville, Kondallila ('rushing waters'), Flaxton and Mapleton. Some of the highlights include very good views of the Glasshouse Mountains from Mary Cairncross; a 'Senses Trail' at Razorback Lookout; Mapleton (estd. 1888) with its pottery and pub; Kondallila National Park, 128 ha (316 acres) of wet and dry eucalypt forest, bunyah pines, pools, whipbirds, and its 80 m (260 ft) falls; Montville (1877) with more crafties, antiquarians and Devonshire teas; and further west, Kenilworth State Forest Park for camping and wilderness walks. Fertile, rainy **Maleny** is perhaps the most authentic of these 'touristic' hamlets, with its doglegged main street, post awnings, and timber town history; it has streets named Beech, Maple, Coral, Cedar and Flame. Nearby, there are lilyponds, falls and the 12 km (7.5 miles) Mapleton Forest Drive of forests and streams. Throughout these towns (average elevation 500 m [1500 ft]) there is plenty of good quality motel, lodge and guest house accommodation available.

To do: Beyond these highlights, the Sunshine Coast and its environs are chocablock with diversions, natural and man-made. A vast number of brochures is available, and advises of everything from the more than 40 bowls clubs on the coast and hinterland, to where to go horseriding, play golf, sleep, eat, sail, and to find lorrikeets and koalas (Buderim Wildlife Park).

Perhaps unique to this area is an obsession with 'Big Things.' Roadside leviathans, erected by competing entrepreneurs in order to lure the tourist dollar leap out of the landscape. A nine metre (29') high dairy cow looms above the highway between Nambour and Yandina. A steady stream of tourists can be seen climbing a ladder and disappearing inside near its udders (free admission). Nearby is an enormous fibreglass Big Pineapple at Sunshine Plantation, and at Glenview, the Ettamogah Pub. The latter is a blow-up of an exaggeration of a parody of a comic strip version of a mythically Aussie Outback pub, including crows that fly backwards in army boots and a Tiny Lizzie (Model T Ford) quaintly parked on the roof.

To see something slightly more real, visit **Eumundi**, with its old 'gunfighter town' style mainstreet, the trendied-up Imperial Hotel and Eumundi Lager Brewery (there are tours of the plant several times a day); and the town's Saturday morning market, a long standing event. Or you can even visit **Gympie**, the main administrative and industrial town of the region, which seems unique in having almost no tourist attractions at all.

On the Blackall Ranges behind the Sunshine Coast, creativity is a booming industry.

TO CAIRNS BY ROAD

The drive from Brisbane to Cairns is gruelling but rewarding, a journey through Queensland as it is, was, and will be: from red soil and eucalypt bush, to canefire nights, and tourism's To-morrowland. But first, ask: 'Why *drive* to Cairns?' If you have sufficient time (say, two weeks) to really enjoy the drive, and you don't mind junk food, in-different accommodation and worse roads, then proceed. If not, catch a plane, train or bus to the Far North, breaking your journey where you will, and arrive in Cairns refreshed, to rent or buy a car for your northern excursions.

The road distance from Brisbane to Cairns, via Highway One, the **Bruce Highway**, is about 1,800 kilometres (1,115 miles), and around 22 hours of straight-through driving. By interna-tional standards, the roads are poor, especially north of Townsville. (There is much maintenance evident - but the potholes and crumbling edges keep coming back for more.) Although it is a coastal highway, very rarely are you within sight of the shore, and mostly you're many kilometres from it. The hazards include trucks, speed limits and cops; cane toads and other suicidal wildlife in your path and the occasional snake in your suspension; highway narcosis on the long, long bits (such as from Rockhampton to Mackay); bushfire and canefire smoke; and that all-Australian six-wheeled disaster, Norm and Norma in the family sedan, towing a caravan. The plusses are: free-wheeling days at your own pace, plenti-ful camping sites or overnight 'vans in good camp grounds, and the stars above. There's also access to magnifi-cent beaches, rain forests, islands, country pubs, splendid fishing and div-ing, and encounters with beings uncon-ventional to the point of bizarre, such as bronze bulls, canetoads, and crocodiles.

Advice Dept: Keep in mind that dis-tances are long and towns may be far between. The Bruce Highway is sealed all the way, however you don't have to get very far off it to find yourself on dirt roads. The law says keep your seat belt fastened at all times, whether driving or a passenger. The speed limit in a built-up area is 60 km/h (37 mph), and in the country 100 km/h (62 mph). Australian drivers are not the best in the world - nor the worst. The accident rate has been lowered by the introduction of random breath testing: if you exceed .05 percent blood-alcohol level, a hefty fine and loss of licence is automatic. Petrol (rather than 'gasoline') comes in regu-lar and super grades and is sold by the litre. Prices start around 70 cents per litre (or $3 per Imperial gallon) and head meaningfully upwards as your location becomes more remote. Foreign driver's licences are valid, although an international permit is preferred.

Remember, northern Queensland experiences a monsoon (known as 'the wet') from December to April, so time your journey accordingly, i.e., prefera-bly at some other time. Allow up to two weeks for a good look-see from Coolan-gatta to Cairns. A four-wheel drive vehicle is ideal, but unless you plan lots of off-roading or beach driving, not necessary. Hardy station wagons or sedans, especially older Valiants, Hold-ens and Falcons (Australian-built, and cheap spare parts) are favourites with younger travellers. The fast food on this route is really drab: white bread, anae-mic coffee, extremely post-mortem chicken, and heat-exhausted salad. 'Slow food' found in fruit and vege-table shops is fresh and cheap-enough, but the roadside fruit stands are great, often working on a weigh-and-pay honour system. You won't need food rations, but do carry plenty of extra water for both car and occupants, and additional oil.

Driver and passengers will find the following personal equipment comes in handy: insect repellent (against sand-flies and 'mozzies'), heavy duty UV blockout cream, long sleeved shirt, raincoat, sunhat, old sneakers for reefwalking, extra long tent pegs for beach camping, face mask, snorkel and fins (in Australian known as flippers), and a basic first aid kit. During the sugar cane harvest farmers rid their crops of undergrowth by torching the field. At such times it's worth keeping an eye out at picnic areas and during those quick roadside stops for venomous snakes, irate at being flushed from their homes in the cane-rows.

Australian hostel accommodation leaves much to be desired in terms of general cleanliness and freshness of bedding; but the company is fun, with up to 75 percent of the clientele being foreign travellers. Average prices starts around $10 per night for dorm accommodation. Camping sites cost about the same; overnight 'vans and country pubs a little more, but the facilities and privacy can be a welcome change. It is important to be aware that most of the island resorts and many hotels are often fully booked, particularly during Australian school holiday periods and the peak holiday season of December and January.

Accommodation bookings should be made as far in advance as possible. Special packages and discounts are often available through Queensland Government Tourist Offices, and these can be much cheaper than booking directly with resorts. For a holiday with a difference, you can stay as a paying guest with Queensland families or on a working farm, or 'station.' (See 'Homestays' in the Travel Tips – these can be booked through Queensland Government Travel Centres.)

In order to star most effectively in your own road movie, make sure that your car in good repair (at least at the beginning), has basic tools, a working jack and a spare tyre (or two). The Royal Automobile Club of Queensland (RACQ) service is highly recommended; a $30 joining fee can save you hundreds of dollars if you need towing or emergency breakdown assistance. Their offices will readily supply you with excellent maps and literature, and provide a telephone service on road conditions. (See 'Motoring Advice' in the Travel Tips.) Contact the RACQ at GPO Box 1403, Brisbane, QLD 4001, tel. (07) 253 2406.

Queensland's 'green gold', sugar cane.

Alternatives: If you plan to hire a car, you'll really only need four wheel-drive for the beaches of Fraser Island and the river crossings of Cape York. There is plenty of national and local competition in the rent-a-car market, so shop around. (Also read the 'Vehicle Rental' section in the Travel Tips) Campervans are available for hire, as are motor-cycles in a number of locations.

Hitchhiking is another way of getting there. The usual rules apply: use your common sense; don't carry too much luggage; look clean; the best place for rides is on the outskirts of town at a point where vehicles can stop easily; don't travel in a group of more than two; don't stand on the road; women shouldn't hitch alone; be prepared for long waits on stretches like Rockhampton-Sarina and Bowen-Townsville; and use your common sense.

By bus: The coach trip from Brisbane to Cairns takes from 23 to 27 hours. There is lively competition between bus companies, and bargains can be found by shopping around. The Brisbane-Cairns fare starts at around $120, which gets you lay-back seats, videos, wash-rooms and air-conditioning. The two major operators, Ansett Pioneer and Greyhound Australia offer discount passes for extensive bus travel over various periods, and sometimes throw in discounts on accommodation and rental cars. Other companies on this route include McCafferty's, Sunliner, and Advance Express, and many companies also offer excursions and discounts. (See 'Buses' section in the Travel Tips)

By rail: The least arduous way of 'driving' to Cairns is to put your car on the train at Brisbane: about 30 hours later, you and it are in Cairns. This serv-ice, which departs every Sunday, costs $190 for your vehicle, plus $107 for your seat. The main coastal rail services to Cairns are the 'Sunlander' (on week days) and the luxurious 'Queenslander' (on Sundays); and, to Rockhampton, the 'Spirit of Capricorn' or 'Capricor-nian.' The Brisbane-Cairns fares start at $107 for a seat, and peak around $290

Yet another roadside attraction – the pub straight out of a cartoon, near Nambour.

for a first-class sleeper berth. Other train routes travel inland from Brisbane, Rockhampton and Townsville, and you can break your journey at any point. All long-distance Queensland trains have sleeping berths and dining cars. For full details, contact Queensland Railways, Central Reservations Bureau, 208 Adelaide Street, Brisbane 4000, tel. (07) 235 1122. (Also see 'Railways' section in the Travel Tips)

The trip: Having cleared the neon shoals and bikinied sirens of the Gold and Sunshine Coasts, your voyage on the narrow road to the deep north gets real at Gympie, a one-time gold mining settlement, and at **Maryborough** (pop. 22,000) on the Mary River, one of the state's oldest cities (settled 1843, and shipped its first wool back in 1847). Check the historical colonial buildings such as the court house, the Royal Hotel and Geraghty's store. Maryborough and Hervey Bay are the places from which to organise barge trips or group tours to **Fraser Island** or the less known **Woody Island**. For Fraser Is-

land, a four-wheel drive vehicle is a necessity; these can be hired locally. Don't underestimate Fraser; it's over 120 km (75 miles) long and has a deep freshwater lakes, extensive rain forests and hundreds of bird species, marsupials and reptiles. A one-day excursion is not sufficient: give yourself at least two days. There are rental cabins on the island and camping facilities.

Hervey Bay, 34 km (21 miles) north of Maryborough, boasts the 1.4 km (.85 mile) Urangan pier, a 70-year-old sugar-loading structure which is very good for fishing; and is known as the 'caravan capital of Australia' - which is perhaps a good reason to avoid it. On the other hand, it offers a relaxed beach life, and is one of the best places in the world for whale-watching: as many as 40 whales at a time rest in the bay for periods of up to three days. Each year, about 400 whales enter Hervey Bay during August-October on their southern migration to Antarctica. A good inn is the Colonial Log Cabin.

Bundaberg, at the mouth of the

The sun doesn't always shine on cane farmers – it's a tough industry to profit in.

Burnett River, sees one fifth of Australia's sugar grown in its hinterland. This town may be relatively small (33,000) but its name is universally recognised by Australians because of its most famous product, Bundaberg Rum, known affectionately as 'Bundy,' which, among other things, is celebrated in the town's September 'Rum, Reef and Harvest Festival.' Nearby Bargara, Burnett Heads and Eliott Heads (the latter offering very good coral reef diving) are Queensland's most northerly stinger-free beaches, and thus offer year round swimming. Mon Repos Environmental Park is the country's largest accessible turtle rookery: from November to March turtles come ashore in their hundreds to lay eggs in the dunes. In short, there's good beaches, cheap accommodation, and lots of nature. Bundaberg is the access point for air transfers to Lady Elliot Island and for day cruises to Lady Musgrave Island.

Meanwhile, back at the Bruce Highway ... you've hit Childers and Gin Gin, then the long stretch up towards Gladstone. At Calliope, just before Gladstone and south of the highway, petrophiles can look for chalcedony and petrified wood, not to mention old diggings from the 1860s gold rush. On the coast, also just south of Gladstone, there are good beaches and the quiet life at Boyne Island and Tannum Sands, only 10 km (6 miles) off the Bruce Highway.

Gladstone,' Aluminium City' has the world's largest alumina plant ($355 million worth) and a general industrial dreariness, relieved somewhat by a large new marina complex. Nearby Port Curtis handles 200,000 tonnes of grain, coal and alumina per hour. For most visitors, these are, predictably, less fascinating than the beaches south or the islands east. Gladstone is the departure point, by launch or helicopter for Heron Island. Campers wishing for an island sojourn should check with the Gladstone National Parks and Wildlife Service, Tel: (079) 76 1621, for full details. No camping is possible on Heron Island (although P&O that operates the resort does have upmarket camping facilities on nearby Wilson Island), but on Masthead, Tryon, North West, Lady Musgrave, Eurimbula and Deepwater islands, camping is usually permitted.

Sprawling only a few kilometres north of the Tropic of Capricorn (which is marked by a roadside spire), Rockhampton is the commercial heart of Queensland's central coast and of the state's beef industry. A baggy-necked Brahman bull cast in bronze standing at the northern entrance to the city and a bronze Hereford at the south, lets you know you've hit Rockhampton. Souvenir hunters frequently 'knacker' the bull, stealing its impressive bronze testicles, for which the wily city fathers have a supply of pre-cast replacements.

'Rocky' is a sprawling city of 75,000 with modern pubs and office blocks interspersed among the old. There is plenty of accommodation, and the YHA Rockhampton hostel is a clean change from some of the other coastal crashpads. It can be insufferably hot in town, so just slip quietly away on the 40 km (25 mile) detour to **Yeppoon** ('Where

The drinking code of Queensland.

the Outback meets the Reef') on the coast for a dip, some excellent local seafood and a look at the Iwasaki tourist development. Try **Keppel Sands** and **Emu Park**, south of Yeppoon, for a quiet change from the big deal tourist resorts; this is one of the prettiest corners of the coast, offering spectacular views of the coastal dunes. (Why isn't there a 'Dune Coast'?) Yeppoon is a departure point for the distant Swain Reefs and nearby Great Keppel Island, and also for various diving trips.

From Rockhampton, the adventurous traveller might consider a lengthy (500 km round trip - but reasonably fast) detour west through Blackwater to the Central Highlands and gemfields around **Emerald.** From here you can continue to **Longreach** and its famous Stockman's Hall of Fame. A detour to Mackay via Emerald means avoiding the worst section of the Brisbane-Cairns route: the 400 long weary kilometres (250 miles) between Rockhampton and Mackay.

Sarina, 37 km (23 miles) south of Mackay is the jumping-off point for several good 'Sugar Coast' beaches and camping spots. You'll know **Mackay** is nigh when you spot a full-sized Taiwanese fishing junk mounted on a rock pedestal beside the highway, *Shin Hsun Yuan No. 3*, which was captured by the Navy in 1976. Fanned by tropical breezes and surrounded by a sea of sugar cane, Mackay is a pleasant city of wide streets and elegant old hotels. It was settled in 1862 by Capt John Mackay, and its first cane was harvested in 1865.

Mackay is the access point for the following Cumberland-Whitsunday islands: Hayman and Hamilton (by air), Lindeman and Brampton (by air or sea) and Newry (by sea). Try a diversion to Eimeo, Bucasia and Shoal Point, just north of Mackay, for a quiet alternative to the full-bore resorts of the Whitsunday region; and further north at Cape Hillsborough, Ball Bay and Seaforth for more of the same.

From **Proserpine** it is only about 30 kilometres (18 miles) to the Whitsun- **A 'vantasy' vehicle.**

day Coast, with its azure sea and islands in the beautiful Whitsunday Passage. This region is the yacht charter capital of Australia and launching pad (by air and/or sea) for guests to Daydream, Hamilton, Hayman, Hook, Lindeman, Long, South Molle and Whitsunday islands. **Airlie Beach**, the main centre on the Whitsunday Coast, is cluttered with competing tourist traps whose lust for publicity gives the place the atmosphere of a circus-by-the-sea in the on-season. Both Airlie Beach and nearby Shute Harbour offer good restaurants and a degree of sophistication. Excellent day trip (and longer) excursions are available from **Shute Harbour**, with your choice of emphasis on diving, snorkelling, fishing, sailing, picnicking, rainforests or scenic flights. Sea-kayaking to the nearer islands is highly recommended, as is an adventurous week on square-riggers such as *Coral Trekker*. In this region, the peaceful alternatives are at Cannonvale beach, and - much quieter still - south of Proserpine, at Conway (camping) and Cedar Creek Falls.

Bowen is your next non-stop. This 'salad bowl of Australia,' is temporary home for four million cartons per season of mangos, melons, chillis, tomatoes and more each year Pressing ever northwards you hit Home Hill, then Ayr, before taking a detour to Alva Beach, about 30 minutes off the Highway, for a swim (stingers permitting) or a snooze. Cape Bowling Green is one of the world's great billfishing areas, and the big tournament in this sport is held here in September.

And so to **Townsville**, Queensland's second largest city, and commercial hub for the area's rich sugar, copper, beef and refining industries. The city is built around a picturesque harbour at the base of Castle Hill, from which a lookout provides fine vistas. The main thoroughfare is notable for its extensive late 19th century architecture. Picturesque Magnetic Island is so close to Townsville that it is regarded as a suburb, and can be reached by ferry or charter boat. The rich hinterland is bor-

Horse riders easily get away from the crowds.

dered by steamy mountain ranges and offers such attractions as the Crystal Creek-Mount Spec National Park, (with spectacular tracts of rainforests and lagoons) and the Valley of Lagoons. Townsville is the departure point, by air, for Dunk, Bedarra, Hinchinbrook and Orpheus islands.

From Townsville the highway sticks close to the coast, offering plenty of spots for picnics, camping, fishing and water sports. West of Ingham are the Wallaman Falls, at over 280 metres (915 ft), the highest single-drop falls in Australia. About 30 kilomertres (18 miles) north-east of Ingham on the coast is Lucinda, sea access point to the luxurious Orpheus Island - and to the far less luxurious Aboriginal reserve of Great Palm Island, to which the Queensland government used to banish 'wrong-doers.' The coastal road for about the next 50 km (30 miles) flanks the Hinchinbrook Channel, through which some old salt once said it was impossible to sail and not believe in God. Dump the car at either Lucinda or Cardwell, hop on the launch for the island and see if he was right. There's a resort on the northern tip of this, the world's largest island national park, which caters for only 30 people. If they can't fit you in, or your wallet can't fit them in, get a camping permit from the National Parks and Wildlife Service and go bush.

Tully used to be famous for rain. The rain hasn't stopped, but now there are other things happening there, too. White water rafting on the Tully River gorge is a recommended one day of thrills. Most travellers go to Tully en route to **Mission Beach** (See chapter). Turn off the highway 80 km (50 miles) south of Cairns at Mirriwinni to find quiet **Bramston Beach**, which has a golf course, camp ground and a very reasonably priced retreat. This is the site of Australia's oldest commercial coconut plantation.Getting seriously 'troppo' now, you soon find yourself at Innisfail, only 65 km (40 miles) south of Cairns. Also famous for rain (3.64 m [143"] p.a.), the Innisfail district offers good boating on calm waters, rainforest

Canoeing the Mary River near Bundaberg.

at Palmerston National Park, Nerada Tea Plantation, and access to the Atherton Tableland (see chapter). Bramston Beach 23 km (14 miles) north of Innisfail has a long palmy beachfront. Also about the same distance north on the highway is Bellenden Ker National Park with Queensland's two highest mountains, Bartle Frere (1612 m., or 5287 ft) and Bellenden Ker (1593 m., or 5225 ft). About 45 minutes south of Cairns, in some of the most ruggedly beautiful terrain along the route, you'll come across a little town of **Babinda**. If it's hot - and it usually is - the traveller may be tempted to detour from the highway through Babinda to the much-signposted rainforest picnic and swimming area called 'The Boulders.' It's breathtakingly lovely, and has claimed at least 25 lives by drowning this century. Resist the urge to dive in. You're almost at your destination.

Fish Junction? – Ceratodus is the proper name of the Queensland lungfish.

And then you're there, **Cairns**, 'Far North Queensland' - as the locals like to write it. Cairns FNQ is access point for the following islands (by air for some,

sea for others): Hinchinbrook, Bedarra, Dunk, Fitzroy, Green and Lizard. Cairns has its own international airport and is the centre of a tropical region of such diversity that it's hard to know what to do first. It's a chapter in itself - while you're there and before you hit the Reef, the beach and the bar, see a quintessentially Australian institution, the headquarter of the Flying Doctor Service and the School of the Air.

Along the so-called Marlin Coast north of Cairns is a collection of resort hotels and apartments packed along Machan's, Trinity, Clifton and Palm Cove beaches. Beyond the Daintree River the road traveller ought to be in a four-wheel-drive vehicle. For trips to Port Douglas, the Atherton tableland or other black-top destinations, a conventional vehicle will have no trouble but further afield, negotiating the river crossings, ruts and washouts can vary from difficult to impossible without 4WD. And the FNQ Banana Benders aren't too polite when hauling yet another tourist out of the river or the bog.

FRASER ISLAND

On old maps this is 'Great Sandy Island,' but to the world it's **Fraser Island**. Once made infamous by the fabulations of the shipwrecked Mrs Eliza Fraser, this great strand of silica and time was thought until 1822 to be part of the Australian mainland, and was known as the Great Sandy Peninsula.

Perfumed isle, or sleeping lizard in the sun - it's hard to capture Fraser Island in word, lens or imagination. The world's largest sand island, it has been formed over millions of years by silica washed down from the Great Dividing Range and then pushed up the coast of NSW and southern Queensland, and blown in by prevailing south-easterly winds and tides onto the few outcrops of continental rock which anchor this dreaming dragon to Earth's surface.

Statistics are rarely vital, but Fraser Island's involve figures of 123 km (76 miles) by 14 km (8.7 miles) average width, and 184,000 ha (440,000 acres) of area. There are 206 species of birds (including peregrine falcons, kingfishers and jabirus) as well as echidnas, wallabies, the purest dingos remaining in eastern Australia, and brumbies, the wild horses descended from those introduced in the late 19th century by timber cutters. Fraser Island has 40 freshwater lakes, of two kinds, 'window' and 'perched.' Window lakes include **McKenzie, Yankee Jack, Wabby** and **Birrabeen**. At **Lake Wabby** a massive 'sandblow' is advancing westwards at about 3 m (10 ft) annually into the lake. Perched (i.e. in the dunes, above sea level) lakes include **Bowarrady** and **Boomanjin**.

Much of the island is flat land covered in wallum heathlands, scribbly gum and banksia; cypress pines are found on the western side of the island behind a rich mangrove fringe. Picabeen palms, prehistoric Angiopteris ferns, tall satinay trees (with which the banks the Suez Canal were re-lined in the 1920s) and giant kauri are but part of the complexity of the island's rainforests.

Teewah (coloured) sands are a feature of the northern east coast beach. Despite terms like 'Rainbow Sands,' the shades are subtle, being predominantly cream, ochre and umber, salmon and beige. The only rock headlands (of volcanic rhyolite) on the east coast are at Indian Head (named so by James Cook who saw 'Indians' on it), Middle Rocks and Waddy Point.

The island was known as as 'K'gari' - Paradise - to the Badjala Aborigines, one of the three tribes who inhabited it. With the arrival of whites - fishermen, missionaries and loggers - Paradise soon passed on, and the black inhabitants were decimated by disease, then exiled to the mainland, a practice which continued until the late 1930s. All that remains now of those original inhabitants are middens of shells.

Notoriety came to the Great Sandy Island in 1836 when Captain James Fraser's ship *Stirling Castle* was wrecked on Swain Reefs, some 300 km (180 miles) to the north. His wife, Eliza Fraser later told several versions of their ordeal, none regarded as reliable. Having drifted in the ship's longboat to Great Sandy Island, the weakened survivors were found by Dulingbara Aborigines. Within a fortnight the seriously injured James Fraser and his first mate were dead, the former slain by his captors. Eliza, who during the sea voyage had given birth to a child which died soon after, lived under harsh conditions with the island Aboriginals for some months, until assisted in escape to the mainland by an escaped convict who had 'gone native.' She returned to civilisation with exaggerated tales and hints about 'a fate worse than death' for any audience who would listen, and later, who would pay.

In 1863, a Yankee, Jack Piggott began kauri logging at Wanggoolba Creek on the western side, from where the logs were rafted to a mainland mill. The logging of hoop pine, kauri and white beech continued until these softwoods were exhausted; the hardwoods were then taken, the limited logging of which still continues. A lighthouse was built on northermost point Sandy Cape in

Left, the buttress roots of a Fraser Island fig tree.

1870 because of many wrecks occuring.

A titanic 'greenies vs. greedies' contest commenced in 1971 over the mining of black mineral sands on the island. With one side and the state government believing the highest human achievement to be either strip-mining or clearfelling, this was probably the high-tide point of environmmental vandalism in Australia. Multinational miner, Murphyores Dillingham had churned up 160 hectares before the Federal government refused an export licence for the extracted minerals. The project was abandoned in 1976.

Today, Fraser Island is almost all Crown Land (that is, state owned and protected) and the northernmost third is National Park. The only townships (more like hamlets) are at **Eurong** and **Happy Valley**, where accommodation, food, petrol, telephone, post, beer, bait and other essentials are available. There are no doctors on the island.

Driving: There are plenty of commercial day trips to Fraser from Noosa, (a full 12 hour round trip) and from Hervey Bay. The best way of enjoying the island is to drive one's own (or better, someone else's) four wheel drive vehicle. 4WD is essential. Vehicular ferries depart from Hervey Bay and from Inskip Point (north of Rainbow Beach), and cost from $15 to $25 per vehicle each way. Don't believe the advertised times of the last barge; the service ceases when the captain feels like calling it a day. The National Parks and Wildlife Service charges $15 for a car permit for the island, and a further $7 per night camping fee, all of which must be paid before departing from the mainland. The address is P.O. Box 30, Rainbow Beach, 4581; the office is open 7 - 4 daily.

The short passage across to the island brings you to another green world, where you are greeted by cadging dingos. Drop your tyre pressure to 100-120 Kpa (15-18 psi). Put your vehicle into 4WD, low range, for getting onto and off the beach, then drive assertively, avoiding the beach at high tide plus or minus two hours. (Get a tide chart or **Just plain horse sense.**

check the notices displayed in shops, etc.) North of the *Maheno* wreck, exhibit real care, also at Eli Creek, both on the east coast. The west coast is far less drivable. The sand track from Waddy Point to Orchid Beach is especially deeply rutted and is no place for a low clearance sedan, even if it claims to be 4WD.

To Do: Allow at least two days to see the island. The only nightlife is a few frogs jumping, the ambient surf-song, and the electricity of creeks and crickets in the moonlight - and a good restaurant at the Happy Valley Resort. At **Central Station** (centre of logging activities from 1918 to 1960), there are rainforest boardwalks and strangler figs, a beautiful green gloom and creeks so clear above the sandy bottom that the water seems invisible; also a forestry Information Centre and Museum. Main attractions are, the 5000-ton former luxury liner, *Maheno* which beached here in 1935 en route to Japan for scrapping - it is 10 km north of Happy Valley; the **Eli Creek** boardwalk; and the '**Cathe-**drals,' cliffs and spires of coloured sand, for about 35 km north of Happy Valley. And of course the great rainforest and lake interior. **Lake Boomanjin** - well, here is peace on earth. Wildflower season is July to September.

The island's resorts are at **Happy Valley, Eurong** and **Orchid Beach** (overlooking Marloo Bay), all on the east coast. These cater for fishing guests and will also arrange 4WD hire for guests who may prefer to fly in.

There are numerous serviced camping grounds, as well as bush sites. Along the beach, fishermen set up their own temporary canvas 'resorts' camps wherever they like in the soft green verge, beside some freshwater flow. Beach fishing, especially during winter, is very good; also estuarine and offshore angling. No domestic animals are allowed on the island. Plants stabilize the fragile dune system, so please obey all signs which indicate areas closed for revegetation - the island depends upon it.

Exploring the Fraser Island greenery.

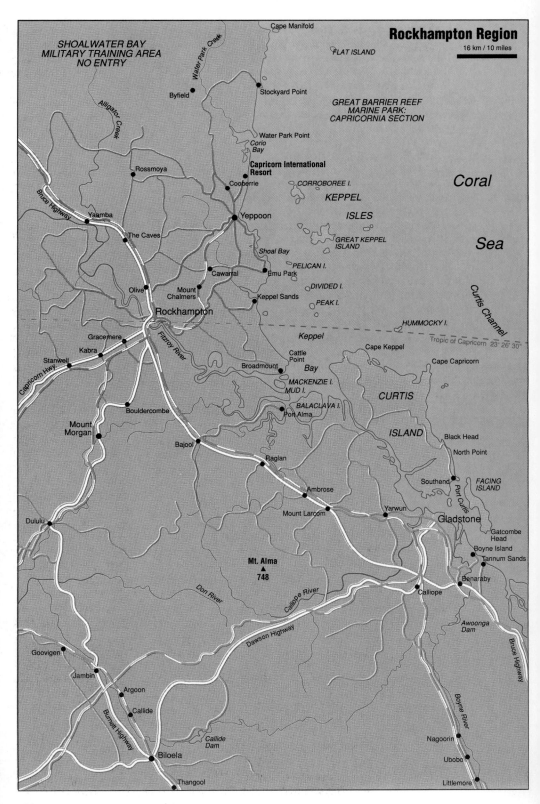

Rockhampton Region

16 km / 10 miles

SHOALWATER BAY
MILITARY TRAINING AREA
NO ENTRY

Cape Manifold

FLAT ISLAND

Water Park Creek

Byfield

Stockyard Point

GREAT BARRIER REEF
MARINE PARK:
CAPRICORNIA SECTION

Alligator Creek

Water Park Point
Corio
Bay

Rossmoya

**Capricorn International
Resort**

Cooberrie

CORROBOREE I.

Coral

Bruce Highway

Yaamba

Yeppoon

KEPPEL

ISLES

The Caves

GREAT KEPPEL
ISLAND

Sea

Shoal Bay

PELICAN I.

Cawarral

Olive

Mount
Chalmers

Emu Park

Curtis Channel

Rockhampton

Keppel Sands

DIVIDED I.

PEAK I.

HUMMOCKY I.

Tropic of Capricorn 23° 26' 30"

Gracemere

Fitzroy River

Keppel

Cattle
Point

Cape Keppel

Cape Capricorn

Kabra

Broadmount

Bay

Stanwell

Capricorn Hwy

MACKENZIE I.
MUD I.

CURTIS

Bouldercombe

BALACLAVA I.
Port Alma

ISLAND

Mount
Morgan

Black Head

North Point

Bajool

Raglan

Southend

FACING
ISLAND

Port Curtis

Ambrose

Yarwun

Dululu

Mount Larcom

Gladstone

Gatcombe
Head

Boyne Island

Tannum Sands

Mt. Alma
▲
748

Calliope River

Calliope

Benaraby

Don River

Awoonga
Dam

Googigen

Dawson Highway

Bruce Highway

Jambin

Argoon

Boyne River

Callide

Burnett Highway

Callide
Dam

Nagoorin

Biloela

Ubobo

Thangool

Littlemore

ROCKHAMPTON

One of the easiest places in the world to place on a map is **Rockhampton**. Just look for the point where the Queensland coast is bisected by the Tropic of Capricorn and you'll find it. However, you are unlikely to hear many Australians talk about it: in the land of the indiscriminate abbreviation Rockhampton is simply "Rocky".

For those making the long drive north, the large modern (well, relatively speaking, on both counts) city of Rockhampton is the start of the Queensland tropics. The tourist blurbs claim it's "where the Outback meets the Reef". However, this country centre of some 75,000 people on the Fitzroy River has a feeling of solidity more in keeping with its Outback roots than the "party industry" feeling of much of the Barrier Reef coast. In a way, it seem as if Rockhampton is a lot further from the coast than the actual 40 kilometre (25 mile) drive. Rockhampton is the hub of central Queensland, with rail connections to the west. This is Australia's largest cattle producing district and the city has two beef export works, as well as several other industries.

Rockhampton was first settled, in 1853, by the brothers Charles and William Archer at "Gracemere", 9 kilometres (5 miles) west of the present city. (The Gracemere Saleyards continue to handle more cattle than any other in Australia.) Like so much of the New World, the real boost to its development came when gold was found in 1858. Soon, more reliable finds were made at Mount Morgan but these didn't detract from Rockhampton as the growing regional capital.

Rather, since last century there has been strong local pressure for Rockhampton to be the capital city of a new Capricornia State. With the independence sentiment for which Queenslanders are noted, the township had barely begun in 1864 when there was talk of secession. After all, they argued, what right did the "southerners" in Brisbane have to govern and tax the residents of the north? However, although the rumblings of discontent have continued ever since, the separatists seemed doomed to disappointment.

Reminders of Rockhampton's past are most evident at **Quay Street** down on the Fitzroy River. This is one of Australia's best preserved Victorian commercial streetscapes and more than 20 of the buildings have National Trust status. On the southern side of the city, a spire marks the **Tropic of Capricorn** and the location of the tourist office. Rockhampton's **Botanic Gardens** have an excellent collection of tropical plants plus an orchid house and fern house spread over 4 hectares (10 acres) of grounds.

A more recent addition to the city's attractions has been the establishment of the **Dreamtime Cultural Centre** to promote understanding of the culture of Aborigines and Torres Strait Islanders. This is the largest Aboriginal cultural centre in Australia and features art displays and dance groups.

Rockhampton is the gateway for the **Capricorn Coast** that extends for about 50 km (30 miles) from Keppel Sands in the south to the Byfield area in the north. The major town of this tourist region is **Yeppoon** with a population of about 20,000. However, the Capricorn International Resort is the single most notable feature of this part of the mainland coast. Situated on 8,500 hectares north of Yeppoon, this resort, which now caters for perhaps a thousand visitors a week, has been surrounded with controversy since it was first announced in 1972. Developed by the Japanese hotelier Yohachiro Iwasaki, only the first stages of the resort have been opened so far - it is to have a total of 12,000 rooms when fully completed. Catering for both Japanese and Australian holiday-makers, its attractions include a giant freshwater pool and a superb 18-hole golf course.

Rosslyn Bay south of Yeppoon is the starting point for many reef tours and visits to nearby Great Keppel Island. Great Keppel Island can also be reached by a short flight from Rockhampton.

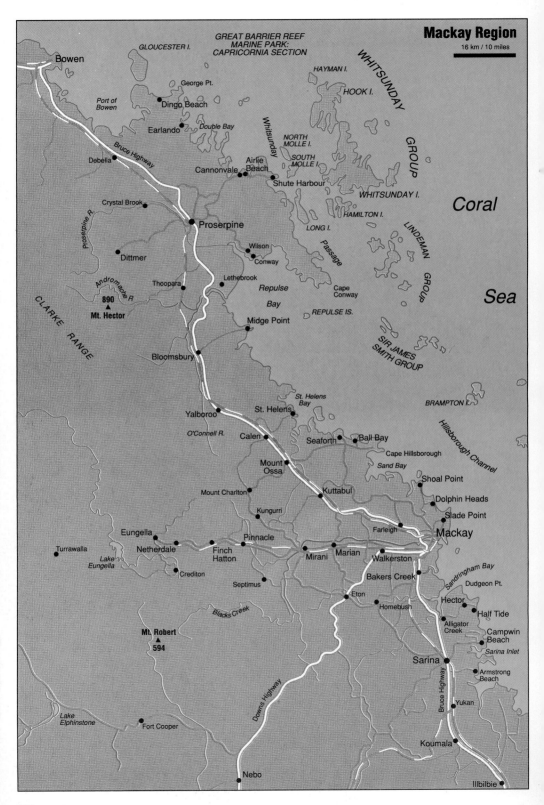

MACKAY

Mackay is just the way one imagines a Queensland city should be - a relaxed place of fine old pubs, wide streets and no traffic jams. Until a few years ago, this town of around 50,000 residents was regarded as a largely a sugar port with some tourist trade. However, depression in the world sugar markets and burgeoning tourism along the coast have of late changed that balance.

Mackay is used to change - even its name and site aren't the originals. The area was explored first in 1859 by a party led by John Mackay who was looking for new grazing land. After finding what is now the Pioneer Valley, he returned home to Armidale, NSW for two years, then came north again with 1200 cattle, to choose a site that he named Greenmount on the banks of a river - which he called, without any false modesty, the Mackay. However, there was already a Mackay River elsewhere, so the Queensland government changed the name to the Pioneer River. The tiny community came to be known as Mackay, not Greenmount. Then in 1866 the whole settlement moved downstream to its present location and became a port.

The most propitious event in Mackay's history took place in 1865 when John Spiller planted some sugar cane he'd brought from Java. That produced a 100 ton crop which sold for 400 pounds ($800 dollars): the Mackay sugar industry was born. Today, the port has sugar storage facilities with a capacity of 677,000 tonnes, the largest in the world. As a bonus for sweet tooths, visitors to Mackay during the cane crushing season (June to December) can tour the bulk sugar terminal.

Mackay, is a low key, low rise place that operates at an ideal holiday pace. The streets are lined with palm trees and there are parks scattered around the town, including **Queens Park** that still has its original band rotunda. The city has several historic buildings from the early days; of note are the Customs House and the Commonwealth Bank Building. John Mackay's **Greenmount Homestead**, is a museum showing the more gracious side of homestead life a century ago.

One of Mackay's best known sights is a fishing junk perched by the side of the highway south of the city. This was one of many confiscated from Taiwanese crews illegally fishing the Reef waters. For several years from 1976 the junk served as Mackay's tourist office, but an information centre was opened alongside it a few years ago.

Near the sugar terminals in the port area lies the ever-expanding fleet of Mackay's tourist vessels. The longest running is Captain Tom McLean's Roylen Cruises. The company started after World War II with a converted gunboat: it now operates a fleet of sleek, large catamarans. Besides five-day cruises of the islands these vessels also operate day tours to Brampton Island and on to the Reef itself. Another cruise boat, the *Elizabeth E II* also operates four-day cruises out of Mackay harbour.

Mackay locals and visitors alike enjoy a beachside ride.

AIRLIE BEACH AND SHUTE HARBOUR

As gateways to the 74 islands of the Whitsunday group, **Airlie Beach** and **Shute Harbour** are probably the most seaward-oriented places on the entire Queensland coast.

Just as Airlie and Shute are stepping off points for the islands, the township of **Proserpine** is the point of access to them for air travellers. Derivations of the statement that "Proserpine and its airport are just 22 kilometres from Airlie Beach" is among the most often used phrases in Australian tourist literature. Yet, strangely enough, Proserpine is both a quiet farming community and the administrative centre for the tourist bustle of the Whitsunday group.

However, the orientation of the Whitsundays has shifted since Hamilton Island was developed with its multi-million dollar airport. No longer do air travellers ned to shuttle to the coast from Proserpine then onto a boat bound for the islands. The same criss-cross pattern of ferry routes can now transfer all those passengers, bound for other Whitsunday islands, who land at Hamilton from Sydney, Brisbane or Melbourne. It remains to be seen what the final effect will be on the coastal townships, no longer essential staging posts.

The backdrop to this stretch of coast is the **Conway Range National Park.** This is the rugged spine of the Whitsunday Peninsula with walking trails overlooking the islands. It is also a good place to discover rich rainforests and tiny creeks, a world away from the tourist trammel at its doorstep.

Hemmed in by the forested mountains behind and forced to grow by the tourist boom of recent decades, Airlie Beach has extended along the coast to almost link up with the town of **Cannonvale** to its immediate north. However, the character of the two towns is quite distinct: Airlie Beach is unashamedly a resort town full of souvenir shops and day tour agencies while Cannonvale, which used to be the main departure point for the Whitsunday Islands, still serves its traditionally rural customers and local residents.

Even if the Whitsunday Islands weren't just a boat transfer away, **Airlie Beach** would be a pleasant place to visit in its own right. The main street is the sort of place where a pair of long pants or a tie look out of place. Unlike the nearby islands, Airlie Beach and Cannonvale offer a good range of accommodation down to relatively inexpensive family apartments and backpacker hostels, yet still have largely the same infrastructure and recreational opportunities as the islands. There are many more restaurants in Airlie than its size would suggest, providing an eating range from basic snacks to good meals.

The permanent population of Airlie Beach is only a couple of thousand or so but that's still more than Cannonvale. On the other hand, **Shute Harbour** has a negligible population - it's little more than an embarkation point for the many cruises and ferries and the heart of the Whitsunday bare boat charter industry - one of the largest in the world. In fact, based on the number of shipping movements, rather than the tonnage involved, Shute Harbour is one of the busiest ports in Australia. However, don't expect much here by way of shops and other facilities - there aren't. The 15 km (9 mile) drive from Airlie Beach is along a meandering road through the edge of the Conway Range National Park.

Shute Harbour is an excellent natural harbour, well protected on all sides. It's an incredibly busy place in the mornings as day trips depart and again in the afternoon when they return. The possibilities for excursions are just about endless, as long as you want a water-based activity. Long trips on fast boats, sailing on a square rigger, picnics on Whitehaven Beach, diving and snorkelling trips, a camping holiday on an island, or setting off as skipper of your own (hired) sailing vessel are just some of the options. Others are limited only by your imagination in this aquatic playground. The Whitsunday Islands have the Queensland coast's greatest concentration of tourist activities and this is very much their access port.

Left, Airlie Beach, the hub of the Whitsunday coast.

TOWNSVILLE

There must be many moments when the city fathers of **Townsville** puzzle over what it takes to make a city a hit on the tourist circuit. Townsville has a casino, quaint colonial tropical architecture, an international airport, a dry pleasant climate and even a suburb that's an offshore island resort. But still it is overlooked in the rush to Cairns to the north.

From the top of **Castle Hill**, the bare granite knob that rises 286 metres (915 feet) from the middle of the city, the character of Townsville falls into perspective. On the seaward side, the casino is dwarfed by the port of Townsville, one of the busiest in Australia, exporting ore from Mount Isa and beef and sugar from the hinterlands. To the west stretch the rapidly expanding suburbs of Thuringowa and the campus of the James Cook University.

Unlike some communities along the Queensland coast, Townsville is a real city where people live and work without giving obsessive thought to the tourist dollar. Therein lies its appeal.

With a population of about 112,000, Townsville is Queensland's second largest city, and the largest tropical city in Australia. (The title sounds more impressive than it is: the only other major population centres north of the Tropic of Capricorn are Cairns and Darwin.) It is also one of the country's most important defence centres with the air force base at Garbutt and the very large army base at Lavarack Barracks. Townsville also houses the headquarters of Great Barrier Reef Marine Park Authority, the CSIRO Tropical Agricultural Research Station and Australian Institute of Marine Science.

Castle Hill provides one of Townsville's most notable folk tales. At 286 metres it's a mere metre short of being classified as a mountain. So, several years ago a retired citizen decided to devote his spare time to raising the height of the hill. This Herculean task was to be achieved by hauling barrows

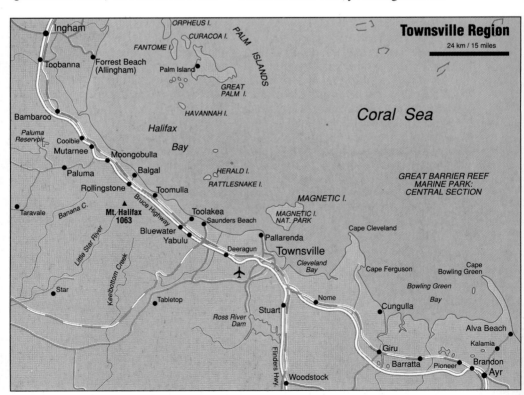

full of soil and rock from the car park to the summit above. Unfortunately, the elements rebelled against this reversal of the natural order of things and the foundations of an "instant mountain" scheme that could have been the beginning of a worldwide trend were washed away. The ambitious quasi-mountaineer battled on but a few years ago admitted defeat and retired from the task. (Don Quixote didn't beat the windmill, either.) And Castle Hill - rather than Castle Mountain - remains a spectacular backdrop to this flat city.

Townsville takes its name from Robert Towns, a Sydney businessman who, with his agent John Melton Black, founded the settlement in 1864 as a focal point for the potentially rich farming areas nearby. Towns only spent a short time in the community that bears his name but we must be grateful to him that Australia wasn't saddled with yet another town called "Blacktown". However, it was Towns who first imported natives from the Pacific islands (known then as "Kanakas") to work his cotton plantations and cane fields. Exploiting this cheap labour, Black soon had the town and port well established with a thriving trade in cattle, sheep, timber and cotton. Then the gold boom of nearby Charters Towers and Ravenswood provided the new community with a healthy boost - this was the beginning of a long term relationship between Townsville and the mining industry. The local gold deposits petered out long ago, but the rail line from Mount Isa continues to pour ore through the port. Today over 1.5 million tonnes of ore, meat and sugar passes through the Port of Townsville.

Despite the entrepreneurial manner of its founding, Townsville has proven to be relatively conservative in development. When most Australian towns were squandering their architectural heritage, Townsville maintained its unique collection of notable buildings in the heart of town. Many of these have now been restored - from the classic colonial pub of the Tattersalls Hotel to the art deco tower of the T&G building.

The bluff of Castle Mountain dominates Townsville.

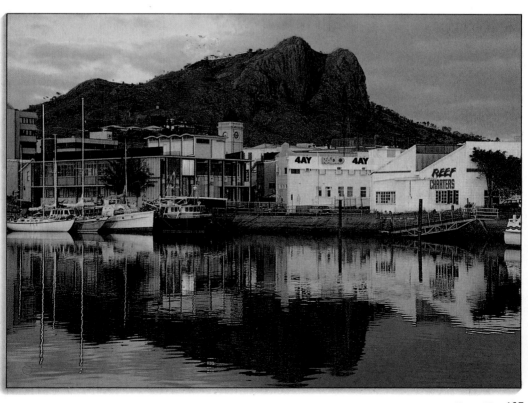

The main thoroughfare of **Flinders Street**, now a pedestrian mall, also has the Townsville Post Office, an impressive building with a restored clock tower. The Strand features the old Queens Hotel which, fittingly, is now serving as a television station, and the Customs House that served the port.

A major boost to the tourist industry in Townsville has been the opening of the **Sheraton Breakwater Casino-Hotel** in the mid 1980s. This set new standards of accommodation in Townsville and proved to be very popular as an entertainment venue for the local populace. As the hotel has campaigned for business around Australia and internationally, the profile of Townsville has risen, too. The casino, the only one in tropical Queensland, provides the standard array of international games like roulette, craps, blackjack and keno, plus the very Australian game of two-up.

A rather tacky four metre (13 feet) high figure, reputed to be a model of a Muttaburrasaurus, a type of dinosaur, marks the entrance to the **North Queensland Museum/Great Barrier Reef Wonderland** complex. This is an impressive showcase of the special features of Queensland, with a large aquarium, Omnimax theatre, museum and an array of speciality shops and food outlets. It also houses an office of the National Parks and Wildlife Service. The aquarium was conceived and is operated by the Great Barrier Reef Marine Park Authority and its large transparent tunnel allows you to "walk through" a living, self-supporting coral reef. A computer terminal at the aquarium allows visitors to find out about the activities possible in each section of the marine park. There is also a wealth of interpretive material on the Reef, how it was formed and the nature of its many inhabitants. The section of reef in the aquarium has some 1500 fish representing 300 species and about 150 species of hard and soft corals. The Wonderland display is an excellent introduction to the Reef for visitors.

The Omnimax theatre within the complex was Australia's first. This is a **Lawn bowlers in action.**

138

new generation of movie theatres that displays a very clear image onto a domed roof. Patrons sit in steeply raked chairs and feel surrounded by the giant action all around them, a feeling enhanced by the high quality sound system. One of the films shown follows divers through the coral canyons of the Great Barrier Reef.

The nearby branch of the Queensland Museum houses displays of the birds and animals of North Queensland, Aboriginal art, local shipwrecks and fossils from the important palaentological research being conducted in Queensland.

Magnetic Island: From Townsville, the horizon is interrupted by the mountainous profile of Magnetic Island 8 km (5 miles) off shore. Its proximity to Townsville has ensured that it's more a suburb of the city than an island apart - but its a special suburb. With a population of only 2300 and much of its 5184 hectares (12800 acres) being national park, Magnetic Island has managed to stay low key as a holiday destination.

There are some starred resorts but there are also many holiday apartments and backpacker lodges.

The island was named by Captain Cook after his compass seemed affected by it (he actually called it "Magnetical Island") but modern day compasses can't reproduce the effect. That's probably fortunate as there are several ferry companies making some thirty crossings a day to the island - the ride takes 20 minutes. Although there are bus services on the island, the most common way for visitors to get around is by open-topped Mini Mokes, motor scooters and bicycles. It's a popular weekend destination for Townsville residents too, but the lengthy shoreline is indented with many tiny beaches and coves so there's always a chance to escape the crowds. There's horse riding, water skiing and most of the other activities found at resorts, plus some pleasant bushwalks within the national park - including the strenuous hike to the top of the 500 metre (1600 ft) peak of Mt Cook.

Gleaming colonial architecture.

MISSION BEACH

If there were such a thing as Thomas Cook's Paradox, it might say: 'the more successful tourism's promotion of a natural attraction, the more assured is that attraction's unnatural demise.' The cassowaries of **Mission Beach** are the living (and dying) proof of this hypothesis. This giant tropical bird with the colourful head is being eliminated by traffic on the major road, Cassowary Drive, named in its honour (or memory), and by the clearing of its rainforest habitat to accommodate the people who have come here to see the natural attractions, like cassowaries.

Beside the late, lamented jungle bird, the 14 km (8.7 miles) string of snoozey settlements known collectively as Mission Beach still has a lot going for it. Garner's Beach, Bingil Bay, Narragon Beach, Clump Point, Wongaling Beach and South Mission Beach comprise this holiday and residential enclave about 130 km (80 miles), or two hours drive south of Cairns. Half-way between Townsville and Cairns, this unspoiled, un-secret spot is 20 km off the Bruce Highway. The area has very good accommodation, ranging from the Mission Beach Resort (at Wongaling Beach, set amid its own 46 acre seafront rainforest), Castaways Resort, the exclusive 'The Point,' and a number of hostels, of which the YHA lodge comes recommended. There are plenty of serviced camping sites along this coast.

The area has a brief European history which commenced with doomed explorer Edmund Kennedy's landing at Tam O' Shanter Point, South Mission Beach in the year1848.'Murdering Point' at Kurrimine Beach got to be that way when in 1878 the ship 'Riser' was wrecked on nearby King Reef. Two crewmen who made it ashore were also doomed, for they were reputedly killed and eaten by a local Aboriginal epicure. The area was opened by the four Cutten brothers who in 1882 introduced pineapple, tea and coffee to far North

Unfortunately many don't make it.

BEWARE
CASSOWARIES
CROSS
REGULARLY
NEXT 10 KM

Queensland with their plantations in this district. An Aboriginal church mission station was established here in 1912, hence the name, Mission Beach.

To do: Just inland is **Clump Mountain National Park**, where you can see (and watch out for) the cassowaries, red and blue giants, up to 1.5 m (5') tall, who have dangerous claws and might be seeking revenge for their impending extinction. In the **Licuala State Forest**, there is a boardwalk through the rainforest ('complex mesophyl lowland vineforest'), swimming, and plenty of Licuala fan palms, epiphytes, elkhorn ferns and plank buttresses. **Dundee Park**, an 'aquaculturally controlled natural environmental park,' is terrific: 'We cage the people, not the animals,' is their motto, and the 12 ha (30 acres) of crocs, barra, cassowaries, snakes, and birds enjoy it, unmolested. There are 100 crocodiles, but don't expect to see display feeding and cinematic saurian frenzy. That is Dundee, Mick's style, not Dundee Park's. Next door to the park is **Island Coast Orchids**, worth a visit for delicate catleya blooms.

Just offshore from Mission beach, Dunk, Bedarra and Family Group islands give this stretch of coast (from Ingham to Innisfail) the title of the 'Tropical Island Coast.' From Clump Point, there are daily cruises to **Dunk** (9 am departure; $10 return) and **Bowden islands**, and the Outer Reef, only 50 mins away. **Kurrimine** ('Beautiful Sunrise') Beach just north of Bingil Bay offers a rare chance to wade out from a mainland beach to extensive coral reefs, those of King Reef. Bring your sneakers. It's great for snorkelling too.

For an inland excursion and a 'cuppa,' try the **Nerada Tea Plantation**, 25 km west of Innisfail, Australia's only commercial tea plantation. On the way, on the Old Bruce Highway between Silkwood and South Johnstone, visit **'Paronella Park'** at Mena Creek, a quixotic 1930 fantasy of early hydro power and romantic decay (and current restoration) built by Spanish immigrant Jose Paronella.

Rafting the Tully River is an action-packed day trip.

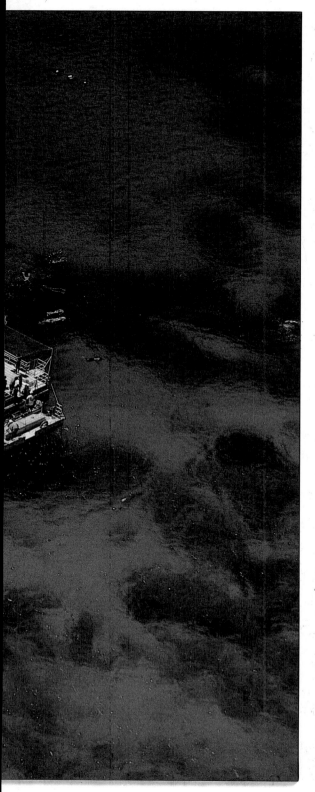

CAIRNS

Until fairly recently the best thing to do in **Cairns** was to leave it. There wasn't anything *wrong* with the town - her orderly streets just couldn't compete with their own backyard of giant skies, fluorescent reefs and bursting forests.

Since the world 'discovered' Cairns in the mid-80s, things have changed. The city centre have been rebuilt in the postmodernist 'Gin Sling School' of architecture: louvres, lattices, fans - all in gin-pink and other 'troppo' pastels. Many attractions has been developed, as well as hotels in which to house all those attracted. "If the hotels get any higher," says one local, "We'll have to raise the mountains." As a result, the visitor ought to allow several days in Cairns, rather than just use the place as a springboard for further excursions.

Cairns International Airport opened in 1984 and is being expanded to accommodate more connections to S-E Asia, Japan, Europe, US, NZ, PNG and interstate. $4.5 billion in tourist projects are scheduled by 1995, and the population (76,500) is growing at 3.7 percent per year, far above the national average. All of which is a long way from the Edenic, cannibalistic coast first sighted by Cook on June 10, 1770, Trinity Sunday (thus was named Cairns' Trinity Bay), prior to his running aground off Cape Tribulation.

For another century, time here had no hour-hands, until in 1873 when the gold rush at Palmer River, north-west of Cairns, flooded the region with a 'river of gold' and a river of hopefuls. The town (named after Governor of Queensland, William Wellington Cairns) was established in 1876 in order to service the closer Hodgkinson goldfields, whose gold died within two years - and so, almost, did the fledgling town. Meanwhile, Port Douglas, also established during the gold rush, was in-

Preceding pages: Cairns overview. Left, a 'wavepiercer' at its outer reef diving pontoon.

tended to be North Queensland's major port. However, when the inland rail service was inaugurated in 1885, it was from Cairns, not 'Port.' The towns' fortunes were reversed: Cairns became the coastal rail terminus, shipping sugar and bananas, while Port Douglas commenced a 90-year decline, until rescued by Australians dropping out and later by foreign tourists dropping in.

The Allied fleet for the Battle of Coral Sea (1942) was launched from Trinity Inlet, and Cairns was the Australian Army's World War II tropical training centre. Otherwise, for a long time the main local activity was watching sugar cane grow. In the 1950s sugar accounted for 60 percent of Far North Queensland's resource-based industries. By the end of the '80s, with diversification into tobacco, timber, maize, tin and tourism, sugar fell to less than 20 percent of the region's industry.

To do: The stroll beside Cairn's Trinity Bay foreshore, along its seemingly endless **Esplanade** is so good that the civic forefathers/mothers who planned

it ought to be posthumously knighted. By night you can sit and watch waves of moonlight pulse slowly towards the shore. At the Esplanade's southern end is the huge new waterfront shopping-sleeping complex called **'The Pier,'** the centrepiece of which is the Radisson Hotel. Check the hotel foyer, a simulated rainforest replete with waterfall and fake snakes - like an Indiana Jones movie set gone AWOL.

Whether you incline towards high life or street life, Cairns offers a democratic range of distractions. On the Esplanade, between Aplin and Shield streets, is a sort of 'Corniche des Eats,' a bright, aromatic gauntlet of cheap eateries, sidewalk tables and backpacker lodges, littered with pizza boxes and cast-off pamphlets. For non-readers, videos tout for rafting and jungle lodges. (Its array of hostels and adventure trips makes Cairns a Backpacker Valhalla - as evidenced by scores of young Scandinavians here, presumably in search of the Land of the Midday Sun.) This highly competitive block

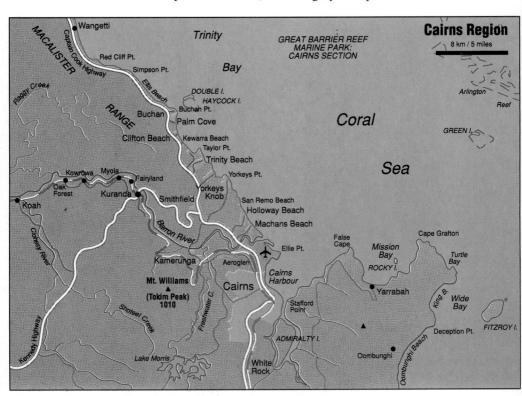

also offers a smorgasbord of adventure travel offices. Over pizza, sort through a pulped forest's worth of brochures on diving courses, reef trips, Cape excursions or white-water thrill. Before heading for these, take a look at a unique Australian institution, the **Royal Flying Doctor Visitors Centre** (070 53 5687).

Dancing: It used to have a nightlife like a coma ward, but nowadays Cairns won't disappoint. For 'house music' there's **Renos Club**, with a good-looking decor and clientele; and for hard rocking and clips, **Tropo's** in the Central Hotel is also loud, well-lit (that is, suitably dimmed) fun. Its classic Queensland pub balcony overlooks the street, perfect for cooling-off. **Johnos Blues Bar**, corner of Florence and Sheridan is for live music; the **Playpen** on Lake Street has a hi-tech aquarium decor. All these have a modest cover charge, around $5, and are good, clean, dirty fun. Sleeker boppers hit **Ribbons Nightclub** (no cover charge) in the new Hilton, while **Magnums** on Grafton Street supplies late, full-bore raging for the backpacker crew. Friday night is the big one in Cairns.

Eating: Some 200 restaurants, ranging from the elegant table in the Cairns International and Raffles in the Outrigger Hotel, to more modest eateries like Barnacle Bill's Seafood Inn on the Esplanade (for 'bugs,' lobster and barramundi). For fresh vegetarian takeaways, eat Greens', 24 hours a day, also on the Esplanade. There are numerous free restaurant guides available, into which, blindfolded, you can poke a pin and come up with dinner.

Hotels: Cairns hosts a minor galaxy of new four- and five-star inns (predominantly Japanese owned): the Cairns International, Holiday Inn, Lyons, Four Seasons, Tradewinds, Ramada Reef (20 km up the road at Palm Cove) and Outrigger - plus scores of more modest sleeperies, van parks, camping grounds and motels. The Radisson and Hilton take full frontal advantage of their dress-circle waterside locations and views over the Inlet, everglades and the sleeping green ranges of Yarrabah. Two

Captain Cook considers what has followed in his wake; for instance, downtown Cairns (<u>right</u>).

recommended mid-range stays are the conveniently located Bay Village Motel on Lake Street, and the spacious, ferny Cairns Colonial Club. Each has a pool, privacy, good service, and large, impeccably clean suites which include a full kitchen. In a sector of the accommodation market more noted for bonhommie than Bon Ami, the Uptown Downunder and Gone Walkabout backpacker hostels are recommended for cleanliness - for which many of their competitors aren't.

Excursions: Inevitably, the rain forest coast, the neon Reef and its islands will tempt you away from Cairns. Tourism's ceaseless search for visual and visceral sensation is well matched by the enterprise of FNQ's excursion operators. The tourist tribes from Munich, Melbourne and Malmo can go up in hot air balloons, down in white-water rafts, rap-jump into Barron Gorge, golf-crazy, and go on a hundred other adventures. A traveller with the money and inclination could take a different commercial day trip for a month of Sundays and never double up on destinations. One particularly good jaunt is a 4WD trip to Cape Tribulation with the incomparable Strikies Safaris, who in one chock-a-block day bring you the Daintree River, mangrove boardwalks, Cape Tribulation's Rousseau-like rainforest and a riverside picnic lunch and swim. Watch your fellow passengers (especially if they're doughty Poms or wide-eyed Americans) be enthralled and appalled by the ecologically well-informed, but robustly 'true blue' crocs-and-all commentary.

Plenty of car rental firms operate out of Cairns, allowing the visitor to make his or her own itinerary, which may range from Mission Beach in the south, to Kuranda, Palm Cove (or any of Cairns' near northern beaches), Atherton Tablelands, or, more adventurously, in a 4WD vehicle, into the Daintree-Cape Tribulation-Bloomfield area. Time and budget are probably the only limitations. As with everything else about FNQ tourism, there is a plethora of printed information available to

Tropical hotel style.

148

guide, beguile or bamboozle the tripper. The FNQ Promotion Bureau, corner of Aplin and Sheridan Streets, Cairns, 4870, tel. (070) 51 3588, is the horse's mouth on most matters. Most operators have courtesy buses to whisk you from even the humblest hostel to the take-off point for their excursions. Rough n' ready backpackers have been heard to moan, 'It's too *easy* travelling here!' - as they slip into the cushioned, airconditioned arms of yet another courtesy coach.

During the September-November marlin season, charter boats take anglers out to the Reef to wrestle with the big black marlin. Five hundred kilogram (half a tonne) fish are not unknown in these waters, and Cairns is regarded as the black marlin capital of the world. About $1000 a day will get you a good craft. Cairns has two islands in its Coral Sea front yard, Green and Fitzroy (see chapters). The former boasts a famous underwater observatory, and Fitzroy is a delightful daytrip or longer stay.

Misdirections.

Outer Reef Trips: As Cairns climbs higher each year, people search further for an Outer Eden. Probably the most popular of all excursions are those to the Outer Reef offered by Quicksilver Connections, Great Adventures and other marine operators. The *Quicksilver* fleet is composed of several 37 m (130') high speed 'wavepiercer' catamarans which leave Cairns and Port Douglas each morning to take up to 300 people on a 28 knot (52 kph) skate to the edge of the known universe. Mooring beside a pontoon, the boat delivers you to a world of bomboras and glowing coral gardens. The crew hand out masks and snorkels, and - plop! - you're in for a close-up of the largest living thing on earth, the Great Barrier Reef. Within inches are all those phantoms of the documentary: brain coral, plate coral, electric day-glo fish, and the whole filigree of life in 350 varieties of coral and 600 species of fish. There are giant clams far older than European settlement in Australia. Time is as suspended as gravity. Coral jungles, coral poems, coral symphonies. Everything is alive, the fish just move faster. A manta ray vacuums its way along the bottom like a Stealth Bomber. Colours that video will never know. An underwater viewing platform and a 'Subsee Explorer' boat, plus optional helicopter flights and scuba dives, make this the best $100 day in history.

The weather: It's about as humid here as above an upturned steam-iron. Then in summer it gets seriously hot and damp. Monsoon season, 'The Wet' (Oct./Nov. - March/April) is just that, wet - no matter what your travel agent in Nagoya or Vladivostock doesn't tell you. (Remember: there's no rain forest without rain.) The cooler months, from April to October offer the most benign climate. It is also during these months that the sea is free of marine stingers, including the potentially fatal box jellyfish. At other times, you are strongly advised while swimming on mainland beaches to do so within the netted enclosures provided at popular destinations. On the islands stingers are not a problem.

PORT DOUGLAS

The beaches, suburbs and resorts packed along the **Captain Cook Highway** immediately north of Cairns are almost good enough to waylay any further progress north. But, keep going. A few million palm trees further up the 'Marlin Coast' (via **Hartley's Creek Crocodile Farm** - feeding time, 3 pm), past those beaches of driftwood and dreams ('if only I ...'), you arrive in tarted-up, but still pretty **Port Douglas**.

In the mid-1870s, bushman-prospector Christy Palmerston blazed an overland trail through intensely thick jungle from the inland Hodgkinson River gold strike out to the coast, arriving at this inlet, which was later named Port Douglas. The new route and port stole the thunder from Cairns and attracted away much of the gold rush commerce. Soon Port Douglas had a Cobb & Co. coach service, 14 licenced hotels and various grog shops. Then the river of

gold faltered, miners left, the Chinese were discouraged from settlement, and Port Douglas declined. In 1911 a cyclone flattened the town, and the rout was complete.

For more than half a century Port Douglas was a myth on a map, somewhere so far north that those who visited went 'troppo' and didn't come back, so hot in 'the wet' that eggs soft-boiled themselves ... and anyway, what's there to do but fish or drink? Which made it very appealing to the dropouts of the 1970s. They turned up, dropped in and bought out. As in scores of other destinations world-wide, the bourgeoisie followed their penurious but trailblazing peers, and soon Port Douglas was experiencing more paint, inflation and that certain gleam in the realtor's eye than it had seen in a century.

In the early '80s a bloke with a great deal of gleam arrived, and painted the town r-i-c-h. Christopher Skase, ex-financial journalist and visionary borrower, did dramatic things like opening the massive and elaborate **Sheraton**

A charming guide at Port Douglas.

Mirage Port Douglas and planting along the road to his Xanadu 1,450 mature palm trees at, it is said, a cost of $5,000 per tree. The Sheraton Mirage now has 121 ha (300 acres) of gardens and an 18-hole golf course, tended by 70 gardeners; all of which (bar the gardeners) is yours for several hundred dollars per night.

By 1989 history was repeating itself, and the boom turned to bust. Skase was bankrupt, and an embarrassment of investment apartments and bungalows clotted the market. Realtors moved to outlaw 'For Sale' signs because it seemed that half the town was for sale.

To do: Visit the **'Rainforest Habitat,'** a superb undercover bird and butterfly sanctuary, with a .8 ha (2 acres) canopied display of 65 species of freewheeling wings: rosellas, sooty terns, ducks, lorrikets, and birdwing and leafwing butterflies; as well Johnstone River (freshwater) crocodiles, wallabies and emus. The antique **'Bally Hooley'** steam loco sugar train rides through mangroves, canefields and forest to the 1897 sugar mill at Mossman. The **'Lady Douglas'** paddle steamer takes a two-hour cruise along Dickson Inlet's concealed waterways and lagoons, returning you to the elaborate Marina Mirage wharf complex

Marina Mirage is the Quicksilver catamaran base, as well as berth for many private and charter cruisers. Its cool arcade of shops and restaurants are ensconced in an elegant structure of decks and white roofs, all of which feel so substantial and consumer-comfortable that the old mangrove dreams of the Inlet upon which the complex is moored seem, by comparison, themselves to be the 'mirage.' **Four Mile Beach** (even pedantic cartographers don't call it 'Six Point Four Kilometre Beach'), is the favourite swimming stretch. During stinger season, a mesh net provides a safe enclosure.

Excursions: About 50 km (30 miles) north of Port Douglas is the deep green world of **Mossman Gorge,** the **Daintree** rainforest and **Cape Tribulation National Park**. En route, the raintrees and strangler figs of **Mossman**, as well

as the town's sugar mill (during the June-November crushing season) are worth seeing. The **Daintree River** with its terrapins, misty mountain views and lurking crocodile eyes, is best seen from a commentary cruise boat. (Thousands of squalling fruit bats hang in the riverside trees, like ranks of tiny demented Batmen.) Through the green fragrance of rain and river you are passing what is (at Noah Creek) the oldest rainforest on earth. 'Smileys' or 'salties' (i.e. saltwater crocodiles) can sometimes be seen sunning on the river bank. Up this way, there are small lodges and motels at Coconut and Pilgrims beaches, and at Cape Tribulation.

Back in Port Douglas there is the elegant and very friendly Reef Terraces (tropicana blooms, room to swing a dozen cats, great coral trout). Or the svelte Radisson Royal Palms, or Club Tropical, a fantasy of colours run rampant. In a different bracket, the Japanese-owned, Australian-run Travellers Hostel is one of the nicest and cleanest on the coast, at only $11 per night.

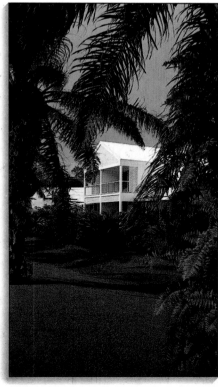

Sheraton Mirage's striking colonial architecture.

KURANDA AND
THE TABLELANDS

You've drifted among its Reefy dreams, eaten Cairns' international cuisine and slept postmodern in its five-star hotels ... and now you'd like to see a bit of *Australia*. It's close at hand - in the **Atherton Tablelands**. This plateau (av. elevation 700 m/2300 ft) is made for ambling. Distances aren't far, roads are good, and the weather is temperate.

Kuranda Train: The first step towards these air-conditioned tropics is **Kuranda**. While not part of the Tablelands proper, this 'village in the rain forest' should not be by-passed. The Scenic Rail train to Kuranda, which everyone takes, because it's such fun, leaves at nine each morning from Cairns' Freshwater Station and climbs over 300 m (1,000 ft), burrowing through 15 tunnels, and stopping at the spectacular **Barron Falls**. One of the great little train journeys of the world, it takes 75 minutes. A lively commentary recounts the 100-year history of the line.

Built between 1886 and 1891, the Cairns-Kuranda line was constructed by Irish and Italian navvies (up to 1,500 of them), who braved landslides, washouts, waterfalls, fever and hostile natives. Passing first through classic wide, open sugar cane lands, the train now traverses foothills, ravines, waterfalls, precipitous drops and trestle bridges to arrive at the Kuranda railway station.

Kuranda: Green, rambling Kuranda deserves at least a day. Once a '70s hangout for mycologically-inclined hippies, but now boutiqued and bistroed, its billion-leafed garden of rain forest is being clipped and Whipper-Snipped to subdivision neatness. On Wednesday, Friday and Sunday the rain forest marketplace erupts with craftworks of a huge variety, good eats, young Aboriginal dancers, and gift bargains. Meanwhile, up the street, one of Australia's most remarkable theatre

<u>Right</u>, the unique Tjapukai Dancers of Kuranda.

companies performs twice daily, every day. Nowhere else will you see the likes of the **Tjapukai Aboriginal Dance Theatre**, whose polished, contemporary corroboree of lore, legend, jokes and animal mime is a delight. This is the most positive, good humoured projection of Aboriginality to reach a mass white audience in a long time.

Kuranda has many attractions, one of the best being its **Butterfly Sanctuary**, the largest in the world. Wear some bright clothing and watch the turquoise Ulysses or Red Lacewings settle upon you as though on a flower. An excellent commentary guides you through this undercover rain forest and its lepidoptery museum. Kuranda offers lots of eating and drinking possibilities - homemade cakes, Devonshire teas, musical pubs - and good accommodation at the Kuranda Rainforest Resort.

The Tablelands: The train continues inland through the Tablelands from here, although travelling by road will allow you more flexibility for excursions. Less than an hour up the Kennedy Highway from Kuranda you reach **Mareeba**, 'the meeting place of the waters.' It's a four-wheel drive town, of wide streets, wide hats and wide shop awnings, with a strong Aboriginal and Italian presence. The annual rodeo, one of the best in Australia, attracts up to 15,000 spectators each July.

You're now on the Tablelands proper, a rich, rain-fed agricultural district (vegetables, rice, mangoes, nuts, etc.), and drug capital of Australia. The annual tobacco crop here is worth over $33 million; other, less addictive mind- and body-altering substances like coffee and tea are also grown. An easy 32 km (20 miles) south of Mareeba is **Atherton** (named after 1870s pioneer John Atherton), the hub of the Tablelands, and another honest, Aussie rural town, where the accents are as broad as the hat brims. 'Fascinating Facets' (at 69 Main Street) is an anomaly here. Amid the stock agents and country cafes, this cavern of crystal jewellery and amethyst geodes offers a range of wearable gifts and has a fascinating gallery of

The morning train on its way to the quaint Kuranda railway station (right).

154

crystals from around the world.

Lakes: Not far from Atherton, the enormous, man-made **Tinaroo Lake** is ideal for waterskiing, sailing and sailboarding. If camping or bushwalking is your forte, Tinaroo is heaven. Two-thirds the size of Sydney harbour, its bays and points provide a combination of picturesque wilderness and well-manicured camp sites. Try **Fong On Bay State Park** for camping and boating. Pelicans, ducks and fish abound. Catch your own 'barra' from a rented Tinaroo Tropical Houseboat. The best accommodation is the Tinaroo Lakes Motel right on the foreshore, a welcoming place whose Village Restaurant presents well-prepared, fresh Queensland fare at a giant dining table.

In the Atherton's **'Lakes District,'** as well as Lake Tinaroo, there are lakes Barrine, Eacham and Euramoo, which feature National Parks, walking trails, wildlife and boat excursions. And the ubiquitous Devonshire teas at **Lake Barrine**. This lake in an extinct 95,000 year-old volcanic crater also has 104 ha (256 acres) of hidden bays, a rainforest-ringed shore, kookaburras, water dragons, and the occasional platypus and pythons. A six kilometre (3.5 mile) ferry cruise of the lake departs daily at 10.15 am and 3.15 pm. Good for swimming too: no stingers in the lakes!

Making the most of its ample rainfall, the Atherton also has a **'Waterfall Circuit'** with lovely names to its falls, like Millaa Millaa, Zillie, Papina, Mungalli and Millstream falls. All of these are good for a short or longer bushwalk, a swim and a picnic, while Millstream in flood can be the wildest falls in Australia. A commercial lodge, Mungalli Falls Outpost conducts a variety of horse trail rides and rainforest treks. But if you're really serious about getting wet, two companies, R 'n R and Raging Thunder, mount very popular white-water rafting trips on the North Johnstone and Tully rivers. Adrenaline on the rocks.

As you meander near Lake Eacham, drop into the **Peeramon Hotel**, a quirky, 1908-vintage pub run by a charming expatriate from Melbourne.

There's an antique motorcycle mounted above the bar, and an equally antique petrol pump, which doesn't work either, on the sidewalk. It's a place to meet friendly locals, whose pubspeak is eminently repeatable, though not always printable. Meandering back to the village of Tolga (between Mareeba and Atherton), visit the Tolga Woodworks for hand-turned and carved wooden gifts. Amble further, to the beautiful old timber town of **Yungaburra** (13 km/8 miles east of Atherton), where cottages and bunyah pines, old churches and the Lake Eacham pub stand as their own eloquent history. Just west of the town is an enormous Curtain Fig Tree, a venerable Tree-beard of a creature. Just don't climb up his beard.

Herberton, about 20 km (12.5 miles) from Atherton, is another historical town, of woodsmoke and grand old timber buildings from tin mining booms gone by. Today its main attractions are an Historical Village (which, unfortunately, permits no cameras) of 28 genuine Queenslander buildings of varying vintages, and nearby Foster's vineyard. Take note: in mid-winter here, the mercury can drop to -10° (in north Queensland!).

En route from Herberton to Ravenshoe is **Hypipamee Crater**, an extraordinary, 140 m (460') deep volcanic hole, formed almost one hundred millenia ago when superheated steam seared out of the earth. Nearby Dinner Falls promises a cooler dip. And so, on to the prettily-named **Ravenshoe** (that's Ravens-ho, not Raven's-shoe), where the streets were built wide enough to turn a horse-drawn wagon. At 904 m (2965 ft) this is the highest town in Queensland. More good teas (try the local Nerada Plantation brew) are available in the main street tea-shops, or a fortifying North Queensland Lager from the pubs.

At **Innot Hot Springs** Village, about 30 minutes drive south-west of Ravenshoe you can scald yourself in a hot river, or simmer comfortably in a spa bath. Mud-baths and massages are available, and it's good for both arthritics and saddle-sore drivers. On the way

Cooling off in the Tablelands.

back, you might stop at **Malanda** for a night in the pub or at the superbly sited Malanda Lodge motel. The sheer oxygen-cleanliness of being here is a joy. You look out from your room to rich pastures and bunyah pines, and know that if there is a place where the grass *is* greener, this is it.

By now, you realise that the Atherton Tableland is a slightly eccentric, certainly historic, and quintessentially Australian (except when it's Chinese or Italian) realm. Fortunes in timber and tin have been won and lost here; nowadays, the forests have been listed for World Heritage preservation, and the money is in other things ... like tourism and Devonshire teas. Much of the country is unspectacular, in that subtle, long-distance Australian way. The mindless bush broken by a quiet pond, or a fire and water sunset. Plains which melt to lakes. Termite mounds and epiphytes; green hills and wooden halls, all removed from the razzamatazz coast; red soil, jocular voices ...

Further excursions: For the traveller who decides to abscond even further, it's possible to just keep driving. Beyond Ravenshoe and Mt. Garnet, there are the dramatic **Blencoe Falls** on the Herbert River. Several hours drive west, near Mt. Surprise is a unique volcanic cave system, the **Undara Lava Tubes**, a 65 km (40 miles) complex of huge tunnels up to 600 m (650 yards) long and 22 m (72 ft) high by 37 m (120 ft) across. At dusk, some quarter of a million bats flock from the cave mouth. Or, 140 km (87 miles) west of Mareeba, the **Chillagoe-Mungana National Park** has limestone caves, Aboriginal painting galleries and abandoned tin smelters. You could keep going to the Gulf of Carpentaria, to the prawn boats and crocs of Karumba, or to Burketown. Or see at close quarters the ramparts of the Atherton, Bellenden Ker Range and **Mount Bartle Frere**, Queensland's highest mountain (1622 m/5320 ft). A rugged 15 km (9 miles) bushwalk including an overnight camp will get you to the latter, via Malanda, Topaz Road and Butchers Creek.

Tinnaburra Waters at dawn.

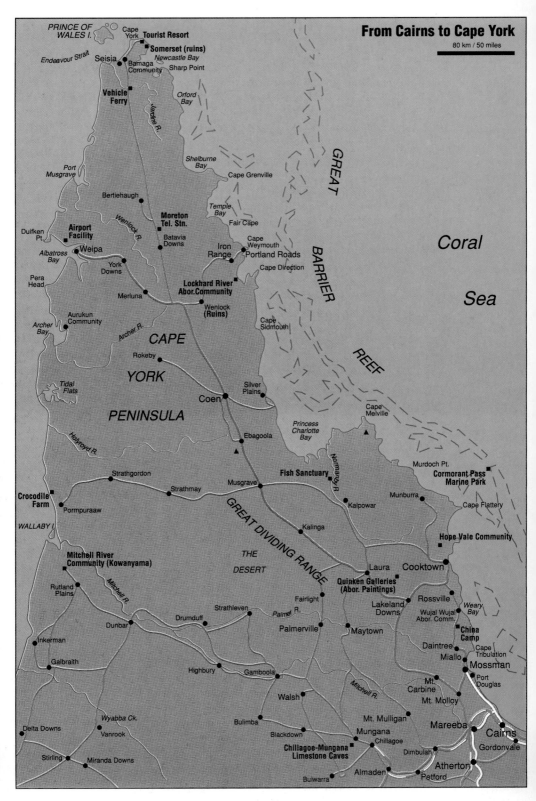

From Cairns to Cape York

80 km / 50 miles

PRINCE OF WALES I.
Cape York
Tourist Resort
Somerset (ruins)
Newcastle Bay
Seisia
Bamaga Community
Sharp Point
Endeavour Strait

Orford Bay

Vehicle Ferry

Jardine R.

Shelburne Bay

Port Musgrave

Bertiehaugh

Cape Grenville

Temple Bay

Moreton Tel. Stn.

Fair Cape

Duifken Pt.

Airport Facility

Wenlock R.

Batavia Downs

Iron Range

Cape Weymouth

Weipa

Portland Roads

Albatross Bay

York Downs

Cape Direction

Pera Head

Merluna

Lockhard River Abor. Community

Wenlock (Ruins)

Archer R.

Cape Sidmouth

Aurukun Community

Archer Bay

CAPE

Holroyd R.

YORK

Rokeby

PENINSULA

Silver Plains

Coen

Princess Charlotte Bay

Cape Melville

Tidal Flats

Ebagoola

Murdoch Pt.

Strathgordon

Cormorant Pass Marine Park

Fish Sanctuary

Crocodile Farm

Strathmay

Musgrave

Normanby R.

WALLABY I.

Pormpuraaw

Kalpowar

Munburra

Cape Flattery

Kalinga

Hope Vale Community

Mitchell River Community (Kowanyama)

THE DESERT

GREAT DIVIDING RANGE

Laura

Cooktown

Rutland Plains

Mitchell R.

Quinken Galleries (Abor. Paintings)

Rossville

Weary Bay

Fairlight

Lakeland Downs

Wujal Wujal Abor. Comm.

Strathleven

Palmer R.

Inkerman

Drumduff

Palmerville

Maytown

China Camp

Dunbar

Daintree

Cape Tribulation

Galbraith

Miallo

Mossman

Highbury

Gamboola

Mitchell R.

Mt. Carbine

Port Douglas

Walsh

Mt. Molloy

Delta Downs

Wyabba Ck.

Mt. Mulligan

Mareeba

Bulimba

Mungana

Cairns

Vanrook

Blackdown

Chillagoe

Gordonvale

Stirling

Miranda Downs

Chillagoe-Mungana Limestone Caves

Dimbulah

Bulwarra

Almaden

Atherton

Petford

Coral

Sea

GREAT

BARRIER

REEF

NORTH TO CAPE YORK

Bigger than the Netherlands or Nebraska, **Cape York** peninsula represents one of the last great wilderness areas on earth. Almost ten percent of its 207,000 square kilometre (80,000 square miles) area is protected within national parks, while an even larger area is proclaimed Aboriginal land. Bounded along its 1200 kilometre (750 miles) eastern seaboard by the Great Barrier Reef Marine Park, at its northern tip are the islands and reefs of the current-wracked Torres Strait, while along its west coast are the shallow and languid waters of the Gulf of Carpentaria. Cape York, along with Mexico's Yucatan, is one of the few major south-to-north peninsulas in the world.

In this expanse less than 25,000 people live - and most of those in the Mossman and Cooktown regions. Elsewhere, scattered towns, Aboriginal communities and huge cattle stations (average size of around 1 million acres or 400,000 hectares) are the only signs of human habitation. Few roads of any significance slice through this vastness and these generally are rough dirt 'washboards' which will shake a normal car to pieces.

The **Peninsula Development Road** heads inland, just south of Mossman, and quickly leaves the rainforest clad ranges behind, immersing itself into the forlorn tropical savannah that is typical of Cape York. Further north at Lakeland the road divides, one arm branching to coastal Cooktown, while the other heads north to the mining town of Weipa and on to the very northern tip of Australia.

The second major artery is the **Burke Development Road** which strikes west from **Mareeba** (65 km inland from Cairns). It meanders west through the old copper mining centre of **Chillagoe** (accommodation, national parks, limestone caves and all facilities), before skirting the mighty **Mitchell River** and heading south to **Normanton** and **Karumba** on Gulf of Carpentaria.

The coast road north from Port Douglas travels through green fields of tall sugar cane, each with a pristine backdrop of forest clad hills. **Mossman**, just 20 kilometres (12 miles) from 'the Port,' is first and foremost a sugar town, and is just 5 kilometres (3 miles) from the fabled Daintree National Park, featuring the **Mossman Gorge**, waterfalls and rich tropical rainforest.

Daintree itself is a small tropical village nestling beside the Daintree River, some 36 kilometres (22 miles) north of Mossman. The locals' houses are garlanded in colorful hibiscus and bougainvillea, and the river bounded by huge shady trees, while all around the evergreen mountains rise supreme, making Daintree a delight to visit. There are regular cruises on the picturesque Daintree River where spotting rare birds, flying foxes and the occasional large crocodile is common. For those who want to stay a while, the Pinnacle Village Van Park offers budget camping, on-site vans and all amenities.

Colourful cassowaries can deliver a nasty kick.

Once across the Daintree River a well graded road can be followed all the way to **Cape Tribulation**, where the rainforest meets the coral reef. 'Tribulation' was the name James Cook gave to the Cape, because that's what his crew experienced from then on, when *Endeavour* ran aground off here on the night of June 11, 1770. For many years this stretch of coast has fascinated travellers with its natural beauty, an intimate mix of white sandy beaches, rocky headlands, blue sea and jungle clad mountains. Tour operators such as Strikies Safaris and Morgans Rainforest Connection offer environmental excursions by foot or four wheel drive vehicle into this rainforest region. Although facilities are limited at 'Cape Trib,' there is a camping ground and a general store, as well as a backpacker hostel offering budget accommodation.

Continuing north the road passes through magnificent rainforest, but is only recommended for four wheel drives. After fording the **Bloomfield River** (possible only at low tide), the route passes through the Wujal Wujal Aboriginal community, before pushing on to **Ayton, Rossville** and finally **Cooktown**. At the mouth of the Bloomfield River is the Bloomfield Wilderness Lodge, a mecca for fishermen and those wanting to get away from it for a while. Access is via a four wheel drive and a short boat ride, while the accommodation is secluded with a relaxed atmosphere.

For those who choose the inland route from Mossman to Cooktown, the Peninsula Development Road via **Mt Molloy** and **Mt Carbine** quickly leaves behind the bitumen and the deep green of the rainforest. Suddenly this is remote country where people wave to one another as they pass. Along the next 240 kilometres (180 miles) there is only the **Palmer River Goldfield Roadhouse** and Caravan Park (fuel, basic supplies and camping) and the small hamlet of Lakeland to break the monotony of the route. **Lakeland** has fuel, a general store, basic repairs and accommodation available at the motel or the small

The controversial road that was cut through the Daintree Wilderness area.

camping ground. Nearby is the **Butcher Hill Homestead**, a cattle station that caters for visitors with beds, country fare meals and outback hospitality.

It is from Lakeland that adventurers can also head north to Australia's northern most tip, through the heart of Cape York Peninsula. Surrounded by some of the most rugged escarpment country in Australia, the tiny township of **Laura**, 60 kilometres (36 miles) north of Lakeland, has gained fame as the centre of one of the world's greatest collections of prehistoric rock art. The **Quinkan Art Reserve** protects many of the 1500 galleries so far discovered, and while a couple are readily accessible to the public (see the ranger based in Laura for details), the best way to view some of the more remote and spectacular galleries is to join Trezise Bush Guide Services at their beautiful Jowalbinna Bush Camp on the Little Laura River. Matt Trezise, who runs the Quinkan Hotel in **Laura,** is not only a rich source of information, but can arrange accommodation at the camp or behind the pub.

A three day Aboriginal Dance Festival, held in Laura at the beginning of July each year, captures much of the magic and the rich tradition of Aboriginal life on Cape York. On the first weekend in July are the Laura Horse Races and Rodeo, and as with any of the annual outback race meets, they are a friendly, kick-up-your-heels social occasion for locals and visitors alike.

Laura is also the gateway to **Lakefield National Park** - the largest park in Queensland. While the park's many rivers and permanent waterholes play host to a wide variety of bird and other animal life, it is the fishing that attracts most people. Long known as one of the places for barramundi (giant perch), Lakefield boasts these sleek, golden fighters up to 30 and 40 kilograms (65-90 pounds), although 5 to 10 kilo ones are much more common.

Maytown, situated on the Palmer River and accessible by a rough track south from Laura, was once the main centre of the Palmer gold rush. Now nothing more than a ghost town, it and

Daintree General store has it all.

the surrounding mines and machinery are protected in a Historic Reserve. **Coen**, more than 240 kilometres (145 miles) north of Laura, is the next major town on the Cape. It has one pub, a motel, camping ground, the Homestead Guest House, a couple of general stores and a garage (to repair your weary vehicle). The Annual Picnic Races, held in August, not only close Coen down for the weekend, but also most of the Cape. The town bulges with visitors, all intent on having a rollicking good hoot.

Rokeby National Park and **Archer Bend National Park** lie to the north-west of Coen. While Rokeby has a number of camping areas, Archer Bend is a true wilderness with no road access and no facilities. **Iron Range National Park**, situated around the tiny hamlet of **Portland Roads** on the east coast (200 km. north-east of Coen), is one of the great natural treasure houses of Australia. Among the verdant rainforest mountains, a wide range of animals and plants can be found, many with ancestry linked more closely to humid tropical New Guinea than dry Australia.

While no facilities exist at Portland Roads, the nearby Aboriginal community of **Lockhart River** has limited services for visitors. There are regular air services to the communities, but no accommodation is available. To visit the area travellers must join an organised safari or be self sufficient. Camping is available in the middle of the rainforest or on the coast at **Chilli Beach**. Facilities are very basic.

Across on the other side of the Cape, 250 kilometres north-west of Coen, is the mining township of **Weipa.** The Peninsula Road (still dirt) heads north from Coen to the Archer River Roadhouse and then north-west to Weipa. Sitting astride one of the world's largest deposits of bauxite, the township has all modern facilities, including the Albatross Hotel-Motel and the Pax Haven Camping Ground. Regular flights service the town, four wheel drive vehicles can be hired or a fishing or crocodile spotting charter can be arranged with Weipa River Safaris. Tours of the vast

Orchids thrive in far north Queensland.

mining complex are conducted each day and give visitors the chance not only to see the mining and processing operations, but also to gape at the sheer size of the machinery used.

Only a rough four wheel drive track pushes on to the very northern tip of the Australian mainland. Crossing rivers, streams and swamps, it is one of the country's great four wheel drive adventures. The route follows the old Overland Telegraph Line, established in the 1880's and used regularly up until the mid 1980's, when a series of microwave links brought modern communication to the region.

While less than 400 kilometres (250 miles) separate Coen from the northern most settlement of Bamaga, there is no other permanent habitation and the route is only open during the dry season, from June to November. For adventurers who love camping beside crystal clear streams, in a region of untouched beauty, this area is beyond all expectations. The **Jardine River National Park** protects all the area around the infamous river of the same name and a number of small camping areas have been established..

Bamaga is the main centre of a large and diverse Aboriginal and Torres Strait Island community, located around the northern tip of the Cape. With its limited facilities (fuel, store and repair facilities), it caters for locals and four wheel drive travellers, but has no accommodation. Camping areas at **Red Island Point** and at **Cowal Creek** cater for those with a tent. The Bamaga Annual Show and Rodeo are held each year in September. These are lively affairs with not only horsemen and rough riding on the draw card, but also local arts and crafts and such fun events as greasy pig catching, which even visitors can enter. Australia's most northern area of rich rainforest, known as the **Lockerbie Scrub**, begins just outside Bamaga and is passed through on the way to 'the Top' or to the deserted government outpost of Somerset.

Somerset, nestling on the steep hills overlooking **Albany Pass**, was the

The remote coastal capes near Cooktown.

original European settlement in the area. Planned as Australia's 'Singapore of the South,' it never grew bigger than a few houses and a military camp. John Jardine, one of the first Government magistrates, carved out a cattle and pearling empire from here from 1863 onwards. His deeds, and those of his sons Frank and Alexander, wrote the family name into the history books and the legends of the Cape. The graves of Frank (who died of leprosy in 1919, with 47 notches upon his rifle) and his Samoan princess wife, remain on the beach below their once grand home at Somerset.

The Top of Australia Wilderness Lodge takes in the northernmost tip of the continent and caters for upmarket travelers in well appointed bungalows around a pleasant bar and reception area. A camping area is also provided. For lodge guests, there are night excursions through the rainforest led by biologist, fishing trips to offshore reefs or to a wilderness camp on the **Jardine River**, as well as historic and picturesque trips to Somerset and Thursday Island. Packaged tours to the lodge can be easily arranged in Cairns or with any travel agent.

Just south of the Wilderness Lodge is Punsand Bay Private Reserve. Not as upmarket as the Lodge, **Punsand Bay** offers camping facilities and accommodation. Again, fishing and other excursions can be arranged for anyone staying at the Reserve, which boasts 12 km (7.5 miles) of sandy beach front, as well as rainforests and swamps alive with birds and other animal life.

Fishing is undoubtedly one of the great attractions of this great Cape. With the rich waters of the Gulf on one side, the Pacific and the Barrier Reef on the other and the islands and reefs of Torres Strait acting as a cauldron pot, it is no wonder the fishing is so exciting. Game fish such as Spanish mackerel, queenfish and giant trevally are common, as are such delectables as coral trout, 'barra' and mangrove jack.

Thursday Island, the government and administrative centre of the fabled

The most 'souvenired' sign in Queensland – leaving unsuspecting swimmers at great risk.

Torres Strait, is a cosmopolitan town seemingly far removed from Australia. Founded as a government outpost when Somerset on the mainland was abandoned, 'T. I.', as it is commonly known, grew as the centre of a rich and widespread pearling industry. Today pearling is still carried on, but other natural wealth is also harvested from the sea. The lifestyle of the locals is laid back and enjoyable and any visitor soon finds him or herself moving to the same beat, rocking on the same boat.

T.I. has a number of hotels and motels catering for travellers. The Federal Hotel, Torres Hotel and the Rainbow Motel are three which have basic, clean facilities - but don't expect anything fancy! Visiting the outlying island communities is possible, but permission must be gained from the local Council on T.I. A couple of the islands have accommodation or camping and a regular air service from T. I. **Saibai** and **Boigu Islands**, which few travellers reach, are just a stone's throw from New Guinea. In this cluster of gem-like islands strewn across the Torres Strait, Australian territory comes to an end.

Touring the Cape: For most visitors the Cape is most easily experienced on an organised safari. The advantages of local knowledge, reliable service and guaranteed Outback experience far outweigh any perceived disadvantages of large groups, timetables, etc. There are several reliable operators offering a variety of 15-18 day drive trips, and 7-8 day drive/fly trips, while some even offer an 8-11 day drive/sail sojourn that takes travelers one way by cruising the northern Great Barrier Reef. All trips originate in Cairns. While in some instances the tours are accommodated (staying in the few motels or lodges along the way), most trips are camping safaris, which is really the only way to fully experience and fully appreciate the region. Major operators include AAT Kings, Australia Pacific Tours, New Look Adventures, Oz Tours and Wildtrack Camping Safaris. Most cater for 10-20 people on each trip and the itinerary is fairly flexible.

Left, a secret waterfall somewhere on the Cape. **Right**, the further north, the more colourful the birdlife.

COOKTOWN

The most spectacular way to visit the historic port of **Cooktown** is without doubt also the most traditional - by boat. In fact, it's a tradition inaugurated (at least among Europeans) by the 'discoverer' of Australia, James Cook R. N. As the country's northernmost east coast town, this eponymous port, until the early 1950's, had no road access at all. Back then visitors arrived by coastal steamer, as did all the town's supplies.

Today there are two roads leading to Cooktown - the inland **Peninsula Development Road** route, a rough 330 km (200 miles) run north from Cairns, or the **coastal route** through the spectacular Daintree rainforest area north of Port Douglas - a shorter, but often closed, and even rougher 240 km (150 miles) jaunt. Despite the different mileages, road conditions ensure travelling times are fairly similar. Coral Coaches operate a regular bus service between Cairns and Cooktown along both circuits.

Those who want to experience the region as the pioneers did (well, almost) and see some spectacular, unspoilt coast along the way, a boat trip is still the real answer. The *Quicksilver* wave-piercer catamaran, operating out of Port Douglas, takes travellers on a two and a half hour jungle coast jaunt north from civilised, tourist orientated Queensland to Cooktown, the very doorstep of the tropical wilderness.

At the Cooktown wharf, just inside the mouth of the Endeavour River, is the spot where, on June 18, 1770, Captain James Cook and his crew beached their crippled barque *Endeavour* for emergency repairs, after having towed it by longboat for four days. Cook departed after seven weeks. As a result of this stay, Cooktown can claim to be the site of the first European settlement in Australia. On the Queen's Birthday weekend in June, Cooktown celebrates with the three-day Discovery Festival.

With the discovery of gold in 1873 on the Palmer River, 160 kilometres (100

Sailing from Cooktown.

miles) inland, Cooktown and the region boomed and during the 1880's the town's population peaked at around 35,000, including large numbers of Chinese in transit to the Palmer 'strike.' Cooktown reportedly had 65 hotels, 20 eating houses and 32 general stores catering for the region's needs. With the decline of the goldfields, Cooktown waned and by the end of World War II it was almost a ghost town. During the '60's, tourism began to breath life into the 'Queen of the North,' as the town is often known, and by the beginning of the '90's the remaining buildings and the parks have been spruced up to look their best for the new wave of visitors.

Cooktown's heritage becomes obvious during even a short stroll around the town. At the wharf end of town there's Cook's Rock and Cook's Monument, erected in 1887. Further along is the Westpac Bank, built in 1878. While its facade has remained virtually unchanged, the main attractions are inside - with its beautiful red cedar interior and 100 year old gold scales. Other sites worth a close look include the James Cook Museum (originally a convent built in 1878), the Cooktown Sea Museum with its collection of maritime history, the 1897 Post Office, the West Coast Hotel (1874), Jackey Jackey Store (1886), the Botanical Gardens, the Hospital (1879), the 'Endeavour Butcher Shop' (1870) and the 1890 Shire Hall. Just outside town is the Cooktown Cemetery with its pioneer graveyard and Chinese Shrine.

Scattered among all this living history is a variety of accommodation to suit all tastes and pockets. There's the Sovereign Resort Hotel, a new building on the site of the original 1874 Sovereign pub. Today's Sovereign offers a range of accommodation from luxury suites to self-contained units with cooking facilities.

Cooktown Backpackers is, as the name suggests, aimed at the ever increasing number of travellers who don't want to spend a fortune on a bed for the night. For them, Far North Queensland is Backpacker Heaven. This reasonably-priced hostel features attractive dorms with a fully equipped kitchen and dining facilities, also a swimming pool, BBQ area and a TV/Video lounge. Other Cooktown accommodation available includes three caravan/camping parks (the Cooktown Mines, Golden Orchid and Peninsula Caravan Parks), and a wide choice of motels including the Cooktown Motor Inn and the Cooktown River of Gold Motel.

There are cruises on the **Endeavour River** or diving and fishing trips to the reef. These charters run from the wharf and trips can be arranged through the Lure Shop in Charlotte Street, or the Cook's Landing Kiosk on the wharf. For swimming and sun baking, **Finch Bay**, only a couple of kilometres from the centre of town, is probably the most popular beach in the region. Further out are Quarantine Bay, Walker Bay and Archer Point.

To discover more of the area's natural beauty, there are four National Parks to explore in the immediate vicinity of Cooktown. Both the **Mt Cook** and **Endeavour River National Parks** protect areas noted during Cook's enforced seven week stay in 1770. Further south is the **Black Mountain National Park**, a huge hill of bare black rock that to the Aborigines was 'Kalcajagga' - The Mountain of Death. **Cedar Bay National Park**, 50 km (30 miles) south of Cooktown, is the largest park in the region, preserving an untamed stretch of coast surrounded by magnificent rainforest. The bay has a wild recent history from the 1970s when it was a haven for feral hippies, anarchist dope growers and various freedom freaks - until it all grew to be too much competition for society's insistent law of 'Averages' and for the Queensland Police.

On the way to Cedar Bay is the small township of **Rossville** with its 130 year-old Lions Den Hotel. The drinkers here are eccentric one-offs, *not* to be patronised as 'colourful locals.' Accommodation is available in the pub, as well as at the camping ground situated right beside the beautiful **Annan River**. Alternatively, there is accommodation or camping at the nearby Home Rule Rainforest Lodge or the Mungumby Lodge.

THE ISLANDS

Work your way up a map of the Queensland coast, attempting to count each island and the enormity of the task soon overwhelms you. These myriad satellites to the Australian continent (itself Earth's largest island) hover upon the horizon of the imagination. No man is one - but each man, and woman, at some time wants one. And with one million visitors per year predicted for the Barrier Reef by year 2000, there's not much chance of *that*.

Queensland's islands range from coral pinpricks to upthrust bones of the continent, thousands of hectares in area. There are 540 continental islands (yes, someone has counted them!), plus 2500 individual reefs and cays. James Cook and Joseph Banks became the first European tourists to set foot among them when in August, 1770, they climbed the peak of Lizard Island, north of Cooktown.

Banks saw remnants of Aboriginal huts. Today, the traveller's imagination might still see a Crusoe-Rousseau island idyll awaiting it somewhere. Well, times have changed - and Lizard Island's 'huts' today are of a very upmarket kind. It is possible to travel 'a month of nights, a year of days' - or longer - among these waking dreams which float upon the larger dream of the Pacific, but, you'll need to be well equipped with credit or supplies, depending upon whether you're slumming it in a $300 a day suite or lording it over the turtles in a tent on the coast of nowhere.

On the developed islands, the list of activities designed to stop you gazing dreamily out to sea for too long includes tennis, golf, sailing, bushwalking, sailboarding, snorkelling, horseriding, scuba diving (bring your certificate!), reef cruises, fishing, discos, reef walking, and drinking. If sailing, you can camp ashore around a bonfire of stars and marshmallows; you can prowl all day like a cat among the sleeping-dog islands; and you can dive among wrecks, drowned mountains or the coral parlours of giant clams and darting, iridescent fish.

The choice is vast. The pages are limited. Thus, the following section covers only the main destinations, and must skip some smaller islands such as Masthead and Tryon in the Capricorn Group, Wild Duck (south of Mackay) and Newry in the Hillsborough Channel. Fraser Island and Magnetic Island have been included within the 'Mainland' section of the book. Islands are presented here as they sail up the coast, a flotilla of choices and chances, from south to north. The Great Barrier Reef Marine Park Authority divides the islands into the following regional groups, and you will find them arranged here accordingly: Mackay-Capricorn Section - Lady Elliot to Brampton Island; Central Section - Lindeman to Dunk Island; Cairns Section - Fitzroy to Lizard Island.

Preceding pages: tropical idyll; which way to the water?; Whitsunday campfire. **Left**, sailing into Heron Island.

Australia is a continent of oddities and marvels, but nowhere else do its wonders form as stunning and cohesive a whole as on the Great Barrier Reef. The Australian government's nomination of the Reef for World Heritage listing reads: "The Great Barrier Reef is by far the largest single collection of coral reefs in the world. Biologically the Great Barrier Reef supports the most diverse ecosystem known to man. Its enormous diversity is thought to reflect the maturity of an ecosytem which has evolved over millions of years ... "

From the moon the Great Barrier Reef appears to justify its name - it is seen as a white line off the north-east coast of Australia, a rampart between northern Queensland and the Pacific Ocean. However, as early European explorers from Captain James Cook onwards learned to their peril, it's a lot more complicated than that. In fact, from its pattern on maps, to the interrelation of its many species, to the life of the most basic creatures, the motto of the Great Barrier Reef could well be, "It's a lot more complicated than that".

This marine wonderland is not a single reef but rather about 2500 reefs strung together with over 500 islands and a further 500 fringing reefs. The whole chain roughly follows the line of the continental shelf for a distance of more than 2000 km (1240 miles). The total area of the Reef is 230,000 square kilometres (88,800 square miles). The southern end of the Reef is the most southerly part of the entire vast Indo-Pacific coralline region, the legendary 'Coral Islands' of the South Seas. The world's next largest reef system is also in this region - off the coast of New Caledonia.

Charles Darwin was the originator of the term "barrier reef" but the name "Great Barrier Reef" was given to the Australian structure by Matthew Flinders, the explorer who first extensively charted these waters in the early nineteenth century. Between July 1802, when the 27 year old Flinders and his crew set sail from Sydney in the *Investigator,* and October of the same year when they emerged through the Reef (by what is now known as Flinders Passage), he charted the east coast in detail. Until very recently his soundings still appeared on nautical charts of the Reef. Flinders, one of the greatest of Australia's scientific explorers, was also the first to use the single word "Australia" for the continent that had earlier been known as "Terra Australis Incognita".

The science of plate tectonics shows that, on a geological time scale, continents waltz around the planet, forming and breaking up more often than one might imagine. Until about 200 million years ago all the land masses formed the single super-continent of Pangaea (the name, logically enough, means "all lands"). Australia was once north of the equator, then it was far south. It commenced its run north about 60 million years ago and is still proceeding north at about a meagre centimetre per annum - don't expect cheaper international airfares in the near future.

The world's climate too has changed much, on a cycle of ice ages and warm periods. When much of the world's oceans are locked up in the polar ice, the sea level falls. During the last ice age that ended about 20,000 years ago, the sea level was some 100 metres lower than today. At that time it would have been possible to walk out to the edge of what is now the outer Barrier Reef. Indeed, the Aborigines who arrived in Australia 50,000 years ago crossed over to Tasmania when it was connected with the mainland. The sea level stabilised only about 6000 years ago.

It's an ever-changing cycle. Some limestone ranges along the Queensland coastal mainland are the remains of ancient reefs. In the Kimberley region of Western Australia are some of the world's best examples of fossil reefs, formed in the Devonian age 350 million years ago. Most Queensland resort islands are continental peaks inundated at the end of the last ice age. Now fringing reefs have formed around them.

To understand how coral reefs come about, one has to zoom in from the grand

Left, no two giant clams look the same.

overview to a microscopic level. The builders of the Great Barrier Reef are coral polyps and algae. A coral polyp is a tiny, simple animal consisting of not much more than a mouth and surrounding tentacles to feed it. The polyp has a limestone skeleton underneath that it withdraws into during the day - it is the remains of these skeletons that form the basis of a coral reef.

There are three main reasons why polyps succeed as nature's greatest architects. Only one of these is their own doing - they breed well. What we see as a single piece of coral is a whole colony of corals, the progeny of a single founder polyp. In a touching display of family togetherness, the whole colony

twice as fast as it otherwise could.

Corals exist in most of the world's oceans - even arctic waters - but can only grow beyond insignificant colonies to form reefs when accompanied by zooxanthellae. This limits the areas in which they are found to places where the water temperature doesn't fall below 18°C (64.4 F), and, as zooxanthellae are like other plants in requiring sunlight, in depths of less than 50 metres (165 feet).

The final contributors to reef development are the algae that bond together the skeletons of dead corals and other animals. Algae is the mortar which binds a reef. Without the algae there would be no reefs, so it has been argued that they could be just as readily called "algal

stay linked together by body tissues so that food caught is the whole colony's bounty.

The second reason is the polyps' little helpers, the zooxanthellae. These are tiny single cell plants that live within the cells of the polyp. Like all plants, zooxanthellae run on photosynthesis, utilising sunlight to turn nitrogen, carbon dioxide and phosphorus into energy. In an excellent symbiotic relationship, a zooxanthellae takes the polyp's waste products and in return provides a majority of the polyp's food requirements in the form of proteins and fats. This gives the coral time to devote itself to reproducing and developing its skeleton at a rate more than

reefs" rather than "coral reefs". However, despite their greater importance, the algae are much less noticeable than corals when one is observing a reef. It's fortunate for a whole school of romantic escapist literature that the exotic coral island was never equated with the algal slime left inside flower vases.

A coral reef is, in fact, a thin veneer of colourful living corals existing on the compacted, bleached remains of their dead ancestors. Coral grows towards sunlight but polyps can't live out of water. Once they reach the water's level at low tide, they spread out rather than grow up.

Coral reproduce both sexually and asexually. Asexual reproduction occurs when part of a colony breaks from the main body, survives and grows independently. As is so often the case, sexual reproduction is much the more spectacular. In late spring there are a couple of nights when many types of coral polyp simultaneously release eggs and sperm into the water. This mass spawning is only now coming to be understood, but it is certainly an impressive sight for the lucky few who witness it- rather like an underwater snowstorm. The fertilised egg eventually settles onto a new surface and lays down a skeleton in which it can hide, then settles into the task of becoming a colony.

There are many different types of coral,

The coral formations created by the "Porites" polyp in massive colonies takes the shape of huge "bommies", some up to 10 metres high, that can support a wide array of reef life forms.

Black coral, the type made into jewellery, isn't normally found on reefs. In fact, these single strand or bush-like corals mainly occur at depths greater than 20 metres (65 feet). When alive, these flexible yellow, brown or grey growths look nothing at all like the finished product in shops. Their only black (or very dark brown) part is the central skeleton revealed when the flesh is removed.

Then there are the soft corals. Contrary to

falling into three main groups: stony corals, black corals and soft corals. Stony (or hard) corals are the basic substance of the reef and any exploration of a reef reveals the many forms they take. Of stony corals, Acropora or staghorn corals are the most common - they grow fast and take a wide variety of forms, from the familiar branch shapes to flat plates. As a rough guide, they are corals which grow out from a base stem. Other types are mushroom corals, and brain corals.

Left and above, soft coral grows in an incredible array of patterns.

often heard stories, these don't become hard when they die and they don't have a hard calcium skeleton, so they contribute little to reef building. However, they are very common and often redominate in the overall appearance of the reef. In fact, they normally occur in very large colonies, so it's hard to miss them. Like the hard corals, most soft corals play the role of symbiotic host to zooxanthellae, and this results in their mainly yellow and brown colourings. As the name suggests, these are soft growths; they come in an incredible array of patterns. In the same octocoral subclass as soft corals are the spectacular gorgonian corals. These often take the form of beautiful Chinese fans or miniature trees or whips in a rainbow of colours. Most have a flexible, firm skeleton called "gorgonin" largely made of protein.

The hydrozoans are a large class of animal that extends from bluebottles to builders of structures virtually indistinguishable from coral. In fact, some are so similar to corals that only scientists and other hydrozoans really care about the difference. The same could be said of bryozoans, some of which are the so-called "lace corals".

All told, there are some 400 types of coral, over 1500 fish species and more invertebrates on the Reef than you can wave a flipper at. Although many are exquisitely

feet) through Michaelmas Cay at the northern section of the Reef. Heron Island was the site of a second bore in 1937 - to 223 metres (730 feet). The aim was to find out how far down the underlying bedrock was. Both sites revealed there was some 125 metres (410 feet) of coral before the drills struck layers of sand and shells. Neither reached bedrock.

There are many different types of reef within the system but the major ones are ribbon, platform, and fringing reefs.

Ribbon reefs are typical of the northern end of the Great Barrier Reef. Although there are some passages between them (as James Cook and Matthew Flinders found, to their relief), there are long stretches where

beautiful (indeed, every plant or animal seems determined to outshine the others), each reef is very much more than the sum of its parts. One can explore the water all day, looking for new species which stand out from the crowd. Alternatively, and eventually more rewarding, is to look closely at a square metre of reef and observe the incredible complexity of life that it supports.

The beginnings of the Great Barrier Reef were about 18 million years ago in the northern end. The southern section probably commenced about two million years ago. In 1926 the Great Barrier Reef Committee sunk an exploratory bore hole 183 metres (600

they line the eastern edge of the continental shelf, forming a seemingly impenetrable barrier. Here the distinction between one side of the Reef and the other is pronounced. The western (mainland) side of the Reef tapers off onto a sandy bottom at around 20 metres (65 feet) depth; the ocean side drops almost sheer for more than 1000 metres (3280 feet). The 1000 fathom line (1850 metres/6000 feet) lies less than five kilometres (three miles) out.

Heading south, the continental shelf becomes much wider - its edge is some 370 km (230 miles) east of Mackay. The Reef, although it's much further from the coast, is well within the continental shelf. The 1000 fathom line is more than 50 km (30 miles) beyond the edge of the Reef. Here are found some of the best examples of platform reefs that, in their ultimate form, eventually become coral cays.

In best metaphysical fashion, the beginning of the formation of a coral reef is the death of the coral polyp. The brittle, dead coral is soon broken by the force of waves and disintegrates into coral sand that calcareous algae binds into a cement. This process of disintegration and cementation continues and a reef rises. Now the waves break off the coral and deposit it on the leeward side of the reef forming a mass of sand and rubble just

cay. At first, the sandbank may move with every tide but gradually it grows and becomes more stable. Eventually the sandbank is exposed at most high tides - only being submerged by the occasional king tide.

At this stage, opportunistic birds may start to use the islet as a staging post and then to nest on it. With them will come plant seeds that germinate and provide the new land with its first vegetation. The roots of the plants further stabilise the sandy mass. Organic material from the vegetation improves the soil quality and the phosphates in the bird guano act as a cement. The cay continues to grow and stabilise.

A form of permanence is reached when the

below the waterline. These flats are normally oval in shape. They can be very extensive and still never become coral cays.

The necessary element for cay formation is a trick of currents or reef shape that results in the waves changing direction as they break over the reef. When this occurs, the sediments will build up higher on one part of the reef flat. Irrespective of the size of this patch of higher sand - it may be no larger than a suburban house block - it's an embryonic

cay has grown large enough to develop a freshwater pool underneath the cay or in a pool near the centre. Once this is established, larger trees can grow on the cay. All this development may be destroyed by a cyclone but it's unlikely - tenuous permanence has been achieved.

There are two major areas for vegetated cays on the Great Barrier Reef. The northern ones are from Green Island north and the southern ones are all below Mackay. That leaves more than 500 km (300 miles) of the central Reef with no fully formed cays.

For most visitors to the Queensland coast, fringing **reefs** are the most important type of

Left and **above**, soft coral polyps.

reef. That's because all but a few resorts are on continental islands, not coral cays, so the nearest reef is likely to be one that's grown up near the resort. Fringing reefs can also occur along the mainland coast but, in practice, the outflow of rivers from the coast limits the number that do form. The variety of corals on fringing reefs along or near the coast appears to have declined this century; it appears likely that farming practices such as use of pesticides and increased land use are having an adverse effect on at least some parts of the Reef.

When the last ice age ended, mountains that had been part of the mainland for 100,000 years became islands as the sea

Waters that could not support any other form of reef can manage to maintain fringing reefs. The most southerly in the world are around Lord Howe Island; that is, on roughly the same lattitude as Port Macquarie, NSW.

Incidently, it's worthy of note that Australia has no coral atolls. An atoll is formed when a continental island is surrounded by a fringing reef then the island subsides through geological activity. Because Australia is geologically very stable and the islands of the Queensland coast are firmly anchored on the continental shelf, atolls are most unlikely to ever occur here.

Fringing reefs can be anywhere from a mere 20 metres (65 feet) wide to expanses of

waters rose. Many of these mountains were, in fact, the remains of ancient reefs formed in the distance past. Since the sea level stabilised about 6000 years ago, fringing reefs have formed around these islands. Much of the visual attraction of areas like the Whitsunday Islands lies in the combination of rocky islands with patches of green vegetation fringed with golden sand beaches, which in turn merge with the pale blues and greens of shallow sands and reefs, before dropping away to the deep royal blue of the open water. The contrasting light band of colour of the reef appears to etch the island firmly into its setting.

reef flats extending over several hundred metres on the lee side of an island. On first sight, a fringing reef can be a disappointment as the inner reef is revealed by a dropping tide with none of the bright corals one expects. It may even be covered in mud. However, its outer edge may teem with life. Because there's less chance of wave damage in sheltered waters, corals of a fringing reef are often more spectacular than those of a ribbon reef at the outer Barrier Reef.

Above, a lagoon walk is a good way to learn about reef life. **Right**, the birth of a cay.

RESEARCH AND CONSERVATION

We are still very much in a learning stage about coral reefs. Most geographical knowledge about northern hemisphere phenomena has been much more deeply studied than these complicated, isolated and vast structures.

The first scientist to view the Great Barrier Reef was Joseph Banks, sailing with Cook on the *Endeavour* in 1770. Many followed after them, though in most cases the prime objective was survey work. Matthew Flinders was the next, then Phillip Parker King in the *Mermaid* and later the *Bathurst* in 1819-21, and Wickham, Stokes and others on the *Beagle* in 1839. However, it could be said that J. Beet Jukes off HMS *Fly* who landed on One Tree Island in 1842 conducted the first scientific investigation of the Reef, mainly from a geological viewpoint.

A Queensland Commissioner for Fisheries, W. Saville-Kent researched much of the Reef for the government and, in 1893 published "The Great Barrier Reef".

In 1904, the Australian Museum conducted an expedition to Masthead Island, which was also the base for the expedition by Royal Australian Ornithologists' Union in 1910. The Queensland branch of the Royal Geographical Society of Australia formed a Great

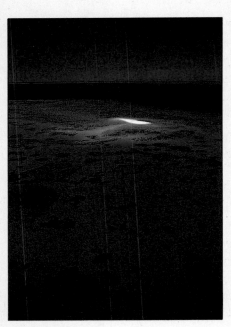

Barrier Reef Committee in 1922. (That committee recently reformed as the Australian Coral Reef Society.) It launched a major expedition in 1928 with the Royal Society of London when it put a team of 23 scientists on a laboratory on the Low Isles off Port Douglas for a full year. The head of that team was Sir C. Maurice Yonge and many of their findings are still being used today.

The first permanent research station came into being when the Great Barrier Reef Committee took a lease of 5 acres of Heron Island in 1950 and established Heron Island Research Station. This facility is now owned and operated by the University of Queensland. The Australian Museum established a field research station on One Tree Island in 1966 - that is now run by Sydney University. The research base on Orpheus Island

is operated by James Cook University, while the Australian Museum controls the one on Lizard Island. In 1972 the federal government established the Australian Institute of Marine Science (AIMS) 50 km south of Townsville. One of the major advances in marine research has been the development of scuba diving equipment and techniques after the Second World War.

Conservation: The development of a comprehensive plan to protect the Great Barrier Reef was long hindered by squabbling between the Queensland and federal governments over the issue of state's rights. This constitutional bunfight lasted for years until more or less settled in 1975 when, under federal legislation, the Great Barrier Reef Marine Park Authority took control of everything below the low tide mark on the mainland and islands for the whole length of the Reef. Until this time, the only parts of the Reef to have any protection under Queensland National Parks legislation were the reefs of Green Island, Heron Island and Wistaria Reef. The first section of national park to be proclaimed was the Capricornia region in 1979.

The catalyst that had raised grave fears for the future of the Reef were plans during the 1960s and early 1970s to drill for oil on the Reef. The Great Barrier Reef Marine Park Act specifically excluded mining (including oil drilling) except for research purposes; however, in 1990 renewed pressure was applied by companies and politicians for oil exploration to commence in areas adjacent to the Marine Park.

In 1982, the Queensland Marine Parks Act established a complementary management scheme to control areas adjacent to the federal areas. Both the federal and state areas of control are administered by the Queensland National Parks and Wildlife Service. A major step to ensure the survival of the Great Barrier Reef was taken on 26 October 1981 when this greatest of Australia's natural wonders was put on the World Heritage List.

REEF LIFE

The inhabitants of the Great Barrier Reef can be lumped largely into creatures to look for and creatures to avoid. Fortunately, the reef nasties are in the minority - they are covered in the following chapter. Here, all sorts of creatures that one part of the world or another regards as food - lobsters, clams, snails, prawns, crabs, turtles and, of course, fish - are seen as part of nature, not just something that arrives on a plate.

However, even a short acquaintance with life and death on the Reef shows that most reef creatures regard most others as something to eat or something that will eat them. It's a glimpse up and down the food chain.

Crustacea: A visitor to the seaside anywhere in the world is likely to see crabs scuttling around the sand and rocks. They and the 30,000 other species in the group called Crustacea are the most populous animal family in the world. True, most of the family are tiny plankton but some are spectacularly visible reef dwellers.

The common family characteristic of Crustacea is that they all have a body consisting of a head, middle and tail, and all come with a protective shell. Otherwise, it's hard to see how creatures as diverse as barnacles and lobsters are related.

The banded coral shrimp is a beautiful, delicate sight - its body is much thinner than commercial prawns and shrimp and it has enormously long white feelers and alternate bands of red and white along its body and nippers.

In many cases, peering under rocks while diving or snorkelling will reveal the face of a timid lobster hidden in the shadows. On the other hand, if you watch a rock pool on the reef flat for a few minutes it will become clear that many of the shells are moving. Closer inspection will reveal that the original inhabitant of the shell has long gone and a hermit crab has taken it over as its home. Other crabs will be seen dashing around the shallows, too.

Sea stars: There is an intellectual neatness to sea stars, with their five radiating arms and

Right, the lionfish looks spectacular but the spines are poisonous.

no real beginning or end, that is very appealing. As some sea stars come in cobalt blue and orange-and-white designer colours, it's hard to miss them in any case.

Their group, echinoderms (meaning "spiny skin"), has several different kinds of members that at first may not seem related. Besides the sea stars with their finger-thickness arms, there are the fragile brittle stars that have very long thin arms more like delicate china than flesh. All sea star have calcareous spines in their flesh and their bodies may hold their form for some considerable time after they die. One notorious member of the family, the crown of thorns starfish is discussed in the following chapter.

or black slug-like forms can be seen in great numbers on many reef flats at low tide. Their skin is much softer than the others in the same group and they are regarded as a delicacy in parts of Asia. The average sea cucumber processes tonnes of sediment through its gut each year.

Shells: The number of molluscs in the reef system is seemingly infinite. Anyone with an interest in shells will delight in seeing what they look like in the wild. The cowries are particularly beautiful, with a wide lip extending well beyond the shell. A highlight of a trip to the Reef is seeing a large nautilus swim past - the marvellous swirled shell contains an animal rather like a squid. The

Feather stars are the most spectacular (and the oldest) type of echinoderms. With feathery arms like fern fronds, they look more like plants than animals. On the other hand, the round, hard sea urchin hardly bears any family resemblance at all, until one examines it closely. Like the other members of the group, sea urchins move around by walking on a mass of tiny tube feet operated by hydraulic pressure.

For such a dowdy creature, sea cucumbers have a remarkable number of aliases. Also known as sea slugs and *bêche de mer*, their collection for food was one of Queensland's earliest export industries. Their large green

nautilus shell also contains gas balance tanks for neutral buoyancy so it need only propel itself forward, not upwards. Surprisingly, the squid and octopus are also molluscs - their shells are completely internal.

The giant clams with bright, individually coloured mantles are most decorative members of the reef population. Matthew Flinders was much taken with them writing that "these cockles did not bury themselves in the sand as their puny English prototypes do."

Fish: The variety and sheer number of fish living on the reef vies with coral as the greatest attraction of a visit to the Great Barrier Reef. There are some 1000 species here, from the relatively plain to the ornately bizarre. A visit to an aquarium or a commercial fish dealer specialising in marine fish. will give you some pale shadow of an idea of what to expect when snorkelling. Also, a look at the price tags will leave you stunned about the value of the innumerable fish filling the coral canyons of every reef.

There are a few reef fish that stand out from the crowd even here. The most maligned are the sharks found all over the reef. One of the most magical encounters a diver can have is meeting a group of manta rays. Manta rays are plankton eaters and harmless to humans. However, coloured grey and white and shaped like a delta winged aircraft

with a wing span of up to 4 metres (13 feet), swimming with these incredibly graceful creatures is a real thrill. If they are feeling very relaxed, they will sometimes allow divers to hitch a ride on their wings.

Turtles: Between October and March, coral cays and other beaches throughout the Reef become breeding grounds for large turtles. These are very important in the world scale - Raine Island near the very top of the outer reef sees more breeding turtles than anywhere else in the world. Thousands of

Left, marine worm (Terebellid) and above, *Loimia medusa*

turtles may crawl up its beach every night during the breeding season. Although access to Raine Island is restricted (there wouldn't be much room between turtles anyway- even they have been known to dig up existing nests to lay their own eggs on this crowded island), other islands do allow tourists to see this primeval performance.

There are seven types of sea turtles and six of these are found in Australia. However, only three of these are common on the Great Barrier Reef. The most often seen is the green turtle that can weigh over 170 kilograms (375 pounds) and have a shell 125 centimetres (4 feet) in length. Unfortunately, green turtles have long been recognised as good to eat and their numbers were decimated on the Reef last century. They are now protected within the marine park.

The loggerhead turtle is also large - its shell can be 110 centimetres (3.5 feet) in length - while the hawksbill turtle is somewhat smaller. The hawksbill turtle favours warmer tropical waters while the loggerhead turtle primarily nests in temperate regions. Sadly, the world's largest turtle, the leatherback, is quite rare and, although widespread, it's an endangered species. Some have been found with shells 170 centimetres (5.5 feet) long. Although they have been known to lay eggs on mainland beaches along the Queensland coast, they mainly breed further south.

Watching female turtles laying eggs reminds one of life's great struggle. From sunset, they arrive to complete the task; often the last return to the water only after sunrise. Each laboriously hauls her vast bulk up the beach slope and into the fringing vegetation. She then uses her flippers to clear a large crater into which she lays 50 or more leathery eggs about the size and appearance of ping pong balls. Now the nest has to be filled in, and as soon as this is completed to her satisfaction, she begins the slow haul back to the water. She will repeat this process several times during the season.

Between January and March turtle hatchlings can be seen on their way across the beach to their first swim. This is a more thrilling sight than the egg laying process. After the sun has set on a moonlit night the sand will suddenly erupt as tiny turtles, still with their soft, fuzzy shells, simultaneously burst out of the nest. Using the reflection of the moon on the water as their beacon, they scamper down the sand and paddle off. However, many predators also know this timetable: many hatchlings never make it to the water and it's estimated that only a few percent reach adulthood.

The Queensland National Parks and Wildlife Service publish a pamphlet on turtle watching, providing guidelines that will ensure watchers won't disturb the cycle. The main points are that flashlights should not be used as the light can disturb a laying turtle or even scare her away. The easiest way to find one is to walk the beach and look for the telltale "tank tracks" where she made her way up the beach. Watchers shouldn't step in front of a laying turtle as the movement may disturb her. Once the turtle has started laying she is not easily baulked and photographs can be taken if you like. However, be aware that other turtles may be coming up the beach, so flash should be used with caution.

Whales and dolphins: It is beyond the scope of this book to detail whale habits. However, the channels of the Great Barrier Reef are used as whale highways and at some times of the year the chances of seeing a pod swim by are high. Dolphins may appear at any time, catching a ride off the bow of a tourist boat or merely putting on an aquatic show alongside. Such heart-warming encounters with marine mammals are common throughout the Great Barrier Reef.

Whale are mammals that returned to the sea at least 50 million years ago. It was a domain they had largely to themselves before man took to hunting them. They fall into two groups - the baleen whales and toothed whales. Baleen whales strain the ocean water through their mouths extracting the plankton or small fish which comprises their diet. Toothed whales actively pursue their prey of larger fish.

The whales one is likely to see in the Great Barrier Reef region are the humpback and minke. The minke whales are sometimes seen here during the winter months, but there is much more likelihood of encountering a humpback whale. In June, humpbacks can be seen heading north, then in early summer they pass the other way returning to Antarctic feeding grounds. A fully grown humpback whale can grow to a length of 15 metres (50 feet) and weigh up to 40 tonnes or more.

Humpback whales were hunted to the edge of extinction until the 1960s, but are now protected in all Australian waters. Seeing one leap out of the water then crash back with a huge splash is a daunting but inspiring sight. This activity (called "sounding") and surfacing to breath with a great exhalation of spray ("blowing") are commonly observed practices. It is most likely that another whale will be sighted alongside: mother and calf are inseperable.

Dugong: The dugong is the world's only marine mammal that lives off plants. These shy animals, like whales, descended from land mammals that returned to the sea.

Seen in the cold light of day it's hard to envisage how these cow-like creatures about three metres long (10 feet) and weighing in at 400 kilograms (1000 pounds) could be the source of persistent mermaid legends, yet it's thought that they were. Mermaids are traditionally half woman, half fish, appearing to sailors and luring them to their doom on hidden reefs. However, a closer examination of dugong behaviour reveals where the stories have sprung from. Being mammals, dugong suckle their young and the mother's nipples are near her flippers. On a moonlit night, the sight of a dugong apparently clasping a baby to its breast could confuse a lovelorn sailor into believing he had seen a mermaid. Still, anything less like Daryl Hannah in *Splash* would be hard to imagine.

Dugong are part of the family *Sirenia*, or sea cows. Of the five known species of sea cows only four survive - the Steller's sea cow, was hunted to extinction last century. The other three survivors are the manatee of the Caribbean, West Africa and Amazon. Dugong populations from Africa through to the Pacific islands have been decimated and likely to become extinct. It's believed that the herds along the Queensland coast number over 10,000, the largest dugong population in the world.

Dugongs are slow breeders, so conservation measures are essential to their survival. They feed on sea grasses and frequently die after being caught in fishing nets. So nets have been banned from the Starcke River north of Cooktown where the largest dugong population is found. Similar measures may have to be introduced in other dugong areas such as Moreton Bay.

Right, jellyfish 'purple stinger'.

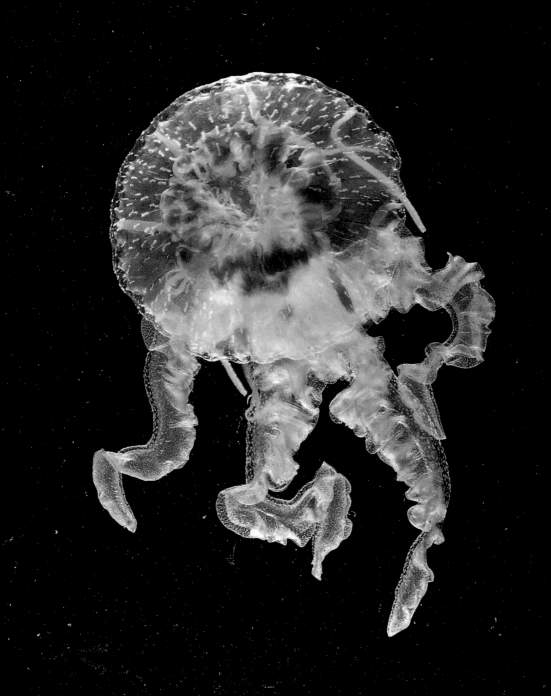

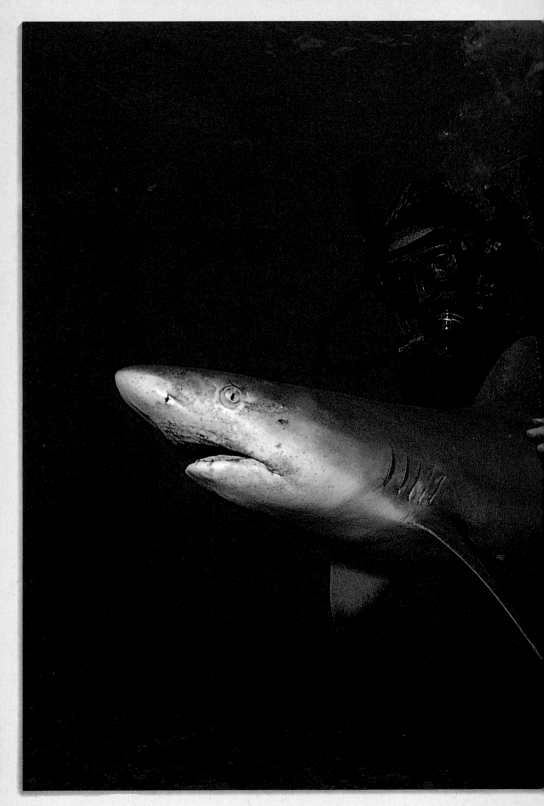

HAZARDS
AND WRECKERS

It must be part of the pioneering psyche of Australians that each of us loves to sit with a visitor to the country and enumerate the ways in which the local wildlife can kill you. As tourism comes of age, this tendency is fading but it's still there. Note that the great Australian box office success of the 1980s was not entitled "Koala (or Kangaroo) Dundee".

There are no animals in Australia that will actively seek you out in order to kill you, but there are a few that might be tempted if you do something foolish. Others may harm you in passing, while the majority can be ignored as non-homicidal. The Great Barrier Reef has a good proportion of all categories.

After reading this chapter, it may well appear that a Great Barrier Reef holiday is fraught with life-threatening hazards. It isn't - but the Reef is an alien environment that needs its dangers pointed out so they can be avoided. Take heart in the fact that hundreds of thousands of visitors come to the region every year without encountering anything more threatening than a crocodile behind a steel-mesh fence.

Sharks: In the Reef's smorgasbord of food, there is little reason for even those rare sharks known to have attacked humans to do so, unless cornered. There is too much to eat to bother tackling anything as big as a person. One diving instructor puts the situation succinctly: "Every student I've ever had professed to be terrified of sharks, but when they saw their first one while diving, every single one has swum over for a closer look. They were fascinated, the sharks were uninterested."

However, as the shark's discrimination is thrown out the window when it senses blood in the water, all bets are off if the person swimming is also spear fishing. Overall, unless you are spear fishing - or do something stupid (one diver's handbook suggests you don't poke at sharks) - the risk of being

Left, who is most surprised?

attacked by a shark on the Great Barrier Reef is minimal. (Note: spearfishing with scuba apparatus is illegal in Queensland.)

The sharks most often seen in the Reef area are the white tip and black tip reef sharks and these are pretty timid. The smaller but more aggressive grey reef whaler is definitely not one to harass. Another type of whaler, the tiger shark, and the hammerhead are two other species to avoid. As sharks are very sensitive to vibrations in the water, splashing furiously in a frenzy to swim away is only likely to attract its attention.

Crocodiles: Of all the islands covered in this book, the only one where crocodiles need be considered a threat is on Hinchin-

that freshies aren't dangerous, except in extraordinary circumstances - and salties are always dangerous. In times of doubt one is unlikely to study the finer points that distinguish one type from the other, so the solution is to avoid swimming anywhere reputed to be a saltwater habitat. Their territory can extend tens of kilometres inland, too.

Since all crocodiles became protected species in Australia their numbers have been increasing. That, coinciding with a rapid growth in tourism is bringing the two groups into more frequent contact. Still, if you follow the advice of local residents and don't swim (or wade) where signs say you shouldn't, you are quite safe.

brook Island, especially on the mainland side. However, the mainland coast north of the Tropic of Capricorn is croc country.

There are two types of crocodiles in Australia: these have long been known as freshwater crocodiles or "freshies," and saltwater crocodiles, "salties". However, in recent years this nomenclature has been considered faulty - visitors have assumed incorrectly that one won't find salties in freshwater streams and have gone swimming where they shouldn't. So more favoured terminology now is Johnstone River crocodiles for freshies and estuarine crocodiles for salties.

The most important point to remember is

Poisons in Paradise

Box jellyfish/sea wasps/stingers: A much more real threat than sharks are the marine stingers known as "box jellyfish" or "sea wasps" that invade tropical coastal waters between October and May. The sting is potentially fatal and always painful.

Box jellyfish are not found far off the coast - they breed in estuaries - but they are a hazard on all mainland beaches north of Rockhampton. They are most commonly found in smooth water and over sandy shores, but the risk can't be overlooked in any conditions. Resorts and beaches that are stinger prone often have stinger-excluding enclosures for the season.

The jelly fish has a small almost transparent body - from about 3 cm to 4.5 cm (1.2 - 1.8 inches) - but it trails tentacles up to 3 metres (10 feet) long. The sting can be avoided by even a thin veneer of clothing, so north Queensland lifesavers used to wear panty hose during the stinger season; these have now been replaced by light, colourful all-covering stinger suits.

The surest way to avoid being stung is to go to a resort island well off the coast, don't come during the stinger season or don't go in the water. Stingers aren't malevolent - in fact they will endeavour to swim out of the way

Blue-ringed octopus: While every other octopus in the world produces ink to hide behind, Australia's small blue-ringed octopus makes a deadly secretion instead. These can be found in rock pools and can look very attractive - especially to children. The effect of its toxin, called tetrodotoxin, is to paralyse muscles; eventually breathing becomes impossible.

In a scenario worthy of an Edgar Allen Poe horror story, the victim of a blue-ringed octopus sting may stay conscious after he or she can no longer breathe. Survivors tell stories of lying immobile as someone conducts mouth-to-mouth breathing, while bystanders advise "Give up. He's obviously dead."

if they sense your presence. However, collisions do occur and it's the most venomous marine animal in the world.

If someone is stung, they will immediately know it. Treatment should be immediate: covering the area stung with liberal doses of vinegar. Wash the area gently with water, but do not rub. A doctor should be called and someone should remain standing by in case mouth to mouth resuscitation or cardiac massage is required.

Left, an estuarine crocodile. **Above**, timely warning.

In fact, continual mouth-to-mouth and speedy medical treatment is remarkably effective in curing a blue-ringed octopus sting. The first thing to do after someone has been stung is to place pressure on the point of entry and immobilise the limb affected - this will slow the spread of the toxin.

Incidently, tetrodotoxin is also present in puffer fish - Captain Cook almost died after eating one. In Japan, the puffer fish is considered a delicacy. It can only be prepared by specially licensed chefs and, even so, several diners die each year.

Stonefish: The bright and beautiful scorpionfish has a near relative, the stonefish, which is both drab *and* deadly. Stonefish are mainly a hazard to reef walkers, as they lie in the reef rubble perfectly camouflaged and, if stepped on, their spines exude a toxin. There are no reported cases of death from a stonefish sting in Australia, although there have been overseas. There is an antivenin available, but the best strategy is to wear shoes while reef walking and step carefully.

The good looking side of the family, the many different scorpionfish also produce a venom in their spines; they too should be approached with care and never handled. The venom, however, is merely very painful to humans, not potentially fatal.

Cone shells: On the Great Barrier Reef,

toxin. Immediately seek medical aid and be ready to administer resuscitation.

Sea snakes: There are some 15 sea snakes in Great Barrier Reef waters. All have a fatal venom but they aren't aggressive. On the other hand, they are very curious, which is almost as bad. They will normally be discouraged if you rise through the water and they will drift away. Even if you are bitten by a sea snake, it's unlikely to inject any venom. So far, there are no reported fatalities from sea snake bites on the Great Barrier Reef.

Coral cut infections: It would be difficult to envisage an environment that has more bumps and sharp edges than a coral reef. One resort has flippantly suggested free accom-

shell collecting is not just anti-social because it deprives others of the chance to see that shell, it's also downright dangerous. Cone shells often have beautiful geometric designs which make them particularly attractive. However, the animal living inside the shell fishes have toxic harpoons it holds in its flesh. Picking one up or putting it in your pocket leaves you wide open to being stabbed. Several people have died from handling cone shells. Like the sting of a blue-ringed octopus, the best immediate treatment for a cone shell sting is to place pressure on the point of entry and immobilise the limb affected - this will slow the spread of the

modation - levying instead an "iodine surcharge" for every scratch its guests receive.

The warm waters of the Reef are alive with micro-organisms, so any cut or scratch is likely to be instantly infected. In fact, recent research has shown that the great majority of infections in coral cuts are from bacteria that resist penicillin, ampicillin and carbenicillin but are sensitive to tetracyclin and erythromycin. But rather than enter into a lengthy course of antibiotics, one is best advised to diligently try not get scratched and to treat even minor abrasions with iodine.

Crown-of-thorns starfish: The crown-of-thorns starfish hasn't got much going for it in the popularity field. It is a glutton that presses its stomach against a piece of coral and eats the coral polyps. To add insult to injury, it will then hide under the coral to avoid its own predators during the day, then return to its feast each night until the entire colony is dead. It leaves behind a white empty patch of dead coral.

If you touch a crown-of-thorns starfish with bare hands, the coating on the sharp spikes gives a sting which subsides to an itch that can last for a week or more. No, this is not a nice creature and, until thirty years ago one could rest assured that it was fortunately rare. When only a few were around, it was easy to ignore its depredations. However, in

reaching the reefs around Bowen by 1988. It became clear that this wasn't just an Australian phenomenon - similar outbreaks had occured throughout the reefs of Asia and the Pacific around the same time.

Surveys between 1985 and 1988 established that about 31 per cent of the Australian reefs examined had been affected. A regional breakdown showed 20 per cent of the southern third of the Reef was affected, 65 per cent of the central section and some 5 per cent of the northern third.

Even after millions of dollars worth of research no-one knows what caused the proliferation of the crown-of-thorns starfish. Further, no economic way to get rid of the pests

the early 1960s the pattern changed. Instead of a few inconspicuous crown-of-thorns starfish, suddenly there were millions on a single reef. As they marched and munched on, they left devastation in their wake.

Green Island was, in 1962, the first part of the reef to see the plague. From there it spread as far as the top of the Whitsundays before apparently dying out. Then it started again in 1970. Again it was at Green Island that it first appeared, to spread southwards,

Left, stonefish are ugly and deadly. **Above**, the crown-of-thorns starfish is a reef destroyer.

has presented itself. Many people have assumed that, somehow, human occupation has caused the plague, and various theories have been put forward. Indications are that it's happened before, but, we don't know how extensive the earlier outbreaks were and whether these latest ones have been exacerbated by our use of the Reef and mainland.

Research continues, but the overwhelming conclusion is that the Reef isn't as stable as we had supposed. In geological terms, it is very young and perhaps, like coral cays that disappear in a cyclone, it could be destroyed by upsetting the balance or an act of nature like a crown-of-thorns starfish plague.

CAPRICORNIA SECTION ISLANDS

The Southern End of the Reef: As one drives north from Melbourne, Sydney or Brisbane there is a feeling of anticipation in approaching the southern tip of the Great Barrier Reef. The first indications are bits of coral among the beach sands. Then, there is no longer surf breaking onto the beaches - the Pacific swells are dissipated against the outer Reef.

Like a point at the bottom of an exclamation mark, Lady Elliot Island stands alone at the southernmost reach of the Great Barrier Reef, separated by 40 km (24 miles) of azure water from Lady Musgrave Island to the northwest. These and the other islands of the **Capricornia and Bunker Groups** are the tops of a series of platform reefs well away from the mainland. While Lady Elliot Island has a resort, Lady Musgrave is restricted to day visitors and campers only.

Straddling the Tropic of Capricorn are the two Reef resorts owned by the P&O company: the near-legendary Heron Island and the newly-developed permanent camp of Wilson Island. Heron also has an important role in developing knowledge about the Reef - it's the site of the University of Queensland's Research Station.

From Lady Elliot Island north past Heron to Great Keppel and Brampton Islands is known as the **Mackay/Capricorn Section**. As the Reef extends so far off shore in this region (up to 300 km/ 180 miles), it covers by far the largest area of any section: some 137,000 sq kilometres (53,000 s miles).

This southern part of the Reef is special. For a start, none of the islands in this section is typified by year-round sweltering heat. In fact, as anyone who visits in winter can attest, on a cloudy July day the wind can have a distinctly chilly bite to it.

The other unusual feature of this area is the number of coral cays. Most of the resorts along the reef are on sunken mountains with fringing reefs but Lady Elliot, Lady Musgrave, Heron and Wilson islands are all true coral cays. (The only other cay resort is Green Island off Cairns.) A pilot could crisscross the lower quarter of this area at tree top level with eyes closed and without fear of running into a mountain. The tallest structures around are the occasional lighthouse and the masts of sailing vessels.

However, anyone closing their eyes while flying here should be charged with criminal disregard and immunity to beauty. All the islands are far enough from the polluting influence of mainland rivers that they stand out as sandy pearls against the backdrop of the emerald sea. In most cases, the island is at one end of a much larger coral lagoon, so in effect, the appearance is of a small pearl in a jade teardrop. The English language is bereft of words to cover all the shades of green, blue and turquoise which sparkle here.

A major advantage of the southern end of the Reef is its proximity to the rest of Australia. Driving from Sydney to Bundaberg, for example, is a feasible holiday project, not a major expedition - as the road trip to Cairns is. Thus, for those who drive, the saving on mainland airfares may bring the cost of an island holiday within reach.

The continental islands of Great Keppel and Brampton are hilly and beautiful with walking trails through forests to tranquil sandy bays. Their resorts are among the best known on the coast. The southern cays have long lured visitors whose interests lie more beneath the waves than around a pool, nightclub or bars.

From October until March the cays offer an extra bonus - nightly visitations of giant female sea turtles that lay their eggs well above the high tide line. If their chosen site is near your tent or, worse, the sand under your cabin this is like being advanced upon by a tank corps.

LADY ELLIOT ISLAND

A stroll along the coral sand beach that fringes **Lady Elliot Island** leads past numerous wrecked vessels. Part of the decor in the main resort complex is part of *Apollo I* - the famous Australian ocean racing yacht which ended its days on the island's coral teeth in 1980. The bar too is formed from a section of another wrecked vessel. No, Lady Elliot isn't a good place to visit by boat.

Fortunately, at 54 hectares (133 acres) Lady Elliot Island is the largest of the Reef's cay resort islands and the only one to have an airstrip - so, access is remarkably easy. The 80 km (50 mile) flight from Bundaberg takes about 35 minutes. In the moments before touch-down, the plane swoops low over the reef, just above the heads of guests wading in the coral lagoon. Right from the start visitors are aware that this is to be a marine experience. The coral that makes Lady Elliot a shipping hazard

Left, a diver prepares for the plunge.

also provides what is arguably the Reef's best island-based snorkelling and diving experience.

Until the early 1980's Lady Elliot was a basic camping resort. When it was expanded with the addition of simple motel-style units, stringent guidelines for the new resort were set down by the marine parks authority. For example, the maximum number of people on the island is 100; and no amplified music is permitted because it could disturb nesting - thus, the evening's entertainment is more directed towards a few quiet drinks or a slide show about the manta rays or turtles, who are local residents.

Anyone seeking a glittering, glamorous resort experience would find Lady Elliot deeply disappointing. On the other hand, for a very informal, relaxed holiday surrounded by underwater marvels, Lady Elliot vies with Heron Island for the title of the best destination on the Reef.

Lady Elliot has a distinct advantage over Heron - it has several beach dives. Rather than load all the requisite scuba paraphernalia onto a boat, chug offshore and backflip into the water, you merely put your gear into a little handcart, haul it to the western side of the island and then walk into wonderland. (This benefit only applies to divers - snorkellers or those in glass bottomed boats will find little difference in water access between the two islands.)

Since it was first sighted and named by Captain Abbott of the *Lady Elliot* en route from India to Sydney in 1816, the island has had a chequered history. The exploitation of its prolific *bêche de mer* (sea slug/sea cucumber) population in the 1830s to supply the Asian markets was one of Queensland's earliest export industries. The natural vegetation of the island was stripped to provide cooking fires for the harvest. Then, between 1863 and 1873 Lady Elliot Island was mined for guano, and the height of the already low-profile island decreased by about a metre. To complete the devastation, goats were left on the island to provide food for shipwrecked mariners - they quickly devoured any new vegetation that arose.

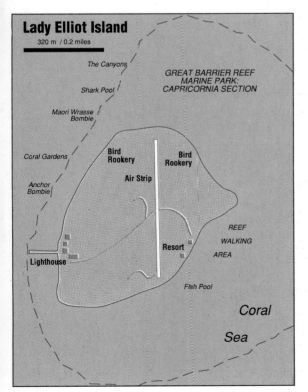

Lady Elliot Island

320 m / 0.2 miles

- The Canyons
- Shark Pool
- Maori Wrasse Bombie
- Coral Gardens
- Anchor Bombie
- Lighthouse
- Bird Rookery
- Bird Rookery
- Air Strip
- Resort
- Fish Pool
- REEF WALKING AREA

GREAT BARRIER REEF MARINE PARK: CAPRICORNIA SECTION

Coral Sea

The first lighthouse was built in 1873 and was replaced by the current one in 1928 (the principal lease over the island is still held by the federal Department of Transport that administers the lighthouse). Had the lights not been installed, one can only imagine the amount of wreckage which would have by now cluttered Lady Elliot's beach!

Entrepreneur and conservationist Don Adams was the salvation of Lady Elliot: he obtained a sub-lease for a small resort in 1969 and replanted the trees and shrubs on the island today. The most notable of his reafforestation projects is the impressive stand of she-oaks around the resort side of the island. (The last goats had been removed about a decade before he arrived.) Adams also constructed the runway which traverses the full length of the island.

Visiting Lady Elliot Island today, it is impossible to detect the effects of the earlier depredations. Indeed, if you wish to avoid others, the island's size, population limitation and relatively dense vegetation combine to make it the best of the Reef's resort cays. Some inhabitants can't be ignored, however. As the bush made a comeback so too did the birdlife. The rookeries of Lady Elliot are growing each year and becoming increasingly important. Although the main nesting time is between October and March, there are many birds on the island year round. As always, if the bird colony falls silent upon your approach or starts shrieking or divebombing you, you are disturbing it and should retreat immediately.

A listing of Lady Elliot's features - no television, phones, or newspapers, few day visitors, no disco or pool, and tents or simple rooms instead of lavish suites - suggests a spartan and unappealing holiday. The reverse is true: it's the perfect place for anyone seeking a relaxed getaway. This is the Reef without hype, and the end result is rather like the ultimate old-fashioned seaside holiday. All meals are provided in the tariff and the food is good and plentiful (an essential when hungry divers are present). Instead of the competition of a singles

Lady Elliot Island is a mere strip on the horizon but (right) it's littered with shipwrecks.

dance floor, evenings tend to be spent in amiable conversations in the bar.

There are 24 rooms in several long buildings scattered along the beach, 18 of which have private showers and toilets. The others share communal facilities with the 10 tents that can each accommodate four people in bunk beds.

The island's surrounding waters can fill every daylight hour. The expansive shallow lagoon in front of the resort on the eastern side is great for reef walking. Take the time to observe the infinite variety of life from tiny anenomes to bright blue starfish and the surprisingly beautiful colours of the lips of each clam. Staff regularly lead reef walks to point out the features. Or, you can take bread out to the fish pool just offshore and hand feed some tame fish there.

The next stage is to don snorkel and flippers and explore the western side of the island. The water is generally very clear with visibility of about 25 metres (80 ft). Snorkelling is best at the **Coral Gardens** where the profusion of coral and the fish life it supports are only a few metres below the surface. However, the way to make the most of Lady Elliot's features is to scuba dive. Those who don't arrive with scuba certificates can complete a five day course on the island. There are enough dive sites to fill a week or more of solid diving and most are sufficiently shallow to allow several dives each day. It is an excellent place to learn to dive, as it avoids the boredom of initial pool dives and the anxiety of boat dives. Instead, there is a channel off the beach near the lighthouse that leads to the **Lighthouse Bommie**. As one student diver put it, "At Lady Elliot there was no time to be nervous - there was too much to explore and experience. The first day was coming to terms with encountering thousands of fish face to face, the next day we met the island's resident turtle and on the next we swam through a group of giant manta rays. On the only day when we had too much theory to allow time for diving we were halfway through a lesson when a pod of humpback whales swam past on their way south."

LADY MUSGRAVE ISLAND

For many tourists, **Lady Musgrave Island** is their first view of a real coral island. There is no resort here - in fact, the sum total of tourist facilities is two very basic toilets - but, several days each week there are relatively cheap day trips to the island by boat from Bundaberg. The catamaran *Lady Musgrave* departs Bundaberg at 7.30 am and Burnett Heads at 8.45 am, taking about 2.25 hours; she returns to the mainland at about 5.45 pm.

Lady Musgrave is a very popular for several reasons. It attracts yachties because of its good anchorage in the middle of its lagoon, and there's good access through a channel cut across the reef by Japanese fishermen earlier this century. And, this is the first chance those sailing north have of staying at an uninhabited coral island. Camping is allowed on the island - the *Lady Musgrave* will bring over your food, fuel and water supplies (like most coral cays, Lady Musgrave has no reliable water supplies) and will pick you up when you're ready to leave.

There is a maximum of 50 campers permitted on the island at one time - after all, it's less than half a kilometre across. This is one of the few islands where portable generators and (more importantly for divers) compressors are allowed, so it also attracts groups of divers drawn here by the excellent coral and fish life of the reef. The day trippers also have the opportunity to dive, snorkel, wade, or cruise the waters of the island in a glass bottomed boat moored to a permanent pontoon in the lagoon. Lady Musgrave Barrier Reef Cruises also operate a seven-seater Canadian Beaver float plane to the island. And for Brisbane or Gold Coast visitors who only have one day to see "The Reef", there are return flights to Lady Musgrave Island available through Seair Pacific.

Like Lady Elliot to the south, late last century Lady Musgrave suffered the twin indignities of guano mining and then being populated by goats to provide meals for the shipwrecked. However, the sailors' appetites must have been poor because by 1928 Lady Musgrave Island was low on vegetation but waist deep in goats. Fortunately, after the goats were removed the vegetation returned, although it is not as dense as on other islands in the Bunker and Capricornia group. Still, shade is provided by the pisonia and casuarina trees of the island.

There is a certain uniformity to coral cays - all were formed the same way, all are very low and don't have much by way of green grass or shade trees, but do come with hectares of lagoon and surrounding reefs. All have great appeal as a venue to experience island life at its most basic. Lady Musgrave takes that one step further than its neighbours Heron or Lady Elliot by requiring all those staying on the island to camp. The juxtaposition of a simple camping holiday on land only metres away from a complexity of marine life that defies the imagination is infinitely appealing.

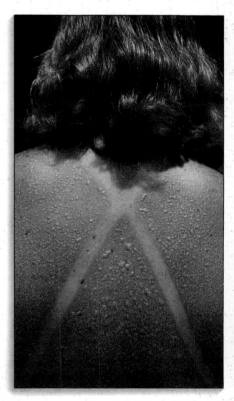

Left, exploring Lady Musgrave's best scenery. Right, you should snorkel wearing a T-shirt.

HERON ISLAND

A tiny islet of a mere 16 hectares (40 acres) set in a massive lagoon of over 3700 hectares (9100 acres), **Heron Island** is - as its advertisements declare - "just a drop in the ocean". However, its remarkable setting and diving have given Heron Island a reputation out of all proportion to its size. During a prolonged airline dispute in 1989, when occupancy rates plummetted all along the Queensland coast, Heron Island stayed relatively busy: people will overcome almost any obstacle to come here.

Never was an island more aptly named. If Alfred Hitchcock's movie "The Birds" gave you the chills, avoid Heron Island during the Christmas period. At this time thousands of sea birds such as black noddies, mutton birds and wedge-tailed shearwaters set up nesting colonies. Words won't describe the sight of every tree weighed down by hundreds of birds, and island paths crowded with stumbling mutton birds. And, although the nightlife of Heron Island is meant to be relatively tame, no-one has told the birds this. Their squabbles and far-from-discreet courting rituals can be ignored only through closed windows. This avian proliferation must be to a bird watcher as a smorgasbord is to a glutton.

In some ways Heron Island encapsulates the Great Barrier Reef. It's certainly part of the Reef. But more than that, through the work of the marine research station established on the island in 1950 by the Great Barrier Reef Committee and run today by the University of Queensland, much of our knowledge of the total Reef system comes from Heron Island-based data.

Heron Island was named by Joseph Jukes, a geologist on board HMS *Fly*, which anchored off the island on January 12, 1843. The island was left to the birds until 1923 when it became the site

Left, Heron Island's pool overlooks the larger one of its giant lagoon.

of a turtle soup factory owned, aptly enough, by the Australian Turtle Company. However, by the late 'twenties the company had so depleted its namesake that it had to scour nearby islands to keep operating. The enterprise foundered in 1932 when the Depression reduced the world's tastes for luxuries like turtle soup.

In that year, Captain Christian Poulson took a lease on the island for a resort. Oddly enough, the lease listed the area of the island as '140 acres' (56 ha) - almost 100 acres (40 ha) greater than its actual size. This error was only corrected when the research station was established in 1950. Captain Poulson was drowned off the island in 1947, but his family remained connected with the island until 1977. P&O became the sole owner-operators in 1980.

Heron Island today is a finely balanced compromise between an international resort island and a spectacular natural environment. The rooms are well appointed, yet not luxurious; there is a main swimming pool, but it isn't huge; there are floodlit tennis courts, but signs by every light switch stress the need to turn lights off so that turtle hatchlings won't become disorientated. Overall, the balance works well.

Access to the island is from Gladstone, 80 km (50 miles) to the south west. The catamaran *Reef Adventurer II* travels to the island twice daily, dropping day visitors at nearby Wistaria Reef on the way through. No day visitors are permitted on Heron Island.

The alternative to the two hour boat ride is a 35 minute helicopter flight. Although much more expensive, the flight provides an excellent vista of the island and its lagoon. If a compromise is required between panorama and pocket, the flight back to Gladstone is better value than the trip out because on the return journey the chopper normally circles the island while it gains height.

The resort can sometimes feel crowded. It houses up to 300 guests in the handful of large Point Suites, 41 Heron Suites along the beach, 32 mid-priced Reef Suites and the much cheaper Lodge units with bunk beds and

share facilities.

It's an old cliche that life in the tropics runs by a different clock, and at Heron Island it's the truth - the resort runs on its own time, one hour ahead of the mainland. This may make sense to maximise daylight useage, but it's certainly confusing when the research station, the Marine Parks authorities and the radio in your room all run on mainland time.

Rooms are comfortably appointed with refrigerator, radios, and ceiling fans. The rooms have no telephones but there are public phones by the office. Telex and fax machines are available to those who can't ignore the rest of the world. Newspapers arrive daily.

As one would expect with meals included in the tariff, breakfast and lunch is served buffet-style. However, the evening meal is a la carte most nights - the pattern is broken by seafood buffet nights. Fishing is available offshore and the chef will cook the catch for any lucky anglers.

Only the most enthusiastic fisherper-

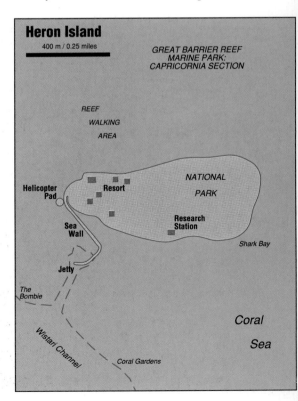

Heron Island

400 m / 0.25 miles

GREAT BARRIER REEF MARINE PARK: CAPRICORNIA SECTION

REEF WALKING AREA

Helicopter Pad

Resort

NATIONAL PARK

Sea Wall

Research Station

Shark Bay

Jetty

The Bombie

Wistari Channel

Coral Gardens

Coral Sea

son could long stay enthusiastic about the challenge of fishing on Heron Island. It offers about as much sport as firing a shotgun into a barrel of fish. Some of the coral canyons here need traffic lights, as schools of blue fish cross paths with yellow and purple ones while other speed-hogs disappear overhead in a flash of silver. After a day snorkelling among these iridescent crowds, or merely observing them through the underwater windows of the so-called "Yellow Submarine", they still taste good - but the act of hunting them down seems bad form.

In an effort to make the Reef more accessible, there was pressure by the marine park for Heron Island to be opened to day trippers. However, the management felt this was inappropriate for a resort which most guests regarded as a very special personal experience. There is such an "all in together" feeling here that the rooms don't have locks. That mood would be shattered by the introduction of daily passers-by. Instead, P&O developed **Wistaria Reef**

Heron Island, a sea-dream pearl in a blue oyster.

across the channel for day visitors. There is a large well-shaded permanent pontoon moored here and, after being dropped off by the *Reef Adventurer II* on its way through to Heron Island, this is the day-visitors' base for snorkelling, diving and glass-bottomed boat trips. Morning and afternoon tea is served on the boat and lunch is a smorgasbord or barbecue on the pontoon.

Heron Island guests have their own diving and snorkelling sites around the island. The best known is the famous **Heron Bommie** to the north of the island's Reef channel. This giant coral head is crowded with fish life, all well used to being hand fed. However, there are more than a dozen other sites with other features such as extensive displays of gorgonia or staghorn coral, resident turtles or moray eels. These are only a few minutes by boat from the resort. Visibility ranges from about 10 to 20 metres (32 to 34 ft) and water temperature is a balmy 17°C (64°F) in winter to a positively warm 23°C (73°F) in summer.

WILSON ISLAND

Wilson Island was made for living out a tropical island fantasy. This very small coral isle, less than an hour by boat from Heron Island, is everyone's image of the desert island which awaits the shipwrecked mariner. It would certainly be a tiny private kingdom for such a Robinson Crusoe - one can walk slowly right around the edge of the island in less than 15 minutes.

Wilson Island has long been available as a day trip for guests from Heron Island who want to snorkel its crystal waters. However, P&O Resorts (who also operate Heron Island) have set up eight tents, scattered around the island, so that a few guests - never more than 15 - can stay overnight.

As more and more of Queensland's islands are burdened by brick work and boutiques, Wilson is an island where the emphasis is on the Reef, not the facilities. Accommodation is in basic-but-comfortable permanent tents, that the P&O brochure describes as "canvas bungalows". Regardless of nomenclature, these are walk-in, two bed dwellings with a wooden floor extending out to a verandah overlooking the beach and reef. Of necessity, there isn't much on Wilson Island that doesn't overlook the beach!

The only other two structures on Wilson Island are a roofed sand floor dining area and a small block containing the hot showers, toilets and the storage/refrigerator room. From the sea, there is no sign that anyone has ever set foot on the island.

Prospective Robinson Crusoes don't have to look for the footprints in the sand. Man Friday's role is admirably fulfilled by the Heron Island staff member who pilots the boat over to Wilson Island, cooks the meals, and takes guests out in the glass-bottomed boat when required. But this is no resort Activities Organiser - the staff realise that anyone coming here wants the island to themselves, so they stay very **Turtle makes tracks.**

210

much in the background.

Surprisingly, the nightlife on Wilson Island can be exhausting. The island is an important bird rookery with thousands of birds in attendance at times of the year. Unsuspecting guests may spend a few nights learning that the moaning, grunts and squeals of mating mutton birds only stop at dawn. If the noctural activities of the flying squads go unnoticed, the tank corps can't be ignored. Between October and March, loggerhead and green turtles lumber up the beach to lay their eggs. Between the moans of mutton birds and the gasps of tired turtles, the Wilson Island soundtrack can seem more blue movie than Blue Lagoon movie.

In the first months of the year, when Wilson Island is the site of the southernmost large breeding ground for Roseate Terns, the island may be closed briefly to ensure they aren't disturbed. Otherwise Wilson Island is an all-year delightful destination.

There are three ways to plan a holiday on Wilson Island. The cheapest is to find a friend and book a canvas bungalow - the tariff includes all meals, glass bottomed boat, snorkelling and surf skis. The most riotous would be to find another fourteen people and book the whole island. Most romantic would be to book out the whole island - for yourself and one very good friend. The cost of doing this is negotiable - it depends on demand - and, it would certainly be a unique experience.

In all cases, access to Wilson Island is through Heron Island. Normally, the trip from Heron Island to Wilson is by boat, but a helicopter transfer can be arranged.

The first time this tiny atoll appeared on a map was during the survey by Captain F. P. Blackwood of *HMS Fly* in 1845. However, it was named later, and no-one can remember who Wilson was. Captain Blackwood spent three years of his life charting the Barrier Reef. Most people would settle for a week on Wilson Island: it's the closest thing Australia has to a desert island with butler service.

Wilson Island's tent quarters.

GREAT KEPPEL ISLAND

The promotional slogan is "Get wrecked on Great Keppel Island," and the island does its best to live up to the image. This is party paradise where even the noisiest natural peregrinations would go unnoticed between the output from the band in the Wreck Bar and the general revelry elsewhere.

Still, there is another side to **Great Keppel**, the first big resort north of the Tropic of Capricorn. It exudes a casual friendliness that can't be ignored. Even a hermit would turn bon vivant in this atmosphere. It's significant that, of all the resorts along the coast, this is the one that all ex-staff want to return to - and rue the day they moved on.

The first view of Great Keppel is a surprise - after all the build-up you rather expect one giant bar and dance hall. Instead you find the resort occupies a small corner of a big island of 1454 hectares (3590 acres). The other

Left, back from the depths.

surprise is that there are two resorts on the island - the predominant one owned and operated by Australian Resorts, a division of Australian Airlines, and another much smaller camping ground called Wapparaburra Haven alongside it, with a 50 bed Youth Hostel attached.

"Wapparaburra" was the Aboriginal name for this hilly island which lies about 20 km (12.5 miles) from the mainland, due east of Rockhampton - the name apparently means "resting place". It was named by Captain Cook in honour of Admiral Augustus Keppel (who become First Lord of the Admiralty in 1782, 12 years after Cook charted and named the island), and is known as "Great Keppel" to distinguish it from the much smaller North Keppel Island. There is also a nearby Keppel Bay on the mainland.

Matthew Flinders charted the island in 1803, but the first white man to land was Mr McGillivray, a naturalist off *The Rattlesnake* who arrived in 1847. He noted the presence of several Aboriginal women and children. Serious settlement and farming was attempted in 1880s, and by 1903 the Aborigines had been driven off.

The homestead of the Leeke family, who grazed sheep on the island from the 1920s to the 1940s, still stands near the middle of the island. It is now mainly visited by resort guests coming to its stables to commence horse riding excursions. Looking out over Leekes Beach from the verandah of the old homestead, the resort might well not exist and the events of the past 40 years forgotten. However, the gauntlet of the resident peacocks and territorial geese - neither being native to these parts - soon brings one back to reality.

The first resort on the island opened in 1967, and in 1975 was purchased by Australian Airlines. Like other Australian Airlines' resorts, meals are included in the tariff and most activities are free. Naturally enough, considering the young and energetic clientele, there is a wide smorgasbord of activities including archery, badminton, basketball, catamaran sailing, cricket, fishing, golf, netball, paddle skiing, sailboarding,

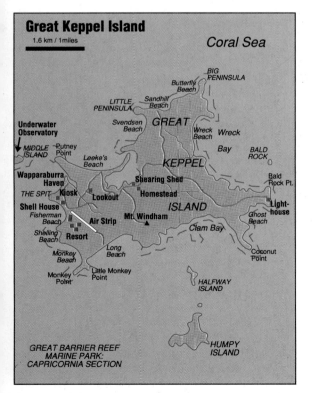

Great Keppel Island

1.6 km / 1 miles

Coral Sea

BIG PENINSULA
Butterfly Beach
Sandhill Beach
LITTLE PENINSULA
Svendsen Beach
GREAT
Wreck Beach
Wreck Bay
BALD ROCK
Underwater Observatory
MIDDLE ISLAND
Putney Point
Leeke's Beach
KEPPEL
Wapparaburra Haven
Shearing Shed
Bald Rock Pt.
THE SPIT
Kiosk
Lookout
Homestead
ISLAND
Shell House
Fisherman Beach
Air Strip
Mt. Windham
Ghost Beach
Light-house
Shelling Beach
Resort
Clam Bay
Monkey Beach
Long Beach
Coconut Point
Monkey Point
Little Monkey Point
HALFWAY ISLAND
HUMPY ISLAND
GREAT BARRIER REEF MARINE PARK: CAPRICORNIA SECTION

snorkelling, soccer, squash, tennis, and volleyball. There is also a daily free cruise around the island with an optional visit to the underwater observatory on nearby **Middle Island**. The activities which cost extra are the glass-bottomed boats, dinghies with outboards, horse riding, para-sailing, off-shore snorkelling trips, water toboganning, water skiing, scuba diving and day cruises to the outer Barrier Reef.

These days the promotional emphasis is very much on Great Keppel's 17 beaches with their total of 28 kilometres (17.3 miles) of pristine white sand. Indeed, the island's beaches are among the very best on the Queensland coast.

It would be possible to have a lazy holiday by the pool at Great Keppel, but you'd have to avoid studiously the frenetic energy around you. The mostly-young staff must have great stamina: they are normally among the last to leave the Wreck Bar in the early hours, yet they are alert and bright eyed the next morning when the first bleary guests stumble in for breakfast. Fortu-

nately, when the raging pace becomes too much there are long bushwalks and deserted beaches to explore. The walk to the lighthouse at the opposite end of the island takes about 2.5 hours one way, while climbing to the top of **Mt Wyndham**, Great Keppel's highest peak, takes about 1.5 hours. Great Keppel also provides the chance for one of the great equine experiences - galloping a horse along the water's edge of a wide sandy beach.

Various boats leave daily from Rosslyn Bay on the mainland for Great Keppel Island. The other option is to fly in from Rockhampton - the airstrip is almost within the resort itself! The flight and voyage times are similar: about 20 minutes. There are numerous day trippers on the island each day but, like the guests of the campground and hostel, their access to many of the resort areas is limited.

The **Wapparaburra Haven** camping resort is made up of 36 permanent tents, 12 cabins and 55 tent sites. The cabins have their own cooking facili-

Beachfront units at Great Keppel Island.

ties; the others use communal ones, and all use communal toilets and showers. There is a store and restaurant within the camp grounds.

Three types of accommodation are available for the main resort's 400 guests. These are the Beachfront Units, the cheaper Garden Units and the new, very modern Ocean View Units up on the hill overlooking the beach and airstrip. All rooms have private bathrooms, refigerator, tea and coffee making facilities, ceiling fans and radios. Each block has a free guest laundry. There are no telephones in the rooms, but there are public phones within the resort. In 1990, the large main block opened with bigger space for restaurant patrons and evening entertainment.

Children are welcome and there is free child minding each evening after the special children's meal time, so that parents may have dinner in peace. At other times there is a charge for baby sitting. During school holidays there is a special roster of activities for the Keppel Kids Cub.

Adults are equally well organised. As guests arrive they are given an A-Z Guide to Great Keppel and each morning the **Daily Wrecker** sets out the organised activities of the day. These are written in terminally cute phraseology that refers to the Wreckreation Office, Kaptain Cook, the Kafe, Klicker the photographer and the Keppel Korral. However, once the crimes against the English language are overlooked, there is a wealth of information which helps greatly in planning the day.

Although the advertising and resort orientation suggests that no-one except those between the ages of 16 and 29 will be allowed on the island (or, if they are, may feel out of place) the truth is that it attracts a wide range of age groups all seeking an active tropical holiday. The age disparity is much greater outside school and university holidays. The secret of Great Keppel's success is that although not everyone will fit in with all activities, no-one will feel left out of what is certainly the Barrier Reef's most exhausting resort.

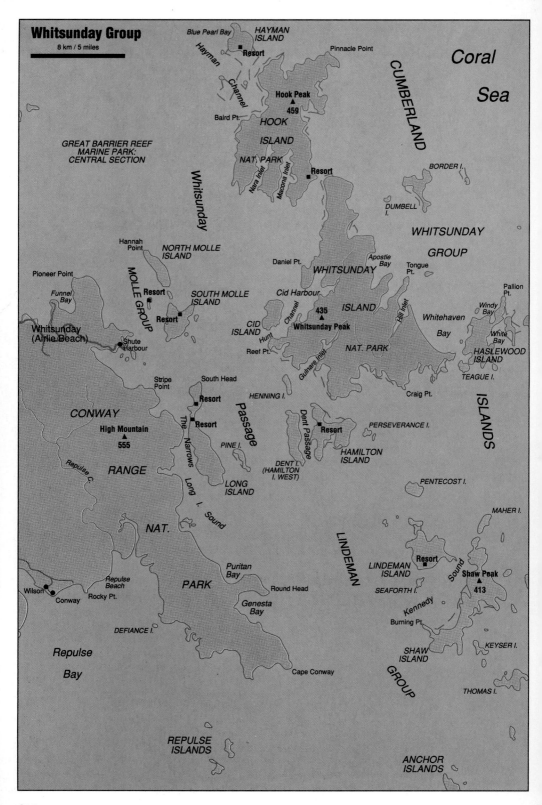

Whitsunday Group

8 km / 5 miles

Blue Pearl Bay

HAYMAN ISLAND

Hayman

Resort

Channel

Pinnacle Point

Coral

Sea

CUMBERLAND

Hook Peak
459

Baird Pt.

HOOK ISLAND

NAT. PARK

Nara Inlet

Macona Inlet

Resort

BORDER I.

DUMBELL I.

GREAT BARRIER REEF MARINE PARK: CENTRAL SECTION

Whitsunday

WHITSUNDAY

GROUP

Hannah Point

NORTH MOLLE ISLAND

Daniel Pt.

Apostle Bay

Tongue Pt.

Pallion Pt.

Pioneer Point

MOLLE GROUP

Resort

SOUTH MOLLE ISLAND

Cid Harbour

WHITSUNDAY

Windy Bay

Funnel Bay

Resort

CID ISLAND

Channel

435
Whitsunday Peak

ISLAND

Hill Inlet

Whitehaven Bay

White Bay

Whitsunday (Airlie Beach)

Shute Harbour

Hunt

Reef Pt.

Gulnare Inlet

NAT. PARK

HASLEWOOD ISLAND

TEAGUE I.

Stripe Point

South Head

Resort

HENNING I.

Craig Pt.

ISLANDS

CONWAY

The Narrows

Passage

Resort

Dent Passage

Resort

PERSEVERANCE I.

High Mountain
555

PINE I.

HAMILTON ISLAND

RANGE

Repulse C.

Long I. Sound

LONG ISLAND

DENT I. (HAMILTON I. WEST)

PENTECOST I.

MAHER I.

NAT.

LINDEMAN

Resort

Puritan Bay

Round Head

LINDEMAN ISLAND

Shaw Peak
413

Wilson

Repulse Beach

Conway

Rocky Pt.

PARK

Genesta Bay

SEAFORTH I.

Sound

Kennedy

KEYSER I.

Repulse Bay

DEFIANCE I.

Cape Conway

Burning Pt.

SHAW ISLAND

GROUP

THOMAS I.

REPULSE ISLANDS

ANCHOR ISLANDS

CENTRAL SECTION ISLANDS

The islands of the Central Section of the Great Barrier Reef Marine Park extend from Lindeman in the Whitsunday group to Dunk in the north, and cover an area of 77,000 square kilometres (30,000 square miles).

Dominating this group are the 74 continental islands of the **Whitsunday Group**. Located just north of Mackay, within the larger cluster of the Cumberland Islands, the Whitsundays were named by James Cook as he threaded his way north on the feast of Whit Sunday on June 3, 1770. Cook named the shipping course between the mainland and the principal islands "Whitsunday Passage", and the adjacent islands, the Cumberland Group after the Duke of Cumberland. However, usage has changed and now all the islands are lumped together as "the Whitsunday Islands" or simply "the Whitsundays".

Prior to European contact, Nagro Aborigines, arriving from the mainland in canoes frequently sought food here. Today, many of the Whitsundays, now National Parks, are still much as the Nagro (if they still existed) might remember them, while other privately owned ones are unrecognisably altered - waxed to golf course glossiness and studded by hotel towers.

Recent movements upmarket in resort development have seen once-sleepy resorts like Brampton, Hayman, Lindeman, Bedarra and Dunk islands tarted up with mega-dollar surgery. The results are often excellent: 'The Xanadu of Australian resorts, Hayman Island,' said the *Bulletin* magazine, 'is a short-list candidate for the world's finest island hideaway.' Predictably, the private resort islands do not allow camping.

There are also more modest accomodation options which vary from mid-range resorts to modest cabins to National Park camp sites. These include South Molle, Long, Whitsunday, Hook, Newry and the beautiful Hinchinbrook, which generally do allow camping. Each one has its own identity, from whispering she-oaks to heavy hormones. Most resorts target particular market cohorts (the dreaded 'demographics'): couples, singles, families, convention groups, etc. Some are crowded, disco-driven enclaves; others somnolent places where you just sit and watch the sun tan, the day glow.

If you're visiting from the mainland, attitudes to day-visitors range from encouragement to 'not permitted', so check before departure. While camping is permitted on 19 of the Whitsunday islands, many do not have water, and all require camping permits. For further details, contact the Airlie Beach National Parks and Wildlife Service office. Tel: (079) 46 9430.

Mackay, Proserpine, Shute Harbour, Airlie Beach are the mainland conduits to the busy Whitsunday islands. A web of transport routes connects the Whitsundays to the mainland. Summarised, they are: Flights to Hamilton Island - from Sydney, Melbourne, Brisbane, Gold Coast, Mackay, Townsville, Cairns, Mt. Isa and Ayers Rock. Launch connections from Hamilton - to Shute Harbour, Hayman, Daydream, Lindeman and South Molle islands. Flights to Proserpine - from Brisbane and Mackay. Helicopter connections from Proserpine - to Daydream, Long, South Molle and Hamilton islands. More information is available from the Whitsunday Tourism Association, PO Box 83, Airlie Beach, QLD 4802. Tel: (079) 466 673. Fax: (079) 467 387

These islands are visitable year-round, though April to October is the optimum time. Day temperatures then are 20-24°C (68-75.2°F) and nights 14-18°C (57.2-64.4°F); the water temp. is always 20-22°C (68-71.6°F).

One Cumberland Group hideaway, **Newry Island** (a National Park) is not actually part of the Whitsundays. Little-publicised, it offers rainforest, good beaches, a small number of family cabins, and night-life of starlight and crickets' songs. Another, **Wild Duck Island** (south of Mackay), has received a $160 million infusion which will transform it from a low-key retreat to a 150-room international resort.

BRAMPTON ISLAND

This hilly, beach strewn island can well claim to be one of the most beautiful in Queensland. **Brampton Island** is another Australian Airlines' resort and, like its siblings, has an airstrip running right past the resort. This provides a spectacular vista for new arrivals - just before the aircraft lands it flashes over the windsurfers and catamarans on the waters in front of the resort.

Brampton Island perhaps sells itself short, relying largely on soft-focus advertising images of a well-dressed couple walking hand in hand along a deserted beach at sunset. Brampton presents itself primarily as a honeymoon destination - and only slowly are people discovering there's a lot more to do here than take sunset strolls.

Brampton lies off the coast, about 35 kilometres (22 miles) north east of Mackay and slightly south of the Whitsunday Islands. It is separated from Carlisle Island by a narrow channel that runs alongside Brampton's airstrip. Both islands are part of the 70-island **Cumberland Group**, so named by Captain Cook in 1770 after the Duke of Cumberland, King George III's brother.

The islands were then largely ignored by white Australia for the next century. In 1879 the Cumberland Group islands were surveyed and named after places in England's Lakes District which these flooded continental peaks were said to resemble. The Queensland coast was a hazardous place for early mariners, so the government had a policy of stocking islands with plants and animals that could provide food for shipwrecked sailors. In the late nineteenth century Brampton Island was the site of a government coconut palm plantation to supply these stocks. The original nuts were brought from Indonesia, and many of the coconut trees seen today along the coast came from Brampton ancestors.

The Busuttin family who first settled on St Bees Island to the south of Brampton early this century later obtained the pastoral lease to Brampton. The first paying guests of the Busuttins came to Brampton Island in December 1933. **Carlisle Island** and Brampton Island in 1936 and 1939 respectively were declared national parks. Today most of these islands are under the care of the Queensland National Parks and Wildlife Service and rough camping (with permits) is allowed on Carlisle Island. In 1962 Roylen Cruises bought Brampton Island Resort. Australian Airlines purchased it in May 1985 and have since virtually rebuilt it.

Both Brampton and Carlisle islands are rugged and covered by vegetation, including patches of dense rainforest. Besides the northern section of Brampton where the resort is located, there isn't much flat land and even the numerous sandy beaches are separated by rocky headlands. Carlisle Island has the only mountain - **Skiddaw Peak** (389 metres/1265 feet) - but Brampton rises to **Brampton Peak** (219 metres/712 feet). There is a 2 km (1.25 mile) walking track to Brampton Peak that is about

Left, the Carlisle Room restaurant.

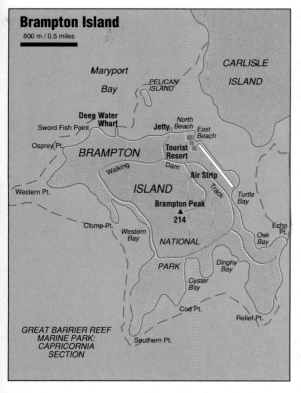

Brampton Island

800 m / 0.5 miles

Maryport Bay

CARLISLE ISLAND

PELICAN ISLAND

Deep Water Wharf

Sword Fish Point

Jetty North Beach
East Beach

Osprey Pt.

BRAMPTON

Tourist Resort

Walking

Dam

Air Strip

Western Pt.

ISLAND

Track

Turtle Bay

Brampton Peak
▲ 214

Clump Pt.

Western Bay

NATIONAL

Oak Bay

Echo Pt.

PARK

Dinghy Bay

Oyster Bay

Cod Pt.

Relief Pt.

GREAT BARRIER REEF
MARINE PARK:
CAPRICORNIA
SECTION

Southern Pt.

two hours return from the resort. Brampton is 907 hectares (2230 acres) and has some 11 km (7 miles) of walking tracks that include an island circuit and many which lead to quiet sandy beaches. There are seven bays with beaches around the island.

Brampton Island resort is a very casual affair. Accommodation is in two-storey blocks and the 108 units (for about 200 guests) are all of the same standard, with most of the usual resort necessities: air conditioning, private bathrooms, fridge, irons and boards, etc. They didn't have televisions or telephones but, these are on the way.

The resort is a very friendly place where guest, staff and management all mingle on a first name basis. Besides newly-weds, it is also favoured by families - there are special early meal times for kids, babysitting facilities and a whole children's activity schedule that comes into effect during school holidays. Everyone eats in the main upstairs dining room, the Carlisle Room, which has a rather Polynesian atmosphere.

Most of the activities on Brampton are free and the sailboards, water trikes, surf skis and catamarans lined up along the front beach have strong allure. There is the daily **Brampton Bugle** detailing the times of organised activities from archery to golf on the six hole course, playing tennis, learning sailboarding or a boat trip out to the Reef.

At low tide, it's possible to walk across the channel to Carlisle Island and the part of the channel that remains underwater has the island's best fringing reef. At high tide guests can take sailboards and catamarans into the azure blue passage and make the most of the breezes that blow through this gap between the islands.

Besides a freshwater pool, Brampton Island has a most unusual saltwater swimming pool. There is an excellent sandy beach that stays stinger free all year round and the pool is at one end of it, perched up on what looks like a tiny breakwater. Lazing around this pool while the sun sets behind Pelican Island just off shore is a good way to end the

Rainbow lorikeet feeding time at Brampton Island.

day. Brampton's beach is the focal point of the resort and even at low tides remains usable although some activities like sailing may be curtailed until there is more water over the sand bar.

Perhaps the subdued nightlife of Brampton is due to exhaustion after a hectic day of water sports. The steps to the restaurant certainly seem to be steeper by dinner time than they were for breakfast.

Dawn on Brampton Island is a magical time. Scores of wallabies feed on the golf course and along the edges of the airstrip; they hardly move aside as people walk past. Early joggers are likely to find they have a companion on the run, Yvonne, Brampton's tame but rather neurotic emu, whose dark form has scared witless many a guest as they leave the bar late at night.

Every morning flocks of rainbow lorikeets are fed near the reception area. This is a remarkably colourful spectacle and a boon for photographers as the birds appear to lose all fear of humans in the presence of food. It's not unknown for photographers to endeavour to photograph someone with lorikeets sitting all over their arms, head and shoulders only to find that they themselves have a bird sitting on their own head and another couple on the lens.

The flight to Brampton Island from Mackay takes about 20 minutes in one of the ubiquitous Twin Otter aircraft. Alternatively, one can come across with the day trippers aboard the Roylen catamaran that departs Mackay outer harbour each morning. For those who come in by boat, there is the extra thrill of riding the Brampton Island train. This leads from the deepwater jetty (a popular fishing spot) to the centre of the resort. The jetty was built in 1965 and the railway tracks laid the following year. The whole operation looks for like a fun park ride, but it's very efficient in moving a lot of people and supplies in an entertaining vehicle. Besides bringing guests and day visitors in, the train also runs guests down to the jetty to join the Roylen cruises that regularly run out to Reef for the day.

A fringing reef lines the Brampton Island coast.

LINDEMAN ISLAND

For most of its period of human habitation, **Lindeman Island** rejoiced in the name of "Yarrakimba", meaning snapper bream. Even today, long after the Aborigines who lived here have departed, there are clear signs that these early inhabitants didn't rely solely on fish and other harvests of the sea for their survival. Lindeman Island's pleasant grassy expanses (that even Captain Cook commented upon) are the result of generations of Aborigines periodically engaging in the practice of burning off. This probably served the multiple purposes of clearing forests so that edible plants would grow and of removing the undergrowth so that animals could be more readily seen. No matter what the reason, the end result is a beautiful island with lots of open grasslands.

Although we may find many Aboriginal names a little difficult to spell and pronounce, we must rue their pass-

Preceding pages: sailing the ocean blue. Left, coming into Lindeman Island.

ing. Yarrakimba, the fish, is a much more pleasant and poetic name than "Lindeman", which is merely the unremarkable surname of an obscure English naval officer.

Lindeman Island is the main island of the Lindeman Group of islands adjoining the Whitsunday Islands. As befits its grassy slopes, the first industry to be established on Lindeman Island by white settlers early this century was sheep farming. However, by the late 'twenties, Angus Nicholson who owned the island, had opened a resort here, the first in the Whitsunday region. For the next several decades Lindeman Island was known as a beautiful, relatively quiet family resort island. The resort site here may be one of the oldest along the coast, but the present resort is brand new and upmarket. Opened in 1987 after a complete rebuild, it is yet another rebirth of an operation which has been in business since 1927.

The new resort has two levels of accommodation - the old quarters, now known as the Hillside Units and the new Seaforth Units. The design of the new resort is striking, with an open-plan lobby overlooking the pool and beach. Use of natural timbers, paving in the bar area matching that by the pool and lighting that draws pool, bar and dining room into a single indoor-outdoor unit, all show considerable creativity.

There is an airstrip on the island so that guests have the option of flying here directly from Proserpine (20 minutes), Mackay (25 minutes) or Hamilton Island (five minutes). Or one can transfer by boat: it takes about two hours from Proserpine or 25 minutes from Hamilton Island. Most guests elect to fly in - which provides a good initial overview of the island and resort.

Lindeman Island is quite large - 790 hectares (2000 acres) and it is a national park. The Queensland National Parks and Wildlife Service have established a number of tracks that lead to beaches on secluded bays on the north, east and west sides of the island - the resort is on the western side of the most southern point. Apart from forests and grasslands, the 20 kilometres (12 miles) of

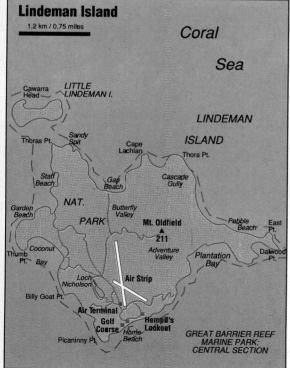

Lindeman Island

1.2 km / 0.75 miles

Coral

Sea

Cawarra Head

LITTLE LINDEMAN I.

Thoras Pt.

Sandy Spit

Cape Lachlan

LINDEMAN

ISLAND

Thora Pt.

Staff Beach

Gap Beach

Cascade Gully

Garden Beach

NAT.

Butterfly Valley

PARK

Mt. Oldfield

211

Pebble Beach

East Pt.

Coconut Bay

Thumb Pt.

Adventure Valley

Plantation Bay

Dalwood Pt.

Loch Nicholson

Air Strip

Billy Goat Pt.

Air Terminal

Golf Course

Hempa's Lookout

Picaninny Pt.

Home Beach

GREAT BARRIER REEF MARINE PARK: CENTRAL SECTION

walking trails will take you past the island's dam, into a forested valley inhabited by butterflies or climbing a grassy rise that leads to **Mt Oldfield**, the highest point of the island, 210 metres (689 feet) above sea level.

There is a full-sized nine hole golf course next to the resort and two floodlit tennis courts. The freshwater pool is a feature of the resort - it's large and provides a strong visual link between the main complex and the beach. The beach itself is quite well protected and can be used in all tides, quite a bonus in these reef-strewn waters. There's a reef in front of this beach too - it just has the good manners to stay decently submerged at low tides. In fact, a channel had to be cut through the fringing reef so that vessels could get into the resort's jetty. Diving and snorkelling aren't wonderful here as visibility can frequently be a problem, but nearby Seaforth Island is a more likely venue; there are also regular trips to the Reef by boat and seaplane.

There's a dive school on Lindeman Island that can take you through to full open water certification.

This is not a frenetic "let's party" resort but rather one for couples and families. The resort conducts a unique "Adventure Island" program for children between eight and 14 in which they go camping and learn about nature and the bush. For adults, a full range of facilities and activities are available, but there is no peer pressure to participate if you'd prefer to be lounging by the pool.

The tariff (which includes all meals) covers the use of all water sports equipment that doesn't require petrol, so chances are that you'll try several or all of the possibilities on hand. These range from archery and boomerang throwing to tennis, golf or cricket, softball or aerobics. Down on the beach there are catamarans, paddle skis, and sailboards. Or one can pay extra to go waterskiing, parasailing, jet skiing, or out in a outboard-powered dinghy.

Although the original units of the resort have been refurbished, these Hill-

Lindeman's choices – fresh water or ocean.

side Units still show their origins as good quality family units from an age when a resort room wasn't supposed to come with all the "mod cons" such as air conditioning, colour television and videos and direct-dial telephones. However, they are perfectly comfortable and do have fans, tea and coffee making facilities, and mini bars.

There are two levels of tariffs for the Seaforth Units: one for those right on the beach and another cheaper rate for those set back from the beach near the pool. All the Seaforth Units have private balconies or terraces, radios and those symbols of a new age mentioned earlier - colour TV and VCR, air conditioning and IDD telephone.

The total capacity of the resort is 400 guests in 104 Seaforth Units and 48 Hillside Units. The resort also has convention facilities with two meeting rooms, the largest of which can seat up to 180 delegates.

Two restaurants cater to the varied needs of guests. Nicholsons is a small à la carte restaurant seating 60 and serv-

ing international dishes in a relatively intimate upstairs setting. The Islander Restaurant has both buffet and set menu meals - it's at ground level and in good weather is opened out onto the pool. By the pool during the day a bar and coffee shop are operating and there's also a lounge bar open in the evenings. Juliet's is the resort's nightclub.

The motto for Lindeman Island Resort is, "where you can't see the luxury for the trees". To the extent that it's a low-rise resort built with some sympathy for the environment (indeed, the resort can be said to set it off), that is quite true. In a more general way, it could be said that potential guests of the resort haven't been able to see the benefits of Lindeman Island for the wood pulp consumed by other resorts extolling their own virtues.

It was not without good reason that Lindeman was selected as the site of the first island resort in the whole Whitsunday group. Its most recent incarnation deserves to put it back in a position of pre-eminence.

A clown fish hides amid an anenome that's poisonous to other fish.

HAMILTON ISLAND

As your jet floats in, **Hamilton Island**'s waters are a wide-angled ultramarine vision etched by the white wakes of powerboats. With silica sand and tower hotels, this is a polarised image of the wild and the mild, of dawn sublimeness and Day-Glo ridiculous.

The largest and most aggressively marketed resort in the Whitsundays, Hamilton, with its 200-berth marina and pseudo-'Barbary Coast' main street (likened by some to a yachties' Disneyland or a pirate's playpen), is more a 'scene' than an island retreat. Access by air is from the major mainland cities and Proserpine, or by launch from nearby Shute Harbour.

This island epitomises the changes which have come upon the Whitsunday. Compare today's intensive-leisure developments to what James Cook perceived among these waters in 1770: "everywhere good anchorage. Indeed the whole passage is one continued safe harbour ... The land both on the main and islands ... distinguished by hills and valleys which are diversified with woods and lawns that looked green and pleasant." Mainly uninhabited until the 1930s, the 550 ha (1360 acres) Hamilton Island slumbered until 1975, when Gold Coast entrepreneur Keith Williams took over its grazing lease for, well, a bagain rent. In the early '80s work commenced on his $75 million Hamilton Island Resort. Shortly after opening in 1984, fire destroyed the development. Williams, no wimp, turned around and started over again. Eventually his project won the National Tourism Award for the country's best resort.

In addition to establishing the resort, Williams sold blocks of Hamilton's prime land for exclusive residences. Beatle George Harrison bought one, but in 1989 he put his luxury home on the market, quipping, "I couldn't figure out why this fella sold me the land so cheaply. Then he began selling off the land around me, saying 'Be George

Rush hour at Hamilton Island marina.

Harrison's neighbour'."

Hamilton is big on convention and business guests, and is intended to be a 'total destination,' not a two-day stopover on a week-long trip to Australia. Day visitors are welcome; campers, forget it. There's plenty to do (Hamilton's motto is 'A World of its Own'): parasailing, helicopter or seaplane picnic excursions to other islands, scuba lessons in the pool, catamaran sailing, tennis, squash and disco - even walking around the undulating terrain of the island. All except the latter come at a healthy price. A fauna park displays an anomalous mixture of deer, emus and 'roos, koalas, peacocks, dolphins and cockatoos. Variety of choice is one of Hamilton's strengths: in food, everything from fish n' chips to silver service is available. The largest freshwater pool in Australia overlooks Catseye Bay, imported palms and bougainvillea grace the lawns, and the yachts slip in and out of the man-made harbour. Mr. Williams' own adventure in paradise, artificial as it may be, is a huge success.

Northern Bay
FAUNA PARK
Coral Sea
Catseye Bay
Swimming Pool
Hamilton Harbour
Jetties
Hotels
Squash & Tennis Courts
Air Terminal
Passage Peak
Tracks
Tracks
Crab Bay
Runway
Driftwood Bay

GREAT BARRIER REEF MARINE PARK: CENTRAL SECTION
Hamilton Island
1.2 km / 0.75 miles

In its thrust for the watersport buck, Hamilton has nailed its colours literally to the mast. In April there is the Hamilton Island Race Week for ocean racing yachts, and in August, more yacht races and a Concourse d'Elegance. The Dunhill 'Billfish Bonanza' competition is held in December. Cruise craft available for charter (see chapter 'Cruising and Bareboat Charter') from Hamilton include the luxurious *Achilles II,* the *Coral Cat* (which functions as a floating hotel on the reef), *Wave Piercer* and *Southern Spirit.* At Hamilton Harbour, gamefishing charters are also available. Excursions from Hamilton include links to Hayman, Daydream, Lindeman and South Molle islands, plus daytrips to the neighbouring National Park gem, Whitsunday Island. The distance to the Barrier Reef is about 80 km (50 miles).

Hamilton isn't resting on its laurels. Recent developments include upgrading the airstrip to international charter capacity; the spending of $200 million on the 20-storey, 400-room, five-star Hamilton Towers Hotel, which includes 30 penthouse suites (bringing the island's total capacity to 2,000 guests); and the purchase of nearby Dent Island - to be renamed 'Hamilton West' - for an 18-hole golfcourse. More restaurants are being constructed in the harbour area, as well as 300 condos and a 370-room hotel on the north-western peninsula of the island.

Accommodation options are wide and range upwards through the Hamilton Island Apartments, Polynesian Bures, Allamanda Lodge rooms, Bougainvillea Lodge rooms and Hamilton Towers to the top-of-the-line Whitsunday Towers apartments. Maximum peopling of these quarters ranges from three (Bure and Allamanda) to six (Hamilton Island Apartments). If you're missing the high high-rise of home, they even have a 20 storey tower. Standby rates are available. Or, the ultimate address on Hamilton Island - the 4-bedroom Villa Illangi is yours for $1250 a day. For further information and booking details, contact Hamilton Island Resort, toll free on 008 075 110, or (079) 469 144, or fax (079) 469 425.

WHITSUNDAY ISLAND

Not all the wildlife in the Whitsundays involves some Daquiri disaster in the cockpit of a yacht. On Whitsunday Island, turtles, gulls, dolphins, swifts, cockatoos, parakeets, giant goannas and kookaburras remind the visitor of how tramelled nature is on those islands which, unlike Whitsunday, aren't national parks.

The largest in the Cumberland group, **Whitsunday Island** is rugged and wooded (pine, eucalypt, casuarina), almost 11,000 hectares (27,000 acres) in area, and located just 13 kilometres (8 miles) off Shute Harbour. It's an impressive landmass with a deeply indented coastline and rugged hills rising to **Mt Whitsunday** at 435 metres (1415 feet). The only 'resorts' the island boasts are a few picnic tables and toilets at Dugong, Sawmill and Whitehaven beaches.

Beside its own complex ecology of mangroves, fringing reefs and rainforest, Whitsunday doesn't have much recorded history. In 1878 the ship *Louise Marie* put ashore for water, but was attacked and burned by natives. The cook was lost and, it is said, eaten. A decade later, John Withnall and his family settled at Cid Harbour on the eastern side and founded a sawmill which employed many Aborigines, including the alleged consumer of the Louise Marie's cook.

The marine life around Whitsunday Island and the adjacent Central Section of the Great Barrier Reef Marine Park is varied and abundant, with well over 1000 species of fish, and 22 species of sea birds. Reefs in the area host over 400 species of corals. Please note that the five species of turtles in this area are very vulnerable to human interference, as is the dugong. (Dugong are often sighted in the sheltered bays along the mainland coast where they feed on seagrasses.)

The neighbouring islands of Whitsunday and Hamilton provide a pointed contrast, which one Queensland journalist described as: 'You round the point near **Whitehaven** [beach], a silica sand masterpiece ... to look up and see concrete highrise on Hamilton, sticking up like a predatory prick, ruining the landscape.' Such realisations lend poignant emphasis to the 'haven' aspect of Whitehaven. This is the sort of tropical strand from which literature is wrought, be it Mills and Boon or Robinson Crusoe. Here you can swim in cerulean waters, or disappear for half a day down Whitehaven's pearl-white 6 kilometre (3.7 mile) scimitar, and swear you're the first person ever to do so. You're not, of course - Aborigines preceded by millenia those first European loggers of last century.

Today the whole of Whitsunday Island is national park and camping is only allowed with permits. There are a number of camping sites on the island with a range of facilities. **Sawmill Bay** at **Cid Harbour** has a 7000 litre water tank, toilets and five camping sites. It's a sandy beach with good snorkelling of the headland to the south. **Joe's Beach** has toilets, four camping sites but no water tank and poor anchorage. **Dugong Beach** is pleasant with rainforest rising directly behind it, but is only accessible by boat at high tide. There's a track overland from Sawmill Bay, too. A freshwater tank with 4000 litre capacity, 15 camping sites and toilets are all here.

Most visitors to Whitsunday come to Whitehaven on day trip launch excursions from nearby islands such as Hamilton and Hayman or from Shute Harbour. (Be prepared for a sort of BBQ-volley ball-windsurfer crush around midday when the tour boats disgorge their appreciative travelers.) However, if you have the time, a week of camping in this Rousseau postcard world is about as close to heaven as you can get and still see daylight. Permission to camp can be arranged through the National Parks and Wildlife Service ranger station at Shute Harbour (tel. 079 469430). Arrangements for supplies and water, as well travel to and from the island are made with private boat or water taxi operators at Shute Harbour.

Left, beautiful sands of Whitsunday.

HAYMAN ISLAND

Hayman Island really is Fantasy Island - if your fantasy is *Lifestyles of the Rich and Famous*. Take an appealing tropical island and add unlimited amounts of money, if not appropriateness, and you have Hayman Island. Clientele are similarly filtered by the money factor. Unless you associate "budget" with "corporate finances", and not with "accommodation", this is not your type of holiday.

There are only a few island resorts in Queensland aiming at the very top end of the market. Both resorts on Bedarra Island do, but they are geared for those wanting a quiet holiday with privacy and luxury. Lizard Island is another top-of-the-market contender: it is expensive and has several unique features, but the accommodation is best described as "good quality comfortable" rather than "luxurious". Hamilton Island too has some very upmarket accommodation, you'll also be sharing the island with crowds who are paying much less. And then we have Hayman Island.

Hayman Island is a destination where the resort is more important than the location. After all, there are campers looking out over the same Whitsunday waters as guests here, but in many ways they are barely on the same planet.

At 360 hectares (890 acres), Hayman is a relatively small granite island situated at the northern end of the Whitsunday Passage, above the much larger Hook and Whitsunday islands. As the closest point of the Great Barrier Reef is to the north east of the Whitsundays, Hayman is one of the islands nearest to the Reef. It also has some of the Whitsunday's best fringing reefs. The island was named in 1866 after Thomas Hayman, the ship's navigator of the *HMS Salamander*. For much of the next hundred years, Hayman was exploited for its timber, and by a hardy family of

Right, Hayman Island poolside.

goats. In 1933 a school teacher called Monty Emery bought the island and used it for fishing holidays from Cannonvale on the mainland. In 1947, Reg (later Sir Reginald) Ansett bought the island for 10,000 pounds ($20,000) - reputedly calculated at $1 per hundred goats. Reginald Ansett was the founder of the remarkably successful Ansett Airlines company and this was their first Reef resort. Royal Hayman (as it became known) opened its doors in July 1950 and put the Whitsundays on the holiday map.

However, by 1985 other Whitsunday destinations had developed beyond the level that Hayman Island's facilities could match without a facelift or full refurbishment. So Ansett Transport Industries tore down the old resort and erected a new one. Fabulous sums of money were reputed to have disappeared into construction, finishings, furnishings and everything else in the new resort. It is believed that a total of $260 million was spent.

The new Hayman Island Resort was launched with one of the most beautiful brochures the Australian travel industry has ever produced. However, its image was so daunting that Australians presumed the new resort was aimed solely at the international jetset, and they stayed away in droves. Hayman has now toned down its aloofness and has greatly increased occupancy, without compromising its standards.

Hayman Island is about 8 km (5 miles) long by 11 km (7 miles) wide. It's a hilly island with similar vegetation to the mainland - primarily eucalyptus forest. Unlike most of the Whitsunday group, Hayman Island is not a national park. There are several sandy beaches around the island and the resort is at the southern side of the island on a beach within a cove; it occupies the only area of flat land on the island. In front of the resort, the island's main fringing reef extends up to several kilometres out from the shore.

Although there is a helipad and transfers can also be made by floatplane, most guests arrive at Hayman aboard

Parasailing is excitement plus, or...

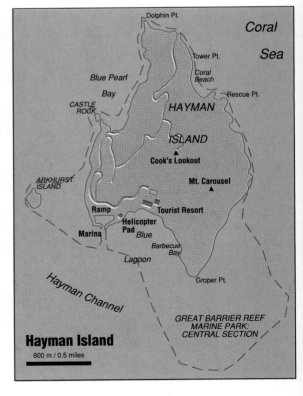

Hayman Island

800 m / 0.5 miles

the resort's vessel the *Sea Goddess* after a 30-minute ride from Hamilton Island. Check-in is completed on the boat.

The resort has 250 rooms and capacity for 480 guests in buildings two to four-storeys high. There are many standards of accommodation from suites down, but even the lowest level is well and truly five-star: all rooms have marble baths and showers, but only the suites have spas. Phones, VCRs, air conditioning and safes are some of the other room facilities.

There are two areas of accommodation: the east wing and west wing, in between which lies the main resort building. The west wing overlooks the huge swimming pool, while the east wing is surrounded by ponds and another pool. Each wing has its own lounge and dining room in a semi-open area with running water and a profusion of plants. Six restaurants cater to the Hayman Island guests, whether they feel like Asian food overlooking a Japanese garden, an Italian cafe complete with whitewashed walls, Polynesian or Australian food in a casual restaurant complete with a piano bar, a Viennese coffee house, or snacks at the thatch-roofed Beach Pavilion. Hayman's best restaurant is La Fontaine, decorated with French classical antiques and serving traditional French cuisine. The wine list is very impressive indeed, and jacket and tie, required.

... you can just muse on the beauty of it all.

Other public areas in the resort are furnished with the same degree of care as the restaurants. This leads to a confusion of styles but the overall effect is more interesting than garish. Prize winning paintings, large sculptures, and expensive hand-woven carpets are all elements of the decor. There is a library and billiard room off the Club Lounge bar, which itself is reminiscent of a traditional London club transported to the tropics.

Outside there are two tennis courts, a half court, both salt and fresh water swimming pools, putting green, archery, and down on the beach a whole line up of paddle skis, sailboards, and catamarans lie waiting to go. Parasailing, waterskiing, and dinghies with outboards are all on hand, too. The unusual design of the pool by the west wing - a large salt water lagoon crossed by several paths leading to a freshwater pool in the middle, all complete with waiter service - could keep most of us occupied for days. For divers, the *Reef Goddess* is the ultimate dive boat and the Hayman Island dive school has staff and facilities to match. Divers' underwater propulsion units can even be hired here. There are excursions for snorkellers and divers to the outer reef most days, and those keen on fishing are equally well catered for by Hayman's superbly-equipped game fishing boat.

Chances are, whatever you want, Hayman Island will have anticipated your wishes. It's as much an experience as it is a holiday. An employee of another, less opulent resort told of how one of their staff left to work at Hayman. A few days later he telephoned his old friends with the message - "You know how you feed the parrots over there? Well, over here on Hayman, we feed the white swans."

LONG ISLAND

A thin channel, no more than a few hundred metres wide stops **Long Island** from being part of the mainland, south of Shute Harbour. Like the thickly-wooded mainland slopes of the national park opposite it, Long Island supports large forests of eucalypts and rainforest species on its basaltic hills. As the name suggests, it's a long thin island, about 40 kilometres (24 miles) in length and ranging in width from 7 kilometres (4 miles) to only a few hundred metres at the narrow neck where Palm Bay Resort is located.

There are two resorts on Long Island. Palm Bay is the older, in both orientation and years. Slightly to the north of it lies Contiki Whitsunday Resort, which is aimed exclusively at those in the 18 to 35 age bracket. Except for the two resort leases, Long Island is a national park and there are some 13 kilometres (8 miles) of walking tracks running north

Left, beachwear for the tropics.

and south of the resorts. The track from Palm Bay to Sandy Bay, a cove on the wider part of the island, is about a 1.5 hour return trip. There is also a path heading north from Palm Bay, over the hill to the Contiki Resort and up to the lookout at the northern point of the island. From Palm Bay, expect to take about two hours. To visit any other points on the island, one must travel around the coast by boat.

Palm Bay: The hill and intervening bay between Palm Bay and Contiki's Happy Bay could well be the division between chalk and cheese. Unlike the youthful, 24 hour headlong rush into hedonism of the latter, Palm Bay Resort is a peaceful, very low key place. It opened in 1933, the year before the first resort at Happy Bay, and progressed along the lines of many other resorts until it was flattened by Cyclone Ada in 1970. (That same cyclone also wiped out the third resort on Long Island, at Paradise Bay. There have been several rumours of potential re-opening of this establishment, but they have so far failed to come to anything.)

Palm Bay Resort today is a decidedly "back to nature" sort of place, a mixture of basic cabins and more basic tents known as a Camp-O-Tel. There are nine cabins, each with absolute beachfrontage, double bed and four bunks. They are equipped with a full kitchen and all utensils, but only two have private bathrooms; the others use a central ablution block. Camp-O-Tel units sleep either two or four, they do have electricity and radios, ice coolers, beds (not stretchers), table and chairs, and a solid floor. There is a central shower and toilet block. Guests can buy meals, cook in their cabins or use the communal cooking facilities.

Like Contiki, Palm Bay Resort welcomes yachts to its sheltered waters, but does not apply an age limit. There are two daily shuttles to bring resort guests to the island. The rates at Palm Bay are very moderate and there is quite a range of activities available. These include surf skis, sailboards, catamarans, water skiing and parasailing. There is a pool and the resort has a small general store,

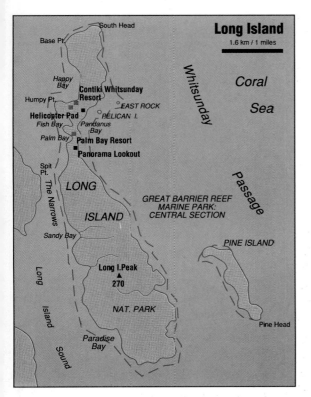

barbecues and a bar.

Contiki Whitsunday Resort: Contiki Whitsunday Resort is marketed as "the world's first resort only for 18 to 35s". Contiki is well known around the world for its bus tours of Europe and North America for young travellers. When his resort opened in July 1988 it just took the concept one stage further.

It's certainly a long way removed from the first use of the island by white Australians. Late last century there was a timber getters' camp here; that development was followed by a banana plantation. The simple, tiny resort first erected at Happy Bay in 1934 continued in ever-expanding form until 1983 when it became known as "Whitsunday 100" which, its brochures claimed had "a laid back atmosphere during the day and raging every night." As an "intimate resort" of 50 units (a great advance on the initial 4!) set amongst tropical foliage on the beachfront, its main attractions included unique "Aussie 12" mini yachts and top live entertainment, followed by dancing till dawn.

However, even the combination of yachts, good entertainment and marathon boogeying had insufficient lure to save the resort, and it closed in 1986. When the Contiki resort opened in 1988 it was largely a brand new resort on the same bay. It can accommodate up to 400 guests, mainly in 145 units housed in a string of two storey buildings, situated mostly along the waterfront. There is only one standard of accommodation within these units so rates vary only by the number of people sharing a room and the length of the stay. All the rooms have private bathrooms and private balconies, ceiling fans, tea and coffee making facilities, radio and telephone. One can hire a television and video movies if required. There are also two lodges providing cheaper accommodation for those on a tight budget. These consist of bunk rooms sleeping four, with ceiling fans and shared bathrooms.

Despite the availability of television sets on demand, one can imagine them gathering dust in the corner of a storeroom. This is not the place to come for

Below, take it easy or (**right**) catch it easily.

a quiet week of watching television. It may be a whole new resort but the new advertisements stress the "nightly entertainment and disco" and "sailing, windsurfing, tennis, volleyball, gym, aerobics and lots, lots more."

Unless the activity you pick requires the expenditure of petrol, it's included in the daily tariff. The tariff also covers all meals and even wine with the meals - a thoughful addition not made by most other resort islands. The sailing boats available on the coral sand beach include the ubiquitous catamarans plus Lazers and the Aussie 12s, a kind of bonsaied 12-metre yacht. There are also sailboards, paddle skis and fishing equipment. The water sports for which you pay extra are parasailing behind a speedboat, waterskiing, dinghies with outboard motors and scuba diving. Even at low tide, the fringing reef in front of the beach remains submerged although it is shallow. The dive school on the island conducts regular courses including introductory ones for beginners uncertain about whether they want to dive. Other sports facilities include tennis courts, games room, archery range, gym, basketball, a large pool, spa and sauna.

Happy Bay is only eight kilometres (five miles) from Shute Harbour so guests can avail themselves of the many tours to the Great Barrier Reef that depart from there. Transfers from Shute Harbour take about 20 minutes; or you can come across by water taxi from Hamilton Island airport if that is your arrival point.

The large bay below Shute Harbour is called Port Molle and it was long the main sheltered anchorage in the Whitsundays. These days, aspiring yachties departing Shute Harbour in their bare boat charter vessels may make Happy Bay or Palm Bay their first night's anchorage. If the crew is 18 to 35-ish and mooring space is available, they're welcome at Happy Bay.

Meals are served buffet style in the Poinciana Room or you can chose to eat at the cafe. There's a bar by the pool; the Sand Bar is the venue for the live music.

SOUTH MOLLE ISLAND

South Molle Island is a middle-sized island with a mid-priced resort.

Unlike some of the other islands of the Whitsundays, South Molle is not rugged. Its highest point is Mount Jeffreys at 197 metres (640 feet) and there are several points around the 150 metres mark (490 feet), but most of the island is undulating rather than craggy. It covers some 405 hectares (1000 acres) and has its only resort on the beautiful sheltered bay at the northern end of the island.

The first inhabitants of South Molle found the island particularly useful as a quarry. Its basalt rock provided Aborigines with a good source of spear heads and other cutting tools such as stone axes. In fact, they named it Whyrriba meaning "stone axe". The first white settler was lured here by its large tracts of grasslands, a legacy of years of Aboriginal burning that had cleared the trees and undergrowth from

Left, Scenery on South Molle.

much of the island. D. C. Gordon arrived here in 1883 to start a sheep station, the first Whitsunday Island to be used in this way. as well as its grasslands, the island's proximity to the mainland must have been a consideration too.

A later resident of the island did a great deal to promote not just South Molle but the entire Whitsunday region. He was Henry Lamond, a farmer who had switched to writing. The change in occupations must have been almost as dramatic as the shift in locations when he and his wife moved to South Molle Island in 1927 after years spent in the Queensland outback. On the island he continued to raise sheep while also writing. Like E. J. Banfield on Dunk Island, his articles on the Whitsundays awoke interest in an area that had largely been ignored by the rest of the world. Ten years later, he exchanged his island for a dairy farm near Brisbane and Ernest Bauer, the dairyman, moved onto the island. It was Bauer who set up the first resort on South Molle Island.

Appropriately, today's resort is located on Bauer Bay and is shaded from the late afternoon sun by Lamond Hill. Both those earlier occupants would probably approve of the way the place is now, for it remains casual but has gone through several stages of renovation and improvement in recent years. One of the early refurbishments was essential: the resort was wrecked by Cyclone Ada in January 1970.

Like Hayman Island, South Molle resort is operated by Ansett Airlines, but is much larger, appealing to a wider clientele. The resort has some 200 rooms in one and two storey blocks and can accommodate up to 500 guests. It's near the coast - only seven kilometres (4 miles) from Shute Harbour.

The resort is quite spread out and has various kinds of accommodation at three price levels, the most expensive being the absolute beachfront Whitsunday Rooms. There are two options in the next price level: individual Beachcomber cabins on the beach, or Reef Unit rooms in a single storey block just back from the beach. The resort's least

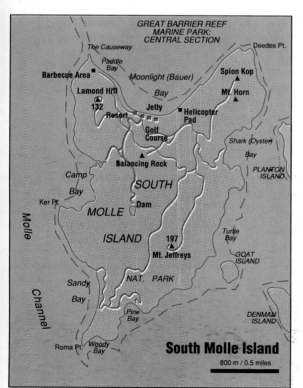

South Molle Island
800 m / 0.5 miles

expensive accommodation is in the Golf units (naturally enough, by the golf course behind the resort), Family units (that can sleep six) and Polynesian units (set back on the hill from the resort). Other than the Golf rooms, which accommodate two people, and the six-person Family rooms, all others accommodate up to four.

The tariff for South Molle Island Resort is inclusive of meals and most activities - guests need only pay for drinks and the cost of some activities. All the rooms have balconies, air conditioning and ceiling fans, refrigerator and mini-bar, iron and board, television (with a video channel) and telephone.

The general facilities are comprehensive, too. There's a half-Olympic size freshwater pool, spa, sauna and gym; a nine-hole golf course, two floodlit tennis courts, an archery range and a squash court. Down on the beach one will find catamarans, paddle boats, snorkelling equipment and sailboards. The sports that require fuel cost extra - aquabikes, water skiing, parasailing,

game fishing, and dinghies with outboards. Scuba diving courses are run on the island and there are regular cruises to the Reef and to other islands in the Whitsundays.

In keeping with the family holiday, that is one side of South Molle's image, there's free child minding for infants and baby sitting for older children. There's also a fun parlour, a children's wading pool and a special daily program of activities for children.

Access to South Molle Island is primarily by means of the daily catamaran services from Shute Harbour; it takes about 20 minutes to cover the 7 kilometres (4 miles). Guests who fly into the airport on Hamilton Island which is 15 kilometres (9 miles) away have the choice of either taking a 40 minute water taxi transfer or a five minute helicopter flight. Either way, your baggage is checked through to the resort.

Day visitors are allowed on the island and yachts can moore in the bay: the island is big enough and the facilities expansive enough to cope with all comers. Most meals are served in the dining room or as a barbecue by the pool. However, there is also the upmarket a la carte Coral Room Restaurant available for dinners. Meals here cost extra, but but it's a change from the main dining room. The resort has lively entertainment in the lounge every night provided by the resident band and based around different themes.

There are a number of walking trails provided by the National Parks and Wilflife Service, so it's easy to explore the island and discover quiet coves. The resort can provide a picnic lunch and one can either make the long trek to **Pine Bay** at the southern end of the island (roughly 12 kilometres/8 miles each way), the climb to the island's summit of **Mt Jeffreys** or shorter climbs to the island's lower peak. The walking trails lead you through the varied vegetation of South Molle Island - from open grasslands to airy eucalyptus forests, and even some patches of dense rainforest in clefts of the hills where vines and wide-leaf vegetation provide an exotic jungle feel.

Left, look – no hands! **Right**, leisurely days.

HOOK ISLAND

From high in the air **Hook Island** looks rather like a sea star with five mutated arms radiating out from Hook Peak. This effect is produced by the peninsulas of the northern part of the island and the deep indentations of Nara Inlet and Macona Inlet to the south. Although most of Hook Island's 5,200 hectares (12,850 acres) are rugged and there are several significant peaks on the island, the highest by far is **Hook Peak**, rising to 408 metres (1,338 feet).

Hook is the second largest island in the Whitsunday Group. A simple tent and cabin resort near the underwater observatory on the south-western point of Hook Island are its claims to "civilisation." There are also very basic , campsites - everything you require (including water) must be brought to the island with you.

About 20,000 years ago, before the sea level rose, the site of Shute Harbour

was on a mountainside overlooking a large valley. On the other side of the valley stood the peaks of what are now Whitsunday and Hook islands.

Hook, like many other continental islands was the site of logging operations early this century and the home of a herd of goats. Although the loggers have long gone, some goats remain. A much more important legacy can be seen at the northern end of **Nara Inlet**: a cave containing Aboriginal paintings. Some of the paintings on this island have been identified as being more than 8,000 years old. The path to the cave has been marked by National Parks and Wildlife Service staff. Nara Inlet and nearby **Macona Inlet** are popular with sailors as they both provide excellent shelter for vessels in times of storms. Macona Inlet is also the location of a small camping area with no facilities beyond 10 basic camping sites.

There is only a narrow passage between Hook Island and Whitsunday Island. This is the site of the resort and **Underwater Observatory** - a boat leaves from Shute Harbour at 8.15 each morning, and many of the other island resorts have day excursions to visit the observatory.

The Hook Island resort consists of 12 basic single storey cabins with six to eight guests in each. For those who bring their own tents, there are also 50 good camping sites here. Meals are available or there are facilities to cook your own. Other facilities include toilets and freshwater showers, refrigerated storage for guest's supplies, a coffee shop and bar, and a store that sells fresh bread and milk as well as other supplies. Bookings for the Hook Island Resort can be made through South Molle Resort.

The best parts of Hook Island's fringing reef are found at the northern end of the island. In fact, these are some of the best coral areas in the Whitsundays. In particular, one should aim for **Butterfly Bay**, **Pinnacle Point** and **Manta Ray Bay**. The last two have no camping facilities, but there is a small camping area at Butterfly Bay with 12 camp sites but no other facilities.

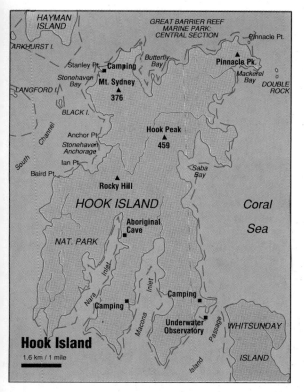

Hook Island

1.6 km / 1 mile

DAYDREAM ISLAND

Shaped like a beckoning finger, **Daydream Island** has great appeal to those who seek a true tropical island experience. Nowhere on this small, long, slender island is more than a couple of hundred metres from the beach. In fact, the resort occupies the whole northern half of the island, with beachfront units almost back to back. Not surprisingly, all guest rooms on Daydream Island have sea views.

We should all offer silent thanks to Paddy Lee Murray. When he and his wife arrived here on board their yacht *Daydream* in 1933, the island was known as West Molle Island. It was lumped in with South Molle Island, North Molle Island and Molle Passage in some of the most confusing nomenclature on the coast. Paddy fell in love with his "Daydream" island, shelved plans for a voyage around the world and bought the island for 200 pounds ($400)

from the retired farmer who owned it. West Molle Island is now almost universally known as Daydream Island.

So who, or what, was "Molle"? The name has nothing to do with Ms Flanders, but belonged to an obscure British army colonel. It was given by one Lieutenant Jeffreys in 1815 to the protected waters south of Shute Harbour, which he called "Port Molle". The name then spread to encompass the group of islands which protected this area of water.

Daydream is only seven kilometres (4 miles) and 15 minutes away from Shute Harbour by water taxi. From Hamilton Island to Daydream takes about 45 minutes by water. Just as the large cruise ships from a more leisurely age used to stop over for a day at Daydream on their way up or down the coast, now the hordes pour out of Shute Harbour each day, and some make Daydream their destination for the day.

Looking at Daydream Island (10 hectares/27 acres) on a map, one could well be mistaken into thinking that it is a coral cay or sandspit. However, like

A whale of a tail.

other islands of the Whitsunday group, this is a flooded continental mountain. The new resort is on the northern half of the island where rough wooded terrain slopes down to grassy natural lawns. Here one finds **Sunlovers Beach** and the island's best fringing reefs. Day visitors are restricted to the southern end of the island - their facilities are within the new Island Plaza.

In 1990, the island was completely redeveloped at a cost of over $100 million. It has reversed the previous layout of facilities - the old resort was down the narrow southern end of the island where the Island Plaza dau activity centre now stands. The new resort can accommodate 600 guests in 4-star comfort. However, some Daydream traditions continue - the old resort was noted for its large saltwater pool and the new layout has two saltwater pools: one exclusively for the resort and another down the day guest end of the island.

All 303 rooms are brand new and modern with private bathrooms, refrigerator, air conditioning, ironing facili-

All you need is a hammock and two trees.

ties, hair drier, radio, television (with in-house movies and Sky channel) and telephone. The 11 larger Sunlover rooms have spas and the best views. There are two suites, each with three bedrooms and full kitchens. There are three bars, a resident band and two restaurants within the resort plus a cafe at the Plaza. The Waterfall Cafe is the resorts main dining area - it takes its name from the waterfall cascading into the lagon round the cafe. Sunlover's Restaurant is more formal and provides panoramic views over Sunlover's Beach to the sun setting behind the mainland. A full range of water activities is provided. This includes tennis, catamaran sailing, sauna, windsurfing, snorkelling, paddle skiing, fishing and coral viewing. Or a launch can take you across to Shute Harbour in the morning to tap into the whole range of activities and cruises out of there. Daydream Island has an accredited scuba instructor and regular courses. Nothing is very far away on Daydream and the atmosphere is very casual.

ORPHEUS ISLAND

Even from the air it's hard to discern the resort among the trees of **Orpheus Island**'s Hazard Bay. Instead, the straggling coastline of this long, thin, hilly island must look much as it did when the island was named by Lieutenant Richards of the Paluma in 1886. Almost as puzzling as the location of its well hidden resort is why the island received this name. This stretch of greenery shining in an azure sea seems to have little in common with the mythical Orpheus, who fetched his wife back from the underworld only to have her turn to a pillar of salt on the threshold. Anyone who has studied Queensland island names will instantly speculate there was a Lieutenant Orpheus on board or a Lord Orpheus back in London. That's close - the namesake, *HMS Orpheus* was an English vessel wrecked in New Zealand in 1883.

Orpheus Island is one of the Palm group of islands north of Townsville. Access to the resort is by seaplane from Townsville in 30 minutes or from Cairns in 1.5 hours. The other options are by helicopter from Townsville or fairly long and complicated transfers by boat. Those who can afford to stay at the resort are unlikely to find the air transfers an intolerable burden. However, the rest of the island is national park and campers (with permits to stay here) will most likely come across on the daily boat operated to Pioneer Bay by Pure Pleasure Cruises. That company also runs a commercial camping site at Yankee Bay down the southern end of the island.

Besides resort guests and staff, the only other people on the island are the scientists at the James Cook University's Research Station in Pioneer Bay. The research station is closely involved with research on the giant clams of the Reef and their farming potential.

Orpheus Island lies about 24 km (14 miles) off the coast and like the other islands in the Palm Group, once sup-

The Orpheus dining experience is a pleasant one.

ported a well-established Aboriginal community. In fact, all the islands of the Palm Group, except Orpheus and her near neighbour Pelorus Island, are now controlled by the traditional owners.

A continental island of some 1,400 hectares (3,500 acres), Orpheus Island is about 44 km (26 miles) long and from one to four kilometres wide (0.6 to 2.4 miles). Its coast is indented with a series of bays - the resort is situated on the beach at Hazard Bay, a third of the way up the island and at its narrowest point.

Its distance from the coast, the limited means of access and the lack of resort islands nearby gives Orpheus Island a sense of remoteness. This has been exploited by the present resort, which commenced operations in 1981. (There had been another resort at a different location in the bay earlier.) Orpheus Island Resort is a sophisticated destination and, in keeping with that, doesn't cater for children under 12 or any day trippers.

The rather Mediterranean-styled resort has 25 individually-designed studios, bungalows and villas, catering for a total of 74 guests. There is plenty of space between the units, resulting in a good feeling of privacy. All units have air conditioning (plus ceiling fans), sound system, refrigerator, tea making facilities and separate vanity areas beside those of the bathroom. The difference between a bungalow and a studio is that the former has all the features of the latter plus a large bath tub in a bathroom which opens onto a private garden courtyard. The fully self-contained villas are the resort's most luxurious accommodation: they are situated on a wooded rise overlooking the water and have two bedrooms and bathrooms, their own kitchens and laundries, a living room and an open entertaining area. The tariff for all units includes all meals and most activities.

This is not a frenetic place where one feels compelled to be doing something every minute of the day. There is no formal entertainment and no activities; the food quality is excellent and a high point of the holiday; and there are hammocks by the pool. Meals, like everything else on Orpheus Island, are informal, and the open-air beachfront restaurant specialises in creative use of fresh local ingredients - especially seafoods and tropical fruits.

However, when one is motivated, there is plenty to do. Coral viewing, either from a boat, snorkelling or diving (there is an informal "course" for non-divers) should be at the top of the list. Orpheus Island has about the best quality fringing reef of any island along the Queensland coast. Another special excursion is to take a powered dinghy and one of the resort's picnic hampers with some chilled wine to one of the island's seven beaches for a quiet lunch. All the beaches along the western side of the island, including Hazard Bay where the resort is located, are well sheltered from the prevailing winds. Mainstream activities include tennis, fishing, catamaran sailing, windsurfing, and walking through the national park to one of the island's ridges for a grand panorama of the surrounding sea and islands.

Orpheus Island

1,6 km / 1 mile

Iris Point

North Reef

Cattle Bay

Mosquito Creek

ORPHEUS ISLAND

NAT.

Pioneer Bay

GREAT BARRIER REEF MARINE PARK: CENTRAL SECTION

Research Station

PARK

Fig Tree Bay

Waterfall

Coral

Fig Tree Hill

Hazard

Captains Rock

Helicopter Pad

Horse Shoe Bay

Jetty

Resort

Bay

Picnic Bay

Rockery Nook

Sea

Yankee Bay

Harrier Point

HINCHINBROOK ISLAND

For some, this is the most beautiful island on Australia's east coast, yet, rarely promoted, most visitors drive or fly right past it in pursuit of glossier, more brochured isles. The Eden which they have missed is, at 39,350 ha (97,200 acres) the world's largest island national park. Its awesome peaks, like the north side of Mt Bowen (1,142 m/ 3,745 ft) drop almost to sea level, its remote beaches and waterfalls bear little trace of human intrusions.

Separated from the nearby mainland for 10,000 years by the moat of a drowned river valley, Hinchinbrook has slumbered in time. This 37 km (23 miles) long island of granite and volcanic stone has an interior of rugged mountains, eucalypt forests, a prolific, mangrove-clad west coast and a sandy beach east coast. Hinchinbrook's diversity of plant and animal life is a great attraction to visitors who love nature without a glass case. It is one of only three Queensland islands to support rain forests (Dunk and Bedarra are the others). Bloodwood, ironbark, Moreton Bay ash, fig trees with buttressed roots, quandong, and pandanus palm all contribute to a canopied mature rainforest. Torresian imperial-pigeons, satin flycatchers and azure kingfishers are among the bird life, while on the ground are possums and echidna and feral pigs.

Jumping-off points for Hinchinbrook are at Cardwell and Lucinda. Visitors wishing to camp must obtain a permit from the National Parks and Wildlife Service that has an office in Cardwell. The Challenger family's boat, *Hinchinbrook Explorer* departs Cardwell 9 a.m. daily except Monday, for guests, day trippers and campers heading to Hinchinbrook. They also hire camping gear, arrange drop-offs and pick-ups for trekkers, and can be reached on (070) 66 8539. The *Tekin III* runs day cruises from Cardwell four times per week; contact (070) 66 8000. The *Searcher* departs daily from from Dungeness

Hinchinbrook Channel grandeur.

(Lucinda) for a Safari Cruise with commentary, and also acts as a 'taxi' service to the island; their contact is (077) 77 8307. A fully equipped houseboat (sleeps 6) for your own cruise in the incomparable mangrove forests, everglades and tidal creeks of the Hinchinbrook Channel starts at $330 for a weekend; call (077) 76 3466 for details. In addition to Hinchinbrook, there are 22 other islands within a half an hour motorboat ride from Cardwell.

Hinchinbrook Island Resort is exclusive (30 guests) and situated on the northern most point of the island, Cape Richards. Staying here comes close to camping on Heaven's door (without the necessity of further knocking). Missionary Bay and its complex ecology of mangroves and everglades is to the south, while to the east is Shepherd Bay and the whole Pacific Ocean. The only things lacking are a raging nightlife (that is, not missed at all) and a coral reef - resort guests are taken to the Brook Islands for reef viewing. The resort address is P. O. Box 3, Cardwell,

Hinchinbrook Island

12 km / 7.5 miles

Queensland, 4816, tel. (070) 66 8585.

The east coast trek: If you're very fit, try this one. If not, try a shorter version. A walking trail along the full length of the east coast from Cape Richards to George Bay has been marked (only roughly in places), and campsites established along the way, the main ones being at Macushla Bay, The Haven (or Scraggy Point) and Zoe Bay. These sites have toilets, tables, fireplaces and water. The campsites at Little Ramsy Bay, the jungle fringed Zoe Bay (with a waterfall and pool) and Mulligans Falls at southern end of trail are more pieces of paradise. Such sites, in combination with the sustained wilderness spectacle of the walk are likely to soon give this trip a reputation as a world-classic walking trail.

The trek is for self-sufficient bushwalkers, and the full excursion takes five days. There are shorter variations, such as a two or three day trip from Ramsay to Little Ramsay Bay. For day trippers, a good 1.4 km hike from the resort to North Shepherd Bay takes 45 minutes. Prior booking for the longer walks is advised as there is a limit to the number of campers allowed at any time. Bookings, permits (maximum seven days), maps and other literature are available from the National Parks and Wildlife Service, Bruce Highway, PO Box 74, Cardwell, Queensland 4816, tel. (070) 66 8601.

As trustees and beneficiaries of this wilderness, walkers on either day trips or treks should keep in mind that dune areas are extremely vulnerable and that tramping kills the sparse, stabilising vegetation. Please stick to the tracks. The longer treks entail walking a very rough trail of loose stones, slippery creek crossings and steep climbs. Trekkers should carry a map and compass, have good footware, a stove (open fires are banned), and be prepared for some scary wading through mangroves. Yes, it is a crocodile-inhabited island. As these waters are prone to sea stingers during the usual November-March wet (and hot) season, it makes sense to do the trek in the cooler months. Also, bring plenty of insect repellent.

BEDARRA ISLAND

When John Donne wrote "no man is an island entire of itself" he was arguing that no-one could live in isolation. Well, **Bedarra Island**'s theme is that an island can be the perfect hiding place from the rest of the world. In this case, all you need is money.

Bedarra is so private that there is one resort at either end of the island, each catering to a maximum of 32 guests. Both are owned by Australian Resorts, an offshoot of Australian Airlines. **Bedarra Bay** and **Bedarra Hideaway** offer the same level of luxury: these are resorts for people who don't bother to worry about money. The tariff is among the highest on the coast, but once paid, everything is included. When guests arrive at their own private cabins, the champagne in the cooler to greet them is *Moet et Chandon* or a choice of the other French champagnes in their refrigerator. For anything else one may wish to

drink, the open bar between the lounge and dining room has a good selection of Australian and imported wines and a wide range of spirits and liqueurs. Guests are free to help themselves and there are spare bottles under the bar in case they chance upon a special drink they may wish to take a sample of when they leave.

Similiarly, the menu for all meals at the silver service verandah and indoor dining rooms is remarkably short. Whatever you feel like, all you need to do is ask. So far the chef has only been caught out twice - and once was by a request for kippers at breakfast! Yes, English visitors (including royalty) are among Bedarra's regular clientele.

Like Dunk only a few kilometres away, Bedarra is a continental island covered in forest. But, unlike its neighbour, Bedarra has had a remarkably idiosyncratic history since it was first sighted by Captain James Cook on June 8, 1770. Cook did not name the island but rather lumped it in with others in the Family Group around Dunk. The metaphor has now been stretched so that Dunk is the Father, Bedarra the Mother and others in the group the twins and triplets. We'll have to wait for another period of geological instability for the in-laws to arrive.

The first name for Bedarra to appear on Admiralty charts was "Richards Island," after Lieutenant G. E. Richards who visited on the survey ship *Paluma* in 1886. However, in 1913 one Captain Allason and his wife arrived in the area from England, seeking the paradise he'd read about in E. J. Banfield's book, *Confessions of a Beachcomber*. He met Banfield on Dunk and went on to buy nearby Bedarra Island from the Queensland Lands Department for 20 pounds. Unfortunately, his idyllic sojourn was short lived - war was declared, Allason was recalled to England and after being injured in France never returned to his island. Even so, Lands Department maps called it Allason Island. However, Banfield had taken to calling the island by what he thought was its Aboriginal name - Bedarra. It's now believed that the correct name was in fact *Biagurra*

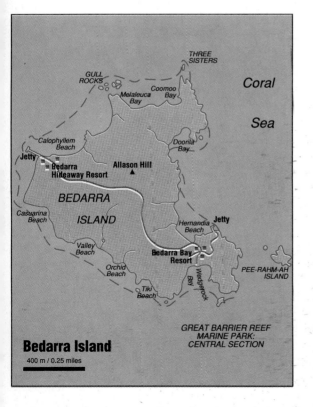

Bedarra Island

400 m / 0.25 miles

(Map labels: THREE SISTERS; GULL ROCKS; Melaleuca Bay; Coomoo Bay; Coral Sea; Calophyllem Beach; Doorila Bay; Jetty; Bedarra Hideaway Resort; Allason Hill; BEDARRA ISLAND; Casuarina Beach; Hernandia Beach; Jetty; Valley Beach; Bedarra Bay Resort; Orchid Beach; Wedgerock Bay; PEE-RAHM-AH ISLAND; Tiki Beach; GREAT BARRIER REEF MARINE PARK: CENTRAL SECTION)

meaning 'place of perennial water'. Nevertheless, Bedarra has stuck as the commonly-used name for this island.

In the 1920s Captain Allason sold the island to a show business personality who wanted to turn it into a home for underprivileged English boys. Inevitably, that plan failed. The London syndicate that bought it out sold a small portion of the island to Noel Wood in 1936. He continues to live at Doorila Bay on the east coast of Bedarra. In 1940, the brothers who had purchased the rest of the island began taking in paying guests at the site of today's Bedarra Hideaway. Eventually they sold their portion to two of their guests - a source of perpetual hope to visitors today who hope that magnanimity will be repeated. The new owners planted the gardens which now cover Hideaway and its surrounds. After several subsequent owners and developments, Australian Airlines bought the resort at Bedarra Bay 1980 as a day resort for guests from Dunk Island. Later that same year, the airline also bought Hideaway Resort.

Both Bedarra Bay and Hideaway resorts have been completely rebuilt and day visitors are no longer welcome, nor are children under the age of fifteen. This is a resort where the privacy and tranquility of guests is paramount. Needless to say, it isn't a wildly active resort. There are bush trails to hike, cruises to take, catamarans to sail, tennis courts to play upon, but most guests are prepared to relax by the pool, take things easy in their rooms or chat in the bar or dining room. At Bedarra, the water is a moat, not a playing field.

The theme of Bedarra is 'your private island in the tropics' and in keeping with this temporary ownership, rules are kept to a minimum and are framed as polite requests. For instance, "there are no dress regulations other than our request that wet swimmers are not worn when dining inside" [for pool chlorine rapidly destroys fabrics], and "please use plastic ware (Guzzini) when drinking by the pool".

Bedarra is clearly aimed at a niche

Bedarra's hallmarks are plushness, pool and peacefulness.

market though it's far too discreet to ever appear on *Lifestyles of the Rich and Famous*. Even the guest list is a well-kept secret, although the manager of Bedarra Hideaway will admit that many of the celebrities reputed to have stayed there, indeed did so.

Among guests, the difference between the two resorts is a hotly contended issue. In fact, both were designed by the same architect and the variances are minimal. The Bay has marginally the better location, but Hideaway is slightly better furnished and maintained. Guests of one resort are free to use the facilities and dining room of the other, although the management asks for some advance notice of your arrival - it gives them the chance to put extra champagne on ice. You can either take the quite rugged wilderness trail or catch a lift with a boat from the resorts to go between the resorts.

From the water, the jetty at each location and the pleasure craft pulled up on the beach are the only intimations that there is a resort at all. The individual villas are well hidden by lush tropical vegetation, and from many of their verandahs one has the feeling of being hidden in the jungle. As one would expect of a first class resort, these villas have been exquisitely designed. They are split level with the bedroom area at the top. The bathrooms at Bedarra Hideaway are unique: they are quite open with sliding paper screen doors separating them from the bedroom and they extend out into a small garden area screened by an outside wall. Each villa has shower and bath, refrigerator, desk, ceiling fans and air conditioning, iron and board, direct dial telephone, radio, hair drier, television and video.

It would have been very easy for the Bedarra Island resorts to have fallen into the trap of taking themselves too seriously. They haven't. They actually succeed in the illusion that one is staying in the holiday home of a millionaire friend. The presence of the Queensland coast and the Barrier Reef by the front door is just one of the lucky breaks.

Both Dunk and Bedarra islands have verdant natural rain forests.

DEPTH
1.0 METRES

DUNK ISLAND

One of the most pedestrian names of all Queensland islands was given to one of the most unusual, **Dunk Island**. However, thanks to its earliest permanent white inhabitant, the author Edmund J. Banfield, it was the first to achieve international fame. Banfield's *Confessions of a Beachcomber*, a classic in escapist literature, and his three other books, related how the 44-year old author, who had come to Australia from England as an infant, quit his job as editor of the Townsville *Daily Bulletin* in 1897 and with his wife Bertha, set up house on Dunk Island. When his first book, *Confessions of a Beachcomber* was published in England in 1908 it hit a responsive chord with every dreamer who had ever thought about going to live on a tropical island. It is an enduring fantasy - his four books are still in print.

The Banfields' cabin was in the forest well back from the beach of Brammo Bay. Edmund died on the island in 1923 and Bertha in 1933; they are buried together in a picturesque gravesite just off the trail near the swinging bridge. Their house has long since disappeared, but was near where the Banfield Units of the resort are today.

At first it seems surprising that their house wasn't right on the beach, in order to make the most of the excellent view across to the mainland. However, that would have been turning their backs on Dunk's major feature, the dense rainforest. Situated halfway between Townsville and Cairns, Dunk is one of only three Queensland islands to have a cover of real tropical rainforest (the other two are nearby Bedarra and the giant National Park, Hinchinbrook). The visitor's first impression of Dunk is of an emerald green jewel rising in facets to the peak of Mt Koo-tal-oo.

The forest gives Dunk Island a dimension other resorts lack. Only a few minutes walk from your palm-shaded deck chair on the beach is a suspension bridge over a small ravine. Swaying above the crystal stream that supplies the resort with water, one looks out over a maze of vines and creepers, fan palms and corkwood trees which is more like a Borneo jungle than a resort's backyard. The wonderful fragrance of the forest pervades the whole island. But the high rainfall that produces Dunk's verdant green adds an element of climatic uncertainty to any holiday here

From the bridge, the trail continues towards the summit of **Mt Koo-tal-oo**, 271 metres (867 ft) above the water. The sunny shoreline is soon forgotten as walkers discover a world of mosses and mist. Indeed, the high humidity in the forest and the effort of the climb,makes it like being in a huge green sauna.

In *My Tropic Isle* Banfield wrote: "Having for several years contemplated a life of seclusion in the bush, and having sampled several attractive and more or less suitable scenes, we were not long in concluding that here was the ideal spot. From that moment it was ours. In comparison the sweetness of previous fantasies became vapid."

Dunk is one of the oldest Queensland

Left, one of Dunk Island's pools.

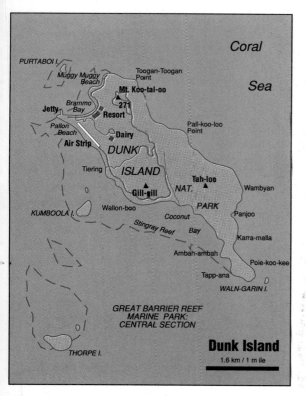

GREAT BARRIER REEF
MARINE PARK:
CENTRAL SECTION

Dunk Island

1.6 km / 1 m ile

resorts and still attracts a very wide clientele. A Townsville businessman opened the Banfields' home as a resort in 1934, the year after Bertha's death, but in the following year sold most of the island to another investor. During the Second World War a radar station was established at the top of Mt Kootal-oo: the ruins are still there today.

In 1976 the resort was purchased by Australian Airlines and P&O, but the later sold its share to the airline in 1978. About 80 per cent of the island is now national park, however the resort continues to operate a dairy at Coonanglebah Farm south east of the airstrip.

At 890 hectares (2200 acres), Dunk Island is the largest in the Family Group. The resort accommodates 375 guests, and many day trippers come to the island on the 15-minute boat ride from Mission Beach. Day guests have their own facilities including a small bar and cafe on the sandy spit known as The Point. Flying time from Townsville or Cairns is 40-45 minutes.

The tariff includes all meals at the Beachcomber Restaurant and most land and activities that don't require petrol. However, the *à la carte* Banfield's Restaurant, open for dinner each evening, is not included within the tariff (nor is alcohol). Dunk is a very pretty resort with low buildings scattered amid the trees. There are three standards of accommodation: 50 Beachfront Units on Brammo Bay, 47 Garden Cabana Units on the lawns back from the beach and the 56 Banfield Units in the older two storey buildings on the fringes of the resort. Every room has private facilities, ceiling fan and air conditioning, a radio, and refrigerator. The Beachfront Units are more expensive and far better appointed than the others. There are no telephones or televisions in the rooms: there are phones by the reception area.

Depending which way you look at it, Dunk has either two or four swimming pools. The one between the beach and the bar provides an excellent vantage point for watching the sun set over the beach and palm trees. The main pool near Banfield's Restaurant is actually a

Left, the graves of the Dunk's first settlers. Below, light through a bamboo grove.

series of three-tiered pools, with a spa as an adjunct to the top one. Away from the pools, other free activities include archery, cricket, fishing, golf, paddle skiing, parasailing, sailboarding, sailing, snorkelling, squash, tennis, and volleyball. The ones that cost extra are: clay-target shooting, horse riding, Reef cruises, motor dinghies, fishing charters, sunset cruises, water toboganning, and water skiing. The day trip to **Beaver Cay** on the outer Reef on the *MV Quick Cat* takes about 50 minutes. Alternatively, the *Neptunius* is a large yacht which cruises the local islands, stopping for lunch along the way. Simply going over to see the permanent artist's colony on the island or dropping by the dairy for a milkshake during afternoon milking adds an extra element to a Dunk Island holiday.

The resort is well geared to children with a range of activities, free supervision during the day, an adventure playground, a early children's sitting for dinner, baby-sitting services and free pony rides at the farm.

The Aborigines who lived on the island called it "Coonanglebah," meaning "isle of peace and plenty". That's certainly a more melodic name than the one Captain Cook gave it. Cook, who did an excellent job of looking after his sponsors, named it (on June 8, 1770) after Lord Montague Dunk, the Earl of Sandwich and previous First Lord of the British Admiralty. Earlier that day Cook had named a promontory of Hinchinbrook Island "Sandwich Point". Although he did well in finding names for everything he discovered, one suspects that if Cook was sailing today his sails and uniform would be covered by sponsors' emblems.

The emblem of Dunk Island itself is the Ulysses butterfly. Its pattern of black and iridescent blue over the 10 cm (4 inch) wing span makes it one of the largest and most beautiful butterflies in Australia. Unlike most of the guests here, it is fast moving and rarely still for long. But it's exotic and visually stunning like the island itself, a suitable symbol for Dunk Island.

Dunk's beachside pool.

Unlike the Central Section of the Great Barrier Reef Marine Park, the Cairns Section is distinctly lacking in major resort islands. In fact there are only three: Fitzroy Island slightly to the south of Cairns, Green Island due east of Cairns and Lizard Island well north of Cooktown. This is also the smallest of the four administrative sections - it's 400 kilometres (250 miles) in length and covers an area of 35,000 square kilometres (13,500 square miles).

Beyond here lies yet another part of the Great Barrier Reef Marine Park, the Far North Section which, as yet, is devoid of any resort islands - and so has not been covered by this guide. That section is about 700 km (430 miles) in length and extends over an area of 83,000 square kilometres (32,000 square miles). It's a rich fishing ground, but otherwise the only recreational visitors are divers.

The three resort islands of the Cairns Section cover a good cross section of Queensland islands: a continental island near the mainland with a relatively low key resort (Fitzroy Island), a coral cay (Green Island) and a first rate resort on a continental island well away from the coast (Lizard Island). There are other islands within this area - **Michaelmas Cay**, an important seabird breeding site, and the **Low Isles** are two that regularly see visitors.

The Great Barrier Reef narrows considerably and comes much closer to the coast in these northern regions. Even by Fitzroy Island the Reef is very close to the coast. Lizard Island is unusual for Queensland: it's a continental island within the Reef area itself.

For all three resorts, Cairns is the natural stepping off point. With a pleasant character, a relaxed atmosphere and a highly developed tourist infrastructure, Cairns is well regarded as a destination in its own right. In fact, one could argue that these islands are adjuncts of Cairns rather than Cairns being merely a stepping stone to them.

In this area the climate is strictly monsoonal. That is, it's hot and humid around the end of the year, and slightly cooler and much drier in the middle of the year. The summer months around Christmas are also the cyclone or hurricane season. Even so, when much of the northern hemisphere is gripped by winter the Great Barrier Reef has great appeal irrespective of climate. So, during Australian summer, the relative proportion of overseas visitors here increases greatly as Australians holiday down in the relatively cool southern states.

In a way, these northern sections represent the future of the reef. It's not just the islands that remain relatively undisturbed: the mainland to the west is the Cape York Peninsula - and that has changed little since Captain Cook visited. As our knowledge of reef systems develops, it looks as if the ramifications of human contact and development may be much more far reaching than originally thought. The section north of Cairns has so far escaped our influence and that may be its long term salvation.

Preceding pages: the edge of the Reef. **Left**, one of Lizard Island's namesakes.

FITZROY ISLAND

The coral beach at **Fitzroy** tinkles on the tide like a wind-chime. This continental island National Park of 880 hectares (2170 acres) of granite, eucalypt bush, freshwater springs and lush rain forest, is a fine combination of Australian bush *and* tropical island, of wildlife and creature comforts.

Mainland Aborigines visited the island to hunt goannas (up to two metres long, and still here) and to fish, but apparently did not live here permanently. Fitzroy Island was sighted on June 10, 1770 by James Cook, who named it after the family name of the third Duke of Grafton. In 1907 Fitzroy Island was used for 'troublemakers' transported from the nearby Yarrabah Aboriginal Mission on the mainland. A plantation of bananas, pawpaw and coconut was established, for which the banished Aboriginals were supposed to care. The venture failed due to the understandable

Left, a ray cruising crystal clear waters.

indifference of its keepers.

Fitzroy is blessed by balmy temperatures (summer max. 32°C [90°F]; winter min. 17°C [62°F]), and its resort is protected from the prevailing southeast winds. Pandanus screw palm and epiphyte orchids; blue Ulysses and giant birdwing butterflies; ospreys, sulphur crested cockatoos and scrub hens ... these are among Nature's creations on shore; while below the sea surface the list barely begins with brain coral, staghorn, beaked coral fish, clown fish, sweetlip and sea anenome.

The island is a quick 50 minutes by sea from Cairns - 8.30 am daily departures. June to October are best months to visit, although the resort (established in 1981) is open year-round. 70,000 visitors per year come to the island, but on any given day, it's hard to find much evidence of them among the shady bush tracks and empty beaches. Day visitors are welcome.

To do: A semi-submersible boat takes visitors for viewing trips among the coral gardens of Fitzroy's fringing reef; and a 20 minute walk to Nudey Beach brings you to sand, a pearl-bright sea and ungarbed freedom. The walk from the resort to the lighthouse and then on to the high point (870 ft/266 m) of the island is a two hour loop which will drench you in sweat, give you a good blast of Aussie bush, and cap it all with great views from the top. Far below, launches tow their white arrow wakes across the ultramarine sea.

Fitzroy Island Resort is one of those rare retreats that gets the balance just right. There is a friendly staff, mainly Australians, and a casual and unpretentious ambience. The choice of accommodation is in cool beachfront 'villas,' or in budget backpacker units, or in a leafy camping ground. Villa units, on a twin share basis, including breakfast and a very good *à la carte* dinner, cost $105 per head. The backpacker bungalows (four per room) cost $18 per head. Peak season is Easter to October, and Christmas through January - booking is advised. These can be made through Great Adventures, P.O. Box 898, Cairns, 4870, tel. (070) 51 5644.

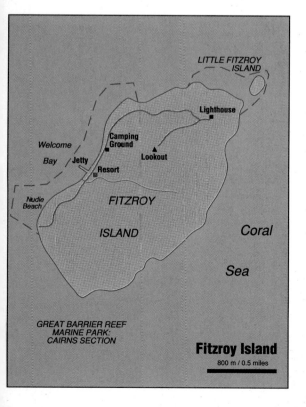

LITTLE FITZROY ISLAND

Lighthouse

Camping Ground

Welcome Bay

Jetty

Lookout

Resort

Nudie Beach

FITZROY

ISLAND

Coral

Sea

GREAT BARRIER REEF MARINE PARK: CAIRNS SECTION

Fitzroy Island

800 m / 0.5 miles

GREEN ISLAND

If Captain Cook sailed past **Green Island** today he would be well pleased with the name he had given it. Unlike most coral cays Green Island has patches of dense rainforest more in keeping with what one expects on the mainland. However, the forest of Green Island today bears little resemblance to the one Cook saw at a distance from the deck of the Endeavour in 1770. In the mid-18th century it became a collecting ground of *bêche de mer*, an Asian delicacy. The island's trees were cut to feed the fires required for treating the food. Since then, replanting and natural reafforestation has produced the pretty, distinctive vegetation of today.

Green Island is a 13 hectare (32 acre) coral cay 27 km (16 miles) east of Cairns. Its proximity to the mainland led to it being the first resort on the Reef - and it's still one of the most popular, attracting around 100,000 visitors each year. Most come on the day trip from Cairns (it's from 45 to 90 minutes each way, depending upon your vessel), but there is also a small resort on the island.

The beginning of modern tourism to Green Island dates from 1922 when the Hayles family built a jetty here and started an infrequent ferry service. In 1937 the Queensland government declared the Green Island reef a national park - Heron Island and Wistaria Reefs were the only others before the Great Barrier Reef Marine Park Authority came into existence in 1975.

In June 1954 the world's first **underwater observatory** opened at Green Island. It took a year to build in Cairns and was carefully lowered into its current position so as to disturb the surrounding coral beds as little as possible. It's held in place by chains and steel pins. As an extra precaution in times of cyclones, the observatory can take on 50 tonnes of ballast to stabilise it. Situated in 5.5 metres/18 feet of water, more than two million visitors have seen the Reef from its bathysphere perspective.

Boat fishing in Cairns.

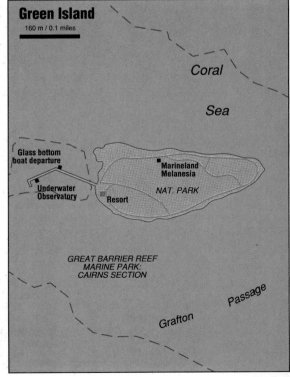

Green Island

160 m / 0.1 miles

Coral

Sea

Glass bottom boat departure

Marineland Melanesia

Underwater Observatory

NAT. PARK

Resort

GREAT BARRIER REEF MARINE PARK: CAIRNS SECTION

Grafton

Passage

However, from most other viewpoints, Green Island isn't a great example of the Reef. Its coral beds - except for the fiercely protected ones within sight of the observatory - have largely been decimated by the crown of thorn starfish plague of past years, although they are now slowly recovering. In addition, the crowds of visitors make it difficult for any to experience the oneness with nature that is so much a part of other coral cays. However, resort visitors have some respite between 4.30 pm when the last boat leaves and 9.15 am when the first of the day visitors arrive.

Nevertheless, there is enough to do on Green Island to make it an enjoyable outing for all who come over. Fish have been fed here for many years, so that many turn up for the daily hand out. The plentiful fish life and some 24 species of hard and soft corals seen from the underwater observatory can also be seen from the snorkel trail near the jetty. In the bush in the middle of the island is **Marineland Melanesia** which has an interesting display of fishing in tanks, and a number of live sharks and crocodiles on display. Sailboards, surf skis and the whole range of snorkelling and diving gear can be hired at Green Island. Besides the facilities for resort guests, there is a bar, barbecue lunch, snack bar, ice-cream parlour and island boutique.

Most of the sporting equipment is available at no charge to resort guests. The resort is set among trees and each villa accommodates up to four people. There's been considerable upgrading of the resort in recent years and room facilities include television, fan and air conditioning, and mini bar. Plans are afoot to completely rebuild the whole resort but the timetable remains uncertain. The resort was closed during 1990 but day visits continued unabated.

The daily Great Adventures Outer Barrier Reef Cruise stops over at Green Island for a couple of hours before continuing to **Norman Reef** at the edge of the continental shelf. There are also day trips from Green Island to **Michaelmas Cay**, one of the largest sea bird rookeries in the southern hemisphere.

Arriving at Green Island.

LIZARD ISLAND

Lizard Island is Queensland's most northerly island resort. It is also internationally famous as the centre of the anual Black Marlin season, which runs from August to December when it attracts well-heeled fishing enthusiasts from around the world, the bay is full of fishing boats and the Lizard Island Game Fishing Club is full of talk. Unless one is a keen angler or has inexhaustible patience for fishing stories, this is not the time to visit the island.

However, there is good fishing of other varieties here year round, and much more to the island than just fishing. Indeed, Lizard Island is the goal of everyone from divers to holiday makers to students of history.

The flight to Lizard is a travel highlight in itself. It's a long flight of 250 km (155 miles) from Cairns - one hour on the daily Twin Otter service of Australian Regional Airlines - and unless the weather is bad, the pilots keep the aircraft at about 500 feet (160 metres) for the whole journey. This takes you over Palm Cove and the Coral Coast, past the Sheraton Mirage resort at Port Douglas and then over a series of beautiful reefs. Finally, Lizard Island appears - a large green expanse of some 1,000 hectares (2,470 acres) rising to 259 metres (850 feet) at Cooks Look with attendant smaller isles linked to it by brilliant turquoise coral lagoons.

At journey's end, the resort of Lizard Island (operated by Australian Resorts/ Australian Airlines) is a row of 32 single storey units fronting a grassy swathe that slopes to the sheltered beach of **Anchor Bay**. There are also two larger deluxe suites each with separate living room and bedroom. The rooms are large and airy with bath and shower, fan and air conditioning, hair drier, fridge and phone. There is no television or radio - just a wall of glass looking onto the beach and bay. The monitor lizards that Joseph Banks noted and after which Cook named the island regularly sun themselves on the lawn.

Inevitably, the large lounge, bar, dining room and reception area are decorated with fishing trophies and the heads of those giants that didn't get away. Meals are relaxed affairs that take place on the balcony, cooled by the on-shore breeze. In fact, the whole resort is very casual. It has to be regarded as exclusive because it's expensive to reach, and costly to stay at (meals and most activities are included in the tariff). Although it does things well, this is definitely not a resort where guests must dress well to keep up appearances.

The range of free activities on hand for Lizard Island guests include: tennis, freshwater pool, archery, sailboarding, water skiing, catamaran sailing, glass-bottomed paddle skis, outboard dinghies, snorkelling and basic fishing gear. Two of the most popular activities for Lizard Island guests are at additional cost: fishing excursions on the resort's well-equipped boat and the diving/ snorkelling excursion to the justly famous **Cod Hole** on the outer Barrier Reef. The Cod Hole lies at the side of a

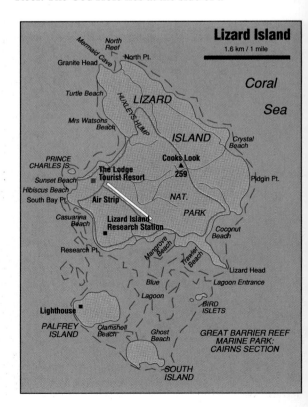

short channel through the last section of Reef before the deep blue Pacific. It's only 40 minutes by boat from the resort. So, less than an hour after leaving your room, you can be 15 metres (50 feet) under water feeding giant potato cod that weigh more than 60 kilograms (130 lbs). The Cod Hole is special because of its concentration of very large fish. Snorkellers can float on the surface and watch the feeding. Tickling a cod under the chin (while thinking how much it looks like Idi Amin) is a unique experience and one that seems hard to improve upon - until the resident moray eel arrives for lunch. Two metres (6.5 feet) long and well endowed with teeth, Merlin the moray eel is a daunting sight: he's reputedly tame, but most divers still flinch as the sinuous shape threads itself through their legs on his way to the food bucket. With luck, a manta ray with a wing span of up to four metres (13 feet) will turn up. The coral along this outer reef is less spectacular than in more sheltered waters, but the fish life is incomparable.

For students of Australian history the most memorable feature of Lizard Island is likely to be its assonant summit, **Cooks Look**. This was the peak James Cook and Joseph Banks climbed when seeking an exit from the Reef that had hemmed them in for more than 1,500 kilometres (930 miles). One still follows the same path to the summit - literally walking in the steps of the great explorer. It's an exhilarating experience, albeit an exhausting one.

The climbing path leads from the far end of a sandy cove to the east of the resort beach; it scales a rocky ridge and passes through a small paperbark forest before emerging onto the grassy slope that leads to the summit cairn. One must respect Cook who completed the climb twice in 24 hours, returning to the summit at dawn to see if the haze of the previous day had abated. It hadn't, but he still saw enough to discern the break in the outer Reef now known as **Cooks Passage**. For Cook, Lizard Island was a means to escape. It still is and it's still on the edge of nowhere.

The Anchor Bay approach.

TRAVEL TIPS

Getting There

BY AIR

Sydney and Melbourne are Australia's major international airports with daily flights from Asia, the Pacific, New Zealand, Europe and North America. Adelaide, Darwin, Perth, Brisbane, Cairns, Townsville and Hobart also have international airports, so check on the gateway options available. Twenty-five international airlines service Australia. (See Appendix: Airlines.)

Several airlines fly direct into Queensland (Brisbane, Townsville or Cairns), rather than utilising the major east coast international airports of Sydney and Melbourne: From the UK, Europe and the Middle East, Qantas and British Airways; from the USA (west coast), Qantas and Continental; from South-East Asia, Qantas, Thai International, Singapore Airlines, British Airways and Philippine Airlines. On other routes carriers include Qantas, Cathay Pacific and Air Niugini from Hong Kong; Qantas and Air New Zealand from New Zealand; Qantas and Air Niugini from Papua New Guinea.

A variety of discount fares is available, but because Australia is a long way from almost everywhere, it can be an expensive journey. Travellers may take advantage of excursion fares, with the price dependent on season of travel. Different rates exist for various travel routes, so seek the advice of a knowledgeable travel agent before purchasing your ticket.

BY SEA

Travel patterns over recent years have changed considerably and most visitors to Australia now travel by air. Before the 1960s, the traditional method of travel to Australia was by ship. A few companies, such as Royal Viking Lines, still offer infrequent and expensive cruises to Australia.

Travel Essentials

VISAS & PASSPORTS

All visitors require a passport and visa to enter Australia. Exception is made only for New Zealanders, who require a passport but no visa. Visas are free and valid for up to six months. Applications should be made to the nearest Australian or British Government representative. (See Appendix: Australian Missions Overseas.)

Visitors must produce an onward or return ticket and sufficient funds to support themselves; employment is not permitted for those on tourist visas. Under a reciprocal arrangement, British, Canadian, Irish, Dutch and Japanese visitors aged between 18 and 25 (or, in exceptional circumstances, up to 30 years) are eligible for a Working Holiday Scheme visa. This entitles them to a maximum stay of 12 months and some casual employment during that time. The emphasis of the trip is meant to be on "holiday", not "work." Such visas can only be applied for in the home country.

MONEY MATTERS

Australia's currency is in dollars and cents. Coins come in one- and two-cent copper pieces; 5, 10, 20 and 50-cent "silver" pieces; and one and two dollar "gold" coins. Notes are $5, $10, $20, $50 and $100. You may bring in as much foreign currency as you like. Before 1966, Australia used a pounds, shillings and pence system, like the UK.

Travellers' cheques (in all major currencies) can be readily cashed at international airports, banks, hotels, motels, and other similar establishments. All well-known international travellers' cheques and major credit cards are accepted. The most widely recognized and accepted are American Express, Diners Club, Mastercard, Visa Card and JCB. Difficulties may be encountered with other less-known overseas cards.

VACCINATIONS

Vaccinations are not required if you're flying directly to Australia and have not come from an endemic zone or from a smallpox, yellow fever, cholera or typhoid-infected area in the 14 days prior to your arrival in Australia.

WHAT TO WEAR

Generally, Australians are informal dressers. However, for special occasions like dining at better-class hotels or restaurants in the larger cities or at the most exclusive resorts, a tie and jacket are recommended. If you visit Australia during summer, include at least one warm garment for the occasional cold snap, but Queensland attire is generally light (cotton is preferable) and casual. Swimsuit, sunglasses, a hat and suntan lotion are essentials. Good walking shoes are necessary if you intend to go bushwalking, and for exploring the Great Barrier Reef, an old pair of sneakers is mandatory.

CUSTOMS

For visitors over 18 years of age there are no customs charges on personal belongings intended for use during your stay. You may import 200 cigarettes or 250 grams of cigars or tobacco, one litre of alcohol and dutiable goods to the value of $400 in personal baggage.

Before arriving in Australia the interior of your aircraft will be sprayed. This is not a happy introduction, but is a necessary part of the strict control on the importation of insects, animal or plant products, fruit, vegetables and seeds. Australia is free from many exotic insect pests and intends to stay that way. Also note that, once inside Australia, there are various restrictions on taking fruit, vegetables and other foodstuffs between states.

Australia is free of rabies, anthrax and foot-and-mouth disease, thus all incoming animals are placed in quarantine. Dogs (including Seeing Eye Dogs) and cats are quarantined for up to nine months. If you have any other type of pet, check with Customs in your country well in advance. In short, the best advice is to leave them at home.

DEPARTURE TAX

A departure tax of A$10 must be paid (in local currency only) by all travellers departing Australia.

GETTING ACQUAINTED

GOVERNMENT & ECONOMY

Since 1901 the six former British colonies of Australia have been governed as an independent federal commonwealth with a Westminster-style bi-cameral parliamentary system based on a mixture of British, American, Canadian and Swiss democracies. Australia is a member of the British Commonwealth group of nations. There is a three-tiered system of government: federal, state and local. The prime minister heads the federal government and is the leader of the party holding the greatest number seats in the lower house, known as the House of Representatives. The upper house is the Senate. The Head of State is the Governor-General, nominated by the federal government and appointed by the Queen. Voting in Australia is compulsory and employs a preferential voting system, whereby each candidate is ranked in order of preference.

To halt the rival cities of Sydney and Melbourne battling for the honour of being the nation's capital, the city of Canberra was founded. The federal parliament has been based there since 1927, and like Washington, D.C., Canberra is in its own administrative zone, the Australian Capital Territory.

A premier leads each state government. There are two main political groups, the Australian Labor Party and the coalition of the Liberal Party and the National Party. Governors in each of the states, along with the Governor-General, represent the British Crown in Australia, in what is generally a symbolic, top hat-wearing, fete-opening sort of role - which occasionally gets out of hand, such as in 1975 when the "G-G" dismissed the elected Government. Australia has a robust free-market economy with a fairly extensive social welfare system.

TIME ZONES

Australia has three time zones. Eastern Standard Time (Tasmania, Victoria, New South Wales, Queensland) is 10 hours ahead of Greenwich Mean Time. Central Australian Time (Northern Territory and South Australia) is 9½ hours ahead and Western Standard Time (Western Australia) is eight hours ahead. So, when it's noon in Perth, it's 1.30 p.m. in Darwin and Adelaide, and 2 p.m. from Cairns to Hobart.

During the summer things get even more complicated. Daylight Saving does not operate in Western Australia, so this state is then one hour behind Eastern and Central Summer Times.

Not taking Daylight Saving into consideration, international times are staggered as follows:

When it's Eastern Standard Time noon in Sydney, Melbourne and Brisbane, it's -

11.30 am in Adelaide/Darwin
11 am in Tokyo/Seoul
10 am in Hong Kong/Manila/Singapore/Perth
9 am in Jakarta/Bangkok
7.30 am in Delhi/Calcutta
3 am in Paris/Rome/Frankfurt/Amsterdam
2 am in London/Lisbon
11 pm yesterday in Buenos Aires
9 pm yesterday in New York/Washington
8 pm yesterday in Mexico City/Chicago
6 pm yesterday in San Francisco/Los Angeles
4 pm yesterday in Honolulu

CLIMATE

The first thing to remember is that Australia's seasons are the reverse of those of the Northern Hemisphere: September to November is spring; December to February summer; March to May autumn and June to August winter.

Queensland's climate is best described as semi-tropical to tropical, with large amounts of sunshine all year round. The further north you go, it the hotter it will be. North of the Tropic of Capricorn, the coastal areas experience hot humid summers, and winter daytime temperatures rarely fall below 27°C. The southern regions have warm to hot summers (26-28°C is common), while the winters are mild to warm with cool nights. The seasonal variations become less as you head north, until in northern Queensland there are only two seasons: hot and dry, or hot and wet. As a rule, assume that from November to March, it's warm to boiling everywhere. Far northern Queensland during the monsoon ("the wet": December-March) season is pretty damp but the winter offers ideal touring weather — warm days, clear blue skies and cool nights.

METEOROLOGICAL CHART

Brisbane	J	F	M	A	M	J	J	A	S	O	N	D
Maximum °C	29	29	28	26	23	21	20	22	24	26	28	29
Minimum °C	21	20	19	17	13	11	10	11	13	16	18	19
Rainfall mm	162	164	145	87	69	69	57	47	48	75	95	130
Water Temp. °C	25	25	25	24	22	20	20	19	20	21	22	24
Cairns	J	F	M	A	M	J	J	A	S	O	N	D
Maximum °C	32	31	30	29	27	26	25	27	28	29	31	31
Minimum °C	24	24	23	22	20	18	17	18	19	21	22	23
Rainfall mm	399	441	464	177	91	51	30	26	36	35	84	167
Water Temp. °C	28	28	28	26	26	23	22	23	24	25	27	28

CULTURE & CUSTOMS

Queensland, despite its huge tourist population, is known as the most 'morally' and politically conservative state in Australia. The bare facts about topless and nude sunbathing on public beaches are that it is technically illegal and can attract a $100 fine. In practice, no one cares much about topless, but be much more circumspect about total nudity. There are at least 50 unofficial nude beaches between the Gold Coast and Cairns.

WHAT IT COSTS

Below is a rough guide to some 1991 Australian prices. These are typical of Brisbane, but may vary from city to city. Concessions for pensioners and students are available. All prices are in Australian dollars.

Bus sightseeing tour	$20 half-day; $35 full-day
Theatre	$20 and up
Opera or ballet	$25 and up
Rock concert	$30 and up
Movie	$10
Museum, art gallery	free to $4
Sports match	$10 and up
City hotel per day (single)	$160-$280 international $90-$160 premier $50-$90 moderate $10-50 budget
Hostel (share dorm)	$15
Breakfast (per person)	$8 and up
Lunch at cafe	$10 and up
Dinner at good restaurant	from $30, without wine
Australian wine, per bottle	$8 and up
Glass of beer in pub	$1.50
Cocktail	$6 -$10
City bus fare	$2 and up
Ferry ride	$2, one way

Tipping is not the general custom in Australia. Porters at airports, taxi drivers and hairdressers do not expect to be tipped (but appreciate it when you do). At railway terminals porters have set charges; but not at hotels, where you may tip porters for service. In better restaurants it is usual to tip waiters up to 10% of the bill for special service. At any time tipping is your choice: no tip sends the message that you thought the service was below par.

WEIGHTS & MEASURES

Australia uses the metric system of weights and measures. Fruit and vegetables are bought by the kilogram, petrol and milk by the litre; distance is measured by the metre or kilometre, and speed limits are in kilometres per hour.

Despite the change from the imperial to the metric system in the 1970s, a 183 cm person is still frequently referred to as being "six feet tall" and many people still give their weight in stone (14 lb to the stone). The main conversions are:

1 metre = 3.28 feet
1 kilometre = 0.62 mile
1 kilogram = 2.20 pounds
1 litre = 1.5 pints (US) = 1.8 pints (UK)
0°C = 32°F; 25°C = 77°F

ELECTRICITY

The domestic electrical supply in Australia is 240 volts and 50 hertz alternating current. Universal outlets for 110 volts (for shavers and small appliances) are usually supplied in leading hotels and motels. For larger appliances such as hairdryers, bring along or buy a converter and a flat three-pin adaptor plug to fit into outlets.

BUSINESS & BANKING HOURS

General retail trading hours for Queensland stores are from 8.30 am to 5.00 pm, Monday to Friday, and 8.30 am to noon Saturday. Late shopping (until 9 pm) takes place in Brisbane, Townsville and Cairns on Fridays. Many Gold Coast shops and stores are open seven days.

Restaurants and snack bars, bookshops and local corner stores are open until later in the evening and sometimes all weekend. Australians still enjoy the tradition of the weekend holiday and most offices are closed on Saturday and Sundays.

Banks are open from 9:30 a.m. to 4 p.m. Monday to Thursday and until 5 p.m. on Friday. All banks, post offices, government and private offices, and most shops close on public holidays. (See below). Transport reservations and hotel bookings are heavily affected by public holidays and some restaurants and hotels may raise their prices.

EMERGENCIES

HEALTH

Doctors, dentists and hospitals all have modern equipment, high-level training, extensive facilities, and are expensive. Health insurance cover is available but there is usually a three-month waiting period after joining before claims can be made. A wise investment is the purchase of a health and accident insurance policy before arrival in Australia. Chemists or pharmacies are staffed by qualified professionals who dispense medication according to doctors' prescriptions. These stores also carry general medications, cosmetics and toiletries.

HOLIDAYS & FESTIVALS

Queensland Public Holidays

January 1	New Year's Day
January 26	Australia Day Holiday
March/April (variable)	Good Friday
" " "	Easter Saturday
" " "	Easter Monday
April 25	Anzac Day
May (1st Monday)	Labour Day
June (2nd Monday)	Queen's Birthday
August (2nd Wednesday)	Queensland Royal Show Day (Brisbane only)
December 25	Christmas Day
December 26	Boxing Day

QUEENSLAND SCHOOL HOLIDAYS

If visiting Queensland during the following school holiday periods, it is recommended that you book all accommodation and travel arrangements well in advance:

Mid to late April
Last two weeks of June
Middle two weeks of September
Mid December to end January

QUEENSLAND FESTIVALS/SEASONAL EVENTS

Listed below are some of the varied and unusual events held in Queensland each year.

JANUARY

•State-wide
Australia Day Celebrations
•Brisbane
Sheffield Shield cricket
•Gold Coast
Magic Million thoroughbred sales and races

FEBRUARY

•Brisbane
Chinese New Year celebrations
•Brisbane
Redcliffe yacht classic

MARCH

•Bundaberg
Autumn Show
•Burleigh Heads
Surf lifesaving championships
•Gladstone
Harbour Festival
•Gold Coast
Gold Coast Cup (horse racing)
•Ipswich
Queensland Eisteddfod
•Stanthorpe
Stanthorpe Apple and Grape Festival

APRIL

•State-wide
Heritage Week

- Brisbane
Brisbane to Gladstone Yacht Race
(Easter)
- Brisbane
Easter Cup (horse racing)
- Gold Coast
World Cup Triathlon
- Hervey Bay
Bay to Bay Yacht Race
- Maroochydore
Endurance Horse Ride
- Rockhampton
Autumn Orchid Show
- Sunshine Coast
Open Golf Championships
- Toowoomba
Royal Show and Gardenfest
- Whitsundays
Hamilton Island Yacht Race Week

MAY

- Airlie Beach
May Day Regatta
- Brisbane
Queensland Oaks and Queensland
Guineas (horse racing)
- Bundaberg
Bundaberg Show
- Gold Coast
Prime Minister's Cup (horse racing)
- Hervey Bay
May Festival
- Maryborough
Maryborough Show
- Proserpine
Proserpine Rodeo
- Rockhampton
City of Rockhampton Dance Festival
Maryborough Show

JUNE

- Brisbane
City Anniversary Celebrations
- Brisbane
Queensland Derby/ Brisbane Cup/
Castlemaine Stakes (horse racing)
- Coolangatta (Gold Coast)
Wintersun Festival
- Fraser Island
Orchid Beach Fishing Competition
- Gympie
Rainbow Beach Fishing Competition
- Nambour

Sunshine Coast Show
- Proserpine
Proserpine Show
- Rockhampton
Rockhampton Show
- Townsville
Townsville Show

JULY

- Atherton
Atherton Show
- Burketown
Burketown Races
- Cairns
Cairns Show
- Mareeba
Mareeba Rodeo Festival
- Mission Beach
Banana Festival
- Townsville
Townsville Show
- Townsville
Winter Racing Carnival

AUGUST

- Brisbane
Royal National Agricultural Show
- Cooktown
Amateur Races (horse racing)
- Gladstone
World 'Cooee' Competition
- Gold Coast
Gold Coast to Sydney Yacht Race
- Noosa (Sunshine Coast)
Festival of the Waters
- Townsville
Townsville Pacific Festival

SEPTEMBER

- Airlie Beach
Whitsunday Mardi Gras
- Atherton
Maize Festival
- Birdsville
Birdsville Races
- Brisbane
Warana Festival
- Brisbane
Winfield Cup (Rugby League) Grand
Final
- Brisbane
Australian Rules Football Grand Final

•Bundaberg
Rum, Reef and Harvest Festival
•Cairns
Amateurs Race Meeting (horse racing)
•Gold Coast
Gold Coast Show
•Kuranda
Kuranda Spring Festival
•Mackay
Sugartime Festival
•Maryborough
Spring Festival
•Mission Beach
Mission Beach to Dunk Island Canoe
Race
•Rockhampton
Rockhampton Rodeo
•Stradbroke Island
Stradbroke Island Festival
•Toowoomba
Carnival of Flowers
•Townsville
Oktoberfest

OCTOBER

•Ayr
Burdekin Water Festival
•Bundaberg
Art and Folk Festival
•Cairns
Fun in the Sun Festival
•Gold Coast
Tropicarnival Festival
•Mission Beach
Aquatic Festival and Sailing Regatta
•Noosa Heads
Picnic Races
•Proserpine
Harvest Festival
•Yeppoon
Pineapple Festival

NOVEMBER

•Airlie Beach
Whitsunday Game Fishing Champion-
ships
•Brisbane
Brisbane Handicap (horse racing)
•Bowen
Coral Coast Festival
•South Molle Island
Golf Week
•Tully
Watermelon Festival

DECEMBER

•Airlie Beach
Carols by Candlelight
•Brisbane
Carols by Candlelight
•Brisbane
XXXX Trophy (horse racing)
•Surfers Paradise
New Year's Eve Celebrations

DISABLED VISITORS

Australia is very aware of the need for facilities for disabled people.
    Advance notice with relevant details of
your disability will ensure the best possible
assistance from the airline, hotel or railway
office. A publication listing facilities in
Australia is available from the Australian
Council for Rehabilitation of the Disabled
(ACROD), PO Box 60, Curtin, ACT 2605.
Tel: (062) 82 4333. Detailed information on
Queensland holiday accommodation and
facilities is available from Disabilities Services, GPO Box 806, Brisbane, QLD 4001.
Tel: (07) 224 8031.

PHOTOGRAPHY

Australia is a photographer's delight and the
cost of film and processing is not too expensive, although it will be cheaper to buy your
film duty-free prior to arrival, if possible. If
flying with film, be careful not to have it
ruined by the cumulative effect of airport X-
rays - no matter how 'film safe' the signs
protest the machines to be: insist on hand
inspection of your film. Processing in most
towns is no problem, and many places offer
rapid service on colour print film.

COMMUNICATIONS

MEDIA

Brisbane has two major daily newspapers - *The Courier Mail* and *The Sun*. The only national daily papers are *The Australian* and *The Financial Review*. Numerous weekly magazines are sold alongside local editions of international publications, such as *Newsweek* (included in Australia's major weekly review magazine, *The Bulletin)* and *Time*. Airmail copies of overseas newspapers and journals are readily available at specialist newsagents and bookstores.

Throughout Queensland the number of television stations varies from place to place. In some remote areas the ABC (Australian Broadcasting Corporation) may be the only station. This is the national, advertising-free, television and radio network — the equivalent of the BBC. Brisbane has the ABC and three commercial television stations, while major centres such as Cairns, Townsville,and Rockhampton also offer both the ABC and commercial television. Brisbane radio features the ABC plus various AM and FM commercial and public broadcast stations, offering everything from rock to classical, and talkback to so-called "beautiful music." The ABC broadcasts in all major Queensland outback and coastal centres.

EMBASSIES & CONSULATES

Anxious to see how your taxes are being spent abroad or to read the latest newspaper from home? Most countries have diplomatic representations in Australia, with embassies located in Canberra. (See Appendix: Embassies and High Commissions in Canberra.)

There are also a number of consular representatives in Brisbane, which are also listed in the Appendix.

POSTAL SERVICES

'Australia Post' offices are open 9 am to 5 pm Monday to Friday, and the service is reasonably efficient, although the rates are not particularly cheap. Post offices will hold mail for visitors (c/- Poste Restante), as will American Express offices for its members.

Electronic post: Post offices provide a full range of E-Post and facsimile services at urgent or ordinary rates; the cost obviously depends on the rate selected and the destination.

The front pages of telephone directories give further information on all services, in addition to telephone interpreter services, community service, and recorded information service. In an emergency, dial 000 for the police, ambulance or fire brigade.

TELEPHONES

Australia's phone system is run by the government body known as Telecom. Public telephones are located throughout cities and towns and are found in most hotel rooms. Local calls from a public phone booth cost 30 cents for a unlimited time. Subscriber Trunk Dialling (STD) for long distance calls is available on all private and most public telephones. STD calls are cheapest after 10 pm and before 8 am, and from 6 pm Saturday to 8 am Monday.

International Calls: International Direct Dialling calls may be made from any IDD-connected private or public phone. International public phones may be found at city GPOs, rail terminuses and airports, as well as many other locations. There are off-peak rates to most countries which, generally, apply all day Saturday and 11 pm to 6 am Sunday to Friday.

Getting Around

DOMESTIC AIR TRAVEL

Australia has two major national domestic airlines, and with deregulation in 1990, a number of new operators also challenging them. Of the big operators, Australian Airlines is government-owned while Ansett Australia, its chief competitor, is private. Both operate regular scheduled flights between all capital cities and regional centres throughout Australia, and both have their own terminals. Flying is expensive but very safe. Some approximate direct flying times to Queensland airports are:

Sydney-Brisbane	1.15 hours
Melbourne-Brisbane	1.55 hours
Canberra-Brisbane	1.30 hours
Adelaide-Brisbane	2.15 hours
Perth-Brisbane	4.10 hours
Darwin-Brisbane	3.50 hours
Sydney-Gold Coast	1.10 hours
Melbourne-Gold Coast	2.00 hours
Adelaide-Gold Coast	2.15 hours
Sydney-Cairns	3.10 hours
Melbourne-Cairns	4.20 hours
Canberra-Cairns	3.05 hours
Adelaide-Cairns	4.10 hours
Perth-Cairns	5.00 hours
Darwin-Cairns	2.30 hours

Booking is advisable on all domestic airline services unless you wish to fly standby, which is available on most routes and can save around 20 percent of the regular economy fare. Various discount and special offer fares apply at different times. Below are listed the major categories and conditions; however, check with your travel agent for the latest fares.

An Apex fare discount of up to 35 per cent is available when purchasing return economy fares in advance. You must book and pay for your Apex ticket at least 30 days in advance and you cannot alter your booking within those 30 days or you lose 50 percent. You must be away for a minimum of seven days.

The highest discounts (45 percent) apply on Excursion 45 tickets These must be registered and paid for on the same day, 14 to four days before departure. You nominate the day but not the time of departure; then find out which flight you're on at noon the day before departure. The same cancellation rules apply as for Apex tickets. You must be away for a minimum of one night and a maximum of 21 days.

Ansett and Australian also offer a 25 percent discount on internal fares to international visitors. The distance to be traveled must be more than 1,000km; tickets are one-way only; no cancellation penalties apply; no children's fares. Bookings may be made before arriving in Australia or within 30 days of arrival. Travel must be completed within 60 days of arrival. If booking after arrival in Australia, a passport and an international airline ticket must be produced.

Round-Australia fares are offered by both airlines and are excellent value if you wish to see a lot in a short time. A number of round-trip routes are available and may be started at various points, while stopovers can be arranged to suit your itinerary, provided the round trip is completed in 90 days.

Qantas also provides cheap domestic travel for international travellers, not just those flying into Australia with the national carrier. These domestic flights can be purchased either outside Australia or within 30 days of arrival upon production of international ticket and passport. Although the range of routes is limited (Qantas doesn't fly between all Australian cities) and departure is through the international terminals, the savings are considerable: about 40 to 50 percent below regular economy domestic fares. Other excursion fares, discounts and packages are available from time to time.

A number of secondary airlines operate scheduled flights from the main cities and country towns, to link with the major trunk services. Secondary airlines which operate flights to and from Queensland are:

Ansett New South Wales
East-West Airlines
Eastern Australia Airlines
Hazelton Airlines
Oxley Airlines

In addition to the major and secondary airlines mentioned there is a third group of smaller regional and local airlines. These mainly fly intra-state routes and give access to more remote destinations, islands and tourist areas. Such airlines operating in Queensland include:

Flight West Airlines
Helijet
Queensland Pacific Airlines
Seair Pacific
Sunbird Airlines
Sunstate Airlines

Some approximate Queensland intrastate flying times are:

Brisbane-Cairns	2.05 hours
Brisbane-Coolangatta	
(Gold Coast)	25 minutes
Brisbane-Mackay	1.20 hours
Brisbane-Maroochydore	
(Sunshine Coast)	30 minutes
Brisbane-Proserpine	
(Whitsunday region)	1.25 hours
Brisbane-Townsville	1.45 hours

BUSES

Lively competition between the major bus companies and numerous independent competitors means many bargains are to be had when travelling by bus in Australia. The two major nationwide bus operators are Ansett Pioneer and Greyhound Australia. The standard of coaches is high with most having lay-back seats, videos, washrooms and air-conditioning. If you plan extensive bus travel in Australia there are several discount plans available. Greyhound's Eaglepass offers unlimited travel on Greyhound routes for either 30 or 60 days. Ansett Pioneer's Aussiepass allows 15, 30 or 60 days unlimited travel. In some cases these passes allow free access to local bus services and discounts on accommodation and rent-a-cars. Although both companies go to all major centres, Greyhound has a more exten-

sive network and more frequent services. Bus terminals are well equipped with toilets, showers and shops and are generally very clean.

There are many other bus companies, such as McCafferty's Express Coaches, Sunliner Express, and Advance Express Coaches, operating into and within Queensland. These companies operate runs from Brisbane to Cairns and include centres in between. There is also a variety of package tours available (which include transportation and accommodation) departing regularly from capital cities. These tours can range from three to 50 days and are run by various companies. Some even feature camping out, rather than hotels, and this proves considerably cheaper.

RAILWAYS

A wide network of modern, air-conditioned trains operates from coast to coast. The principal lines follow the east and south coasts linking the cities of Cairns, Brisbane, Sydney, Melbourne and Adelaide. Brisbane is linked with regular services from Perth, Adelaide and Melbourne via the 'Brisbane Limited' from Sydney.

Within Queensland, the main coastal rail routes are the 'Sunlander', and the luxurious 'Queenslander', from Brisbane to Cairns; and the 'Spirit of Capricorn' or 'Capricornian', from Rockhampton to Brisbane. Other routes travel inland from Brisbane, Rockhampton and Townsville. Queensland trains all feature sleeping berths and dining cars. Details are available from:

Queensland Railways
Central Reservations Bureau
208 Adelaide Street
Brisbane 4000
Tel: (07) 235 1122

WATERWAYS

Most Queensland maritime services are day-trips and commuter services between mainland centres such as Brisbane, Shute Harbour and Cairns, and the Great Barrier Reef or islands. Coastal cruises also operate between Cairns and Port Douglas, Cooktown and Cape York. Local tourist offices can provide details.

VEHICLE RENTALS

Australia has three nation-wide **car rental companies** and numerous local Queensland ones, and competition between them is fierce. The big three are Avis, Hertz and Budget and their rates are just about identical. The small outfits are cheaper and offer special deals, but may not provide all the service and extras of the major companies. The big three have offices in almost every town and at airports and rail terminals. They offer unlimited kilometre rates in the city but when travelling outback it's usually a flat charge, plus so many cents per kilometre. When you collect the car, rental firms ask for a deposit payable by cash or credit card, which is refunded on return on the vehicle. Compulsory third-party insurance is included in car rentals and comprehensive insurance plans are available for an additional fee. You usually must be over 21 to hire a car although some companies have 25 as their minimum age. Look for special deals such as weekend and standby rates.

Campervans are available for hire through companies such as Newmans Campervans, Sunrover Rentals, Holiday Motorhome Rentals and Apollo Motorhomes. Four wheel drive vehicles are useful for motoring in areas like Fraser Island and far north Queensland, and Avis and Budget, as well as many other local companies, provide these for hire. **Motorcycles** are also available in a number of locations and many Queensland cities, such as Brisbane, Cairns and the Gold Coast towns now offer bicycle hire if you are feeling energetic.

MOTORING ADVICE

If exploring Queensland by car, keep in mind that beyond the cities, distances are long and towns may be few and far between. Highways linking principal towns and cities are sealed and vary from good to 'bloody awful' standard. You don't have to get very far off these to find yourself on dirt roads. Drive on the left-hand side of the road, and the law requires you to keep your seat belt fastened at all times, whether driving or a passenger.

The speed limit in a built-up area is 60 km/h (37 mph), and in the country 100 km/h (62 mph). Australian drivers are not the best in the world - nor the worst - although the once-appalling accident rate is now being lowered by the introduction of random breath testing in most states. If you exceed .05 percent blood-alcohol level, a hefty fine and loss of licence is automatic.

'Petrol' (the usual name for gasoline) comes in regular and super grades and is sold by the litre. Prices start around 65 cents per litre and head upwards - in the case of remote areas, a long way upwards. Overseas drivers licences are valid throughout Australia, although an international driving permit is preferred. For extended touring you may wish to buy a new or used car and this involves much the same hassles as anywhere in the world. Queensland's automobile association will readily supply you with excellent maps and literature, and provide road reports. For a small membership fee it will also provide a free emergency breakdown service. If you intend travelling long distances by car, this membership in the Royal Automobile Club of Queensland (RACQ) is highly recommended:

Royal Automobile Club of Queensland
GPO Box 1403
Brisbane, QLD 4001
Tel: (07) 253 2406

Road reports can be obtained by telephoning the following numbers:

Brisbane	(07) 11655
Bundaberg	(071) 72 6300
Cairns	(070) 51 6711
Mackay	(079) 51 2299
Rockhampton	(079) 27 7177
Townsville	(077) 75 3600

HITCH-HIKING

Hitchhiking in Queensland is legal, though generally discouraged by the police, but it can be quite easy. Successful hitching depends on your common sense. Don't carry too much luggage, don't hitch with any more than one partner, do look clean, and display a sign announcing your destination. The best place to get rides is on the outskirts of a town at a junction where vehicles travel slowly and can stop easily.

WHERE TO STAY

HOTELS

(Key. FB = full board; M = motel facilities)

Australian hotels are widely classified into four categories: International, Premier, Moderate and Budget.

• International hotels are usually those of the well-known chains (Sheraton, Hilton, Hyatt, etc), as well as individual establishments (some of the island resorts, for example) which provide 5 star facilities and service.

• Premier establishments offer a good range of services, up to 4 or 4.5 star standard.

• Moderate hotels are well-kept and pleasantly furnished with comfortable accommodation providing most of the amenities required by travellers.

• Budget properties are simple and modest, catering to the needs of budget travellers.

Backpacker hostels, offering dormitory and multiple-bed rooms have become, in recent years, very popular in Australia. These are generally too numerous to list, other than the selection found under "Budget" listings. Several magazines, available in newspaper shops, give up-to-date information on these frequently changing establishments. There are also a great many caravan and camping parks, details of which can be provided by Queensland Government Travel Centres, or the regional tourist offices.

Below is a limited selection of accommodation available. Charges, although accurate at time of publication, are subject to seasonal fluctuations, and constitute the cost of room only. In the case of many island resorts, rates are inclusive of all meals, and this is indicated by (FB). Motel facilities are indicated by (M).

In addition to the accommodation listed below, areas such as the Gold Coast, Sunshine Coast and Cairns/Port Douglas offer a wide range of self-contained, serviced flats and apartments. For details of these, please contact the regional Tourism Queensland offices, which are listed under 'In the Know - Tourist Information'.

It is important to be aware that most of the island resorts and many hotels are often fully booked, particularly for Australian school holiday periods and during December and January. Accommodation bookings should be made as far in advance as possible. Special packages and discounts are often available through Queensland Government Tourist Offices, and these can be considerably cheaper than booking direct with resorts.

Price Categories:
(Prices are per room, in Australian Dollars)

International
Single: $160-280
Twin: $170-280

Premier
Single: $90-160
Twin: $100-170

Moderate
Single: $50-90
Twin: $55-100

Budget
Single: $10-50
Twin: $15-55

THE MAINLAND

GOLD COAST AND SURROUNDS

INTERNATIONAL

ANA Hotel Gold Coast
22 View Avenue
Surfers Paradise 4217
Tel: (075) 59 1000

Conrad International Hotel/Jupiters Casino
Broadbeach Island
Gold Coast Highway
Broadbeach 4218
Tel: (075) 92 1133

Gold Coast International Hotel
Cnr Gold Coast Highway and Staghorn
Avenue
Surfers Paradise 4217
Tel: (075) 92 1200

Hyatt Regency Sanctuary Cove
Manor Circle
Casey Road
Hope Island 4212
Tel: (075) 30 1234

Pan Pacific Gold Coast
Surf Parade
Broadbeach 4218
Tel: (075) 92 2250

Ramada Hotel
Paradise Centre
Cnr Gold Coast Highway and Hanlan
Street
Surfers Paradise 4217
Tel: (075) 59 3499

Sheraton Mirage Gold Coast
Sea World Drive
Broadwater Spit
Main Beach 4217
Tel: (075) 91 1488

PREMIER

Ocean Blue Resort (M)
122 Ferny Avenue
Surfers Paradise 4217
Tel: (075) 59 4444

Sea World Nara Resort Hotel
Sea World Drive
Main Beach 4217
Tel: (075) 91 0000

MODERATE

Admiral Motor Inn (M)
2965 Gold Coast Highway
Surfers Paradise 4217
Tel: (075) 39 8759

Equinox Sun Resort
3458 Main Beach Parade
Surfers Paradise 4217
Tel: (075) 38 3288

Greenmount Beach Resort
Hill Street
Coolangatta 4225
Tel: (075) 36 1222

Mayfair (M)
Cnr Gold Coast Highway and Enderley
Avenue
Surfers Paradise 4217
Tel: (075) 31 7324

BUDGET

Backpackers Inn
45 McLean Street
Coolangatta 4225
Tel: (075) 36 2422

Burleigh Heads Motel
12 The Esplanade
Burleigh Heads 4220
Tel: (075) 35 1000

The Hub Motel (M)
21 Cavill Avenue
Surfers Paradise 4217
Tel: (075) 31 5559

Riviera Motor Inn
2871 Gold Coast Highway
Surfers Paradise 4217
Tel: (075) 39 0666

Tropicana Motel
2595 Gold Coast Highway
Mermaid Beach 4218
Tel: (075) 39 8151

SOUTH STRADBROKE ISLAND

MODERATE

Tipplers Resort
South Stradbroke Island 4216
Tel: (075) 57 3311

• **Gold Coast Hinterland**

PREMIER

Binna Burra Mountain Lodge
(Lamington National Park)
Beechmont
via Nerang 4211
Tel: (075) 33 3622

Kooralbyn Valley Resort
Routley Drive
via Beaudesert 4285
Tel: (075) 44 6222

O'Reilly's Guest House
(Lamington National Park)
Green Mountain
via Canungra 4211
Tel: (075) 44 0644

BRISBANE

INTERNATIONAL

Brisbane Hilton
190 Elizabeth Street
Brisbane 4000
Tel: (07) 231 3131

Brisbane Parkroyal
Cnr Alice and Albert Streets
Brisbane 4000
Tel: (07) 221 3411

Sheraton Brisbane Hotel and Towers
249 Turbot Street
Brisbane 4000
Tel: (07) 835-3535

The Heritage
Cnr Edward and Margaret Street
Brisbane 4000
Tel: (07) 229 8022

PREMIER

The Abbey All-Suite Hotel
160 Roma Street
Brisbane 4000
Tel: (07) 236 1444

Brisbane City Travelodge
Roma Street
Brisbane 4000
Tel: (07) 238 2222

Club One
293 North Quay
Brisbane 4000
Tel: (07) 236 1440

Gateway Hotel
85 North Quay
Brisbane 4000

Tel: (07) 221 0211

Gazebo (M)
345 Wickham Terrace
Brisbane 4000
Tel: (07) 831 6177

Lennons Brisbane
66-76 Queen Street
Brisbane 4000
Tel: (07) 222 3222

Mayfair Crest International
Cnr Roma and Ann Streets
Brisbane 4000
Tel: (07) 229 9111

Ridge Hotel (M)
Cnr Leichhardt and Henry Streets
Brisbane 4000
Tel: (07) 831 5000

MODERATE

Airport International (M)
528 Kingsford Smith Drive
Hamilton 4007
Tel: (07) 268 6388

Albert Park Motor Inn (M)
551 Wickham Terrace
Spring Hill 4004
Tel: (07) 831 3111

Ascot (M)
99 Racecourse Road
Brisbane 4007
Tel: (07) 268 5266

Bellevue Hotel Brisbane (M)
103 George Street
Brisbane 4000
Tel: (07) 221 6044

Embassy
Cnr Edward and Elizabeth Streets
Brisbane 4000
Tel: (07) 221 7616

Metropolitan Motor Inn (M)
106 Leichhardt Street
Brisbane 4000
Tel: (07) 831 6000

Olims Kangaroo Point Motor Inn
355 Main Street
Kangaroo Point 4169
Tel: (07) 391 5566

Parkview
128 Alice Street
Brisbane 4000
Tel: (07) 229 6866

Story Bridge Motor Inn
321 Main Street
Kangaroo Point 4169
Tel: (07) 393 1433

Tower Mill Motor Inn
239 Wickham Terrace
Brisbane 4000
Tel: (07) 832 1421

BUDGET

Homestead Hotel
114 Zillmere Road
Boondall 4034
Tel: (07) 265 1555

Kingsford Hall Private Hotel
114 Kingsford Smith Drive
Hamilton 4007
Tel: (07) 262 4514
(Cooking facilities
available)

Marrs Town House (M)
391 Wickham Terrace
Brisbane 4000
Tel: (07) 831 5388

Ruth Fairfax House
(Country Womens Association Club)
89 Gregory Terrace
Brisbane 4000
Tel: (07) 831 8188

Soho Club (M)
333 Wickham Terrace
Brisbane 4000
Tel: (07) 831 7722

MORETON BAY ISLANDS

• North Stradbroke Island

Also contact the Stradbroke Island Accommodation Centre. Tel: (075) 49 8255

PREMIER

Anchorage Village Beach Resort
East Coast Road
Point Lookout
North Stradbroke Island 4183
Tel: (075) 49 8266

MODERATE

Stradbroke Hotel
East Coast Road
Point Lookout
North Stradbroke Island 4183
Tel: (075) 49 8188

• Moreton Island

PREMIER

Tangalooma Island Resort
Tangalooma
Moreton Island 4025
Tel: (07) 48 2666

• Bribie Island

MODERATE

Bribie Waterways
155 Welsby Parade
Bongaree 4507
Tel: (075) 48 3000

Koolamara Resort
Boyd Street
Woorim 4507
Tel: (075) 48 1277

SUNSHINE COAST

For self-contained apartments and flats, contact:

Accom Noosa
Hastings Street
Noosa Heads 4567
Tel: (071) 47 3444

INTERNATIONAL

Hyatt Regency Coolum
Warran Road
Yaroomba 4573
Tel: (071) 46 1234

Sheraton Noosa Resort
Hastings Street
Noosa Heads 4567
Tel: (071) 49 4888

PREMIER

Netanya Noosa (M)
75 Hastings Street
Noosa Heads 4567
Tel: (071) 47 4722

Noosa International (M)
Edgar Bennett Avenue
Noosa Heads 4567
Tel: (071) 47 4822

MODERATE

Jolly Jumbuck Homestead
44 Noosa Drive
Noosa 4567
Tel: (071) 47 3355

Noosa Haven Motor Inn
119 Noosa Parade
Noosa Sound 4567
Tel: (071) 49 9211

Noosa Lakes Motel
3 Hilton Terrace
Noosaville 4566
Tel: (071) 49 7333

Noosa Parade Holiday Inn
Cnr Noosa Parade and Key Court
Noosa Heads 4567
Tel: (071) 47 4522

BUDGET

Claribe Hotel (M)
David Low Way
Noosa Heads 4567
Tel: (071) 47 3486

Noosa Court Beachfront (M)
55 Hastings Street
Noosa Heads 4567
Tel: (071) 47 4455

Rainbow Waters Lodge
Carlo Road
Rainbow Beach 4570
(071) 86 3200

SUNSHINE COAST HINTERLAND

PREMIER

Eumundi Guest House
1 Black Stump Road
Eumundi 4562
Tel: (071) 42 8948

MODERATE

Headland Crest Lodge
Golf Links Road 4556
Buderim
Tel: (071) 44 5755
Fax: (071) 44 7323

Maleny Lodge
58 Maple Street
Maleny 4552
Tel: (071) 94 2370
(No children)

HERVEY BAY

PREMIER

Susan River Homestead
PO Box 516
Maryborough 4650
Tel: (071) 21 6846

MODERATE

Delfinos Bay Resort (Units)
383 Esplanade
Torquay 4655
Tel: (071) 24 1666

Hervey Bay Resort Motel (M)
249-251 Esplanade
Pialba 4655
Tel: (071) 28 1555

Kondari Resort
49-63 Elizabeth Street
Urangan 4655
Tel: (071) 28 9702

BUDGET

Colonial Log Cabin Backpackers Resort (Units)
Cnr Blackall and Pulgul Streets
Urangan 4655
Tel: (071) 25 1844

Fraser Gateway Motor Inn (M)
68 Main Street
Pialba 4655
Tel: (071) 28 3666

Golden Sands Motor Inn (M)
44 Main Street
Pialba 4655
Tel: (071) 28 3977

Hervey Bay Backpackers
195 Torquay Terrace
Torquay 4655
Tel: (071) 28 1458

FRASER ISLAND

PREMIER

Orchid Beach Resort (FB)
c/o Mail Bag 4
Maryborough 4650
Tel: (071) 27 9185
Fax: (071) 27 9145

MODERATE

Happy Valley Resort
Happy Valley
Fraser Island 4650
Tel: (071) 27 9144
Fax: (071) 27 9131

BUDGET

Dilli Village Recreation and Fitness Camp
Fraser Island 4650
Tel: (07) 237 1268

Eurong Beach Resort (FB)
c/o PO Box 100
Maryborough 4650
Tel: (071) 27 9122

BUNDABERG

MODERATE

Don Pancho Beach Resort (M)
62 Miller Street
Kellys Beach
Bargara 4670
Tel: (071) 79 2146

Park Lane Motel (M)
247 Bourbong Street
Bundaberg 4670
Tel: (071) 51 2341

BUDGET

Kalua Hotel (M)
4A Hinkler Avenue
Bundaberg 4670
Tel: (071) 71 3049

Pacific Sun Motor Inn (M)
11 Bauer Street
Bargara 4670
Tel: (071) 59 2350

GLADSTONE

MODERATE

Country Comfort Inn (M)
100 Goondoon Street
Gladstone 4680
Tel: (079) 72 4499

Highpoint International (M)
22-24 Roseberry Street
Gladstone 4680
Tel: (079) 72 4711

BUDGET

Ocean View Hotel
35 Yarroon Street
Gladstone 4680
Tel: (079) 72 2166

Queens Hotel (M)
Cnr Goondoon and William Streets
Gladstone 4680
Tel: (079) 72 1055

ROCKHAMPTON/YEPPOON

PREMIER

Capricorn International Resort
Farnborough Road
Yeppoon 4703
Tel: (079) 39 0211

MODERATE

Ambassador on the Park (M)
161-163 George Street
Rockhampton 4700
Tel: (079) 27 5855

Bayview Towers (M)
Cnr Adelaide and Normanby Streets
Yeppoon 4703
Tel: (079) 39 4500

Country Comfort Inn (M)
31 Bolsover Street
Rockhampton 4700
Tel: (079) 27 7488

Duthies Leichhardt Hotel
Cnr Denham and Bolsover Streets
Rockhampton 4700
Tel: (079) 27 6733

BUDGET

Castle Court Motor Inn (M)
75 Gladstone Road
Rockhampton 4700
Tel: (079) 27 5377

Criterion Hotel
Cnr Quay and Fitzroy Streets
Rockhampton 4700
Tel: (079) 22 1225

MACKAY

PREMIER

Dolphin Heads Resort (M)
Beach Road
Dolphin Heads

Mackay 4740
Tel: (079) 54 6963

Ocean International Resort
1 Bridge Road
Illawong Beach
Mackay 4740
Tel: (079) 57 2044

MODERATE

Four Dice Motel (M)
166-170 Nebo Road
Mackay 4740
Tel: (079) 51 1555

Ko Huna Village Resort
The Esplanade
Bucasia Beach 4750
Tel: (079) 54 8555

Lantern Motor Inn (M)
149-151 Nebo Road
Mackay 4740
Tel: (079) 51 2188

BUDGET

Backpackers Retreat
21 Peel Street
Mackay 4740
Tel: (079) 51 1115

Bazza's Backpackers
37 Milton Street
Mackay 4740
Tel: (079) 57 2530

Boomerang Hotel (M)
South Nebo Road
Mackay 4740
Tel: (079) 52 1755

AIRLIE BEACH/SHUTE HARBOUR

PREMIER

Whitsunday Terraces Resort
Shute Harbour Road
Airlie Beach 4802
Tel: (079) 46 6788

Whitsunday Coral Sea Resort
25 Ocean View Avenue
Airlie Beach 4802
Tel: (079) 46 6458

MODERATE

Coral Point Lodge
Harbour Avenue
Shute Harbour 4802
Tel: (079) 46 9552

Shute Harbour Motel (M)
Shute Harbour Road
Shute Harbour 4802
Tel: (079) 46 9131

Whitsunday Village Resort
Shute Harbour Road
Airlie Beach 4802
Tel: (079) 46 6266

Whitsunday Wanderers Resort
Shute Harbour Road
Airlie Beach 4802
Tel: (079) 46 6446

BUDGET

Airlie Beach Hotel
16 The Esplanade
Airlie Beach 4802
Tel: (079) 46 6233

Airlie Beach Motor Lodge (M)
Lamond Street
Airlie Beach 4802
Tel: (079) 46 6418

TOWNSVILLE

INTERNATIONAL

Sheraton Breakwater Casino/Hotel
Sir Leslie Thiess Drive
Townsville 4810
Tel: (077) 22 2333

PREMIER

Colonial Gardens Resort (M)
The Lakes
Woolcock Street
Townsville 4810
Tel: (077) 25 2222

Townsville Ambassador (M)
75 The Strand
Townsville 4810
Tel: (077) 72 4255

Townsville International
Flinders Mall
Townsville 4810
Tel: (077) 72 2477

MODERATE

Seagulls Holiday Inn (M)
74 The Esplanade
Belgian Gardens 4810
Tel: (077) 21 3111

South Bank Motor Inn (M)
23-29 Palmer Street
South Townsville 4810
Tel: (077) 21 1474

Townsville Reef International
63 The Strand
Townsville 4810
Tel: (077) 21 1777

BUDGET

Coolabah Motel (M)
75 Bowen Road
Townsville 4810
Tel: (077) 79 2084

The Strand (M)
51 The Strand
Townsville 4810
Tel: (077) 72 1977

MAGNETIC ISLAND

PREMIER

Latitude 19 Resort
Mandalay Avenue
Nelly Bay
Magnetic Island 4816
Tel: (077) 78 5200
Fax: (077) 78 5806

MODERATE

Arcadia Holiday Resort
1 Marine Parade
Arcadia
Magnetic Island 4816
Tel: (077) 78 5177

Island Palms Resort
The Esplanade
Nelly Bay
Magnetic Island 4816
Tel: (077) 78 5571

Radical Bay Resort
Radical Bay
Magnetic Island 4819
Tel: (077) 78 5294

Tropical Palms Inn
34 Picnic Street
Picnic Bay
Magnetic Island 4819
Tel: (077) 78 5076

BUDGET

Alma Den Beach Resort
11 Olympus Crescent
Arcadia
Magnetic Island 4816
Tel: (077) 78 5163

Backpackers Headquarters
32 Picnic Street
Magnetic Island 4816
Tel: (077) 78 5110
(Dormitories and private rooms)

Foresthaven
11 Cook Road
Arcadia
Magnetic Island 4816
Tel: (077) 78 5153

Geoff's Place
40 Horseshoe Bay Road
Horseshoe Bay
Magnetic Island 4816
Tel: (077) 78 5577
(camping ground also)

TOWNSVILLE TO CAIRNS
PREMIER

The Point
Mitchell Street
South Mission Beach 4854
Tel: (070) 68 8154
(No children under 12 years)

Tradewinds Castaways Beach Resort
(M)
Cnr Pacific Parade and Seaview Avenue
Mission Beach 4854
Tel: (070) 68 7444

MODERATE

Mission Beach Resort
Cnr Mission Beach and Wongaling Beach
Roads
Mission Beach 4854
Tel: (070) 68 8288

CAIRNS

In addition to the hotels, motels and back-packers hostels listed below, there is a wide variety of apartments and houses to let. Contact the Far North Queensland Promotion Bureau, Tel: (070) 51 3588; or Accom Cairns, Tel: (070) 51 3200 for details.

INTERNATIONAL

Cairns International
17 Abbott Street
Cairns 4870
Tel: (070) 31 1300

Hilton International Cairns
Wharf Street
Cairns 4870
Tel: (070) 52 1599

Holiday Inn
Esplanade and Florence St.,
Cairns 4870
Tel: (070) 313 757

RadissonPlaza
Marlin Pde
Cairns 4870
Tel: (070) 311 411

PREMIER

Cairns Colonial Club Resort
18-26 Cannon Street
Manunda 4870
Tel: (070) 53 5111

Four Seasons Cairns
The Esplanade
Cairns 4870
Tel: (070) 31 2211

Pacific International
43 The Esplanade
Cairns 4870
Tel: (070) 51 7888

Quality Harbourside
209 The Esplanade
Cairns 4870
Tel: (070) 51 8999

Rodeway International
Cnr Grafton and Spence Streets
Cairns 4870
Tel: (070) 51 0333

Tradewinds Esplanade
137 The Esplanade
Cairns 4870
Tel: (070) 52 1111

Tradewinds Outrigger
Cnr Lake, Florence and Abbott Streets
Cairns 4870
Tel: (070) 51 6188

MODERATE

Bay Village Tropical Retreat (M)
227-229 Lake Street
Cairns 4870
Tel: (070) 51 4622

Acacia Court (M)
230A Lake Street
Cairns 4870
Tel: (070) 51 5011

Cairns Holiday Lodge
259 Sheridan Street
Cairns 4870
Tel: (070) 51 4611

Cairns Tropical Garden Motel (M)
312 Mulgrave Road
Cairns 4870
Tel: (070) 31 1777

G'Day Tropical Village
7 McLachlan Street
Cairns 4870
Tel: (070) 53 7555

High Chaparral (M)
195 Sheridan Street
Cairns 4870
Tel: (070) 51 7155

BUDGET

Cairns Backpackers Inn
255 Lake Street
Cairns 4870
Tel: (070) 51 9166

Pacific Coast Budget Accommodation
100 Sheridan Street
Cairns 4870
Tel: (070) 51 1264

Silver Palm
153 The Esplanade
Cairns 4870
Tel: (070) 51 2059

Tropicana Lodge
158C Martyn Street
Cairns 4870
Tel: (070) 51 1729

Uptop Down Under Holiday Lodge
170 Spence Street
Cairns 4870
Tel: (070) 51 3636

CAIRNS-NORTHERN BEACHES

INTERNATIONAL

Ramada Reef Resort
Palm Cove
Cairns 4870
Tel: (070) 55 3999

Eden Coral Coast Resort
Coral Coast Drive
Palm Cove 4879
Tel: (070) 59 1234

Kewarra Beach Resort
Kewarra Beach 4879
Tel: (070) 57 6666

Reef House International
103 Williams Esplanade
Palm Cove 4879
Tel: (070) 55 3633

MODERATE

Paradise Village Resort
117 Williams Esplanade
Palm Cove 4879
Tel: (070) 55 3300

CAIRNS HINTERLAND

MODERATE

Tinaroo Lakes Motel
Palm Street
Tinaroo 4872
(070) 95 8200

Malanda Lodge
Millaaa Millaa Road
Malanda 4885
(070) 96 5555

Chambers Rainforest Holiday Apartments
Eacham Close
Lake Eacham
Atherton Tableland 4883
Tel: (070) 95 3754

Kuranda Rainforest Resort
2 Greenhills Road
Kuranda 4872
Tel: (070) 93 7555

PORT DOUGLAS

INTERNATIONAL

Sheraton Mirage Port Douglas
Port Douglas Road
Port Douglas 4871
Tel: (070) 99 5888

Club Tropical Resort
Cnr Wharf and Macrossan Streets
Port Douglas 4871
Tel: (070) 99 5885

PREMIER

Reef Terraces
Port Douglas Road
Port Douglas 4871
(070) 99 3333

Radisson Royal Palms Resort
Port Douglas Road
Port Douglas 4871
Tel: (070) 99 5577

MODERATE

Lazy Lizard Motor Inn (M)
121 Davidson Street
Port Douglas 4871
Tel: (070) 99 5900

Rusty Pelican Inn (M)
123 Davidson Street
Port Douglas 4871
Tel: (070) 99 5266

BUDGET

Coconut Grove Travellers Palm Motel
Macrossan Street
Port Douglas 4871
Tel: (070) 99 5124

Port Douglas Travellers Hostel
111 Davidson Road
Port Douglas 4871
Tel: (070) 99 5922

PORT DOUGLAS TO COOKTOWN

PREMIER

Bloomfield Wilderness Lodge (FB)
c/o 18 Grove Street
Cairns 4870
Tel: (070) 51 9687

Heritage Lodge (FB)
(Cape Tribulation)
Turpentine Road
Cooper Creek
via Mossman 4873
Tel: (070) 98 9138

Silky Oaks Colonial Lodge
Finlay Vale Road
Mossman River Gorge
Mossman 4873
Tel: (070) 98 1666

MODERATE

Punsand Bay Private Reserve
(Cape York Peninsula)
c/o PO Box 2097
Cairns 4870
Tel: (070) 31 2644

The Rainforest Resort
Coconut Beach
Cape Tribulation
Tel: (070) 52 1311

BUDGET

Crocodylus Village Budget Resort
Buchan Creek Road
Cow Bay
Cape Tribulation
Tel: (070) 31 1366

COOKTOWN

MODERATE

Cooktown's River of Gold Motel (M)
Cnr Hope and Walker Streets
Cooktown 4871
Tel: (070) 69 5222

Sovereign Hotel
Charlotte Street
Cooktown 4871
Tel: (070) 69 5400

BUDGET

Backpackers Cooktown
Charlotte Street
Cooktown 4871
Tel: (070) 69 5166

Cooktown Motor Inn (M)
Charlotte Street
Cooktown 4871
Tel: (070) 69 5357

Sea View (M)
Charlotte Street
Cooktown 4871
Tel: (070) 69 5377

CAPE YORK

PREMIER

Cape York Wilderness Lodge (FB)
c/o Australian Airlines
247 Adelaide Street
Brisbane 4000
Tel: (07) 229 8333

YOUTH HOSTELS

Youth Hostels Australia has over 20 Youth Hostels and associated hostels in Queensland. These hostels welcome members affiliated with the International Youth Hostel Federation. Fees vary, but average around $10 per night. Coastal Queensland Youth Hostels are located in the Gold Coast, Brisbane, the Sunshine Coast, Hervey Bay, Great Keppel Island, Mackay, Magnetic Island, Mission Beach and Cairns. For full details, contact the Queensland YHA Office - details below.

You may obtain an International Youth Hostel membership card at your local YHA or when you arrive in Australia.

National YHA Office
60 Mary Street
Surry Hills NSW 2010
Tel: (02) 212 1512
or 212 1151

Queensland YHA Office
462 Queen Street
Brisbane QLD 4000
Tel: (07) 831 2022

HOMESTAYS

For a holiday with a difference, you can stay as a paying guest with friendly Australian families in private home accommodation or on a working farm. In addition to the booking agencies listed below, station and farm holidays can also be booked through Queensland Government Travel Centres.

Agtour Australia
PO Box 754
Rockhampton QLD 4700
Tel: (079) 22 5788

Queensland Host Farm Association
c/o Cherry Sawyer
Go Connection
72 Victoria Park Road
Kelvin Grove QLD 4059
Tel: (07) 832 6799
Fax: (07) 369 4824

Key. NP = National Park; FB = full board

In addition to the major resort islands detailed below, there are many uninhabited islands, particularly in the Whitsunday region, on which permission to camp may be obtained from the National Parks and Wildlife Service.

SOUTHERN GROUP

•Lady Elliot Island (NP)

Access: by air ex Bundaberg
Number of guests: 100 maximum
Day visitors: no facilities
Camping: permitted

Moderate:
Lady Elliot Island Resort (FB)
LMB 6
via Bundaberg 4670
Tel: (071) 71 6077

(Cabin and tent accommodation)
Bookings can also be made through Sunstate Airlines offices.

•Lady Musgrave Island (NP)

Access: by sea ex Bundaberg
Camping: permitted

(Bush camping only - contact the National Parks and Wildlife Service for details and permits)

•Heron Island (NP)

Access: by air or sea ex Gladstone
Number of guests: 300 maximum
Day visitors: no
Camping: not permitted

Premier:
Heron Island Tourist Resort (FB)
via Gladstone 4680
Tel: (079) 78 1488
Fax: (079) 78 1457

•Great Keppel Island

Access: by air or sea ex Rockhampton
Number of guests: 400 maximum
Day visitors: yes
Camping: permitted away from the resort

Premier:
Great Keppel Island Resort (FB)
PO Box 108
Rockhampton 4700
Tel: (079) 39 1744

(Reservations should be made through Australian Airlines offices)

Moderate/Budget:
Wapparaburra Haven
Great Keppel Island
Tel: (079) 39 1907

(Timber cabins and camping - guests use day facilities at the resort)

WHITSUNDAY AND CUMBERLAND GROUPS

•Brampton Island (NP)

Access: by air or sea ex Mackay
Number of guests: 200 approximately
Day visitors: yes
Camping: not permitted

International:
Brampton Island Resort (FB)
Brampton Island
via Mackay 4740
Tel: (079) 51 4499
Fax: (079) 51 4097

(Reservations should be made through Australian Airlines offices)

•Newry Island (NP)

Access: by sea ex Mackay

Budget:
Newry Island Resort
via Seaforth 4741
Tel: (079) 59 0214

•Lindeman Island (NP)

Access: by sea ex Mackay, or air from Proserpine, Shute Harbour, Mackay or Hamilton Island
Number of guests: 350 approximately
Day visitors: occasionally
Camping: not permitted

Premier:
Lindeman Island Tourist Resort (FB)
Lindeman Island
via Mackay 4740
Tel: (079) 46 9333
Fax: (079) 46 9598

•Hamilton Island

Access: by air from major cities, or sea ex Shute Harbour
Number of guests: 2000
Day visitors: yes
Camping: not permitted

International/Premier:
Hamilton Island Resort
Hamilton Island 4803
Tel: (079) 46 9144
Fax: (079) 46 9425

International:
Villa Illalangi (FB)
Hamilton Island 4803
Tel: (079) 46 9144
Fax: (079) 46 9144

•Long Island (NP)

Access: by sea ex Hamilton Island or Shute Harbour
Number of guests: 400 approximately
Day visitors: not encouraged
Camping: not permitted

Premier:
Contiki Whitsunday Resort (FB)
Long Island
PMB 226
Mackay 4740
Tel: (079) 46 9400
Fax: (079) 46 9555

(18-35s only)

Moderate/budget:
Palm Bay Island Resort (FB)
Long Island
PMB 28
Mackay 4740
Tel: (079) 46 9233

(Cabins and permanent tents)

•South Molle Island (NP)

Access: by sea ex Shute Harbour or Hamilton Island
Number of guests: 500 approximately
Day visitors: yes
Camping: not permitted

Premier:
South Molle Island Resort (FB)
PMB 21
Mackay Mail Centre 4741
Tel: (079) 46 9433
Fax: (079) 46 9580

•Daydream Island

Access: by sea ex Shute Harbour or Hamilton Island
Number of guests: 600
Day visitors: yes
Camping: not permitted

Premier:
Daydream Island International Resort
PMB 22
Mackay 4740
Tel: (079) 48 8488
Fax: (079) 48 8499

•Whitsunday Island (NP)

Access: by sea from Shute Harbour
Camping: permitted

•Hook Island

Access: by sea from Shute Harbour
Number of guests: 72 maximum
Camping: permitted

Budget:
c/o South Molle Island Travel
Airlie Beach
Tel: (079) 46 6900

(Camping and cabins only)

•Hayman Island

Access: via Hamilton Island, or by sea ex
Shute Harbour
Number of guests: 480
Day visitors: no facilities
Camping: not permitted

International
Hayman Island International Hotel
Hayman Island
via Shute Harbour 4801
Tel: (079) 46 9100
Fax: (079) 46 9410

NORTHERN ISLANDS

•Orpheus Island (NP)

Access: by air ex Townsville or Cairns; by
sea from Townsville
Number of guests: 74 maximum (no children under 12 years)
Day visitors: no facilities
Camping: permitted away from the resort

International:
Orpheus Island Resort (FB)
Private Bag
Ingham 4850
Tel: (077) 77 7377
Fax: (077) 77 3377

•Hinchinbrook Island (NP)

Access: by air ex Townsville or Cairns; by
sea from Cardwell and Lucinda
Number of guests: 50
Day visitors: yes
Camping: permitted away from the resort

Premier:
Hinchinbrook Island Resort (FB)
PO Box 3
Cardwell 4816
Tel: (070) 66 8585

•Bedarra Island

Access: by air via Dunk Island; by sea ex
Dunk Island or Mission Beach
Number of guests: 32 at each resort
Day visitors: no
Camping: not permitted

International:
Bedarra Bay Resort (FB)
Bedarra Bay
Bedarra Island 4854
Tel: (070) 68 8233
Fax: (070) 68 8215

Bedarra Hideway Resort (FB)
Bedarra Island 4854
Tel: (070) 68 8168
Fax: (070) 68 8552

(Reservations for both resorts should be
made through Australian Airlines offices)

•Dunk Island (NP)

Access: by air ex Townsville or Cairns; by
sea from Mission Beach
Number of guests: 375 maximum
Day visitors: yes
Camping: permitted

International/Premier:
Dunk Island Resort (FB)
Brammo Bay
Dunk Island
via Townsville 4810
Tel: (070) 68 8199
Fax: (070) 68 8528

(Reservations should be made through
Australian Airlines offices)

•Fitzroy Island

Access: by sea ex Cairns
Number of guests: 200 approximately
Day visitors: yes
Camping: permitted

Premier/Moderate:
Fitzroy Island Resort
PO Box 898
Cairns 4870
Tel: (070) 51 9588
Fax: (070) 52 1335

•Green Island (NP)

Access: by sea or seaplane ex Cairns
Number of guests: 80
Day visitors: yes
Camping: not permitted

International:
Green Island Reef Resort (FB)
Green Island 4871
Tel: (070) 51 4644
Fax: (070) 51 3624

•**Lizard Island (NP)**

Access: by air ex Cairns
Number of visitors: 70 (no children under
6 years)
Day visitors: not encouraged
Camping: permitted away from resort

International:
Lizard Island Lodge (FB)
c/o Australian Airlines
PO Box 2572
Cairns 4870
Tel: (070) 50 3711
Fax: (070)

(Reservations can also be made through
any Australian Airlines office)

Things to Do

NATIONAL PARKS

If you intend to visit national parks in
Queensland general information may be ob-
tained from the Division of Conservation,
Parks and Wildlife (DCPW). PLEASE
NOTE THAT YOU WILL NEED A
CAMPING PERMIT IN ORDER TO
STAY IN ANY MAINLAND OR ISLAND
NATIONAL PARK. Fees range from $2 to
$7 per site per night. Permits are obtainable
from the DCPW office or local rangers in
each region. Contact the Brisbane office for
a list of DCPW offices in the area you're
heading to.

**Division of Conservation,
Parks and Wildlife.**
166 Anne Street

Brisbane
Tel: (07) 227 8185
PO Box 155
North Quay, QLD 4002

HISTORIC BUILDINGS

If you plan to visit a number of Queensland's
historic buildings, it is worth joining the
National Trust, which is dedicated to preserving these buildings in all parts of the
State. The Trust owns a number of properties
which are open to the public, and as a trust
member, you are entitled to free entry to any
of these. Annual membership costs $33 for
individuals and $44 for families. You'll
soon find that this pays off. The Queensland
National Trust office is open from 9 am to 5
pm, Monday to Friday, at:

Old Government House
George Street
Brisbane QLD 4000
Tel: (07) 229 1788

GETTING AROUND

BRISBANE

For hotels and accommodation, please refer to the Where To Stay section of the book.

Nature reserves and historical sights are listed below:

The Australian Woolshed
148 Samford Road
Ferny Hills
Tel: (07) 351 5366
Sheep shearing, craft shop etc.

Bunya Park Wildlife Sanctuary
Bunya Park Drive
Eatons Hill
Tel: (07) 264 1200
Open: 9.30 am to 5 pm, daily
Wildlife park.

City Botanic Gardens
Alice Street
Tel: (07) 221 4528
Open: Sunrise to sunset

City Hall Tower
King George Square
Open: 9 am to 4 pm
Views of Brisbane.

Earlystreet Historical Village
75 McIllwraith Avenue
Norman Park
Tel: (07) 398 6866
Open: 9.30 am to 4.30 pm Mon-Fri
10.30 am to 4.30 pm Sat/Sun
Early Queensland buildings.

Lone Pine Koala Sanctuary
Jesmond Road
Fig Tree Pocket
Tel: (07) 222 7278
Open: 9 am to 5 pm daily
Koalas, kangaroos, wallabies.

Mt Coot-tha Botanic Gardens
Mt Coot-tha Road
Toowong
Tel: (07) 377 8893
Open: Daily, 7 am to 5 pm

Mt Coot-tha Reserve and Lookout
Sir Samuel Griffith Drive
Toowong
Open: Daily
Views of Brisbane.

National Trust Properties
Tel: (07) 229 1788
A variety of historic buildings in and around Brisbane.

Queensland Cultural Centre
Southbank
Tel: (07) 840 7200
Open: Daily
Queensland Art Gallery, Museum, State Library and Performing Arts Complex.

Queensland Maritime Museum
Stanley Street
Southbank
Tel: (07) 844 5361
Open: 10 am to 5 pm, daily.

ISLANDS

Brisbane is the access point for the following Moreton Bay islands:

Bribie by road.
Coochiemudlo by ferry.
St Helena by ferry.
Moreton by air or sea.
North Stradbroke by sea.

NATIONAL PARKS

Contact the **Brisbane National Parks** and **Wildlife Service** for further details. Tel: (07) 202 0200

Brisbane Forest Park camping permitted.
Fort Lytton no camping.
Glass House Mountains no camping.

TOURS

Bushranger Tours
Tel: (07) 300 5381
Heritage, wildlife and botanic gardens tours.

Lovely! Champagne Balloon Flights
Tel: (07) 844 6671
Hot air balloon flights.

Q Guide
Tel: (07) 268 4630
City walking tours.

CRUISES

Brisbane River Cruises
Tel: (07) 221 6149
Cruises to Moreton Bay and islands

Koala Cruises
Tel: (07) 229 7055
River cruises and trips to St Helena Island.

Kookaburra Queen
Tel: (07) 221 1300
Paddlewheeler river trips.

FOOD DIGEST

WHERE TO EAT

The Cat's Tango
242 Hawken Drive
St Lucia
Tel: (07) 371 1452
International.

Chulio's
293 Sandgate Road
Albion
Tel: (07) 262 7494
Spanish/seafood.

Daniels's Steakhouse
145 Eagle Street
Tel: (07) 832 3444
Steak and seafood.

Emperor's Palace
31B Duncan Street
Fortitude Valley
Tel: (07) 252 3368
Chinese.

Little Tokyo
Bowen Street
(Between Wharf and Boundary Streets)
Tel: (07) 263 3940
Japanese.

Oxley's Wharf Restaurant
Coronation Drive
Milton
Tel: (07) 368 1866
Seafood.

Pasta Pasta
242 Hawken Drive
St Lucia
Tel: (07) 371 1403
Italian.

CULTURE PLUS

THEATRE

Brisbane Arts Theatre
210 Petrie Terrace

La Boite Theatre
57 Hale Street
Petrie Terrace
Tel: (07) 369 1622

Performing Arts Complex
Tel: (07) 846 4646
(Various theatre, ballet and opera performances at the Concert Hall, Lyric Theatre and Cremorne Theatre).

Royal Queensland Theatre Company
Suncorp Theatre
Turbot Street
Tel: (07) 221 5177

NIGHTLIFE

Alice's Rock Cafe
15-23 Adelaide Street
Tel: (07) 221 7719
Disco and live music.

Brisbane Tavern
347 Ann Street
Tel: (07) 229 5288
Live entertainment.

The Caxton Hotel
38 Caxton Street
Petrie Terrace
Tel: (07) 369 5971
Rock and roll, jazz, etc.

The Melbourne
2 Browning Street
West End
Tel: (07) 844 1571

JAZZ

Reflections
Sheraton Hotel
249 Turbot Street
Tel: (07) 835 3535
Night club.

Rosie's Tavern
Rowe's Arcade
Edward Street
Tel: (07) 229 4916
Upmarket disco.

SHOPPING

The Boardwalk
Cnr Durong and Breakfast Creek Roads
Newstead
Tel: (07) 252 2973
Shopping centre, restaurants, etc.

Brisbane Arcade
(Joins Queen and Adelaide Streets)
Gifts, souvenirs etc.

Fortitude Valley
Chinatown, boutiques and specialty
shops.

National Trust Gift Shop
The Mansions
40 George Street
Tel: (07) 221 1887
Quality Australian gifts.

Paddington Circle
Petrie Terrace
Paddington
Arts, crafts, boutiques.

Rowes Arcade
Edward Street
Prestige specialty shops.

Queen Street Mall
Main city shopping centre

Wintergarden on the Mall
Queen Street Mall
Specialty shops.

SPORTS

GOLF

Indooroopilly Golf Club
Tel: (07) 870 2012

MORETON BAY ISLANDS

National Parks

St Helena Island
No camping
Tel: (07) 396 5113

Moreton Island
Camping permitted
Tel: (075) 48 2710

Blue Lake (North Stradbroke Island)
No camping
Tel: (07) 202 0200

Moreton Island
Most of the island's tourist facilities centre around the Tangalooma Island Resort. Access is by launch from Brisbane. Camping is permitted.

North Stradbroke Island
The island is reached by launch from Cleveland (south of Brisbane) or the Gold Coast, with vehicular ferry access also possible from Cleveland. Most tourist facilities are based around Anchorage Village Beach Resort, which also features the Quarterdeck Restaurant. Camping is permitted.

GETTING AROUND

GOLD COAST

Sightseeing

Currumbin Sanctuary
28 Tomewin Street
Currumbin
Tel: (075) 34 1266
Native fauna sanctuary -
National Trust member.

Dreamworld
Dreamworld Parkway
Coomera
Tel: (075) 53 1133
Open: Daily
Theme park, rides and shows.

Koala Town
Pacific Highway
Coomera
Tel: (075)
Open: Daily, 9.30 am to 5 pm
Koalas and other native fauna.

Olson's Bird Gardens
Currumbin Creek Road
Currumbin Valley
Tel: (075) 33 0208
Open: Daily
Botanic gardens and aviaries.

Sea World Australia
Sea World Drive
Main Beach
Tel: (075) 32 1055
Open: Daily
Marine theme park.

SOUTH STRADBROKE ISLANDS

From the Gold Coast, South Stradbroke Island is reached by sea from Runaway Bay Marina north of Southport or by seaplane from Paradise Waters.

NATIONAL PARKS

For further details, contact the local **National Parks and Wildlife Service** - Tel: (07) 202 0200 or 227 8185.

Burleigh Head
No camping.

Fleay's Fauna Centre (Fauna reserve)
No camping.

Pine Ridge
No camping.

Tamborine Mountain (Hinterland)
No camping.

Springbrook (Hinterland)
Camping permitted.

Natural Arch (Hinterland)
No camping.

Lamington (Hinterland)
Vamping permitted.

AIR TOURS

Paradise Helicopters
Tel: (075) 36 9422

Tiger Moth Joy Rides
Tel: (075) 96 2662

OTHER TOURS

Hinterland Experience 4WD Bush Tours
Tel: (018) 73 2936
4WD day tours of the hinterland.

Lovely! Champagne Balloon Flights
Tel: (075) 92 0330
Hot air ballooning.

BOAT CHARTER & HIRE

Sunshine Cruiser Hire
Tel: (075) 46 1177
Skippered or self-drive cruisers.

CRUISES

Chevron Princess Cruises
Tel: (075) 39 0444
Canal and harbour cruises.

Shangri La Cruises
Tel: (075) 51 0888
Stradbroke Island day cruises.

Sir Bruce Cruises
Tel: (075) 92 0505
Varied calm water cruises.

FOOD DIGEST

WHERE TO EAT

For other dining out suggestions, call the Restaurant Infoline on (075) 91 6699.

Ginza
2909 Gold Coast Highway
Surfers Paradise
Tel: (075) 92 2884
Japanese/Korean.

Horizons
Sheraton Mirage Hotel
Sea World Drive
Main Beach
Tel: (075) 91 1488
A la carte international.

Oskars on the Beach
Marine Parade
Coolangatta
Tel: (075) 36 4621
International.

The Paddle Steamer
Cnr Cavill Avenue and
Gold Coast Highway
Surfers Paradise
Tel: (075) 31 7159
Seafood.

River Inn
Wahroonga Place
Surfers Paradise
Tel: (075) 31 6177
Seafood.

Tandoori Taj
3100 Gold Coast Highway
Surfers Paradise
Tel: (075) 39 9433
Indian.

NIGHTLIFE

Cocktails and Dreams
The Mark
Orchid Avenue
Surfers Paradise
Tel: 9075) 92 1955
Upmarket nightclub.

Conrad International Hotel
and Jupiters Casino
Broadbeach Island
Broadbeach
Tel: (075) 92 1133
Casino and other entertainment.

Melba's on the Park
46 Cavill Avenue
Surfers Paradise
Tel: (075) 38 7411
Cabaret/restaurant.

SHOPPING

Galleria Fashion Shopping Plaza
Cnr Gold Coast Highway and
Elkhorn Avenue
Surfers Paradise
Tel: (075) 92 1100
Shopping centre.

Marina Mirage
Sea World Drive
Main Beach
Tel: (075) 91 4955
Upmarket shopping complex.

Pacific Fair
Nerang Road
Broadbeach
Tel: (075) 39 8766
Shops, department stores, etc.

Presenting Australia
Raptis Plaza
Cavill Mall
Surfers Paradise
Tel: (075) 92 1823
Australiana, gifts and souvenirs.

Sanctuary Cove
Caseys Road
Hope Island
Tel: (075) 30 8400
Upmarket shopping complex.

MARKETS

Burleigh Heads Markets -
Last Sunday in every month
(Marine Parade, Burleigh Heads)

Coolangatta Markets -
2nd Sunday in every month
(Marine Parade, Coolangatta)

Flea Market -
Every Saturday and Sunday
(Nerang Coast Road)

SPORTS

DIVING

Gold Coast Dive Centre
Tel: (075) 32 8820

GOLF

Carrara Golf Centre
Tel: (075) 58 4400

Palm Meadows
Carrara
Tel: (075) 94 2800

Sanctuary Cove
Tel: (075) 30 8400

Windaroo Golf Course
Beenleigh
Tel: (07) 287 4555

GETTING AROUND

SUNSHINE COAST

Sightseeing

Buderim Wildlife and Koala Park
Cnr Bruce Highway and Brisbane Road
Buderim
Tel: (071) 45 1670
Open: 9 am to 4.30 pm, daily
Native fauna park.

Forest Glen Deer and Wildlife Sanctuary
Bruce Highway
Forest Glen
Tel: (071) 45 1274
Open: 9 am to 5 pm, daily.

Queensland Reptile and Fauna Park
Glasshouse Mountains Tourist Road
Beerwah
Tel: (071) 94 1134
Open: daily.

Underwater World
The Wharf
Parkyn Parade
Mooloolaba Spit
Tel: (071) 44 8088
Open: daily.

The Wharf
Mooloolaba Spit
Maritime Museum, shops, restaurants, boat hire.

NATIONAL PARKS

Full details can be obtained from the Noosa National Parks and Wildlife Service. Tel: (071) 47 3243

Peregian no camping.
Kondalilla no camping.
Noosa no camping.
Cooloola camping permitted.

BOAT CHARTER & HIRE

Luxury Afloat
Tewantin
Tel: (071) 49 7611
Houseboats

Noosa River Houseboats
Tewantin
Tel: (071) 47 1411

O Boat and Catamaran Hire
Noosaville
Tel: (071) 49 7513

CRUISES

Cooloola Cruises
Noosaville

Tel: (071) 49 7884
Half and full day cruises on the Noosa river and lakes.

Everglades Water Bus Co
Noosa
Tel: (071) 47 1838
Half and full day Everglades cruises
4WD tours of Cooloola National Park.

TOURS

Balloon Aloft
Nambour
Tel: (071) 41 5020
Hot air balloon flights.

Budget Chauffeur Drive
Tel: (071) 93 3321
Personalised tours.

Clip Clop Treks
Tel (071) 49 7408
Horse riding.

Lookaburra Tours
Alexandra Headland
Tel: (071) 43 4821
Coach tours

O'Loughlans Coach and Travel Service
Tel: (071) 43 7880
Full and half day coach tours of the area.

Sunshine 4WD Hire
Noosa Heads
Tel: (071) 47 3702.

FOOD DIGEST

WHERE TO EAT

China World
1 Sunshine Beach Road
Noosa Heads
Tel: (071) 47 4725
Chinese.

Going Pasta
The Sound Shopping Place
Noosa Sound
Tel: (071) 47 5366
Italian.

Pavilions
Netanya Noosa
75 Hastings Street
Noosa Heads
Tel: (071) 47 4722.

Sanosa
Bay Village Shopping Centre
Hastings Street
Noosa Heads
Tel: (071) 49 2200
Japanese.

Troppo
Noosa Harbour Resort
Quamby Place
Noosa Sound
Tel: (071) 47 5021
Oyster bar.

NIGHTLIFE

Sheraton Noosa Resort
Hastings Street
Noosa Heads
Tel: (071) 49 4888
Bars and restaurants.

SHOPPING

Australia House
15 Sunshine Beach Road
Noosa Junction
Australiana, souvenirs, maps etc.

Bay Village on Hastings
18 Hastings Street
Noosa Heads
(Shopping Centre).

Maroochydore Shopping Centre
Cnr Duporth Avenue and Horton Parade
Maroochydore.

Noosa Fair Shopping Centre
Lanyana Way
Noosa Junction.

SPORTS

FISHING

Gemini Reef Cruises
Tel: (071) 92 1035
Reef fishing trips.

GOLF COURSES

Cooroy Golf Club
Tel: (071) 47 6051

Noosa Valley Golf Club
Tel: (071) 49 1364

Tewantin-Noosa Golf Club
Tel: (071) 47 1407

GETTING AROUND

FRASER ISLAND

Access to Fraser Island is from Rainbow Beach, Hervey Bay or Maryborough.

FACILITIES

The island's only townships are at Eurong and Happy Valley, which have restaurant, bar, petrol, bait and shopping facilities, while Orchid Beach Resort features a licensed restaurant, bar and shop. There is also the Sarinay restaurant at Happy Valley Resort.

TOURS

Fraser Flyer Adventure Tours
Tel: (071) 25 1755
Catamaran/4WD day tours.

Fraser Island Fishing and Tours
PO Box 13
Rainbow Beach
Tel: (071) 27 9126.

Fraser Island Top Tours
Tel: (071) 28 2577
Comprehensive coach tours

Fraser Venture Day Tour
Tel: (071) 28 1900
Cruises.

MV Islander
Tel: (071) 28 9370
Day cruises

4WD HIRE

Bay City Rentals
Tel: (071) 25 1955
Bay 4WD Centre
Tel: (071) 28 2981
Vehicle and camping equipment hire.

Fraser Island 4WD Hire
Tel: (071) 86 3227.

NATIONAL PARKS

Great Sandy National Park
Vehicle access permits are obtainable from the National Parks and Wildlife Service - Tel: (071) 22 2455 or 86 3160.

Getting Around

ARLIE BEACH/SHUTE HARBOUR

Sightseeing

In addition to the islands and waterways of the Whitsunday region, the following are popular attractions:

Crocodile and Wildlife Park
Shute Harbour Road
Orchid Valley
Tel: (079) 46 7155
Open: Daily

Proserpine Sugar Mill
Tel: (079) 45 1755
Open: July to December for tours

WHITSUNDAY REGION

Islands

The Proserpine/Airlie Beach/Shute Harbour area provides access to the following resort or camping islands:

Daydream by sea.
Hamilton by sea or air ex Proserpine.
Hayman by sea via Hamilton Island.
Hook by sea.
Lindeman by air.
Long by sea.
South Molle by sea.
Whitsunday by sea.

NATIONAL PARKS

For further details, contact the Airlie Beach National Parks and Wildlife Service office. Tel: (079) 46 9430.

Conway camping permitted
Whitsunday Islands camping permitted on 19 islands.

AIR TOURS

Seair Pacific
Tel: (079) 46 9336
Seaplane Barrier Reef tours.

BOAT CHARTER & HIRE

Australian Bareboat Charters
Tel: (079) 46 9381
Yachts and power cruisers.

Cumberland Charter Yachts
Tel: (079) 46 7500
Bareboat or crewed charters.

Mandalay Boat Charters
Tel: (079) 46 6298
Bareboat or crewed yacht charters.

Queensland Yacht Charters
Tel: (008) 25 1217 (toll free)
Crewed or bareboat charters.

Whitsunday Escape Houseboat Charters
Tel: (079) 46 7301
Bareboat charters.

Whitsunday Rent a Yacht
Tel: (079) 46 9232
Bareboat or crewed charters.

CRUISES

Coral Trekker
Tel: (02) 264 3366
7 day cruises on a 70' square-rigger.

Fantasea Cruises
Tel: (079) 46 9357
Catamaran reef trips.

Golden Plover Tall Ships Safaris
Tel: (079) 46 6049
7 day cruises on a 100' brigantine.

Southern Spirit
Tel: (02) 498 5622
7 night luxury cruises ex Hamilton Island.

Trinity Cruises
Tel: (079) 46 6255
Trimaran day trips.

OTHER TOURS

Tropical Rainforest Tours
Tel: (079) 46 6224
Half day 4WD tours.

FOOD DIGEST

WHERE TO EAT

KCs Char Grill
382 Shute Harbour Road
Airlie Beach
Tel: (079) 46 6320
Char grilled steaks and seafood.

La Perouse Seafood Restaurant
The Esplanade
Airlie Beach
Tel: (079) 46 6262
A la carte French.

Manollis Greek Taverna
The Esplanade
Cannonvale
Tel: (079) 46 7533
Greek and seafood.

Romeos
Shute Harbour Road
Airlie Beach
Tel: (079) 46 6337
Italian.

Spice Island Bistro
378 Shute Harbour Road
Airlie Beach
Tel: (079) 46 6585
Asian and Indian.

NIGHTLIFE

Airlie Beach Hotel/Motel
The Esplanade
Airlie Beach
Tel: (079) 46 6233
Live bands, discos etc

Reef Oceania Village
Shute Harbour Road
Cannonvale
Tel: (079) 46 6137
Restaurant and live entertainment

Whitsunday Village Resort
Shute Harbour Road
Airlie Beach
Tel: (079) 46 6266
Restaurant and live entertainment

Tricks Nightclub
325 Shute Harbour Road
Airlie Beach
Tel: (079) 46 6465
Bistro, dancing, etc

SHOPPING

Jilly's at the Jetty
The Jetty
Shute Harbour
Gifts and souvenirs.

Naturally Australiana
Spalla Centre
Shute Harbour Road
Airlie Beach
Opals, souvenirs, jewellery etc.

Sunny Koala
Spalla Centre
Shute Harbour Road
Airlie Beach
Gifts and souvenirs.

Whitsunday Centre
Cnr Shute Harbour Road and Coconut Grove
Airlie Beach
Restaurant and shopping complex.

SPORTS

DIVING

Barrier Reef Diving Adventures
Tel: (079) 46 9232
Instruction and 5 day trips.

Barrier Reef Diving Services
Tel: (079) 46 6204
Instruction and trips.

H2O Sportz
(Hamilton Island)
Tel: (079) 46 9144
Courses and dive trips.

Tropical Reef Dive Charters
Tel: (079) 46 6996
Courses, dive trips, boats for charter.

FISHING

Hamilton Island Charters
Tel: (079) 46 9144
Gamefishing charters ex Hamilton Island.

GOLF

Proserpine Golf Club
Tel: (079) 45 1315.

Whitsunday Golf Club
Cannonvale
Tel: (079) 46 6588.

GETTING AROUND

MARYBOROUGH/HERVEY BAY

Sightseeing

Baddow House
364 Queen Street
Maryborough
Tel: (071) 23 1883
Open: 10 am to 4 pm, daily
Historic home.

Hervey Bay Historical Museum
Zephyr Street
Tel: (071) 28 1271
Open 1 to 5 pm, Fri-Sun.

Hervey Bay Wildlife Park
Main Highway
Tel: (071) 24 1733
Open: 9 am to 4.30 pm, daily
Native fauna park.

Maryborough Sugar Museum
Lower Kent Street
Maryborough
Tel: (071) 21 2361
Open: 8am to 4 pm, Mon-Fri
Sugar industry museum.

Neptune's Marine Aquarium
Dayman Point
Urangan
Tel: (071) 28 9828
Open: 9 am to 4 pm, daily
Living coral, fish, etc.

The Nut Factory
Cnr Bruce Highway and Owanyilla
Boundary Road
Maryborough
Tel: (071) 29 2154
Open: 9 am to 5 pm, daily
Macadamia nut plantation and factory.

Queens Park
Sussex Street
Maryborough
Park and model railway.

FRASER ISLAND

Hervey Bay is the main departure point for Fraser Island, with both air and vehicular ferry connections.

NATIONAL PARKS

For details, contact the local National Parks and Wildlife Service - Great Sandy NP, Tel: (071) 86 3160; other parks, Tel: (071) 23 7711.

Mt Walsh camping permitted.
Great Sandy (Fraser Island) camping permitted.
Woody Island camping permitted.

BOAT CHARTER & HIRE

Mary River Houseboats
Tel: (071) 21 2648

Fraser Island Rent a Yacht
Pacific Marina
Tin Can Bay
Tel: (071) 86 4153

Sandy Straits Rent-A-Cruise
Tel: (071) 28 9031
30' cruiser hire.

CRUISES

Hervey Bay Whale Watch
Tel: (071) 28 1847
Half or full day whale watch cruises.

Krystal Klear
Tel: (071) 28 9537
Glass bottom boat coral viewing.

Maryborough Heritage Cruises
Tel: (071) 23 1462
Mary River cruises.

Colony Room Restaurant
Mineral Sands Motel
Cnr Ferry and Albert Streets
Maryborough
Tel: (071) 21 2366.

Don Camillo
Cnr Crown Street and Esplanade
Urangan
Tel: (071) 25 1087
Italian and seafood.

Delfinos Bay Resort
383 Esplanade
Hervey Bay
Tel: (071) 24 1666
Bistro and cocktail bar.

Seven Seas
573 Esplanade
Urangan
Tel: (071) 28 9699
Seafood.

NIGHTLIFE

Royal Hotel
Kent Street
Maryborough
Tel: (071) 21 2241
Bars and night spot.

Also live music at the following hotels:
Hervey Bay Hotel, **Pialba Hotel-Motel**,
Torquay Hotel.

SHOPPING

Bottlebrush Crafts
320 Albert Street
Tel: (071) 22 2533
Craft exhibitions and shop.

Maryborough Markets
Kent and Adelaide Streets
Thursday: 10 a.m. to 8 p.m.

Pialba Place Shopping Centre
Main Street
Pialba
Hervey Bay's major shopping centre.

Pollyannas
352 Esplanade
Scarness
Tel: (071) 28 4166
Gifts and souvenirs.

SPORTS

DIVING

Boomerang Cruises
Tel: (071) 28 3218
Diving trips.

Divers Mecca
Tel: (071) 25 1626
Instruction and dive trips.

FISHING

Boomerang Cruises
Tel: (071) 28 3218
Fishing trips.

Fraser Princess
Tel: (071) 25 1522
Fishing trips.

Super Cat Reef Fishing Trips
Tel: (071) 25 1900
Day or evening trips.

Tasman Venture
Tel: (071) 28 1847
Day or extended fishing charters.

GOLF

Craignish Country Club
Dundowran
Tel: (071) 28 7186.

Eagles Nest Golf Course
Urangan
Tel: (071) 25 2728.

Hervey Bay Golf Club
Pialba
Tel: (071) 28 4249.

GETTING AROUND

BUNDABERG

Sightseeing

Bundaberg Distillery
Avenue Street
East Bundaberg
Tel: (071) 52 4077
Open: Mon-Fri
Rum distillery tours.

Bundaberg Historical Museum
Bundaberg Botanic Gardens
Mt Perry Road
North Bundaberg
Tel: (071) 52 0101
Open: Daily, 10 a.m. to 4 p.m.

Hinkler House Memorial Museum
Bundaberg Botanic Gardens
Tel: (071) 52 0222
Open: Daily, 10 a.m. to 4 p.m.

Pennyroyal Herb Farm
Penny's Lane
Branyan
Tel: (071) 55 1622
Open: 9 a.m. to 5 p.m. daily.

ISLANDS

Bundaberg is the access point for **Lady Elliot Island**. Transfers are by air. Cruises are also available to **Lady Musgrave Island**.

NATIONAL PARKS

For full details, contact the National Parks and Wildlife Service on (071 26 8810 or 59 2628.

Woodgate camping permitted
Mon Repos Environmental Park No camping.

TOURS

Bundaberg Coach Tours
Tel: (071) 53 1037.

CRUISES

MV Lady Musgrave
Tel: (071) 72 9011
Day cruises to Lady Musgrave Island.

FOOD DIGEST

WHERE TO EAT

Alexandra's Seafood Restaurant
66 Quay Street
Tel: (071) 72 7255.

Il Gambero
57 Targo Street
Tel: (071) 52 5342
Seafood.

The Rendezvous
Sugar Country Motor Inn
Cne Bourbong and Burrum Streets
Tel: (071) 53 1166.

NIGHTLIFE

Krystal's Place
East End Hotel
58 Princes Street
Tel: (071) 52 6388
Restaurants and live entertainment.

SPORTS

DIVING

Anglo Diving Services
Tel: (071) 71 6422
Dive trips

Bundaberg Dive Centre
Tel: (071) 72 6707
Tuition and dive trips

GOLF

Bargara Golf Club
Tel: (071) 59 2221

Bundaberg Golf Club
Tel: (071) 52 6765

GETTING AROUND

GLADSTONE

Sightseeing

Auckland Hill Lookout
Views of Gladstone and islands

Gladstone Art Gallery and Museum
Cnr Goondoon and Bramston Streets
Tel: (079) 72 2022
Open Mon-Fri, 10 a.m. to 5 p.m.;
Sat, 10 a.m. to noon.

Gladstone Marina

Tondoon Botanic Gardens
Open: daily, 8.30 a.m. to 5.30 p.m.

HERON ISLAND

Gladstone is the access point for Heron Island. Transfers are either by launch or helicopter.

NATIONAL PARKS

Full details can be obtained from the Gladstone National Parks and Wildlife Service. Tel: (079) 76 1621.

Heron Island no camping.
Masthead and Tryon Islands camping permitted.
North West and Lady Musgrave Islands camping permitted.
Eurimbula camping permitted.
Deepwater camping permitted.

BOAT CHARTER & HIRE

Coral Reef Booking Service
Tel: (079) 72 2982
Snorkelling, diving, fishing, cruising.

Gladstone Marina Services
Tel: (079) 72 4033
Fishing, diving or day trips.

Lady Elliot
Tel: (079) 75 7162
Charters for fishing, snorkelling, etc.

OTHER TOURS

CQ Safari Tours
Tel: (079) 72 1644
Personalised tours of Gladstone and surrounding areas.

CRUISES

Wistari Reef Adventures
c/o Reef Adventureland Travel
Tel: (079) 72 2866
Day trips to the reef.

FOOD DIGEST

WHERE TO EAT

Brass Palm
100 Goondoon Street
Tel: (079) 72 4499.

Capone's Pasta and Pizza
Windmill Centre
Phillip Street
Tel: (079) 78 2911.

Clancy's Family Restaurant
19 Tank Street
Tel: (079) 72 1171.

Park Lane International Restaurant
4th Floor
Cnr Goondoon and Tank Streets
Tel: (079) 72 5545.

Swaggy's Australian Restaurant
56 Goondoon Street
Tel: (079) 72 1653
Steaks, seafood, crocodile steaks.

NIGHTLIFE

Gladstone City Theatre
Tel: (079) 72 2822
Regular show and events.

SPORTS

GOLF

Gladstone Golf Club
Tel: (079) 78 1310

GETTING AROUND

ROCKHAMPTON/YEPPOON

Sightseeing

Aquatic Adventureland
Cnr High Street and Bruce Highway
North Rockhampton
Tel: (079) 28 3344
Water slides, mini golf, barbecue and picnic areas.

City of Rockhampton Art Gallery
Victoria Parade
Southside
Tel: (079) 27 7129.

Cooberrie Park
Woodbury Road
Yeppoon
Tel: (079) 39 7590
Native fauna park.

Dreamtime Cultural Centre
Bruce Highway
North Rockhampton
Tel: (079) 36 1655
Open: Daily except Wednesday, 11 a.m. to 5.30 p.m.

Aboriginal cultural centre,
art gallery and shop.

Koorana Crocodile Farm
Emu Park Road
(North of Rockhampton)
Tel: (079) 34 4749
Open: Thursday-Monday.

Old Glenmore Homestead
Belmont Road
Tel: (079) 36 1033
Open: Sun-Thurs, 11 am. onwards
Historic homestead an.d evening
dinner dances.

Olsens Caverns
Barmoya Road
Tel: (079) 34 2883
Open: Daily, 8.30 a.m. onwards
Limestone caves.

Quay Street
National Trust classified historic
buildings.

GREAT KEPPEL ISLAND

Rockhampton is the access point for Great
Keppel Island.

NATIONAL PARKS

For full details, contact the Rockhampton
National Parks and Wildlife Service: Tel:
(079) 76 1621.

Keppel Group Islands camping permitted.
Capricorn Coast no camping.
Mt Archer no camping.

TOURS

Flexi Tours
Tel: (079) 27 1111
Private taxi tours.

Rotherys Coaches
Tel: (079) 22 4320
Coach tours of Rockhampton and sur-
rounding area.

CRUISES

Capricorn Reefseeker
Tel: (079) 33 6744
Day reef cruises ex Yeppoon.

Denison Star
Tel: (079) 22 4334
Great Keppel Island ferry service.

Great Keppel Island Tourist Services
Tel: (079) 33 6744
Day tours to Great Keppel Island and the
reef.

FOOD DIGEST

WHERE TO EAT

Berserker Tavern
Dean Street
North Rockhampton
Tel: (079) 28 4888.

Central Park Restaurant
224 Murray Street
Rockhampton
Tel: (079) 27 2333
Seafood and steak.

Pickles
75 High Street
Rockhampton
Tel: (079) 28 6490
Buffet and smorgasbord.

Riverside International Restaurant
Country Comfort Inn
31 Bolsover Street
Rockhampton
Tel: (079) 27 7488.

Wah Hah
70 Denham Street
Rockhampton
Tel: (079) 27 1659.
Chinese

NIGHTLIFE

Ambassador on the Park Cocktail Bar
161 George Street
Rockhampton
Tel: (079) 27 5855.

The Factory Niteclub
The Headrick's Building
189 East Street
Rockhampton
Tel: (079)

La Bamba Nightclub and Simons Restaurant
16 Hill Street
Yeppoon
Tel: (079) 39 3212.

SHOPPING

Rockhampton's main shopping area is the City Heart Mall, located on East Street. Other shops are:

Biroo Gallery
Cnr Agnes and Spencer Streets
Rockhampton
Pottery, crafts and jewellery.

Rockhampton Markets
Saturday and Sunday from 8 a.m.

SPORTS

DIVING

Rockhampton Diving
Tel: (079) 28 0433
Diving trips to Heron Island and the reef.

GOLF

Capricorn International Resort Golf Course
Yeppoon
Tel: (079) 39 0211.

Rockhampton Golf Club
Tel: (079) 22 4098.

GETTING AROUND

MACKAY

Sightseeing

Illawong Fauna Sanctuary
Illawong Beach
Tel: (079) 57 7591
Open: Daily, 10 a.m. to 10 p.m.
Native fauna sanctuary.

Muddies Crab and Prawn Farm
Illawong Drive
Far Beach
Tel: (079) 57 2402
Open: Daily
Australia's only crab farm-tours and restaurant.

Polstone Farm
Homebush Road
Tel: (079) 59 7359
Open: Tours from May to June
Working sugar cane farm.

Sugar Mill and Bulk Sugar Terminal
Tel: (079) 52 2677
Open: Monday-Friday
Sugar industry tours.

ISLANDS

Mackay is the access point for the following islands:

Hayman by air.
Hamilton by air.
Lindeman by air or sea.
Brampton by air or sea.
Newry by sea.

NATIONAL PARKS

Full details are available from the Mackay National Parks and Wildlife Service. Tel: (079) 51 8788

Brampton Island no camping.
Cape Palmerston camping permitted.
Eungella camping permitted.
Cape Hillsborough camping permitted.
Newry Island camping permitted

AIR TOURS

Air Pioneer
Tel: (079) 57 6661
Reef trips.

Fredericksons Aerial Services
Tel: (079) 42 3161
Reef trips.

Seair Pacific
Tel: (079) 57 2505
Reef trips.

CRUISES

Elizabeth E Coral Cruises
Tel: (079) 57 4281
Extended Barrier Reef cruises

Roylen Cruises
Tel: (079) 55 3066
One or five day cruises.

FOOD DIGEST

WHERE TO EAT

The Banquet House
68 Victoria Street
Tel: (079) 51 1003
Chinese.

Harbour Lights
Outer Harbour
Tel: (079) 55 1203
Seafood and cocktail bar.

Jakades Restaurant and Steakhouse
Cnr Shakespeare and Sydney Streets
Tel: (079) 51 1119
Australian fare.

Romeo and Juliet's
309 Shakespeare Street
Tel: (079) 53 1111
International.

NIGHTLIFE

Fathoms
Bridge Road
Illawong Beach
Tel: (079) 57 2044
Over 25s club.

Paradise Nights Niteclub
85 Victoria Street
Tel: (079) 51 4365.

Valentino's
Victoria Street
Tel: (079) 57 3965.

SHOPPING

P. Comino and Sons
14-16 Sydney Street
Tel: (079) 57 4370
Bush clothing, Akubra hats, etc.

Gumleaf Gifts and Souvenirs
126 Victoria Street
Tel: (079) 51 3861
T-shirts, souvenirs, etc.

Tourism Mackay
'The Junk'
Nebo Road
Tel: (079) 52 2677
Souvenirs, postcards, videos etc.

Woolly Fleece
20 Evans Avenue
North Mackay
Tel: (079) 51 2649
Sheepskin products.

SPORTS

DIVING

Barnes Reefdiving
Tel: (079) 51 1472
Courses and island trips.

Little Aussie Dive Shop
Tel: (079) 57 2028
Courses and dive tours.

Mackay Diving
Tel: (079) 51 1640
Courses, day trips, extended trips.

GOLF

Mackay Golf Club
Tel: (079) 42 1521.

GETTING AROUND

TOWNSVILLE

Sightseeing

Anderson Park Botanical Gardens
Gulliver Street
Mundingburra
Gardens, conservatory, picnic areas.

Billabong Sanctuary
Bruce Highway
(17 km south)
Tel: (077) 78 8344
Open: Daily - 9 a.m. to 5 p.m.

Native animal sanctuary, tropical gardens

Castle Hill Lookout
Views of the city, coastline and islands.

Great Barrier Reef Wonderland
Flinders Street East
Tel: (077) 21 2411
Open: Daily - 9.30 a.m. to 5 p.m.
Coral reef aquarium, Queensland Museum, specialty shops.

Jezzine Military Museum
Kissing Point Battery
Open: 9 a.m. to 3 p.m., weekdays 2 to 4 p.m., weekends.

Maritime Museum
Port of Townsville
Open: 10 a.m. to 4 p.m., weekdays 1 to 4 p.m., weekends.

Mount Stuart Lookout
Flinders Highway
(2 km south)
Views of the Townsville area.

National Trust Historic Houses
5 Castling Street
West End
Tel: (077) 72 5195
Open: Saturday/Sunday - 1 to 4 p.m.
Worker's dwelling, farmhouse and villa residence.

Townsville Museum
Sturt Street
Open: 10 a.m. to 3 p.m.,
weekdays 10 a.m. to 1 p.m., weekends.

Perc Tucker Regional Gallery
Flinders Mall
Open: 10 a.m. to 5 p.m.
Art gallery.

ISLANDS

Townsville is the access point for the following islands:

Dunk by air
Bedarra by air via Dunk Island
Hinchinbrook by air
Orpheus by plane or helicopter
Magnetic by launch

NATIONAL PARKS

Full details of national parks in the Townsville area can be obtained by contacting the Queensland National Parks and Wildlife Service: Tel: (077) 74 1411.

Bowling Green Bay camping permitted.
Magnetic Island no camping.
Townsville Town Common no camping.
Mt Spec camping permitted.
Orpheus Island camping permitted.
Herbert River (Ingham district) camping permitted.
Wallman Falls (Ingham district) camping permitted.
Jourama Falls (Ingham district) camping permitted.
Hinchinbrook Island (Cardwell district camping permitted.
Edmund Kennedy (Cardwell district) camping permitted.
Dunk Island (Cardwell district) camping permitted.

AIR TOURS

Rundle Air Service
Tel: (077) 79 6933
Air charter service.

Seair Pacific
Tel: (077) 25 1470
Scenic reef flights, services to Orpheus and Hinchinbrook Islands.

OTHER TOURS

Brolga Tours
Tel: (077) 21 2266
Day and evening bus tours of Townsville and surrounding areas.

Raging Thunder
Tel: (077) 72 5022
Whitewater rafting: 1/2 to 7 day trips.

BOAT CHARTER & HIRE

Breakwater Boat Charter and Rentals
Tel: (077) 71 3063
Fishing or pleasure boats.

CRUISES

Coral Princess Cruises
Tel: (077) 21 1673
4 day cruises from Townsville to Cairns or reverse.

Pure Pleasure Cruises
Tel: (077) 21 3555
Day cruises to the outer Barrier Reef. Diving, snorkelling and fishing available.

Reef Link
Tel: (077) 72 5672
Day trips to the outer reef.

Westmark Reef and Island Cruise
Tel: (077) 21 1913
MV 'Magnetic Explorer' day trips to Magnetic and Orpheus Islands. Dive facilities available on board.

Worripa Cruises
Tel: (077) 71 3063 or 78 5937
Catamaran day trips from Magnetic Island to the Reef.

FOOD DIGEST

WHERE TO EAT

Admirals Seafood Restaurant
Cnr Blackwood and Sturt Streets
Tel: (077) 21 1911
Seafood and other dishes.

Affaire de Coeur
1 Sturt Street
Tel: (077) 72 2742
Seafood and other dishes.

Cassis Restaurant and Cocktail Bar
Townsville Ambassador Hotel
The Strand
Tel: (077) 72 4255.

Higgins
141 Flinders Street
Tel: (077) 72 4337
International BYO restaurant.

Pasini's
2 Archer Street
South Townsville
Tel: (077) 71 6333
North Italian.

Seagulls
74 The Esplanade
Tel: (077) 21 3111
Seafood and steaks.

NIGHTLIFE

Dance North
Arts Centre
Cnr Stanley and Walker Streets
Tel: (077) 72 2549.

North Queensland dance company
New Moon Theatre Co
Tel: (077) 72 2311

Sheraton Breakwater Casino
Sir Leslie Thiess Drive
Tel: (077) 22 2333
Open: Noon to 2 a.m. daily.

Townsville Civic Theatre
Boundary Street
South Townsville
Tel: (077) 71 4188.

SHOPPING

Flinders Mall is Townsville's main shopping area, while Flinders Street East contains galleries, souvenir and art/craft shops.

Aussie Original Designs
88 Primrose Street
Belgian Gardens
Tel: (077) 72 1008
Screenprinted gifts and t-shirts.

Australian Precious Opals
223 Flinders Street East
Tel: (077) 72 7300.

Djilbalama Arts and Crafts
Hollimans Arcade
435 Flinders Street
Tel: (077) 72 1481
Aboriginal artefacts.

Flinders Mall Cotters Market
Flinders Mall
Open: Sundays - 8.30 a.m. to 12.30 p.m.
Arts and crafts market.

David Jones
313-335 Flinders Mall
Tel: (077) 71 3041
Department store.

SPORTS

DIVING

Mike Ball Watersports
Tel: (077) 72 3022
Diving courses and dive tours to the reef.

The Dive Bell
Tel: (077) 21 1155
Diving school, dive trips, charter boat.

Pro-Dive
Tel: (077) 72 7288
Dive courses and reef trips.

FISHING

Aussie Game Fishing Agencies
Tel: (077) 73 1912
Game fishing charters.

Australian Pacific Charters
Tel: (077) 72 4205
Game fishing charters.

GOLF

Rowes Bay Country Club
Tel: (077) 74 1188.

Townsville Golf Club
Tel: (077) 79 0133.

GETTING AROUND

MAGNETIC ISLAND

Sightseeing

Arcadia Pottery Gallery
Horseshoe Bay Road
Tel: (077) 78 5600
Handcrafted pottery studio.

Koala Park Oasis
Horseshoe Bay
Tel: (077) 78 5260
Koalas and other wildlife.

Sharkworld
Nelly Bay
Tel: (077) 78 5187
Tropical aquarium.

TOURS

Horseshoe Ranch
Tel: (077) 78 5109
Horse riding and bicycle hire.

Magnetic Diving
Tel: (077) 78 5799
Courses and reef trips.

Nelly Bay Sail Hire
Tel: (077) 78 5748
Catamaran and sailboard hire.

Reef Link
Tel: (077) 72 5733
Cruises.

FOOD DIGEST

WHERE TO EAT

Alla Capri
Arcadia
Tel: (077) 78 5448
Italian.

The Bounty Restaurant
Horseshoe Bay
Tel: (077) 78 5208
Seafood.

Latitude 19 Resort
Nelly Bay
Tel: (077) 78 5200
Licensed restaurant.

Skipper's Restaurant
Arcadia Resort
Tel: (077) 78 5177
A la carte.

SHOPPING

Captain Kidd's Treasure Chest
Horseshoe Bay
Gifts and souvenirs.

Figtree Gift Shop
The Mall
Picnic Bay
T-shirts, souvenirs, etc.

GETTING AROUND

CAIRNS AND SURROUNDING AREA

Sightseeing

BEACHES
South and north of Cairns (with distances from Cairns):

South:
Kurrimine Beach	120 km
Mission Beach	130 km

North (Marlin Coast):
Machans Beach	10 km
Holloways Beach	12 km
Yorkeys Knob	16 km
Trinity Beach	21 km
Kewarra Beach	22 km
Clifton Beach	23 km
Palm Cove	26 km

KURANDA
Wildlife Noctarium, Australian Butterfly Sanctuary, Tjapukai Dance Theatre, river cruises.

ATHERTON TABLELAND
Chillagoe Caves; Lakes Barrine, Eacham and Euramo; several waterfalls.

CAIRNS

Cairns Historical Museum
Top Floor
Cnr Shields and Lake Streets
Tel: (070) 51 5582
Open: 10 am to 3 pm, Mon-Fri.

Flecker Botanical Gardens
Collins Avenue
Edge Hill
Open: sunrise to sunset, daily.

Hartley's Creek Crocodile Farm
Cook Highway
Tel: (070) 55 3576
Open: 9 am to 5 pm, daily
(40 km north of Cairns).

Royal Flying Doctor Service Visitors Centre
1 Junction Street
Edge Hill
Tel: (070) 53 5687
Open: Daily.

Wild World
Cook Highway
Palm Cove
Tel: (070) 55 3669
Open: Daily
Australian wildlife park
(22 km north of Cairns).

ISLANDS

Cairns is the access point for the following islands:

Hinchinbrook by air, or sea ex Cardwell
Bedarra by air or sea, via Dunk Island
Dunk by air, or sea ex Clump Point
Fitzroy by launch
Green by launch
Lizard by air

NATIONAL PARKS

For full details, contact the Cairns National Parks and Wildlife Service. Tel: (070) 51 9811

Clump Mountain (Mission Beach area) no camping
Bellenden Ker camping permitted
Eubenangee Swamp no camping
Mt Whitfield no camping
Barron Gorge no camping
Michaelmas Cay no camping
Green Island no camping
Davies Creek camping permitted
Lake Eacham (Atherton Tableland) no camping
Lake Barrine (Atherton Tableland) no camping
Mt Hypipamee (Atherton Tableland) no camping
Malanda Falls (Atherton Tableland)

no camping
Millstream Falls (Atherton Tableland)
no camping
Palmerston (Atherton Tableland)c a m p-
ing permitted
Chillagoe (Atherton Tableland) camping
permitted

AIR TOURS

Aquaflight Airways
Tel: (070) 51 3893
Reef and charter flights.

Cairns Seaplane Airways Australia
Tel: (070) 50 5777
Air tours and charters.

DC3 Queensland
Tel: (070) 32 1900
Cooktown and other day tours.

Heliventure
Tel: (070) 53 5765
Reef and rainforest scenic tours.

CRUISES

Quicksilver Connections
Marina Mirage
Port Douglas 4871
Tel: (070) 99 5500.

Great Adventures
Tel: (070) 51 0455
Cruises to the outer reef.

Ocean Spirit
Tel: (070) 31 2920
Catmaran cruises to the outer reef.

Royal Tropic Cruise Line
Tel: (070) 31 1844
Cruises to Cape York.

OTHER TOURS

Strikies Safaris
27 Macrossan Street
Port Douglas 4871
Tel: (070) 99 5599.

Australian Wildlife Tours
Tel: (070) 51 4911
Wildlife tours in the Cairns region.

Balloon Flights Australia
Tel: (070) 51 7366
Atherton Tablelands ballooning trips.

Cairns-Kuranda Railway
Tel: (070) 55 2222
Scenic rail trip.

Down Under Tours
Tel: (070) 31 1355
Coach tours.

New Look Adventures
Tel: (070) 51 7934
4WD adventures.

Raging Thunder
Tel: (070) 51 4911
Whitewater rafting.

Dundee Park
South Maria Creek Road
Mission Beach
Tel: (070) 685 348.

Island Coast Orchids
South Maria Creek Road
Mission Beach.

FOOD DIGEST

WHERE TO EAT

Backpackers Restaurant
24 Shields Street
Tel: (070) 51 9323.

Breezes
Hilton International Hotel
Wharf Street
Tel: (070) 52 6786
Seafood and international cuisine.

Cock and Bull
6 Grove Street
Tel: (070) 31 1160
Traditional English food.

Fuji
Tradewinds Esplanade
Cnr Minnie and Abbott Streets
Tel: (070) 31 1134
Japanese.

Omar Khayyam
82A Sheridan Street
Tel: (070) 51 5871
Lebanese.

Rio's
141 Grafton Street
Tel: (070) 31 1035
Mexican, steaks and seafood.

Trinity Wharf Tavern
Trinity Wharf Complex
Wharf Street
Tel: (070) 31 1922
Bars and bistro.

NIGHTLIFE

Chatz Nightclub
91 Esplanade
Tel: (070) 31 3699
Nightclub and pasta bar.

Jabiru Cabaret Restaurant
Level 2, Parkroyal Shopping Village
Lake Street
Tel: (070) 31 3211
Aboriginal and islander dancing, etc.

Playpen International
2 Lake Street
Tel: (070) 51 8211.

Scandals Night Club
Tradewinds Sunlodge
Cnr Lake and Florence Streets
Tel: (070) 51 5733.

Renos
Palm Court

Lake Street
(070) 52 1480.

Magnums
70 Abbott Street, and
139 Grafton Street.

SHOPPING

The Australiana Aspect
Shop 1, Hilton International Hotel
Wharf Street
Tel: (070) 31 2040
Quality Australian gifts.

Gallery Primitive
1st Floor
26 Abbott Street
Tel: (070) 31 1641
New Guinea and Aboriginal artefacts.

Opal World
Hilton International
Wharf Street
Tel: (070) 31 2466
Opals and opal jewellery.

Palm Court
34-42 Lake Street
Upmarket shopping centre.

Parkroyal Shopping Village
Cnr Abbott and Lake Streets
Tel: (070) 51 1489
Upmarket shopping centre.

Presenting Australia
The Conservatory Shopping Village
Lake Street
Tel: (070) 51 1798
Gifts, souvenirs, t-shirts, etc.

Rusty's Bazaar
Grafton Street
Market: open Saturday, 5 a.m. to 1 p.m.

SPORTS

DIVING

Ausdive
Tel: (070) 31 1255
Courses and dive trips.

Deep Sea Divers Den
Tel: (070) 51 2223
Courses and dive trips.

Down Under Aquatics
Tel: (070) 31 1588
Courses and dive trips.

FISHING

Cairns Reef Charter Services
Tel: (070) 51 3893
Fishing trips and private charters.

GOLF

Cairns Golf Club
Tel: (070) 54 1494.

Paradise Palms Golf Course
Tel: (070) 59 1166.

GETTING AROUND

PORT DOUGLAS

Sightseeing

The Rainforest Habitat
Port Douglas Road
Tel: (070) 99 3235
Rainforest sanctuary.

Access to Cape Tribulation, Mossman Gorge, Daintree, Cooktown and Cape York.

ISLANDS

Access to most of the northern group of islands is from Cairns. From Port Douglas, day trips can be made to the Low Isles.

NATIONAL PARKS

For full details, contact the Cairns National Parks and Wildlife Service. Tel: (070) 51 9811.

Daintree no camping
Cape Tribulation camping permitted
Cedar Bay no camping
Lizard Island camping permitted
Flinders Island Group no camping
Lakefield (Cape York Peninsula) camping permitted
Iron Range (Cape York Peninsula) camping permitted
Rokeby (Cape York Peninsula) camping permitted
Jardine River/Heathlands (Cape York) camping permitted

TOURS

Daintree Bloomfield Explorer
Tel: (070) 99 5599
4WD tours

Trail Blazer Tours
Tel: (070) 99 5031
4WD tours

CRUISES

Hardy's Courier Sailaway
Tel: (070) 99 5599
Low Isles sailing trips.

Quicksilver Connection
Tel: (070) 99 5500
Reef and Low Isles cruises.

Willow
Tel: (070) 88 0234
Low Isles sailing trips.

FOOD DIGEST

WHERE TO EAT

Terracehouse Restaurant
Reef Terraces
Port Douglas Road
Tel: (070) 99 3333.

Dannys Restaurant
Wharf Street
Tel: (070) 99 5535
Tropical fare.

Marina Mirage
Sheraton Mirage
Tel: (070) 99 5775
Various restaurants.

Nautilus
17 Murphy Street
Tel: (070) 99 5330
Seafood.

Sassis Island Point
2 Island Point Road
Tel: (070) 99 5323
Italian.

Marina Mirage
Sheraton Mirage
Tel: (070) 99 5775
Upmarket shopping centre-
souvenirs, Australiana, etc.

SPORTS

DIVING

Dive Centre
Tel: (070) 99 5327
Dive courses and trips.

Fantasy Dive Charters
Tel: (070) 98 5195
Extended reef diving trips.

Quicksilver Diving Services
Tel: (070) 995050
Dive courses and outer reef trips.

FISHING

MV Stingray
Tel: (070) 99 5599
Reef fishing and snorkelling, also
private charter.

GOLF

Sheraton Mirage
Tel: (070) 98 5888.

LANGUAGE

AUSSIE SLANGUAGE

ABC	Australian Broadcasting Commission
ACT	Australian Capital Territory (Canberra)
ACTU	Australian Council of Trade Unions
ALP	Australian Labor Party
ASIO	Aussie CIA
Abo	Aborigine (impolite)
Across the ditch	Across the Tasman Sea: New Zealand
Air fairy	Flight steward
Alf	Stupid Australian
Alice, The	Alice Springs
Amber fluid	Beer
Anzac	Australian & New Zealand Army Corps (World War I)
Arse	Ass, bum, bottom
Arvo	Afternoon ('the'sarvo' - this afternoon)
BHP	Broken Hill Proprietary, giant mining corporation
Babbler brook"	"babbling cook
Back o' Bourke	Far Outback
Back o' beyond	Farther Outback
Bail up	To rob, hold up
Banana bender	Queenslander
Barbie	Barbecue
Barrack	To cheer for, encourage
Bastard	Term of endearment (when it's not a term of dislike)
Battler	One who struggles hard for a living
Bazza	Barry; also a "Barry McKenzie," a gauche and gross expatriate Australian cartoon character created by satirist Barry Humphries
Beaut	Short for "beautiful" (very good, great, fantastic)
Beergut	Self explanatory
Bible basher	Minister of the Church
Bikey	Biker
Billabong	Water hole in semi-dry river
Billy	Tin container used for boiling water to make tea
Bitsa	Mongrel dog ("Bits a this and bits a that")
Black Stump, The	Where the back of Bourke begins, way beyond Bulmakanka)
Blacktracker	Aboriginal bush tracker
Blind Freddie could have seen it	Unable to see the obvious
Bloke	Man, fellow: used like "guy" in the U.S.
Bloody	Universally undeleted expletive, as in "up at Tumba-bloody-rumba

	shootin' kanga-bloody-roos"	Dag/daggy	Dreadful looking
Blowie	Blowfly	Daks	Trousers
Bludger	Sponger, ne'er do well	Damper	Unrisen bread (bush tucker q.v.)
Blue	A fight. Also a redhead	Dead 'orse	Tomato sauce
Bonzer	Terrific	Deli	Delicatessen
Bookie	Bookmaker	Demo	Demonstration (political or practical)
Boot	Trunk of a car		
Buckley's Chance	One chance in a million	Dero	Derelict person, bum
Bugs Bunny	Money		
Bulamakanka	Mythical, far distant place	Didgeridoo	Aboriginal droning instrument
Bumper crop	Good harvest		
Bunch of fives	A fist	Digger	Australian soldier, but used by for eigners to mean any Australian (Australians prefer "Aussie")
Bunyip	Australia's Yeti, Big Foot or Loch Ness monster		
Bush	Countryside outside cities and towns		
Bushranger	Highwayman, outlaw	Dill	Idiot
		Dingo	Australian native dog
Cacky hander	Left hander	Dinkie-di	The truth
Chemist	Pharmacist	Dinkum	Genuine or honest (also "fair dinkum")
Chips	French fries		
Chook	Chicken		
Chuck	Throw	Do yer block	Lose your temper
Chuck a Uey	Do a U-turn		
Chunder	Vomit	Don't come the raw prawn	
Clap trap	Useless talk		Don't try and fool me
Cobber	Friend		
Cockie	Farmer	Drongo	Idiot
Come a gutser	Make a bad mistake	Dumper	A heavy surf wave
Coolabah	Box eucalyptus tree	Dunny	Toilet ("Use less as a glass door on on dunny")
Cop it sweet	To take the blame or the loss agreeably		
Corker	A good one	Eau de cologne	Phone
Corroboree	Aboriginal ceremonial gathering	Fair dinkum	Same as "Dinkie-di" and "dinkum"
Chrissie	Christmas		
Crook	Broken, sick or no good	Flash as a rat with a gold tooth	Showing off
Cropper, to come a	To come undone, have a spill	Flat out	As fast as possible
		Flog	To sell
Cuppa	Cup of tea	Footpath	Pavement or sidewalk

Footy	Football	Knackers	Testicles
Funnel web	Poisonous spider	Knee trembler	Sexual intercourse standing up. *Coitus verticalis*
G'day	Good day		
Galah	Fool or idiot (after the parrot of same name)	Knock	To criticise
		Knuckle	To punch
		Knuckle sandwich	A punch
Garbo	Garbageman		
Get stung	To be over charged	Lair	A show-off
		Larrikin	Wide boy, street hoodlum
Getting off at Redfern	*Coitus inter ruptus* (Redfern being the last railway station before Sydney Central)	Lingo	Language
		Loaf	To do nothing (" just loafing about"). Also means one's head.
Gift of the gab	The gift of persuasive speech	Lob	To arrive; also to throw.
Give it the flick	Get rid of it	Loo	British/Australian slang for toilet
Gloria Soame (Strine)	Glorious home		
Gong, The	Wollongong	Lousy	Mean
Greenie	A conservation ist	Lucky Country, The	Name (ironic) for Australia, coined by author Donald Hume
Grizzle	To complain		
Grog	Alcoholic drink		
Gurgler, down the	Down the drain, wasted		
		Lurk	A racket, a "dodge" or illegal scheme
Heart starter	First drink of the day		
Home unit	Apartment, flat	Mate	Friend (does not mean spouse)
Hoon	Loudmouth		
Humpy	Aboriginal shack	Mick	A Roman Catholic
Job	To punch	Middy	Ten-ounce beer glass (in NSW)
Joey	Baby kangaroo		
Journo	Journalist	Mob	A group of persons or things (not necessarily unruly,etc.)
Jumbuck	Lamb		
Kangaroos in his top paddock	A bit crazy		
Karked it	Died		
Kick	Pocket orwallet	Mozzie	Mosquito
Kick the bucket	To die	Mug	A gullible fool.
Kip	To sleep. Also an instrument used to toss pennies in "two-up"	Neck oil	Beer
		Never-never	Desert land far off in the Outback. Also means to pay by instalment plan
Kiwi	New Zealander		
Knackered	Tired		

New chum	Newly arrived British immigrant	Pseud	Poseur, pseudo-intellectual (coined by Barry Humphries)
Nick	Steal		
Nip	A Japanese person. Also a bar measure for spirits	Pub	"Public house", bar, drinking establishment
Nipper	Small child, or junior lifesaver	Quack	Doctor
Nit	Fool, idiot		
No hoper	Same as above, but worse	RSL	Returned Servicemen's League
Nong	Fool	Ratbag	Eccentric character (also a friendly term of abuse)
O.S.	Overseas		
Ocker	Quintessential Aussie bumpkin-loudmouth	Ratshit	Lousy, ruined
Oodles	Plenty of	Red-back	Poisonous spider
Outback	The bush; uncivilized, uninhabited country	Ripper	Good
		Roo	Kangaroo
		Roof rabbits	Possums or rats in the ceiling
Oz	Australia or Australian (ironic term)	Root	Sexual intercourse
		Running round like a chook with its head off	Self-explanatory if you see "Chook"
Panic merchant	Chronic anxiety case		
Penguin	A nun	Sack	To fire, dismiss ("get the sack" - to be fired)
Perve	To watch a person (or part thereof) with admiration (does not mean "perverted")	Salvo	Member of the Salvation Army
		Schooner	Large beer glass (N.S.W.)
Piddle in the pocket	To flatter	Scrub	Bushland
Pie-eyed	Drunk	Scunge	A dirty, untidy person; mess
Pinch	Arrest, or steal		
Pissed	Drunk; or urinated	Semi-trailer	Articulated truck
Plonk	Cheap wine	Septic, Seppo	American (as in "septic tank = Yank")
Point Percy at the porcelain	To urinate (men only!)		
Poker machine	Slot machine (aka "pokie")	Shandy	Beer and lemonade mix ("Two shandies off the horrors" - close to delirium tremens)
Pom or Pommy	English person		
Poof, poofter	Male homosexual		
Postie	Mail person		
Prang	Accident, crash		

She'll be apples	It'll be right	Tassie	Tasmania
She's sweet	Everything is all right	Technicolour yawn	Vomit
Sheila	female	Telly	Television, also the Sydney Daily Tele- graph
Shoot through	Leave unex pectedly, escape		
		Thingo	Thing, thinga mijig, whatcha macallit
Shout	Buy round of drinks (as in 'it's your shout')	Tin lid	Kid
		Togs	Swim suit (sometimes called "bath ers")
Shove off	To depart		
Sidekick	A friend, companion		
Silly as a cut snake	Self explana- tory	Toot	Toilet, lavatory
		Troppo	Demented by tropical life
Silvertail	Member of high society	Trouble n'strife	Wife
Slats	Ribs	Tube	Can of beer, or innermost section of breaking surf wave
Sly drool	Slide rule (Strine)		
Smoke-o	Tea break		
Snags	Sausages		
Speedos	Nylon swim ming trunks	Tucker	Food
		Turps	Any form of alcohol. ("On the turps" - to be drinking)
Sprog	Baby		
Spunky	Good-looking person		
Squatter	Large land holder in early colonial times	Two pot screamer	Person unable to hold their drink
Station ranch	Large farm or	Two up	Popular gambling game involving two pennies thrown in the air
Stickybeak	Busybody		
Sting from	To borrow		
Stockman station hand	Cowboy,		
		Uni	University
Strides	Trousers	Unit	Apartment, flat
Strine Australian	Vernacular	Up the creek	In trouble
		Ute	"Utility" truck - a pickup truck
Stubby beer	Small bottle of		
Swagman	Vagabond, rural tramp	Vegemite	Vile brown yeast sandwich spread which Australians grow up on
Sydney or the bush	All or nothing		
TAB	Totalisator Agency Board, legal offtrack betting shop		
		Walkabout	Travelling on foot for long distances, an Aboriginal tradition
Tall poppies	Achievers; what knockers like to cut down		
		Walloper	A policeman

Whinge	Complain
Whip-round	A collection of money for the benefit of an other or for some celebration
Wog	Minor disease; also impolite term for darker-skinned foreigner - a "Worthy Oriental Gentleman"
Wop	Southern European (again impolite)
Wowser	Bluenose, prude, killjoy
Yabber	Chatter
Yack	To talk
Yahoo	An unruly type
Yakka	Work
Yobbo	Hoon, loud mouth

USEFUL ADDRESSES

INTERNATIONAL AIRLINE OFFICES

•Air Caledonie
436 Queen Street, Brisbane, QLD 4000
Tel: (07) 832 5344

•Air India
21st floor, Lennons Plaza, 68 Queen Street, Brisbane, QLD 4000
Tel: (07) 229 4088

•Air New Zealand
Watkins Place, 288 Edward Street, Brisbane, QLD 4000
Tel: (07) 229 3044

•Air Niugini
127 Creek Street, Brisbane, QLD 4000
Tel: (07) 229 5844
4-6 Shields Street, Cairns, QLD 4870
Tel: (070) 51 4177
Townsville: Tel: (077) 21 3142

•Air Pacific
199 Adelaide Street, Brisbane, QLD 4000
Tel: (07) 833 3750

•Air Zimbabwe
199 Adelaide Street, Brisbane, QLD 4000
Tel: (07) 833 3752

•Alitalia
247 Adelaide Street, Brisbane, QLD 4000
Tel: (07) 229 6400
Lake Street, Cairns, QLD 4870
Tel: (070) 50 3711

•British Airways
243 Edward Street, Brisbane, QLD 4000
Tel: (07) 223 3123

•Cathay Pacific Airways
8th Floor, 40 Queen Street, Brisbane, QLD 4000
Tel: (07) 223 3123

•Continental Airlines
19th Level, Riverside Centre, 123 Eagle Street, Brisbane, QLD 4000
Tel: (07) 221 7961

•Japan Airlines (JAL)
13th Floor, Santos House, 215 Adelaide Street, Brisbane, QLD 4000
Tel: (07) 229 9916
33 Lake Street, Cairns, QLD 4870
Tel: (070) 31 2700

•JAT-Yugoslav Airlines
247 Adelaide Street, Brisbane, QLD 4000
Tel: (07) 229 7855

•KLM Royal Dutch Airlines
Suite 304, 231 George Street, Brisbane, QLD 4000
Tel: (07) 229 5811

•Lufthansa
380-386 Queen Street, Brisbane, QLD 4000
Tel: (07) 229 2666

•Malaysian Airline System
Jackman House, 247 Adelaide Street,
Brisbane, QLD 4000
Tel: (07) 229 9888

•Olympic Airways
217 George Street, Brisbane, QLD 4000
Tel: (07) 854 2832

•Philippine Airlines
141 Queen Street, Brisbane, QLD 4000
Tel: (07) 229 6022

•Qantas Airways
262 Adelaide Street, Brisbane, QLD 4000
Tel: (07) 833 3747
13 Spence Street, Cairns, QLD 4870
Tel: (070) 50 4000
3047 Gold Coast Highway, Surfers Paradise, QLD 4217
Tel: (075) 38 5766
280 Flinders Mall, Townsville, QLD 4810
Tel: (077) 71 6902

•Singapore Airlines
100 Eagle Street, Brisbane, QLD 4000
Tel: (07) 221 5744
Mid-City Arcade, Cnr Flinders and Ogden
Streets, Townsville, QLD 4810
Tel: (077) 71 3171

•Thai Airways International
167 Eagle Street, Brisbane, QLD 4000
Tel: (07) 832 2778
38-40 Lake Street, Cairns, QLD 4870
Tel: (070) 31 2755

•United Airlines
23rd level, 307 Queen Street, Brisbane,
QLD 4000
Tel: (07) 221 7477

•UTA French Airlines
201 Edward Street, Brisbane, QLD 4000
Tel: (07) 221 5655

INFORMATION FROM ABROAD

The Queensland Tourist and Travel Corporation has the following overseas promotional offices which will refer the intending
visitor to local travel agents with a good
knowledge of Queensland:

•UK (for UK, Ireland and Scandinavia)
Queensland House
392/3 Strand
London WC2R 0LZ
Tel: (01) 836 1333
Fax: (01) 836 5881

•Germany (for Europe)
Postbox 330743
8000 Munich 33
Tel: (089) 260 9693
Fax: (089) 260 3530

•USA
611 North Larchmont Boulevard
Los Angeles
CA 90004
Tel: (213) 465 8418
Fax: (213) 465 5815

New York
9th Floor
645 Fifth Avenue
New York
NY 10022
Tel: (212) 308 5520
Fax: (212) 308 0272

Chicago
Suite 2130
150 North Michigan Avenue
Chicago
IL 60601
Tel: (312) 781 5156
Fax: (312) 781 5159

•Canada
Suite 1730
2 Bloor Street West
Toronto
Ontario M4W 3E2
Tel: (416) 922 2305
Fax: (416) 925 9312

•Japan
Suite 1303
Yurakucho Denki Building NW
7-1 Yurakucho 1 Chome
Chiyoda-Ku
Tokyo 100
Tel: (03) 214 4931
Fax: (03) 211 7904

•Singapore (for South East Asia)
101 Thomson Road, #07-04

United Square
Singapore 1130
Tel: (65) 253 2811
Fax: (65) 253 8653

•New Zealand
PO Box 4410
Auckland
Tel: (09) 39 6421/2/3
Fax: (09) 77 9439

TOURIST CENTERS (AUSTRALIA)

The Australian Tourist Commission can also provide information on Queensland and of course, on Australia in general:

Tourism Australia
80 William Street
Sydney NSW 2000
Tel: 902) 360 1111

Within Australia, Queensland tourist information is handled by the various Queensland Government Travel Centres:

•**Queensland**
196 Adelaide Street
Brisbane, QLD 4000
Tel: (07) 833 5255

•**New South Wales**
75 Castlereagh Street
Sydney, NSW 2000
Tel: (02) 232 1788

309 Church Street
Parramatta, NSW 2150
Tel: (02) 891 1966

516 Hunter Street
Newcastle, NSW 2300
Tel: (049) 26 2800

•**Australian Capital Territory**
25 Garema Place
Canberra City, ACT 2601
Tel: (062) 48 8411

•**Victoria**
257 Collins Street
Melbourne, VIC 3000
Tel: (03) 654 3866

•**South Australia**
10 Grenfell Street
Adelaide, SA 5000
Tel: (08) 212 2399

•**Western Australia**
55 St Georges Terrace
Perth, WA 6000
Tel: (09) 325 1600

These offices are generally open from 9 am to 5 pm weekdays plus Saturday mornings, and will provide brochures, maps, price lists and other information. They will also book accommodation, tours and transport for you.

•**Tourism Queensland** has a state-wide network of regional offices which offer detailed information on local services, facilities and tours. These can be very helpful on local attractions and places of interest:

•**Tourism Brisbane**
Ground Floor, City Hall
King George Square
Brisbane, QLD 4000
Tel: (07) 221 8411

•**Gold Coast Visitors and Convention Centre**
115 Scarborough Street
Southport, QLD 4217
Tel: (075) 91 1988

•**Tourism Sunshine Coast**
Tourist Information Centre
Alexandra Parade
Alexandra Headland, QLD 4572
Tel: (071) 43 2411

•**Fraser Coast** (formerly Sugar Coast-Burnett) Tourism Board
1st Floor, 224 Bazaar Street
Maryborough, QLD 4650
Tel: (071) 22 3444

•**Bundaberg District Development Board**
Cnr Mulgrave Road and Burbong Street
Bundaberg, QLD 4670
Tel: (071) 52 2406

•Gladstone Area Promotion and Development
100 Goondoon Street
Gladstone, QLD 4680
Tel: (079) 72 4000

•Capricorn Tourism Development Organisation
Curtis Park, Gladstone Road
Rockhampton, QLD 4700
Tel: (079) 27 2055

•Tourism Mackay
'The Junk'
Nebo Road
Mackay, QLD 4740
Tel: (079) 52 2677

•Whitsunday Tourism Association
PO Box 83
Airlie Beach, QLD 4802
Tel: (079) 46 6673

•Magnetic North Tourism Authority
303 Flinders Mall
Townsville, QLD 4810
Tel: (077) 71 2724

•Far North Queensland Promotion Bureau
36-38 Alpin Street
Cairns, QLD 4870
Tel: (070) 51 3588

AUSTRALIAN MISSIONS ABROAD

•Afghanistan
No Resident Representative—see Pakistan.

•Algeria
Australian Embassy, 12 Avenue Emile Marquis, Djenane-el-Maik, Hydra, Algiers. Tel: 602 846, 609 321, 601 965

•Argentina
Australian Embassy, Stano Fe 846 Piso 80, Buenos Aires. Tel 326 841 8

•Austria
Australian Embassy, Mattiellistrasse 2-4, A-1040 Vienna. Tel: 512 8580

•Bahamas
No Resident Representative—see Jamaica

•Bahrain
No Resident Representative—see Saudi Arabia

•Bangladesh
Australian High Commission, Dhaka, 184 Gulshan Avenue, Gulshan, Bangladesh. Tel: 600 091, 600 095

•Barbados
No Resident Representative—see Jamaica

•Belgium
Australian Embassy, Guimard Centre, Rue Guimard 6-8, 1040 Brussels. Tel: 231 0500

•Bolivia
No Resident Representative—see Chile

•Botswana
No Resident Representative—see Zimbabwe

•Brazil
Australian Embassy, SHIS QI9, Conj 16, Casa 1, Brasilia D.F. Tel: 248 5569

•Britain
Australian High Commission, Australia House, The Strand, London WC2 B4LA. Tel: (01) 438 8000
Edinburgh: Australian Consulate, Hobart House, 80 Hanover Street, Edinburgh EH2 2DL. Tel: (031) 226 6271/3
Manchester: Australian Consulate, Chatsworth House, Lever Street, Manchester M1 2DL.Tel: (061) 228 1344

•Brunei
Australian Commission, Teck Guan Plaza, Bandar Seri Bagawan, Brunei. Tel: 29435/6

•Bulgaria
No Resident Representative—see Yugoslavia

•Burma
Australian Embassy, 88 Strand Road, Rangoon. Tel: 80 711, 80 965

•Canada
Australian High Commission, The National Building, 130 Slater Street, Ottawa K1P 6E2. Tel: 613/236 0841
Toronto: Australian Consulate-General, Suite 2324, Commerce Court West, Corner of King & Bay Streets, Toronto, Ontario. Tel: (416) 367 0783
Vancouver: Australian Consulate-General, 800 Oceanic Plaza, 1066 West Hastings Street, Vancouver B.C. V6E 3X1.Tel: (684) 1177/8

•Chile
Australian Embassy, Santiago, 420 Gertrudis Echenique, Las Condes, Santiago de Chile. Tel: 2285065

•**China**
Australian Embassy, 15 Donzhimenwai Street, San Li Tun, Beijing. Tel: 522 331 or 522 336

•**Colombia**
No Resident Representative—see Venezuela

•**Costa Rica**
No Resident Representative—see Mexico

•**Cyprus**
Australian High Commission, 4 Annis Komminis Street, (corner Strassinos Avenue), Nicosia. Tel: 473 001/2

•**Czechoslovakia**
No Resident Representative—see Poland

•**Denmark**
Australian Embassy, Kristianagade 21, 2100 Copenhagen. Tel: (01) 262 244

•**Ecuador**
No Resident Representative—see Venezuela

•**Egypt**
Australian Embassy, 5th floor, Cairo Plaza South, Corniche el Nil, Boulac, Cairo. Tel: 777 900

•**Ethiopia**
Australian Embassy, House 710, Kebele 08, Higher 09, Addis Ababa. Tel: 114 500/1

•**Fiji**
Australian High Commission, Dominion House, Thomson Street, Suva. Tel: 312 844

•**Finland**
No Resident Representative—see Sweden

•**France**
Australian Embassy, 4 Rue Jean Rey. 75724 Paris Cedex 15. Tel: 4575 6200

•**Gabon**
No Resident Representative—see Nigeria

•**Germany, Federal Republic of**
Australian Embassy, Godesberger Allee 107, 5300 Bonn 2. Tel: (0228) 81030

•**Ghana**
No Resident Representative—see Nigeria

•**Greece**
Australian Embassy, 15 Messogeion Street, Ambelokipi, Athens. Tel: 775 7650 4

•**Grenada**
No Resident Representative—see Jamaica

•**Guatemala**
No Resident Representative—see Mexico

•**Guyana**
No Resident Representative—see Jamaica

•**Hong Kong**
Australian Consulate-General, Harbour Centre, 25 Harbour Road, Wanchai. Tel: (5) 731 881

•**Hungary**
Australian Embassy, Room 736, Forum Hotel, Budapest V, Apaczai Csere JU 12-14. Tel: 188 100

•**India**
Australian High Commission, Australian Compound, No. 1-50-G Shantipath, Chanakyapuri, New Delhi. Tel: 601 336/9 Bombay: Australian Consulate-General Maker Towers, E Block, Colaba. Tel: 211 071 or 211 072

•**Indonesia**
Australian Embassy, Jalan Thamrin 15, Jakarta. Tel: 323 109 Bali: Australian Consulate, One Jalan Raya Sanur, 146,Tanjung Bungkak, Denpasar. Tel: 25997/8

•**Iran**
Australian Embassy, 123 Shadid Khalid Al-Islambuli Avenue, Abassabad, Tehran. Tel: 626 202

•**Iraq**
Australian Embassy, Masbah 391-335, Baghdad. Tel: 719 3435, 719 3430

•**Ireland**
Australian Embassy, Fitzwilton House, Wilton Terrace, Dublin 2. Tel: 761 517 or 761 519

•**Israel**
Australian Embassy, Beit Europa, 37 Shaul Hamelech Boulevard, Tel Aviv 64928. Tel: 250 451

•**Italy**
Australian Embassy, Via Alessandria 215, Rome 00198. Tel: 832 721, Milan: Australian Consulate-General, Via Turati 40, Milan 20121. Tel: 659 8727 or 659 8729

•**Ivory Coast**
No Resident Representative—see Nigeria

•**Jamaica**
Australia High Commission, First Life Building, 64 Knutsford Boulevard, Kingston 5. Tel: (92) 63550/2

•**Japan**
Australian Embassy, No. 1-14 Mita 2 Chome, Minato-ku, Tokyo. Tel: 453 0251/9

Osaka: Australian Consulate-General, Osaka International Building, Azuchimachi 2-Chome, Higashi-ku, Osaka. Tel: (06) 271 7071/6

•**Jordan**
Australian Embassy, Between 4th and 5th Circles, Wadi Sir Road, Jabel Amman. Tel: 613 246/7

•**Kenya**
Australian High Commission, Development House, Moi Avenue, Nairobi. Tel: 334 666/7

•**Kiribati**
Australian High Commission, Bairiki, Tarawa. Tel: 21184

•**Korea, Republic of**
Australian Embassy, Kukdong-Shell Building, 58-1 Shinmoonro 1-Ka, Chongro-ku, Seoul. Tel: 730 6491/5

•**Kuwait**
No Resident Representative—see Saudi Arabia

•**Laos**
Australian Embassy, Rue J Nehru, Quartier Phone Xay, Vientiane. Tel: 2477

•**Lebanon**
Australian Embassy, Farra Building, 463 Bliss Street, Ras Beirut. Currently not staffed—see Syria

•**Lesotho**
No Resident Representative—see South Africa

•**Luxembourg**
No Resident Representative—see Belgium

•**Madagascar**
No Resident Representative—see Tanzania

•**Malaysia**
Australian High Commission, 6 JLN Yap Kwan Seng, Kuala Lumpur. Tel: 2423 122

•**Maldives, Republic of**
No Resident Representative—see Sri Lanka

•**Malta**
Australian High Commission, Airways House, Gaiety Lane, Sleima. Tel: 338 201

•**Mauritius**
Australian High Commission, Rogers House, 5 President John Kennedy Street, Port Louis. Tel. 081 700/1/2

•**Mexico**
Australian Embassy, Plaza Polanco Torre B-Piso 10, Jaime Balmes 11, Col. Los Morales, 11510 Mexico D.F. Tel: 395 9988

•**Mongolia**
No Resident Representative—see USSR

•**Morocco**
No Resident Representative—see France

•**Nauru**
Australian High Commission, Civic Centre, Nauru. Tel: 5230/1

•**Nepal**
Australian Embassy, Bhat Bhateni, Kathmandu. Tel: 411 578/9

•**Netherlands, The**
Australian Embassy, Koninginnegracht 23, 2514 AB The Hague. Tel: (70) 630 983

•**New Caledonia**
Australian Consulate-General, 18 Rue de Marechal Foch, Noumea. Tel: 272 414

•**New Zealand**
Australian High Commission, 72-78 Hobson Street, Thorndon, Wellington. Tel: 736 411 or 736 412
Auckland: Australian Consulate-General, 7th & 8th floors, 32-38 Quay Street, Auckland. Tel: 32 429

•**Nigeria**
Australian High Commission, Nurse's House, Plot PC 12, off 1 Idowu Taylor Street, Victoria Island, Lagos. Tel: 618 875

•**Norway**
Canadian Embassy, Oscars Gate 20, 0352 Oslo 3. Tel: (2) 466 955

•**Oman**
No Resident Representative—see Saudi Arabia

•**Pakistan**
Australian Embassy, Plot 17, Sector G4/ 4, Diplomatic Enclave No. 2, Islamabad. Tel: 822 115 or 822 111

•**Panama**
No Resident Representative—see Mexico

•**Papua New Guinea**
Australian High Commission, Independence Drive, Waigani, Port Moresby. Tel: 259 333

•**Paraguay**
No Resident Representative—see Argentina

•**Peru**
Canadian Embassy, 130 Frederico Gerdes, Miraflores, Lima. Tel: 444 015, 444 032

•**Philippines**
Australian Embassy, China Banking Corporation Building, Paseo de Roxas (corner Ayala Avenue) Makati. Tel: 817 7911

•Poland
Australian Embassy, Estonska 3/5, Saska Kepa, Warsaw. Tel: 176 081/6
•Portugal
Australian Embassy, Avenida de Liberdale 244-4, Lisbon 1200. Tel: 523 350, 523 421
•Qatar
No Resident Representative—see Saudi Arabia
•Romania
No Resident Representative—see Yugoslavia
•Saudi Arabia
Australian Embassy, Diplomatic Quarter, Riyadh. Tel: (01) 488 7788
Jeddah: Australian Consulate-General, 59 Amir Abdullah, Al-Faysal Street, Al Hamra's District 5, Jeddah. Tel: 665 1303
•Senegal
No Resident Representative—see Nigeria
•Seychelles
No Resident Representative—see Mauritius
•Singapore
Australian High Commission, 25 Napier Road, Singapore 10. Tel: 737 9311
•Solomon Islands
Australian High Commission, Hong Kong & Shanghai Bank Building, Mendana Avenue, Honiara. Tel: 21561
•South Africa
Australian Embassy, 4th Floor, Mutual & Federal Centre, 220 Vermeulen Street, Pretoria 0002. Tel: (012) 325 4315
Capetown: Australian Consulate, 1001 Colonial Mutual Building, 106 Adderley Street, Capetown. Tel: 232 160
•Spain
Australian Embassy, Paseo de la Castellano 143, Madrid, 28046. Tel: 279 850
•Sri Lanka
Australian High Commission, 3 Cambridge Place, Colombo. Tel: 598 767/8/9
•Sudan
No Resident Representative—see Egypt
•Swaziland
No Resident Representative— see South Africa
•Sweden
Australian Embassy, Sergels Torg 12, Stockholm C. Tel: 244 660
•Switzerland
Australian Embassy, 29 Alpenstrasse, Berne. Tel: 430 143

Geneva: Australian Consulate, 56-58 Rue de Moillebeau, Petit Saconnex, 1211 Geneva 19. Tel: 346 200
•Syria
Australian Embassy, 128A Farabi Street, Mezzeh, Damascus. Tel: 664 317
•Tanzania
Australian High Commission, NIC Investment Building, Samora Avenue, Dar-Es-Salaam. Tel: 20244/5/6
•Thailand
Australian Embassy, 37 South Sathorn Road, Bangkok 12. Tel: 286 0411
•Tonga
Australian High Commission, Salote Road, Nuku'Alofa. Tel: 21244/5
•Trinidad and Tobago
No Resident Representative—see Jamaica
•Tunisia
Canadian Embassy, 3 Sénégal Street, Palestine Place, Tunis. Tel: 286 577
•Turkey
Australian Embassy, 83 Nenehatun Caddesi, Gazi Osman Pasa, Ankara. Tel: 361 240/1/2/3
•Tuvalu
No Resident Representative—see Fiji
•Uganda
No Resident Representative—see Kenya
•Union of Soviet Socialist Republics
Australian Embassy, 13 Kropotkinsky Pereulok, Moscow. Tel: 246 5012/6
•United Arab Emirates
No Resident Representative—see Saudi Arabia
•United States of America
Australian Embassy, 1601 Massachusetts Avenue N.W., Washington D.C. 20036. Tel: (202) 797 3000
Los Angeles: Australian Consulate-General, Suite 1742, 3550 Wiltshire Boulevard, Los Angeles, CA 90010. Tel: (213) 380 0980/2
Chicago: Australian Consulate-General
Honolulu: Australian Consulate-General, 1000 Bishop Street, Honolulu, Hawaii 96813. Tel: (808) 524 5050
New York: Australian Consulate-General, International Building, 636 Fifth Avenue, NY 10111. Tel: (212) 245 4000
San Francisco: Australian Consulate-General, Qantas Building, 360 Post Street, San Francisco 94108. Tel: (415) 362 6160
Houston: Australian Consulate-General,

Suite 800, 1990 South Post Oak Boulevard, Houston, Texas, 77056-9998. Tel: (713) 629 9131

•**Vanuatu**
Australian High Commission, Melitco House, Vila. Tel: 2777

•Vatican: Australian Embassy to the Holy See, Corso Trieste 27, Rome 00198. Tel: 852 792

•Venezuela
Australian Embassy, Centro Plaza, Torre C, Piso 20, Primera Transversal, Los Palos Grades, Caracas. Tel: 261 5799

•Vietnam, Socialist Republic of
Australian Embassy, 66 Ly Thuong Kiet, Hanoi. Tel: 52 763

•Western Samoa
Australian High Commission, Fea Gai Ma Leata Building, Beach Road, Tamaligi, Apia. Tel: 23 411/2

•Yugoslavia
Australian Embassy, 13 Cika Ljubina, 1100 Belgrade 6. Tel: 624 655

•Zambia
Australian High Commission, 3rd floor, Memaco House, Sapele Road, Lusaka. Tel: 219 001 or 219 003

•Zimbabwe
Australian High Commission, Throgmorton House, corner of Samora Machel Avenue, and Julius Nyerere Road, Harare. Tel: 794 591/4

EMBASSIES & CONSULATES

IN CANBERRA

(Telephone area prefix is 062 for all numbers)

•**Argentina**
58 Mugga Way, Red Hill, ACT 2603. Tel: 95 1570

•**Austria**
107 Endeavour Street, Red Hill, ACT 2603. Tel: 95 1533

•**Bangladesh**
11 Molineaux Place, Farrer, ACT 2607. Tel: 86 1200

•**Belgium**
19 Arkana Street, Yarralumla, ACT 2600. Tel: 73 2501

•**Brazil**
19 Forster Crescent, Yarralumla, ACT 2600. Tel: 73 1202, 73 2372

•**Britain**
Commonwealth Avenue, Yarralumla, ACT 2600. Tel: 70 6666

•**Burma**
85 Mugga Way, Red Hill, ACT 2603. Tel: 95 0045

•**Canada**
Commonwealth Avenue, Yarralumla, ACT 2600. Tel: 73 3844

•**Chile**
10 Culgoa Court, O'Malley, ACT. Tel: 86 2430

•**China**
247 Federal Highway, Watson, ACT 2602. Tel: 41 2446

•**Cyprus**
37 Endeavour Street, Red Hill, ACT 2603. Tel: 95 2120

•**Denmark**
15 Hunter Street, Yarralumla, ACT 2600. Tel: 73 2195

•**Egypt, Arab Republic of**
125 Monaro Crescent, Red Hill, ACT 2603. Tel: 95 0394

•**Fiji**
9 Beagle Street, Red Hill, ACT 2603. Tel: 95 9148

•**Finland**
10 Darwin Avenue, Yarralumla, ACT 2600. Tel: 73 3800

•**France**
6 Perth Avenue, Yarralumla, ACT 2600. Tel: 70 5111

•**Germany, Federal Republic of**
119 Empire Circuit, Yarralumla, ACT 2600. Tel: 73 3177

•**Greece**
Stonehaven Crescent, Red Hill, ACT 2603. Tel: 733011

•**Holy See**
2 Vancouver Avenue, Red Hill, ACT 2603. (office and residence of the Apostolic Pro-nuncio) Tel: 95 3876

•**Hungary**
79 Hopetoun Circuit, Yarralumla, ACT 2600. Tel: 82-3226

•**India**
3 Moonal Place, Yarralumla, ACT 2600. Tel: 73 3999

•**Indonesia**
8 Darwin Avenue, Yarralumla, ACT 2600. Tel: 73 3222/95 8911

•**Iran**
14 Torres Street, Red Hill, ACT 2603. Tel: 95 2544

•Iraq
48 Culgoa Circuit, O'Malley, ACT. Tel: 86 1333

•Ireland
Arkana Street, Yarralumla, ACT 2600. Tel: 73 3022

•Israel
6 Turrana Street, Yarralumla, ACT 2600 (Embassy and residence). Tel: 73 1309

•Italy
12 Grey Street, Deakin, ACT 2600. Tel: 73 3333

•Japan
112-114 Empire Circuit, Yarralumla, ACT 2600 (Embassy and residence). Tel: 73 3244

•Jordan
20 Roebuck Street, Red Hill, ACT 2603. Tel: 95 9951

•Kenya
33 Ainslie Avenue, Canberra City, ACT 2601. Tel: 47 4688

•Korea, Republic of
113 Empire Circuit, Yarralumla, ACT 2600. Tel: 73 3044

•Lebanon
27 Endeavour Street, Red Hill, ACT 2603. Tel: 95 7378

•Malaysia
7 Perth Avenue, Yarralumla, ACT 2600. Tel: 73 1543

•Malta
261 La Perouse Street, Red Hill, ACT 2603. Tel: 95 0273

•Mauritius
43 Hampton Circuit, Yarralumla, ACT 2600. Tel: 81 1203

•Mexico
14 Perth Avenue, Yarralumla, ACT 2600. Tel: 73-3963

•Netherlands, The
120 Empire Circuit, Yarralumla, ACT 2600. Tel: 73 3111

•New Zealand
Commonwealth Avenue, Yarralumla, ACT 2600. Tel: 73 3611

•Nigeria
7 Terrigal Circuit, O'Malley, ACT. Tel: 86 1322

•Norway
3 Zeehan Street, Red Hill, ACT 2603. Tel: 95 6000, 73 3444

•Pakistan
59 Franklin Street, Forrest, ACT 2603. Tel: 95 0021

•Papua New Guinea
Forster Crescent, Yarralumla, ACT 2600. Tel: 73 3322

•Peru
111 Monaro Crescent, Red Hill, ACT 2603. Tel: 95 1016

•Philippines
1 Moonah Place, Yarralumla, ACT 2600 (Embassy and residence). Tel: 73 2535

•Poland
7 Turrana Street, Yarralumla, ACT 2600 (Embassy and residence). Tel: 73 1208

•Portugal
8 Astrolabe Street, Red Hill, ACT 2603. Tel: 95 9992

•Singapore
Forster Crescent, Yarralumla, ACT 2600. Tel: 73 3944

•South Africa
Corner State Circle and Rhodes Place, Yarralumla, ACT 2600. Tel: 73 2424

•Spain
15 Arkana Street, Yarralumla, ACT 2600. Tel: 95 3872/73 3555

•Sri Lanka
35 Empire Circuit, Forrest, ACT 2603. Tel: 95 3521

•Sweden
Turrana Street, Yarralumla, ACT 2600 (Embassy and residence). Tel: 73 3033

•Switzerland
7 Melbourne Avenue, Forrest, ACT 2603 (Embassy and residence). Tel: 73 3977

•Thailand
111 Empire Circuit, Yarralumla, ACT 2600 (Embassy and residence). Tel: 73 1149

•Turkey
60 Mugga Way, Red Hill, ACT 2603 (Embassy and residence). Tel: 95 0227

•Union of Soviet Socialist Republics
78 Canberra Avenue, Griffith, ACT 2603. Tel: 95 9033

•United States of America
Moonah Place, Yarralumla, ACT 2600. Tel: 70 5000

•Uruguay
Adelaide House, Phillip, ACT 2606. Tel: 82 4418

•Vietnam
6 Timbara Crescent, O'Malley, ACT. Tel: 86 6059

•Yugoslavia
11 Nuyts Street, Red Hill, ACT 2603. Tel: 95 1458

•Zambia
33 Ainslie Avenue, Canberra City, ACT 2601. Tel: 47 2088

IN BRISBANE

(If calling from outside Brisbane, telephone area prefix is 07 for all numbers)

•Austria
24 Sandgate Road, Argyle Place, Breakfast Creek, QLD 4010. Tel: 262 8955
• Belgium
12 Brookes Street, Bowen Hills, QLD 4006. Tel: 854 1920
•Bolivia
Suite 517, 5th Floor, Penney's Building, 210 Queen Street, Brisbane QLD 4000. Tel: 221 1606
•Chile
503 Gympie Road, Strathpine, QLD 4500. Tel: 881 1988
•Cyprus
280 Sir Fred Schonell Drive, St Lucia, QLD 4067. Tel: 371 5105
•Denmark
633 Wickham Street, Fortitude Valley, QLD 4006. Tel: 854 1855
•Finland
Suite 803, 8th Floor, Riverside Centre, 123 Eagle Street, Brisbane, QLD 4000. Tel: 839 8733
•France
Newspaper House, 289 Queen Street, Brisbane, QLD 4000. Tel: 229 8201
•Germany, Federal Republic of
26 Wharf Street, Brisbane, QLD 4000. Tel: 221 7819
•Greece
127 Creek Street, Brisbane, QLD 4000. Tel: 229 3222
•Italy
158 Moray Street, New Farm, QLD 4005. Tel: 358 4344
•Japan
17th Floor, Comalco Place, 12 Creek Street, Brisbane, QLD 4000. Tel: 221 5188

•Mexico
26 Aston Street, Toowong, QLD 4006. Tel: 870 9188
•Nepal
66 High Street, Toowong, QLD 4066. Tel: 378 0124

•Netherlands
10th Floor, Dalgety House, 79 Eagle Street, Brisbane, QLD 4000. Tel: 31 1779
•New Zealand
Watkins Place Building, Edward Street, Brisbane, QLD 4000. Tel: 221 9933
•Norway
633 Wickham Street, Fortitude Valley, QLD 4006. Tel: 854 1855
•Panama
54 Upper Brookfield Road, Brookfield, QLD 4069. Tel: 369 1324
•Papua New Guinea
79 Eagle Street, Brisbane, QLD 4000. Tel: 221 8067
•Portugal
379 Queen Street, Brisbane, QLD 4000. Tel: 221 4833
•Spain
27 Troubridge Street, Mount Gravatt, QLD 4122. Tel: 221 8571
Cairns: 81 Sheridan Street, Cairns, QLD 4870
•Sweden
30-36 Herschell Street, Brisbane, QLD 4000. Tel:236 2797
•United Kingdom
BP House, 193 North Quay, Brisbane, QLD 4000. Tel: 236 2575
•United States of America
4th Floor, 383 Wickham Terrace, Brisbane, QLD 4000. Tel: 839 8955

343

Further Reading

GENERAL

Blainey, Geoffrey. A Land Half Won. Melbourne: Macmillian, 1980.

Borthwick, John & McGonigal David (eds). Insight Guide Australia. Singapore: APA Publications, 1990.

Borthwick, John & McGonigal, David (eds). Melbourne Cityguide. Singapore: APA Publications, 1989.

Burnum Burnum, A Traveller's Guide to Aboriginal Australia, Sydney, Angus & Robertson: 1988.

Clark, Charles Manning. A History of Australia. University of Melbourne Press, 1962.

Clark, Charles Manning. A Short History of Australia. Melbourne: Macmillan, 1981.

Fitzgerald, Ross; From 1915 to the Early 1980s: A History of Queensland; University of Queensland Press, St. Lucia, 1983.

Hornadge, Bill. The Australian Slanguage. Sydney: Cassell, 1980.

Horne, Donald. The Australian People; Biography of a Nation. Sydney: Angus and Robertson, 1972.

Hughes, Robert. The Fatal Shore. New York: Vintage Books, 1988/UK: William Collins 1986.

Isaacs, Jennifer. Australia's Living Heritage: Arts of the Dreaming. Isaacs, Jennifer. Australian Dreaming: 40,000 Years of Aboriginal History. Sydney: Lansdowne Press, 1980.

Lauder, Afferbeck. Strine. Sydney: Lansdowne Press, 1982.

McGonigal, David & Borthwick, John (eds). Sydney Cityguide. Singapore: APA Publications, 1989.

McGonigal, David. Wilderness Australia McRobbie, Alexander. The Real Surfers Paradise, 1988.

Morcombe, Michael. Australia, the Wild Continent. Sydney: Lansdowne, 1980.

Reptiles, Plants of Australia and New Guinea. Sydney: Angus and Robertson, 1966.

Richardson, Michael. Australia's Natural Wonders. Sydney: Golden Press, 1984.

Sinclair, John. Discovering Fraser Island, Australasian Environmental Publications, 1987.

The Australian Adventure, Sydney. Australian Adventure Publications 1987.

The Macquarie Dictionary. Sydney: Macquarie University, 1982.

Warren, Mark; Atlas of Australian Surfing; Sydney: Angus & Robertson, 1987.

Williams, Fred. Written in the Sand: A History of Fraser Island, Jacaranda Press, 1982.

Wilson, Robert. The Book of Australia. Sydney: Lansdowne Press, 1982.

Worrell, Eric. Australian Wildlife: Best-Known Birds, Mammals, Reader's Digest. Wild Australia. Sydney: Reader's Digest, 1984.

Young, C. The New Gold Mountain: The Chinese in Australia. Richmond: S.A. Raphael Arts, 1977.

Young, Nat; Surfing Australia's East Coast; Horwitz, Sydney, 1980.

ART/PHOTO CREDITS

Photographs	
178, 180, 181, 186, 189, 194, 227, 246	**Atkinson, Kathie**
34L	**Australian Museum, Sydney**
56, 66, 67R, 82, 85, 107, 112, 116,	
119, 122, 128, 129, 140, 144/145,	
147L, 150, 151, 154, 164, 170/171,	
193, 228,	**Borthwick, John**
78, 95, 159, 165R, 270	**Bowen, David**
30/31, 35	**Dixson Galleries, State Library of N.S.W.**
64	**Fantini, Piero**
28, 32, 33, 36	**General Reference Library, State Library of N.S.W.**
50, 93, 134, 174, 182, 198, 209, 224,	
230, 240	**Gottschalk, Manfred/ APA**
22	**Heaton, D & J/ APA**
89	**Heritage Hotel, Brisbane**
38	**John Oxley Library, State Library of Queensland**
91	**Kugler, J./ APA**
25, 44/45, 49, 51, 55, 57, 62/63, 67L,	
70, 77, 92, 94, 124, 125, 141, 147B,	
148, 152/153, 200, 202, 203, 205, 206/	
207, 210, 211, 212, 214/215, 218, 220,	
242, 244, 248R, 252, 254, 255, 256,	
258L, 258R, 259, 262, 269	**McGonigal, David**
34R	**National Library of Australia**
cover, 76, 187, 204	**Nissen, Mark**
248	**Orpheus Island Resort**
37	**Qantas Airways**
3, 9, 16/17, 20/21, 42, 43, 48, 52, 53,	
54, 60/61, 65L, 65R, 68, 69, 74, 80,	
81, 84, 101, 102, 103, 104, 106, 118,	
120, 121, 133, 138, 139, 142/143, 149,	
168/169, 172/173, 183, 192, 222/223,	
226, 234L, 235, 236, 238, 243, 247,	
260, 261, 266L	**Steel, Paul**
72	**Stockshots/ Barker, Paul**
96/97, 105	**Stockshots/ Brown, Geoff**
166, 232/233	**Stockshots/ Castleton, Phill**
110/111, 114	**Stockshots/ Foley, Paul**
176, 179, 184/185, 190/191, 195,	
196/197	**Stockshots/ Kohen, Kim**
250	**Stockshots/ Linsey, Ralph**
73, 221, 267	**Stockshots/ Miles, W.L.**
113	**Stockshots/ Monro, Graham**
160, 163	**Stockshots/ Nevin, Paul**
108/109	**Stockshots/ Smitt, Barrie**
155, 161	**Stockshots/ Sullivan, North**
79	**Stockshots/ White, Clifford**
14/15, 18/19, 115, 123, 126, 239	**Sunshine Coast Tourist Board**
58/59	**Tovy, Adina**
26/27	**Tresize, Steven**
156, 165L, 264	**Walker, Harry M.**
86/87, 98, 137, 157	**Walmsley, Murray**
Maps	**Berndtson & Berndtson**
Illustrations	**Klaus Geisler**
Visual Consulting	**V. Barl**

INDEX

D

Daily Wrecker, 215
Daintree rainforest, 151
Daintree River, 125, 151
Daintree-Cape Tribulation, 38
Darwin, Charles, 177
Daydream Island, 66, 245-246
de Quiros, Pedro Fernando, 29
de Torres, Luis Vaez, 30
Deepwater, 121
Dempster, Quentin, 39
Department of Environment and Conservation, 93
Devil's Kitchen, 112
Dillingham, Murphyores, 38, 128
dingos, 127
diving,
    diving safari, 76
    resort dive, 76
    schools of, 75-76
dolphins, 188
Doomben, 92
Double Island Point, 79, 114
Dreamtime Cultural Centre, 131
Dreamworld, 100
Dugong Beach, 231
dugong (marine mammal), 188
Dundee Park, 141
Dunk Island, 72, 124, 125, 141, 217, 257
    accommodation, 258
Dunk, Lord Montague, 259
Dunwich, 94
Duranbah, 78

E

Eager's Swamp, 95
Eagle Farm, 92
Earl of Morton, 92
echidnas, 127
echinoderms, feather stars, sea urchin, 186
Eimeo, 122
El Dorado Syndrome, 37
Eli Creek, 129
Eliott Heads, 121
Elizabeth E II, 133
Elliot, Lady, 31
Emerald, 122
Emery, Monty, 232
Emu Park, 122
emu, 221
Endeavour Butcher Shop (1870), 167
Endeavour River National Park, 167
Endeavour, 30
Esplanade, 146
Ettamogah Pub, 115
Eumundi Lager Brewery, 115
Eumundi, 115
Eurimbula, 121
Eurong, 128

F

Fairweather, Ian (painter), 95
Fairy Pools, 112
farming, sugar, 33
Fascinating Facets, 154
Fig Tree Pocket, 91
Finch Bay, 167
fish, 186
Fishermans Wharf, 101
Fishermans, 79
fishing, 71, 111, 164
    billfish, 73
    reef fish, 72
    Spearfishing, 73
    tackle billfish, 71
Fitzgerald Royal Commission, 39
Fitzgerald, Ross (historian), 37
Fitzroy Island, 68, 125, 263-265
Flaxton, 115
Fleay's Fauna Centre, 101
Flinders Street, 138
Flinders, Matthew, 31, 177, 183, 213
Flying Doctor Service, 125
FNO Promotion Bureau, 149
FNQ Banana Benders, 125
Fong On Bay State Park, 155
Fortitude Valley, 92
Fortunes, 106
Four Mile Beach, 151
Fraser Island (Great Sandy Peninsula), 35, 71, 79, 119, 120, 127, 175
Fraser, Captain James, 127
Fraser, Mrs Eliza, 127

G

Gailes, 81
Game Fishing Club, 268
Garbutt, 136
Garden Cabana Units, 258
Garner's Beach, 140
Geraghty's store, 120
Gin Gin, 121
Gladstone National Park and Wildlife Service, 121
Gladstone, 121, 208
Glasshouse Mountains, 114-115
Gold Coast Burleigh, 80
Gold Coast, 99
    accommodation, 102
    casino, 100
    cruises, 102
    economy, 37
    night spots, 106
Gold Coast, restaurants, 105
    shopping, 104
    takeaway services, 106
    transport, 106
    Car rental business, 106
    taxi service, 106
    climate, 99
gold, 34, 166
    rush, 145
    Canoona gold rush, 32
Golden Stradbroke Wallaby, 94
Golf Culture, 81

U – V

W – X

Y – Z

A
C
D
E
F
G
H
I
J
b
c
d
e
f
g
h
i
j
k
l